IN MY
OWN
WAY

Also by Alan Watts

Behold the Spirit
Beyond Theology
The Book
Cloud-hidden, Whereabouts Unknown
Does It Matter?
The Joyous Cosmology
Myth and Ritual in Christianity
Nature, Man and Woman
Psychotherapy East and West
The Spirit of Zen
The Supreme Identity
Tao
This Is It
The Way of Zen
The Wisdom of Insecurity

Also by Alan Watts from New World Library

Eastern Wisdom, Modern Life
Still the Mind
What Is Tao?
What Is Zen?

IN MY
OWN
WAY

an autobiography
1915–1965

Alan Watts

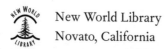
New World Library
Novato, California

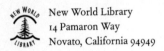 New World Library
14 Pamaron Way
Novato, California 94949

Grateful acknowledgment is made to the following:
James Broughton and The Jargon Society, for permission to use excerpts from *A Long Undressing: Collected Poems 1949–1969.* Copyright © 1971 by James Broughton.

Elsa Gidlow, for permission to use "Let the Wild Swan Singing Go"; and for an excerpt from
"Forgive Us," from *Moods of Eros* (Druid Heights Press).

Text design and typography by Tona Pearce Myers

Library of Congress Cataloging-in-Publication Data
Watts, Alan, 1915–1973.
In my own way : an autobiography, 1915–1965 / Alan Watts. — 2nd ed.
    p.   cm.
Includes index.
ISBN-13: 978-1-57731-584-1 (pbk. : alk. paper)
ISBN-10: 1-57731-584-7 (pbk. : alk. paper)
    1. Watts, Alan, 1915–1973. 2. Zen Buddhists—United States—Biography. 3. Philosophers—
United States—Biography. 4. Zen Buddhists—England—Biography. 5. Philosophers—Eng-
land—Biography. I. Title.
BQ995.T8A3 2007
294.3'927092—dc22   2007006128

First New World Library printing, June 2007
ISBN 978-1-57731-584-1
Printed in the USA on acid-free, partially recycled paper

10 9 8 7 6

To Elsa Gidlow

CONTENTS

FOREWORD

A foreword written by a father to his son's autobiography may not be unique but it must surely be something of a rarity; indeed the only somewhat similar instance I can recall is that of Rudyard Kipling's *Kim*, beautifully illustrated by his father, Lockwood Kipling.

What may appear to be another rather odd circumstance is that a person of Alan's breadth of outlook and depth of thought should have sprung from the parentage of a father who inherited much of the Victorian outlook and tradition and a mother whose family were Fundamentalists to whom the Bible was the Truth, the whole Truth, and nothing but the Truth. And that without any upheaval of the relations between us.

Perhaps this circumstance may qualify me in some way to write this foreword, for I still do not go the whole way with him in some of his views, and it thus enables me to restrain the natural parental pride and admiration which I have for his work from becoming mere adulation.

As a child a gift of narrative showed in him before he could read or write, and an early need was to keep him supplied with material for illustrating tales he invented about an imaginary island and its people situated—appropriately in view of his later interest in the East—in the Pacific Ocean. Plenty of white kitchen paper, pencils, and colored chalks had always to be on hand.

He acquired quite early a characteristic handwriting, and when I went with him to open his first Post Office Savings Bank account, I had some difficulty in convincing the clerk that Alan had himself written the signature on the pass-book. The clerk said he had never seen so mature a signature by a child of that age.

It was while he was at King's School at Canterbury that his thoughts turned to the East and he became interested in Buddhism. He made the acquaintance there of one who had traveled in Japan and the Far East and who introduced him to the works of Lafcadio Hearn. He also corresponded with the Buddhist Lodge—as it was then—and when we attended one of its meetings, to which Alan had asked me to go with him, I remember the astonishment when a lad of sixteen introduced himself as their correspondent.

Incidentally, he wrote and published his first book while still at school.

Another episode of his school days is worth recording as a tribute to the broadmindedness of his Headmaster, Norman Birley. When Archbishop Tempe of York arranged a Convention on Religion in the Public Schools, Mr. Birley suggested to Alan that he should attend as one of the school's representatives, a liberal gesture from a school so closely connected with the Church of England.

It was at this time, during the school holidays and immediately after he left school, that probably the most interesting period developed in the relations between the three of us, mother, father, and son. The house in which we lived had a large room running from front to back which we used for meetings and discussion groups on the various subjects in which Alan was interested. He had now acquired a typewriter and often after an evening spent in composition he would come down and ask us to hear and discuss something he had written. Discussion continued sometimes until late in the night.

I have of course read with great enjoyment all his books and any of his articles which have come my way, and have learned much from them. Visits to the United States have also enabled me to attend his lectures and seminars and to take part in the discussions following upon them, and it is here, I think, that Alan excels. The lucidity with which he speaks—and writes—of matters which are enormously difficult to express in words is amazing. The discussions are to my mind models of what a discussion should be, not an antagonistic debate but an exchange of views in which each side learns something from the other, and here Alan shows the way by his courtesy and open-mindedness. Questions intended seriously are answered seriously, and no questioner is ever made to look or feel foolish. I have no doubt that such consideration, especially when it is extended to the youthful inquirer, accounts largely for the interest taken in his philosophy by the young people of America.

Finally he has done more perhaps than any other writer to open the eyes of the West to the spiritual significance of Eastern religions and philosophies and to show that the Truth is not the monopoly of any one school of religious or philosophic thought.

Perhaps I may analogize this by supposing that four men approach an inaccessible mountain from different directions, and each writes a faithful description of the mountain as he sees it. Inevitably they will differ widely in detail and in opinion as to the best way to reach the summit, and although each account will be true as far as it goes, none will give a true picture of the mountain as a whole. But by putting the four accounts together, each taking from the others what it lacks, surely a much closer approximation to the whole will be achieved.

"The Paths are many but their End is One."

Laurence W. Watts

PREFACE

To be or to get in your own way means all at once to fulfill yourself and to obstruct yourself, for language is full of *double entendre*—as when to cleave means both to split and to adhere, when *sacer* means both sacred and accursed, and *altus* both high and deep. I had thought originally to call this book *Coincidence of Opposites*, but the publishers, rightly, thought it too highbrow and moved me to search for something more simple and direct that would convey the spirit and style in which I have tried to live. For I am committed to the view that the whole point and joy of human life is to integrate the spiritual with the material, the mystical with the sensuous, and the altruistic with a kind of proper self-love—since it is written that you must love your neighbor as yourself.

So I have always done things in my own way, which is at once the way that comes naturally to me, that is honest, sincere, genuine, and unforced; but also perverse, although you must remember that this word means *per* (through) *verse* (poetry), out-of-the-way and wayward, which is surely towards the way, and that to be queer—to "follow your own weird"—is wholeheartedly to accept your own *karma*, or fate, or destiny, and thus to be odd in the service of God, "whose service," as the Anglican Book of Common Prayer declares, "is perfect freedom."

I am, of course, playing with words. But that is the proper business of a philosopher who is also a poet, for the task and delight of poetry is to say what cannot be said, to eff the ineffable, and to unscrew the inscrutable.

I thought I had no business writing an autobiography, because I have been a sedentary and contemplative character, an intellectual, a Brahmin, a mystic, and also somewhat of a disreputable epicurean who has had three wives, seven children, and five grandchildren—and I cannot make up my mind whether I am confessing or boasting. But I have not fought in wars, explored mountains and jungles, battled in politics, commanded great business corporations, or accumulated vast wealth. It seemed to me, therefore, that I had no *story* to tell as the world judges stories. But two women absolutely insisted that I write this tale: the first my publisher's editor, Paula Van Doren McGuire, who has watched over the whole project; and the second my wife, Mary Jane Yates (hereafter known as Jano), who has worked out with me every detail of taste, grammar, spelling, and punctuation.

And, while giving thanks, thanks are also due to the advice of Henry Volkening and to my father, Laurence Watts, who prompted me to avoid certain indiscretions and corrected my memory on sundry matters of detail.

Now it is an essential principle of this book that I am describing myself largely in terms of other people and my reactions to them. The sensation called "self" is unrealizable without the sensation called "other," just as you would not know that you exist unless you had once been dead. Fortunately, there have been very few people in my life who could be regarded as my enemies—so few that I have not mentioned them. Unfortunately, there have been so many that I regard as friends that I have not been able to include them all, without making this book a monstrous compendium of the biographies of other people. Please, therefore, will the many who consider themselves my friends not be offended if I have said nothing about them.

Alan Watts
Sausalito, California
April 1972

IN MY
OWN
WAY

PROLOGUE

As I am also a you, this is going to be the kind of book that I would like you to write for me. It is not going to be in the linear dimension, since I do not subscribe to the chronological or historical illusion that events follow one another on a one-way street, in series. We think about them in that way because that is how we have decided to write and speak, and thus, if I am to communicate with you in words, I must "give you a line," and you must follow this string of letters. But of course, the world itself isn't strung out; it exists in many dimensions. I have, then, a preference for books that I can open at any place and begin to read—books like a garden in which I can roam, and not like a tunnel, maze, or superhighway where I must enter at Point A and come out at Point Z. This will not be so much the history as the mystery of my life, and I write it neither to edify you nor to justify myself, but to entertain both of us.

This next point may sound metaphysical, but like much that is metaphysical, it is rockily practical: I have realized that the past and the future are real illusions, that they exist only in the present, which is what there is and all that there is. From one point of view the present is shorter than a microsecond. From another, it embraces all eternity. But there isn't anywhere, or anywhen, else to be. History determines what we are only to the extent that we insist, now, that it does so. Likewise, the dream—or the nightmare—of the great tomorrow is a present fantasy which distracts us from both reality and eternity. For every sentient being is God—omnipotent, omniscient, infinite, and eternal—pretending with the utmost sincerity and determination to be otherwise, to be a mere creature subject to failure, pain, death,

temptation, hellfire, and ultimate tragedy. One of the most intelligent, pleasant, and scholarly men I know devotes himself to the creed that a noble
human life is simply courage in the face of inevitable disaster and annihilation.
But I won't argue with him, any more than I would argue with a fish for
living in the sea. It's his game, his style, his posture; and he does it very well.

Thus, in telling this nonstory of my own life I shall always begin from the
present, the *Fons et Origo*, Fount and Origin of all happenings, from which
the past trails and vanishes like the wake of a ship. I have said that many times
before, and one of the problems of a well-read author is to be accused of repetition by critics who do not seem to understand that repetition is the essence
of music as, for example, in the *andante* movement of Beethoven's Seventh
Symphony or Ravel's *Bolero*. Each of the twenty books I have had published
arrives at the same destination from a different point of departure, as the
spokes of a wheel converge at the hub from separate points on the rim. Taking the premises of Christian dogmatics, Hindu mythology, Buddhist psychology, Zen practice, psychoanalysis, behaviorism, or logical positivism, I
have tried to show that all are aiming, however disputatiously, at one
center. This has been my way of making sense of life in terms of philosophy,
psychology, and religion.

But—and as yet I am not quite sure whether this is simply a function of
growing older or growing wiser—so many writings in the fields of philosophy, psychology, and religion now seem to me to be meaningless, without
even attaining the charm of deliberate nonsense; and this is even, and perhaps
especially, true of the harangues of logical analysts and scientific empiricists
against poets and metaphysicians. This is not to say that I, as an eccentric
and nonacademic philosopher, am disillusioned with and dejected about my
own craft, since I have always been an intellectual critic of the intellectual life.
What I am saying is that an enormous amount of philosophy, theology, and
even psychology strikes me as a discussion of words and concepts without relation to experience—not exactly as empty words, but as intelligent and
scholarly argument about problems not recognized as creations of grammar
and forms of language, such as the arbitrary distinction between nouns and
verbs, the rule that verb acts must have noun agents, and empty differentiations between substance and form, things and events. There is too little

recognition of the vast difference between the world as described and the world as sensed, too little recognition that what we describe in the physical universe as separate things are of the same order as areas, views, aspects, selections, and features—not *data* but *capta*, grasped rather than given.

My own work, though it may seem at times to be a system of ideas, is basically an attempt to describe mystical experience—not of formal visions and supernatural beings, but of reality as seen and felt directly in a silence of words and mindings. In this I set myself the same impossible task as the poet: to say what cannot be said. Indeed, much of my work is poetry described as prose (with margins adjusted) so that people will read it. As poets value the sounds of words above their meanings, and images above arguments, I am trying to get thinking people to be aware of the actual vibrations of life as they would listen to music.

I would therefore like, again, to approach this ever-entrancing hub of the wheel from a point on the rim which is not formally philosophical, theological, or psychological, but which is simply my own everyday life. Generally speaking, the task of autobiography so embarrasses the writer that he must either boast or confess. Men of action and adventure tend to boast. Men of piety and intellect tend to confess, as witness the *Confessions* of St. Augustine and Rousseau, and Cardinal Newman's *Apologia Pro Vita Sua*. I have nothing to boast about in the way of heroic adventures in war or exploration, and I am certainly not going to make a public apology or confession. Having had considerable experience as a father-confessor, counselor, and amateur psychotherapist, I have come to see that my own "sins" are as normal and as boring as everyone else's—which is not to say that I haven't had some splendid experiences that stuffy people would deem sinful. The point is that beyond boasting on the one hand, or confessing or apologizing on the other, I find my life intensely *interesting*. If it were not so I should probably commit suicide, for, as Camus so bluntly suggested, the only serious philosophical problem is whether or not to commit suicide. (Ultimately, of course, he is wrong, for to be or not to be is *not* the question, since the two states manifest each other. How would you know that you are alive unless you had once been dead?)

Somehow I have come to a place where I see through ideas, beliefs, and symbols. They are natural expressions of life, but do not, as they so often claim, embrace or explain life. Thus I am fascinated with almost all religions, so long as their followers do not try to convert me, in the same way that I am fascinated with the various kinds of flowers, birds, and insects, or with different ways of dressing and cooking. And just as I don't like standard British, American, Mexican, or German cooking, I cannot imagine myself a Jehovah's Witness, a Southern Baptist, a Jesuit father (much as I respect some of those gentlemen), or a Theravada Buddhist monk. Everyone to his taste—but why fight about it? *Because it isn't that important.* Do you suppose that God takes himself seriously? I know a Zen master, Joshu Sasaki, who has let it be known that the best form of meditation is to stand up with your hands on your hips and roar with laughter for ten minutes every morning. I have heard of a sophisticated shaman-type fellow who used to cure ringworm on cows just by pointing at the scars and laughing. Truly religious people always make jokes about their religion; their faith is so strong that they can afford it. Much of the secret of life consists in knowing how to laugh, and also how to breathe. A failure of our schools is that their departments of "physical education" teach only mechanical and mathletic versions of body-play.[1]

Physical education is the fundamental discipline of life, but it is actually despised, neglected, and taught intellectually, because the true intent of our schools is to inculcate the virtues of cunning and calculation which will make money, not so much for the students themselves as for those who employ and govern them, and who, in turn (because they were educated in the same system), do not know how to transform money into physical enjoyment. They were never taught how to husband plants and animals for food, how to cook, how to make clothes and build houses, how to dance and breathe, how to do yoga for finding one's true center, or how to make love. "The

---

[1] In the same connection, it might be asked why the German army has lost two world wars. Because of the goose-step and brass bands, because of military stamp, pomp, and swagger. An effective army is inaudible and invisible; you cannot hear or see it coming. This is also why the French and the Americans have not been able to subdue Vietnam: their methods of war are too affectedly masculine.

establishment" is a class of physical barbarians. Consider simply the dowdy and scrubby masculine dress and appearance of Mr. Nixon, Mr. Heath, Mr. Kosygin, M. Pompidou, and (alas) the Emperor of Japan, who affects the absurdities of Edwardian formal dress or common business suits. When the rich and the powerful are falsely modest and afraid of color and splendor, the whole style of life deteriorates—there being no example to follow save that of cultivated mediocrity. High style and pageantry are then confined to the theater, and—being left out of all such serious domains as religion, government, and commerce—become signs of frivolity, with the disastrous result that seriousness (or, better, sincerity) must always be associated with a drab aspect.

My mother, before she married, was a teacher of physical education and home economics in a school for the abandoned daughters of missionaries who had gone off to India, Africa, China, and Japan under the strange impression that God had called them to teach religion to "the natives." She was a modestly expert cook, a most competent gardener, and a wizard at embroidery. She turned me on, bless her, to color, to flowers, to intricate and fascinating designs, to the works of Oriental art given to her by those missionaries in appreciation of her fosterage of their daughters—and all this despite the wretched fundamentalist Protestantism she had halfheartedly inherited from her parents. She lived in a world of magic beyond that religion—a world inhabited, not by the domineering prophets and sentimental angels upon the stained-glass windows of Christ Church, Chislehurst, but by sweet peas, scarlet-runner beans, rose trees, crisp apples, speckled thrushes, blackbirds, blue tits, and bouncy little robins. By bracken, maidenhair fern, blackberries on the bush, enchanted circles of beech trees on the South Downs, dew-ponds and wells of chalk-cool water in Sussex, and hopfields and oast-houses in the vast and miraculous garden of Kent.

This world was simply *not* the world of the "Bible-black" religion which has, according to my own prejudices, become the curse and menace of the White Anglo-Saxon Protestant (and Irish Jansenist Catholic) culture. The sexy, complex, gambling, diaphanous, ecstatic, and terrifying lilts of nature were no more designed by the biblical God-the-Father than the music of Ali Akbar Khan was composed by Elgar, or the poetry of Dylan Thomas written by Edgar Guest.[2] My mother's world, which she did not have quite the full courage of conviction to set above the world of God *her* father (who really looked like God, beard and all), seemed rather to be designed by Kwan-yin of the thousand arms, the Bodhisattva of compassionate skill, forever trying to show sentient beings that "energy is eternal delight."

I am sure I was—at least until puberty—overly dependent on my mother, though I cannot remember anything even faintly resembling an Oedipus complex. On the contrary, I was disappointed in the fact that she did not seem to me as pretty as other women, and I couldn't abide the expression she wore when she first woke up in the morning. But, at least when I was little, she understood me, and always believed in me—or perhaps in her idea of me, for when I was naughty she would say that it just wasn't like *me* to do such a thing. She also gave me the impression that God had it in mind for me to do a great work in the world, and it is probably just as well that I remember this subtle reinforcement of my ego. It gave me comfort in the face of childhood sicknesses and dangers. Somehow it seemed that she disliked her own body, perhaps because she had had so much sickness just after marriage, and when she spoke of people being very *ill* she would swallow the word as if it were a nasty lump of fat, and take on a most serious frown. As I was an only child (she had two miscarriages and a baby boy who lived only two weeks) I think I picked up her anxiety for my survival and became something of a physical coward.

But she made up in personality for what she lacked in my conception of prettiness, and my father adored her, always. They would hold hands under the dining table at meals, and he would hug her like a bear. Although she never sang and couldn't hold a tune, she had a musical and lilting speaking-voice which held authority without forcing it. Having now become gently cynical about human nature I can say with some amazement that her eyes were as honest as her conscience, and that, though she may have been squeamish about things of the body, she was never at any time malicious, mean, greedy, conceited, or untruthful. I could never imagine what sins she

---

[2] But the biblical God of the Jews is perhaps another matter. He understands Yiddish.

was confessing in church when she joined in saying, "But thou, O Lord, have mercy upon us most miserable offenders." The "us" must have meant me. The only unpleasantness I ever found in her was her annoying habit (especially to an Englishman) of probing for your real emotions when you were trying to keep a stiff upper lip. When I once berated her for this, rather forcefully, she said, "I think I'll go and shed a tear."

Although my parents suffered through two horrendous wars and the Depression, which hit them hard, I cannot imagine being born to a more harmonious and unostentatiously virtuous couple. Yet I feel that I never quite gave them what they wanted. I don't know what that was, and perhaps they didn't either. But I was a weird child. I was a fantast who believed in fairies and magic when all the other children had given them up for twaddle. I preferred watching birds to playing cricket. I adopted a strange and un-English religion, and went off on my own to a far country. They said I had "imagination," which was good but dangerous, and the neighbors would speak of Mrs. Watts as "Alan Watts's mother." I told anyone who would listen endless tales of fantasy and of blood-and-thunder. I would conduct funeral ceremonies for dead birds and bats and rabbits instead of learning tennis. I read about ancient Egypt and Chinese tortures and Aladdin's lamp instead of "good books" by Scott, Thackeray, and Dickens. I have no idea how I came to be so weird, but never for a moment have I regretted that I forgetfully reincarnated myself as the child of Laurence Wilson Watts and Emily Mary Buchan, at Rowan Tree Cottage in Holbrook Lane, in the village of Chislehurst, Kent, England, almost due south of Greenwich, on the morning of January 6, 1915, at about twenty minutes after six, with the Sun in Capricorn, conjuncted with Mars and Mercury and in trine to a Moon in Virgo, with Sagittarius rising, and under bombardment in the midst of the First World War.[3]

---

[3] These details are given for the satisfaction of my many friends who believe in astrology— a primitive science which is correct in theory but inexact and unworkable in practice. Obviously, who and what you are is where and when you are in relation to the whole universe. But the map, or horoscope, is not the territory—or should I say the celestiary? Heaven is a big subject.

CHAPTER ONE

THE STONED WOOD

Topophilia is a word invented by the British poet John Betjeman for a special love for peculiar places. It sounds almost like a disease or a perversion, but it comes close to the Japanese *aware*, which signifies a sophisticated nostalgia. One may love special places either for their beauty, or for their fascinating ugliness, or for their inability to be described. In the first class put the Swiss-Italian lake district and Big Sur, California; in the second put residential North London, Philadelphia, or Baltimore; in the third put Chislehurst, which means a stoned or stony (or even astonished) wood. It is an area on a well-forested and flat-topped hill to the southeast of London, its soil abounding in round and grey-surfaced stones, some of which contain pockets of crystals, and some which, when broken, reveal an image of dark blue sky, dense with clouds. Large sections of this area are commons or public parks, wild and left generally to themselves. In the interstices lie palatial mansions, affluent suburban residences, three small shopping areas, seven churches, seven amiable pubs, and two respectable slums.

Even today it hasn't been too objectionably improved. Indeed, many of the mansions are now schools, offices, or service-flats, and a number of boxy, red-brick, quiet-desperation homes have filled up the old rural lanes. But the Royal Parade, the one-block-long principal shopping center, is almost exactly what it was fifty years ago. I was back there in June 1970 to celebrate my father's ninetieth birthday at the Tiger's Head pub on the village green, across from the ancient parish church of Saint Nicholas—and incidentally, it isn't so widely known that English pubs (as distinct from restaurants) can provide magnificent feasts. But there was the village center in its original order, though ownerships had changed. Close to the prosperous-looking Bull Inn are Miss Rabbit's original sweet shop, and opposite, the incredible Miss Battle is still running the bakery. I can't account for her; she is a young woman about seventy years old. Mr. Walters (Junior) is still running the book, stationery, and greeting-card shop, though Mr. Coffin's excellent grocery has been taken over by a chain—and yet the goods and the service are unchanged. It smells as it always did of flavors of fresh coffee, smoked meats, and Stilton cheese, and is run with a dignity and courtesy which make it, for me, the archetypal grocery designed in heaven.

Mr. Francis's tobacco and barber shop is still there, though he has long joined his ancestors. It was here that I had my one and only personal encounter with that vivacious and ancient priest, Canon Dawson, rector of Saint Nicholas who, as a very High Church Anglo-Catholic, sported a fried-egg hat and cassock around the village. (All I can remember of his sermons is a series of enthusiastic coughs, but everyone loved him, and he lived in a magnificent and mysterious Queen Anne house—The Rectory—kitty-corner from the church, next to the Tiger's Head, and backed by a row of stately trees beyond which lay the acres of Colonel Edelman's spacious farms and crow-cawing pines.) The Rector was in a hurry and very affably asked me to yield place in line for a haircut. Naturally, I was delighted; he, the dignitary, the parson or person of the domain had treated a nine-year-old boy as a human being. I hadn't long to wait, for he was almost bald.

But vanished now is the drapery and dress shop run by the Misses Scriven, two elderly spinsters with put-up hair, bulging, with bun on top, and thoroughly clothed from neck to ankles with long-sleeved frilly blouses and tweedy skirts, granny-style spectacles with thin gold rims insulting their faces. Fashionable young ladies of today should note (since granny spectacles are back in vogue), that constructions of wire upon the face, especially upon ladies with angular figures, have about as much sex appeal as bicycles. To make things worse, the Misses Scriven displayed their frocks and dresses upon "dummies," which were headless, armless, and legless mock-ups of female torsos, having lathe-turned erections of dark wood in place of heads. These hideous objects gave me repeated nightmares until I was at least six years old, for in the midst of an otherwise interesting dream there would suddenly appear a calico-covered dummy, formidably breasted (without cleft) and sinisterly headless. This thing would mutter at me and suggest ineffable terrors, but thereafter it would rumble, and I would have the sensation of dropping through darkness to find myself relieved and awake.

And then, just to the north, was the pharmacy of Messrs. Prebble and Bone, its windows adorned with immense tear-shaped bottles of brightly colored liquids, for ornament and not for sale, where medications were sold in an aromatic atmosphere which has prompted the riddle "What smells most in a chemist's shop?" Answer: "Your nose." Whereas Mr. Coffin's grocery was low and on the level, Mr. Prebble and Mr. Bone's establishment was lofty and looked down at you, and their mysterious bottles with occult labels were stored in high, glass-doored cupboards. They supplied Dr. Tallent's utterly illegible prescriptions in bottles and boxes with formal and punctilious labels entitled "The Mixture," "The Ointment," or "The Pills," followed with such paradoxical instructions as "Take one pill three times a day," which reminds me of a notice once posted on the buses of Sacramento, California: "Please let those getting off first."

Dr. Tallent also lived on the Royal Parade, at Walton Lodge, a pleasant begardened house oddly sequestered in the very middle of the row of shops. He was a confident, kindly, and clean-smelling man who officiated at my birth, upon whose brand-new suit I pissed at my circumcision, and from whom, as soon as I was articulate, I demanded a two-shilling fee (which he paid) for some unpleasant medical attention. His wife was, necessarily, a talented woman—a singer and actress resembling Mary Pickford—and I was secretly in love with his tall brunette daughter Jane without knowing how to do anything about it. She seemed to be on a higher rung in the social ladder, and thus went with the boys who played tennis and cricket (the ultimately boring game), and indulged in the lugubrious dangle-armed dancing of the 1920s. And then I was vehemently in love with a blond kindergarten mate named Kitty, who lived in one of the pretentious mansions near the Rectory, so much so that I got up the courage to propose marriage to her and was so flatly rejected that I didn't have the nerve to make amorous approaches to women until I was nineteen.

I have been told, in later years, that I look like a mixture of King George VI and Rex Harrison, but *then* the boys told me I was a cross-eyed and buck-toothed weakling to whom no girl would ever possibly be attracted. But when I search through the records, like *Who's Who* and even the Greater London Telephone Directory, all those handsome and self-confident sportsmen, scholars, and snobs who were my successful peers in school seem to have vanished. It is unbelievable and awesome that I find no trace of the heroes of my childhood, save one or two whom the system rejected, like poet, travelogist, and (during World War II) Brigadier General Patrick Leigh Fermor, who was expelled from King's School, Canterbury, for taking a walk with the local greengrocer's daughter.

But back to Chislehurst. Rowan Tree Cottage, our home, is one block east of the Royal Parade, and takes its name from a mountain ash or rowan tree which grew in the front garden behind a hedge of sweetbrier and beside an arbor of jasmine and a magnificent tree of green cooking-apples upon which we used to hang coconuts, sliced open for the delectation of wrens and blue tits. The house is a semidetached cottage, that is, a mirror-image structure, one half occupied by ourselves and the other by an astonishingly ugly, garrulous, holy, and warmhearted lady known as Miss Gussy (Augusta Pearce—and may she rest in peace, fanned by the jeweled wings of her Anglo-Catholic angels.) Also let it be said, in passing, that most of the people mentioned in this book are to be recognized as my gurus—people from whom I have learned all that I value—and in this respect Miss Gussy had an important role.

Behind the house my parents had acquired an acre of land which adjoined the playing fields of Farrington's (Wesleyan) school for girls and gave access to the immense fields and forests of Scadbury Manor, where the lords of Chislehurst had lived from at least the thirteenth century. Just at the boundary between our land and Farrington's was a colossal sycamore tree exactly ninety feet high, where the sun rose, and where, in the late afternoon, my mother and I watched glistening pigeons against black storm-clouds. That was the axletree of the world, Yggdrasil, blessing and sheltering the successive orchards, vegetable gardens and (once) a rabbit farm which my father cultivated in time of economic distress. There was also a time when he let the back part of the garden go fallow, with grasses, sorrel, and flowering weeds so well above my head that I could get lost in this sunny herbaceous forest with butterflies floating above. I was so happy in this miniature jungle that I still don't understand why those who have neither time nor skill for real gardening shouldn't just let their land go its own way, rather than insisting on lawn order, whereby grass is forced to imitate a billiard table.

We are compulsively and drearily tidy, and frantically flatten, rectangularize and uniformize the chthonic world into Euclidian patterns, which are wholly bereft of imagination and exuberance. Shouldn't we beg pardon for millions of square miles of cropped, unflowering grass? This was the magic of the Chislehurst commons—that all those acres were simply left alone, save for the attentions of jovial Mr. Cox, the Common-Keeper, who went about with a burlap sack and a spiked stick to pick up human trash—mostly paper. There were open acres covered with curly-ferned bracken and dotted with prickly, yellow-flowered gorse bushes. There were dark dense clusters of rhododendrons, dank mysterious pools under enormous oaks and cedars, sweet, sandy, and sunny groves of pines, and, at the bottom of Pett's Wood—just across the railway tracks—an almost tropical swamp, where the stream Marchristal (named after Margaret, Christine, and Alan, who explored it from end to end) flowed into a larger stream which ran eventually into the Medway River, through Maidstone, and into the Thames at Sheerness.

Margaret and Christine, incidentally, were sisters—two adorably feminine tomboys whom I hadn't the nerve to relate to except on the boy level of adventure and mild naughtiness, such as initiating Christine into smoking cigarettes under a bush on the commons. However, we followed that tiny stream through two miles of thickets, mostly young hazels, elm, and ash, over ground twinkling with wild primroses and celandine and blossoming (if that is the word) with pagodalike layers of tree fungus, with toadstools, and with that formidable red-topped, white-flecked mushroom *Amanita muscaria*—of whose properties we knew nothing except "Don't."

The Marchristal descended across a belt of pines, through a culvert under the tracks, and out into this vividly alive swampy area where flowering weeds grew far above our heads—white umbelliferae, yellow ragweed, something with small but imperially purple flowers, nettles, wild roses, honeysuckle, common bugle, foxgloves, wild poppies, vast thistles, blackberry bushes, and high barleylike grasses—all of which was bewhizzed by kingfisher-blue dragonflies, by bumblebees and tiny pseudowasps called hover-flies, and befluttered by fritillaries, red admirals, swallowtails, painted ladies, tortoise-shells, orange-tips, small coppers, Camberwell beauties, gray-lings, common whites, commas, peacocks, clouded yellows, marble whites, chalkhill blues, and even an occasional purple emperor.

Yes, I am showing off my knowledge of folk entomology. My father was an amateur entomologist, and his guru in this pursuit was an extremely small, affable, and intelligent *bon vivant* named Samuel Blyth—a well-to-do solicitor, stockholder in the Bank of England, and confirmed bachelor, who lived with his splendidly witty mother and two devoted serving-maids in a Churrigueresque house just south of the Royal Parade. Samuel Blyth was one of Canon Dawson's loyal henchmen, a devout and even militant High Churchman who hardly ever discussed religion. His ancestors had sailed with the Royal Navy, and his house was ablaze with the folk art of Africa, India, and Indochina—inlaid tables, silver canisters, an immense basket from Lagos, and all sorts of lacquered and marquetry boxes with images, in bril-liant color, of Shiva, Krishna, Parvati, and Radha dancing it up amid stylized frameworks of creepers and vines. Furthermore, he presided at stately din-ner parties to which a select company gathered in formal dress, where the cuisine—served by Annie I and Annie II—was English cooking at its best, accompanied by the best wines of Bordeaux, for which he had a special liking. Next to my mother, he may be considered my true teacher in the arts of the table, although now—in California—we attend formal dinners in out-rageously imaginative costumes instead of black, silk-lapelled suits with boiled shirts and black bow ties.

Sam's mother was just the sort of woman I hope my own wife will be-come when she is eighty. She was somewhat stout, wore a black velvet choker, and carried a silver-topped ebony walking stick; a lady of wonder-ful presence and dignity who was, nevertheless, given to chuckling. Sam, also, had this particular and important grace for appreciating and giggling about nonsense—important, because I am not fully at ease with those who lack it. At a very early age I was presented with a handsome edition of the nonsense limericks of Edward Lear by the angular, (apparently) acid, and bearded Mr. Chettle who, as headmaster of the school sponsored by the Worshipful Company of Stationers, had been the most respected of my father's teachers. He, then, was responsible for initiating me into a taste for such profound ridiculosities as

There was an Old Man of Vienna,
Who lived upon Tincture of Senna.
    When that did not agree,
    He took Camomile Tea;
That nasty Old Man of Vienna.

So, I told Sam Blyth and his mother about an insane cartoon-film I had seen called *The Worm That Turned* in which an officiously persecuted worm, ordinarily slow and limp in action, became galvanized with energy after drinking from a bottle labeled "Encouragement," and with electric convulsions banged all his persecutors to bits. Thereafter, on our return from night-time entomological expeditions, I was invariably given a Bottle of Encouragement which, as then appropriate for a small boy, was that most pleasant concoction—English ginger beer from a stone bottle. I am drinking some at the moment of writing, and though it comes from a nasty and ecologically pestiferous no-return bottle which says, with incongruous pomposity, "bottled under authority of Schweppes (U.S.A.) Ltd., Stamford, Conn., 06905, from essence imported from Schweppes, London, England," it is very good; though not quite the same thing as served by Samuel Blyth from a stone bottle or bought, homemade, from a rose-engarlanded cottage on an ancient Roman road just south of Canterbury.

Those entomological expeditions after dark were usually conducted in a long and ancient grove of trees on the west side of Pett's Wood, bordered by Colonel Edelman's open fields with their clusters, or spinneys, of pines. Sam and my father would paint the trees with a thin, one-foot strip of molasses mixed with essence of pear. Then, at the bottom of the grove, they would wait and light up their pipes (Sam, who was a perky little man, had the most enormous Dunhill I have ever seen), whereafter we would return with our flashlights examining the various moths which had visited our treacly traps. My father usually called them by their folk names, such as the Silver

Y, from the silvery Y-shaped mark on its upper wing, but Sam, as the guru, used the Graeco-Latin scientific names—in this case *gamma*—always pronounced in the flagrantly British distortions of Mediterranean languages. Thus the very rare and prized oleander hawk moth, which Sam once netted ecstatically over his flowering tobacco plants, is known to the science as *nerii*. He pronounced it "neary-eye." It is a gorgeous mottled green, almost bird-like moth which occasionally reaches the southern shores of England from Africa.

We would carefully identify the various specimens on the treacle, then proceed to capture those not already in our collections by inveigling them into glass-topped pillboxes, and thereafter spiflicate them in glass jars, or "killing-bottles," containing cyanide under a coating of plaster of Paris. Pounded laurel leaves would do just as well.

From all this I learned a love of moths, but I no longer catch, kill, and set them in cabinet drawers under glass. I have found that by talking gently to moths, even calling "Here kitty-kitty-kitty!" I can get them to alight on my hand, where I can inspect them alive and at leisure. I have even persuaded a huge Polyphemus to stay on my head for half an hour. By this means, if you are inclined to the scientific study of moths or butterflies, you can simply photograph them in color instead of killing them—and the sport of making friends with them is far more challenging than going out on the hunt. This applies equally to birds, deer, fish, and bears. I will no longer hunt for any creature which I do not seriously need to eat, although, for reasons which may be—as they say—Freudian, I have constantly practiced the arts of archery and riflery. In an autobiography one must surely be allowed to boast, just for fun. I have, at a range of twenty feet, shot the tobacco out of a cigarette and left the paper intact. At a range of thirty feet, I have split a target, edge towards me, with an air pistol. I am also the world's champion in a game called "You Are the Target," in which anyone better than I would be dead. The game is to shoot an arrow straight up and see how near to you it can be allowed to land. You have to watch its fall very carefully, but I have had it hit the ground exactly between my feet. Of course, there were no witnesses. Had there been, they would forcefully have discouraged the experiment. I was using a fifty-five-pound bow.

My father, although an admirably peaceful man, carefully instructed me in these arts. He made bows for me and taught me how to use his .22 carbine, as well as how to sling arrows with a string. Nature preserved him from the colossal folly of World War I by giving him a carbuncle on the neck, though he did weekly drill with the territorial troops on the local cricket ground with an Enfield rifle—a ritual operation, like the Officers' Training Corps fantasies with which I was later involved in school, which had absolutely nothing to do with the bloody realities of fighting. Drummers and buglers being in attendance, I called the affair "Daddy's Band." (This was 1917.) At that time I was absolutely delighted with sporadic German air raids, which provided me with an excuse for being taken out of bed in the middle of the night and down to the dining room, there to drink cocoa and wave a small Union Jack flag. The nearest hit was plunk in the middle of the village green, which shook everything up but killed no one, and the crater is there to this day, as a sort of memorial. The village was protected by an antiaircraft gun affectionately known as Archibald. I am told that, as I was being wheeled beside this gun in my perambulator, two soldiers came by with a basket of laundry and I convulsed them by saying, "Here come Archibald's nappies."

This is perhaps the place to say that I regard human wars as I regard storms and earthquakes—as totally irrational disasters, or forms of collective madness, which I will do my best to avoid under almost all circumstances, even though I am now living on top of the San Andreas Fault. The mere robber can take what he wants; however, I would probably give violent resistance to anyone attempting physical injury upon myself or my loved ones—although there would always be an element of judo in the tactics employed. But collective banding together for offense or defense is, as is now so obvious, a no-win game. Modern warfare is planetary destruction, a luxury we cannot afford. All offenders proclaim and even believe that they are defending themselves, since it is now becoming increasingly impossible to wage war for the good old-fashioned motive of capturing the territory and the women of other tribes. Nor do we need their men as slaves. We have machinery instead. To take sides in a modern, technological war is to take sides in a lunatic asylum—as between believers, and really ardent believers, in Dottlebonk and Geflugg, both out to prove their manhoodlumism. Call me a physical coward, a sissy, a nervous Nellie, a traitor, a deserter, a chicken, a worm, a slug, a salamander, or anything you like, but I have always used my ingenuity to stay out of these ridiculous uproars. I would rather exercise my manhood in bed with the ladies, though those who do not approve of such delectable imploits say that I am out to "prove" my masculinity, whereas I am simply and innocently enjoying life and *im*proving my masculinity. It is so strange that everyone infected by psychoanalysis regards every form of exuberance as a neurotic excess, and classifies mere happiness under the clinical and diagnostic term "euphoria."

But to go back to Chislehurst. My father and mother brought me up in a garden flutant with the song of birds, especially at dawn and twilight. They decided, however, that I should be educated as a Brahmin, an intellectual, directed towards the priestly, legal, or literary professions. As soon as I was exposed to the ideals of these disciplines, which were studious and bookish, I lost interest and energy for the work of the garden, though I remained enchanted with the flowers and fruits of other people's work, so much so that in my old age I shall probably return to the craft of the garden, but of a very small garden, consisting mainly of culinary, medicinal, and psychedelic herbs, with nasturtiums, roses, and sweet peas around the edges. Alongside there will be a large redwood barn where the various herbs will hang from the beams to dry, where there will be shelves of mysterious jars containing cardamom, ginseng, ginger, marjoram, oregano, mint, thyme, pennyroyal, cannabis, henbane, mandrake, comfrey mugwort, and witch hazel, and where there will also be a combination of alchemist's laboratory and kitchen. I can smell it coming.

The garden at home was what is now called "organic," and, in my mind, I can still taste its peas, potatoes, scarlet-runner beans, and pippin apples which my father stored on wooden racks to last through the winter. (Having made recent tours of inspection, I can report that vegetables from this neighborhood are as good as ever.) But the advantage of being a small child is that you can see vegetables better than adults. You don't have to stoop down to them, and you can thus get lost in a forest of tomatoes, raspberries, and beans on sticks—and from this standpoint and attitude vegetables have nothing to do with the things served on plates in restaurants. They are glowing, luscious jewels, embodiments of emerald or amber or carnelian light, and are usually best when eaten raw and straight off the plant when you are alone, when no one can see you doing it, and when the whole affair is somewhat surreptitious. This is, of course, what happened to Adam and Eve in the Garden of Eden, and perhaps it was an unripe apple that made Eve ill. It is not usually understood that she was a little girl and Adam a little boy, because they are always portrayed as mature adults, but they were obviously a couple of kids scrounging around Big Daddy's garden. Having thoroughly satisfied themselves on gooseberries, raw peas, and green apples, they hid between the tomato plants and began to examine each other's private parts. But just then Big Daddy came along and said, "God damn it, get the hell out of here, you little bastards!"[1]

One of the major taboos of our culture is against realizing that vegetables are intelligent—an insight which I owe to an inspired eccentric named Thaddeus Ashby, who haunts and dismays the general area of Southern California, but who is an undoubted genius. Not so long ago he arrived at my door in the rig of a British field marshal, Montgomery-style, except that the golden badge on his beret proved, on close inspection, to be a Buddhist emblem. He explained that he was a true *field* marshal, representing the interests of the vegetable kingdom, and gave me a long discourse on the intellectuality, cunning, and compassion of the whole world of plants. This was in line with my own suspicion that every living and sentient being considers itself human—that is, as being at the center of the universe and as having attained the height of culture. He went into the amazingly beautiful and varied methods whereby plants disperse their seeds, and pointed out that fruit is sweet or tangy because the plant *wants* it to be eaten, so that seeds will be distributed through the alimentary canals of bugs, birds, or people. He further exemplified our dim view of the plant world by the fact that we call decrepit people "mere vegetables," and deplore homosexuals by calling them "fruits." He pointed out that, as distinct from mammals, birds, reptiles,

---

[1] The vulgar language is, as always, soundly grounded in theology. In the Catholic and Christian scheme of things we are sons of God by adoption and grace, not by nature, since God has only one Son, rendering the rest of us bastards essentially damned and in hell.

and fish, the brain and the sexual organs of plants are in the same place, and that they do not therefore have the problems over which Freud puzzled, namely the conflict between the pleasure principle and the reality principle. He further suggested that the botanical world was so concerned about human misuse of the biosphere that it had decided to turn us on, psychedelically, so that we would come to our senses, or, if that wouldn't work, to turn us off by making itself increasingly poisonous.

Now it is the papal infallibility and orthodox dogma of the present scientific establishment that plants are mechanisms without intelligence, and that they have neither feeling nor capacity for purposeful action. A little child hasn't been told this, and therefore knows better. I knew that plants, moths, birds, and rabbits were *people*—as is exemplified in such tales as *The Wind in the Willows*, *Winnie the Pooh*, and innumerable folk tales from all cultures. Anthropologists and historians of religion dismiss this as animism, the most primitive, superstitious, and depraved of all those systems and beliefs which, in the course of historical progress, eventually blossom into Christianity or dialectical materialism. It is thus that our entire civilization has no respect for plants or for animals other than pets—the flattering dog, the wily cat, the obedient horse, and the mimicking parrot. It is high time to go back, or on, to animism and to cultivate good manners toward all sentient beings, including vegetables, and even lakes and mountains.

In that garden I learned to talk with birds, to whistle all their calls, and, in winter especially, to feed them by hand on the window sill. As Henry Miller has pointed out, the birds of America (excepting perhaps the cardinal and the mockingbird) do not really sing. They squawk, chatter, screech, croak, cluck, and hoot—and he attributes this to our terrible bread and to "the tasteless products of our worn-out soil." We have nothing like a nightingale or skylark, although some years ago the California mockingbirds picked up the first half of the nightingale's song from listening to the record of Respighi's *Birds* being played on suburban patios. In Santa Barbara I whistled this melody back and forth with a mockingbird for about half an hour, and taught him some new variations. But at dawn in Chislehurst or, for that matter, any country place in Western Europe, the birds come on like a choir of angels in praise of the sun, and I used to lie in bed feeling my spirits raised and raised by this bird-symphony of total delight in life. At sunset a solitary thrush would perch at the very top of the rowan tree and go into a solo to which I would rather listen than to even Tebaldi or Sutherland.

May I go into the topography and geography of my home, for it still fascinates me. It was (and is) a semidetached cottage of solid brick, facing west, having two stories and a mysterious attic which I hardly ever visited. There were two rooms on the front ground floor—to the north, an ample dining-room-cum-kitchen with a large black iron stove and oven in a niche under the chimney; to the south—interrupted by the front door, vestibule, and staircase—was the drawing room, used only on special occasions, but to me a place of magic and fascination. For it contained all my mother's Oriental treasures: a round brass mandala-designed coffee table from India, shining with intricate floral patterns; two large Chinese vases on either side of the fireplace (I would guess from the Ch'ien-lung period) showing mandarins in their courts and warriors on the battlefield, and containing raffia fans from Samoa; over the mantelpiece a *turista* Japanese woven picture of a teahouse jutting out over a lake, seen at moonlight; on the mantelpiece, a fine celadon vase from Korea and a tiny wooden coffin from China containing the "corpse" of the aristocratic deceased; on the sofa, two richly embroidered Japanese cushions depicting falcons on flowering trees; an upright piano at which my mother played and my father used to sing arias from Gilbert and Sullivan—and such amazing Edwardian sentimentalities as "Dumbledum Deary" and "I'll Sing Thee Songs of Araby... 'til rainbow visions rise, and all my songs shall strive to wake sweet wonders in thine eyes."

It was in this room, with its flavor of Oriental magic, that my father, in his perfectly unostentatious King's English accent, read to me the tales and poems of that much maligned and misunderstood author, Rudyard Kipling —the *Just So Stories*, *The Jungle Books*, and *Puck of Pook's Hill*. Today, Kipling is largely regarded as an imperialist and jingoist whose writings represented British colonialism at its most aggressive peak. Yes and no. Kipling was one of the major channels through which the high culture of India and the Himalayas flowed back into the west, and persuaded me, for example, through such books as *Kim*, to have more sympathy for Buddhism than Christianity. Kipling was not a Max Müller or an Arthur Waley on the level of fine Oriental scholarship, but he spoke in a subtle and roundabout way to emotions in the solar plexus, the *manipura chakra*, and thus enchanted a small boy with curious, exotic, and far-off marvels that were simply not to be found in the muscular Christianity of the (Low Church) Church of England or in the boiled-beef-and-carrots English middle-class way of life.

It is important that this magical room was on the southwest of the house, although it ornaments were Oriental, for it was here that I acquired an interior compass which led me to the East through the West. I suppose I am some sort of human sunflower, for I always want to follow the sun— to the south, from England, and to the west. To the east of our home in Chislehurst was the wretched town of Sidcup. I called it "Sick-up," for it was a place which I prejudicially despised as I now despise Berkeley and Oakland from the standpoint of westerly Sausalito and Mount Tamalpais, upon whose beneficent slopes I am now writing. Beyond Sidcup there is a cruddy, run-down suburban and industrial area which ends up, believe it or not, in a place called Gravesend. I never went there, but judging from its position on the map,[2] it must be the rectum of England—not, perhaps, a real slum such as one finds in Whitechapel or Liddypool, but something even worse—a sordid monotony of identical babyshit-colored houses, adjoined row upon row.

So I am a mobile sunflower. I find myself incarnated at a pleasant—but often dingy and murky—point on a ball from which the sun is always south and constantly moves west. Being accustomed to the temperate zone, I don't want to live right under the sun, in the tropics, but I want to get a little warmer and to consort with people whose emotions are not quite so cold and standoffish. Look at this from the standpoint of a child who knows only his own immediate area. To the southwest of home there was the wild land of Pett's Wood and Colonel Edelman's sky-open estate. There were those elegant Elizabethan, Queen Anne, and Victorian mansions with their splendid gardens and cedar trees just south of Saint Nicholas's Church. There was the hopeful luminosity of the western sky in the early morning. There was

---

[2] The map of England, Scotland, and Wales shows an American Indian riding on a pig, pursuing the ball of Ireland to the West.

also, right on the edge of the commons, the home of my closest childhood friend, Ronald Macfarlane, who has now most sensibly become a student of Vedanta and breeds chickens on the open field in Cambridgeshire. He lived with his gentle and bewitchingly full-blown-rose-sexy mother and his warm-gruff father in an enormous house, appropriately called Brackenside, which smelled of the particular African tobacco that his father smoked constantly in a silver-lidded pipe. West also, at the bottom of Summer Hill, was Chislehurst Station—which is today almost exactly as it was fifty years ago—the point of departure for adventures in London and, better, for expeditions to the seacoast of Sussex. Much as I loved my home, that station—with the knock-knock sound of tickets being issued, the trring of the bell announcing an approaching train, and the murmuring rails as a train came in from the distance—was a center of liberation.

Like a moth drawn to the light I had to go west and south, following that interior compass which was aligned by the very topography of the place in which I was born—the southwest room of the house, and the southwest pleasantness of the village. Moving in that direction I always felt elated, and returning, depressed. So it was that in due course I discovered the Celtic-flavored Southwest of England, which from my point of departure, took off from the bare grassy hills of Berkshire with their dolmens (of burial mounds) from the days of the Druids, on to Avalon (or Glastonbury) in Somerset, where one felt the lurking presence of the Holy Grail, to Worle Hill—a lofty headland at the mouth of the Bristol Channel, crowned by a small, ruined, and ancient church in which I most earnestly sought the Christian God and didn't find him, and at which point I bought, from a curio shop in Weston-super-Mare, a small image of the Buddha—of the Daibutsu in Kamakura.[3] I liked the expression on his face. It wasn't judgmental or frantic, but stately and serene, and the title "Buddha" went along in my mind with buds.

This interior compass eventually drew me across the Atlantic, first to New York, then to Chicago, and at last to California—at which destination

---

[3] Why has no one ever made a correct reproduction of this extraordinary statue? I have seen hundreds and possess two reasonable facsimiles, but they never get the correct proportions of the head.

I saw a fog-clouded horizon and knew that this was the end of the West. But I felt that I had arrived, that I was comfortable and in my proper place, and that I had only to make up my mind as to whether to go a little way north or a little way south. It might have taken me to Portugal, or to the Riviera, but in those days I could not make a living in such places, and there they were also having their periodic political fits. Of course, through the ravages of commerce and gross misgovernment, California is rapidly being turned into a desert (or a plastic nursery like Disneyland), but I have found myself a quiet forested valley as a retreat for writing, and there isn't a single human habitation in sight. At any moment there might be a formidable earthquake—yet that is the way things are. Elsewhere it might be a tornado, an ice storm, a plane crash, a war, or simply slipping on the soap in the bathroom.

I have carefully considered going back to Chislehurst, because the environment is a much more agreeable place for an adult than a child. But, as everyone knows, the main reason for England's imperial exploits was that its more imaginative natives wanted to escape from its climate and its cooking. Some also wanted to escape its three hundred religions. In winter, which can last most of the year, the east wind brings a damp cold which, although nowhere near as low in actual temperature as a Chicago winter, seems to penetrate and freeze one's very bones, and to perpetrate an affliction, almost unknown in America, called "chilblains," which are red and itchy swellings on the hands.

As for the cooking, this subject has been treated by innumerable authors. I can say only that when I was first sent to boarding school, at Saint Hugh's, Bickley, one of the masters, urgently warned my parents that I was eating nothing but bread. This is not entirely true, for there were also fried pork sausages of a peculiarly scrumptious type that are no longer available, served with mashed potatoes, and also bars of milk chocolate and chocolate-coated marshmallows. We also managed to get down slices of suet pudding smothered in Lyle's Golden Syrup. For the rest, it shall be nameless. And, as was quite otherwise in the good old days, there was no beer. Before children were invented, during the Industrial Revolution, and set off as a special class of subpeople, everyone drank beer—and, despite Löwenbräu, Heidsieck, Kirin,

and Doseches, there is no beer like the beer of England.[4] Yet, anachronisti-
cally, the school song was a drinking song in honor of Saint Hugh of Lincoln,
tamer of wild swans, whose feast day was November 17.

Cold's the wind and wet's the rain,
Saint Hugh be our good speed!
Ill is the weather that brings no gain,
Nor helps good hearts in need.

So—troll the bowl, the jolly brown bowl,
And here, kind friend, "To thee!"
Let's sing a song for Saint Hugh's soul,
And down it merrily.

But if it is impractical physically, I must go back to Rowan Tree Cottage,
Holbrook Lane, in the imagination, because, as I am suggesting, the layout
of this house and garden gave me a compass for a life course. It wasn't forced
on me. I feel, somehow, that I chose it and would not have had it otherwise,
and I cannot find it in me to blame my parents in any way for the mazes and
tangles through which I have had to go to get where I am, doing what I really want to do in this astounding valley. Thus far I have described only
the two front rooms. Behind, and to the east, were a pantry, a larder, and an
auxiliary kitchen. I was gently discouraged from investigating the pantry
and larder too closely, and thus these little storage rooms became places of
pleasant mystery. In the pantry we kept the china and glass, and, in later
years, my father stowed there all the admirable beer which he made from
Kentish hops by his own recipe. The larder was what would now be the re-
frigerator—actually a "cooler"—a solidly walled room with a wire window-
screen where milk, butter, meat, vegetables, bread, and rock salt were kept.
The little kitchen—auxiliary, because much of the baking and cooking was done
on the iron stove in the dining room—was then more of a scullery. Mas-
sively stuffed into one corner was an enormous and formidable institution,

---

[4] America has Rainier Ale and Meisterbrau Dark, the latter available only within a hundred
miles of Milwaukee. The rest might just as well be ginger ale with alcohol added.

never used, known as "The Copper"—a receptacle with a fireplace beneath for boiling anything from laundry to a baron of beef.

Letters, excitement, friends, everything new came in by the western front door. But everything normal and regular came in by the eastern back door of the kitchen, where the representative of Mr. Coffin, the grocer, would call every day to take our orders, and where the milkman—who drove an incredible two-wheeled, horse-drawn chariot—would deliver the milk in metal canisters which, when empty, he would fling with clang and gusto into the chariot's bowels.

There was also in the dining room an amiable and mysterious monstrosity known as the Housetop. Below, it was a mahogany chest of drawers combined with a desk having, instead of a roll top, a hinged panel like one side of a roof. On the inside this panel was covered with green baize, and formed the writing surface when the desk was open. Above, it was a high matching cupboard, reaching almost to the ceiling, in which my mother hid away plum puddings wrapped in cheesecloth, fruit cake, brandy, *eau-de-vie*, and preserved fruits, amid cutglass decanters and such conceits of the Victorian silversmith as a fitted tray for four eggcups, accompanied by two chicks respectively loaded with salt and pepper. (I loved boiled eggs, and when my eyes were no higher than the edge of the table the appearance of eggs would set me to trotting around it saying, "Egg-egg-egg-egg-egg-egg…")

Inside the desk were small drawers and pigeonholes containing such delights as my father's checkbooks, printed in some ink that smelled of wealth and banks; but our olfactory vocabulary is so poor that it cannot be described. There were also drawers of semiobsolete fountain pens (the kind that one filled with a dropper), ordinary dip pens with scratchy points, screw pencils run out of leads, short rulers, compasses, and nameless gadgets with ivory handles for pricking, scoring, and scratching. There was another drawer for playing cards, with a box of Chinese chips in the form of ornate fish cut from mother-of-pearl. Here were Japanese-made gadgets for keeping score at bridge or whist—small rectangular tablets of black lacquer edged with hinged ivory tabs about the size and shape of a thumbnail, each inlaid with a different insect in varying shades of abalone shell.

In the center of this bank of drawers and pigeonholes was a small cupboard flanked by Corinthian columns with gilded capitals. It contained mostly photographs, postcards, and old letters, but there was a secret way of pulling out the whole unit to get access to two hidden compartments behind the columns. I didn't discover this until I was in my teens and, for some reason, have only the vaguest memory of what was kept there. Perhaps it was jewelry. But from as far back as I can remember I always had the fantasy that, somewhere, the Housetop contained some mystery, some hidden treasure, some magical entity that would be a key to the secret of life. The feeling was, of course, intensified because my parents kept me from exploring the Housetop too closely—for the simple reason that they didn't want all their papers disarranged. In 1968, when we had to sell the house because my father was too old to maintain it, I went through every nook and cranny of the Housetop—as well as all the chests of drawers and the attic—for even at the age of fifty-three that childish fantasy still lingered. Indeed, there were lots of interesting treasures and trinkets—but in all such quests and searches, as also in my pull to the West, it keeps coming back to me that the secret is in the seeker.

But it is fascinating to try to specify the external lure. Just what was it that I expected to find by following the sun, or hidden away in a secret box? I am quite certain that the pull to the West and South was the ancient search for the Paradise Garden—somewhere a courtyard with a fountain, set about with roses and magnolia trees, cypresses and willows, as may be seen in Persian miniatures, and with round arches through which one can look down upon an ocean fondling jagged islets with foam. And in this garden the point to which I drift, like a bee bewitched, is some flower—an iris, a jonquil, a crocus, or a morning glory. Indeed, I have sometimes wandered in such paradises with a magnifying glass, to gaze deeply into these translucent coronas of yellow and purple, ivory and coral with a contemplative devotion which is surely mystical. As my mother put it—once when showing me a morning glory—"Doesn't it make you feel jazzy inside!" Indeed, so many human beings have dreamed of this paradise that poets and literary people fear to seem trite in trying to evoke this beatific vision of the bee.

Of course it follows very simply that the thing I am hoping to find in the secret box is a jewel, whether indestructible as a diamond or emerald, or temporary as a dewdrop or crystal of snow. To pass into it through the eyes, to integrate one's consciousness with its ecstatic center of energy, and so enter the point where all one's nerve currents flow back into the place from which they come, where the individual is the universal and the moment eternity. The ecstasy of the jewel and the flower, of the Buddhist *mani padma*, of the jewel in the lotus as in *Om mani padme hum*, is a fascination so widely spread that it must have some unexplored connection with our whole psychophysical structure, and perhaps with the very design of life.

Serious cruelwits may dismiss jewels and flowers as ornaments and baubles for the brief delectation of children and vacuous women. But if so, why are gems worth vast sums of money? Why are focal points of religious aspiration so often represented as the bright centers of mandalas and petaled aureoles? Why the rose windows of cathedrals, the Celestial Rose in Dante's vision of Paradise, the Rose Garden of Our Lady, and the Lotus Throne of Mahavairocana—the great Buddha of the Sun? It adds only another question to see in all this a symbolism of sex, of self-abandonment in the paradise of the vaginal flower, for why, in turn, is *that* so fascinating—for reasons which must go far beyond its function as a reproductive lure?

I carry over from childhood the vague but persistent impression of being exposed to hints of an archaic and underground culture whose values were lost to the Protestant religion and the industrial bourgeoisie, indeed to the modern West in general. This may be nothing but fantasy, but I seem to have been in touch with lingering links to a world both magical and mystical that was still understood among birds, trees, and flowers and was known—just a little—to my mother and perhaps to one or two of my nursemaids. Or was it just I who carried in my genes or in my "collective unconscious" the apprehension of whole worlds of experience which official culture repressed or ignored? The *disciplinum arcanum* of this culture, so easily mistaken in the child for idle reverie, was that intense contemplative watching of the eternal now, which is sometimes revived by the use of psychedelic drugs, but which came to me through flowers, jewels, reflected light in glass, and expanses of clear sky. I get it also from music that is not mechanical and does not march, as from the music of India which I loved at first hearing and which continues, like a lost name on the tip of the tongue, to put me in mind of a long-forgotten afternoon in a sunlit room where magicians were playing on the heartstrings of the universe.

How well, then, is it remembered—for it is hardly mentioned today—that the contemplation of jewels is a way for the mind to understand itself and see its own reflection? I have just turned up the story of the Indian king Kankanapa, who learned yoga by gazing into the diamonds on his bracelet, following the instruction of a sage who told him, "Behold the diamonds of your bracelet, fix your mind upon them, and meditate thus: They are sparkling in all the colors of the rainbow; yet, these colors which gladden my heart have no nature of their own. In the same way our imagination is inspired by multifarious forms of appearance, which have no nature of their own. The mind alone is the radiant jewel, from which all things borrow their temporal reality."[5] A gypsy woman may use a crystal ball to probe the future, but a child who uses it to look into eternity may be better occupied than in memorizing multiplication tables.

All that I have so far described is a world that, to a child, needs no explanation or justification. The routine of shops on the Parade, the clop-clop of horses going by, the trees, fields, and bracken, the flowers, vegetables, and insects; and mother and father playing and singing in the drawing room with its Chinese embroideries—all this was unproblematic, a kind of incarnate music that was sufficient to itself and, as itself, the explanation of life.

Troubles began when you went to the bleak and unheated upstairs—to bed, bathroom, and prayers. Especially prayers. The rooms above had no features of beauty whatsoever—except their view of the garden. The bathroom was so abominable that I have made a drawing of it. It was constructed by a people, by a whole culture, which had never figured out delightful and amusing ways of handling such fundamentals of life as crapulation and bathing. Even an impecunious Japanese farmer has a reasonable bath where you can sit, soak, and laugh with the rest of the family, but it is kept separate from the

---

[5] Lama Anagarika Govinda, *Foundations of Tibetan Mysticism* (New York: E. P. Dutton & Co., 1959), p. 59.

THE BATHROOM AT ROWAN TREE COTTAGE, CHISLEHURST

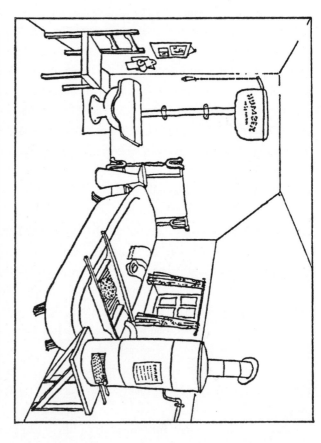

Looking back at it now, it wasn't so bad after all—especially when compared with the washing facilities of most people in the world. But as a child I hated and despised the place. The contraption to the far right is a geyser, for the gas heating of water. The puffy object on the rack over the bath is a natural sponge, then widely used for rinsing oneself. The roll of toilet paper was of a brand called Novio, smooth, hard, and shiny, and almost completely useless for its intended purpose. Just above it is a calendar with a pad of tear-off sheets for each day, giving the day of the week, the date, and a quotation from the Bible.

crapatorium, or *benjo*, which is operated on a system that, instead of wasting millions of gallons of water and requiring complex and ridiculous thrones, enables human excrements to be recycled and returned to the earth. The amount of shit we allow to flow out into the oceans is simply wasted manure—wasted, neglected, ignored because our eyes, noses, and mouths go one way and our assholes another, and because we are "ladies and gentlemen" we do not deign to look backward. But this crick in the neck is killing us. Do not be like serpents. Go on. Go forward. Progress. Remember Lot's wife, who looked backward at Sodom and Gomorrah and was turned into salt—by a one-way God.

All my childhood preceptors—parents, nurses, and physicians—were fascinated, even obsessed, by the problems of constipation. They seemed to want, above all things, to know "Have you *been*?" They invaded the bathroom with an almost religious enthusiasm to discover whether you had made it. They insisted that you "go" every morning immediately after breakfast, whether or not you felt so inclined. If you didn't, they dosed you with "California Syrup of Figs" (which is not to be found in California, just as English muffins are unknown in England), and if that did not produce results the next step was senna tea, the next cascara sagrada, the next calomel, and at last, the final punishment of castor oil—a sickening poison which gives you instant diarrhea. And then, as Dr. Tallent once remarked to one of my constipation-panicked nurses, "There is always some constipation after diarrhea." Thus the vicious cycle of crapulatory anxiety went on and on. As the great Dr. Georg Groddeck, colleague of Freud, once said, "There is a hole at the bottom and it has to come out eventually," and as a fact of historical memorabilia a certain King Ferdinand VII of Spain, who flourished, as I vaguely remember, in the early nineteenth century, existed for twenty-seven days without a bowel movement.

Actually, in this connection I have an early memory of an incident which may be curiously revealing about my father's attitude to life. I had been lying in my crib exploring my body, as infants do, and had recovered a small piece of dry excrement. My father saw me playing with it and asked, "What have you got there?" I held it up. He took it from my fingers, looked at it carefully, and gave it back.

From a child's point of view most adults are plainly irrational. As I get older, I begin more and more to feel that being brought up and "educated" is a form of hypnosis, brainwashing, and indoctrination that is extremely difficult to survive with one's senses intact. For me, being literate and articulate is a form of judo, of overcoming the game by its own method, though I must not be taken too seriously in this respect since I have a certain pride in my style as a Brahmin.

So, in this miserable bathroom I was taught prayers by my mother, and spanked by my mother who, for that purpose, sat upon the crapulatory throne, and told Bible stories by a governess, Miss Hoyle, who was forceful and ugly—unlike three other memorable and lovely nannies, Milly Hills, Miss Nielsen (from Denmark), and Miss Baumer (from the Netherlands), beneficent witches who beguiled me with fairy tales, and subtly represented the archaic resistance of Western Europe to the Christian invasion from Rome. Of course, my mother thought she was doing "the right thing," but she was regarded as the black sheep of her family for lack of true enthusiasm for their dreary and tiresome religion. She would sometimes mock their more lugubrious hymns, such as:

Weary of earth, and laden with my sin,
I looked at heav'n and longed to enter in.
But there no evil [i.e., sexy] thing may find a home:
And yet I hear a voice that bids me "Come."

And they don't seem to realize what doubletalk they are singing. The Misses Hills, Nielsen, and Baumer put—as the Scandinavian saying goes—raven's blood in my mother's milk. They gave me a sense of magic and the weird, which my mother, with her intense sensitivity to floral beauty, had not altogether renounced, and which my father simply compounded with tales from Kipling and the *Arabian Nights*.

In this same bathroom, then, my mother taught me my first prayer, which was not the usual "Now I lay me down to sleep," but

Gentle Jesus, Shepherd, hear me:
Bless thy little lamb tonight.
Through the darkness be thou near me;
Keep me safe 'til morning light.

Let my sins be all forgiven;
[Which I would repeat as: Let my sins be awful given;]
Bless the friends I love so well.
Take me, when I die, to heaven,
Happy there with thee to dwell.

This doggerel inspired in me entirely unnecessary terrors of darkness and death, and made "going to heaven" as depressing as the alternative, "going to hell," was horrendous. For Christians have never had a good idea of heaven.

Be my last thought, "How sweet to rest
For ever on my Savior's breast."

This might be fun for a nun, but for a man it is an invitation to the boredom of a homosexual paradise—which is not to say that I condemn homosexuality, but only that I do not enjoy it. There was also that twisted-head idea of heaven which describes the immense fun of eternity as

Prostrate before Thy throne to lie,
And gaze and gaze on Thee.

Children notice these things and, though they may make jokes about them among themselves, are often seriously troubled by the apparent seriousness with which adults take them.

Children, as well as adults, make humorous, bantering, scurrilous, and abusive uses of the notion of hell as everlasting post-mortem damnation. But I was so appalled by this possibility that I would lie awake at night worrying about it, frightened of going to sleep because of the obvious analogy between sleep and death. People were always talking about someone or other who "died in his sleep." My mother tried to console me by quoting John 3:16, but there seemed to be no way of being really and truly sure that one actually and genuinely did believe in Jesus, or whether one had not inadvertently committed the unpardonable sin against the Holy Ghost by laughing at the limerick

Il y avait un jeune home de Dijon
Qui n'amait pas la religion.

Il dit, "O ma foi,
   Comme drôle sont ces trois:
Le Père, et le Fils, et le Pigeon."

Which, I suppose could be translated into English as

There was a young fellow of Dijon,
Who took a dislike to religion.
   He said, "Oh my God,
   These three are so odd—
The Father, the Son, and the Pigeon."[6]

As one is tempted to fall over a precipice from vertigo, the child exposed to this grotesque Bible religion is apt to mutter compulsively under his breath, "Damn the Holy Ghost," and then suffer from paroxysms of guilt. Do the adults seriously mean that if you whisper this diabolic formula you will, when dead, squirm and scream in unquenchable fire forever and ever and ever, Amen? After all, a child is not theologically sophisticated, and takes this imagery literally.

My own bedroom was on the southwest of the upper floor, overlooking a wide area of vegetable gardens, or allotments, the Workmen's Clubhouse, and—beyond rows of trees—the spire of Saint Nicholas's Church. Until, in early adolescence, I made this room into a congenial den, it was a plain, boring, and purely functional bedroom to which one was sent as a place of punishment because one was being a nuisance on the lower floor, or because it

---

[6] Why translate it? Because most of my American readers, especially the younger, do not understand French, or any language other than their own. Strangely, from a European point of view, they may otherwise be amazingly intelligent people. Also, unless they come from a respectably churchly family (Episcopalian or Presbyterian) or from the Bible-crazed South, they will not have read the Bible at all, and thus will not understand the reference John 3:16, a verse from the Gospel of Saint John in which it is said that "God so loved the world that he gave his only-begotten Son, Jesus Christ, that whosoever believes in him shall not perish, but have eternal life." Even then, an intelligent young American hasn't the faintest idea of what is meant by an "only-begotten Son" or by "eternal life." Neither, for that matter, have most of the clergymen—except some of the very young set, who have recently been getting such excellent theological instruction that they are completely at odds with their parishioners.

was the proper time of evening to GO TO BED or, worse, to "take a rest" in the afternoon. Why don't adults understand that the siesta, however delectable for themselves after an ample luncheon with good wine, and with the companionship of a pleasing lover, is a colossal bore to a child who gets neither wine nor lover? Perhaps one might also ask why children, with their fantastic energy, do not realize how irritating they can be to adults. Of course, the mild and perfectly mannered children of Japan, China, and Mexico are simply undernourished, by our standards. They fill them up with starch. As soon as the children of prosperous and Westernized Japanese go on our diet they become objectionable brats, but so long as they stay on starch and vegetables they are allowed to stay up at night, and to doze off naturally into sleep when they are genuinely tired.

But the culture in which I and almost all whites were raised vainly imagines that hunger, sleeping, and excreting can be regimented. Amerindians have always mocked the palefaces for looking at clocks to know when they ought to be hungry. It is in the same clock-mad spirit that we are all supposed to "work" from nine to five on such preposterous projects as accounting for what we have done upon billions of square miles of paper derived from devastated forests, frittering away our time upon such dreary gambling games as playing the stock market or selling insurance in drab offices, turning out drillions of lines of chatter for people whose minds cannot be at peace unless perpetually agitated with information and misinformation, and manufacturing, selling, and advertising bizarre, noisome, and pestilential automotive contraptions for taking us all to and from these same projects at the same hours—thereby blocking the roads and jangling our nerves, presumably to give ourselves the message that we really exist and are really important.

Thus I could never understand why my beloved father had to dress himself in absurd black clothes, assume an umbrella, and top himself with a fatuous bowler (American: derby) hat to catch the eight-thirty train to the City and bore himself all day by selling tires for Monsieur Bibendum of the Michelin Company, which has, however, somewhat exonerated itself by providing its celebrated guide to the restaurants of France. Therefore, at about the age of twenty-one, I made to myself the solemn vow that I would never by an employee or put up with a "regular job." I have not always been

able to fulfill this vow. I have had to work (in a reasonably independent manner) for the Church and for a graduate school, but since the age of forty-two
I have been a free lance, a rolling stone, and a shaman, as distinct from an
apostolically successed priest. For the shaman gets his magic alone in the
mountains and forests, whereas a priest gets his from being ordained by a
guru or bishop.. The first goes with a culture of nomads and hunters, and the
second with cultures of agrarians or industrialists. Although I am, unofficially and on the side, an ordained priest of the Anglican Communion, my
genes must have come from the nomads of Europe and my reincarnation
from the Taoist poets of China or the *yamabushi*, or mountain hermits, of
Japan. I am gregarious, but I like to be left alone.

I especially remember that bedroom on Sunday twilights. The British
have, even now, a positive and supernatural genius for making Sunday depressing. They roll up not only the sidewalks but everything else, and permit only the celebration of their three hundred dreary religions. Those not
disposed to religion swarm off to the seacoast in miles of traffic jams. But
alone in that bedroom I would hear the bells of Saint Nicholas falling down
through the major scale, ringing the changes forever downwards, to summon the faithful to Evensong, to the closing service of the day, with, as John
Betjemen has put it, undertones of "death and hell at last."

Strangely enough, young people in Japan have the same feeling about
the atmosphere of their parents' Buddhism—the atmosphere which is, to me,
enchanting and magical with booming gong-bells and deep-throated and unintelligible sutrachanting. To them all this is *kurai*—a word which means
deep, dark, dank, musty, gloomy, and sad. This was more or less the way I
felt about the bells of Saint Nicholas on a Sunday evening. They were all at
once sweet, melodious, and *kurai*. I love-hated them.

The day Thou gavest, Lord, is ended,
The darkness falls at Thy behest;
To Thee our morning hymns ascended,
Thy praise shall sanctify our rest.

(Sung to a wobbly, sentimental tune called Saint Clement, composed in 1874.)
It is understandable, therefore, that I have an aversion to bedrooms—

to rooms specifically set aside for sleeping. Usually I curl up on a divan in my library or studio, cuddled up with (*a*) my wife and (*b*) a blanket—preferably a soft one made with vicuña or, according to the weather, one of those substantial Mexican blankets from Oaxaca or Toluca in which the wool of white sheep and black sheep are combined into those fundamental designs where the figure is always interchangeable with the background. The British and the Western Europeans in general, as well as the North Americans, waste the space of their homes with these rooms for ludicrously vast sleeping-machines— some with four pillars and a roof, some with iron fences at each end, topped with brass balls, and some with mahogany headboards whose function I have never yet understood. I would rather follow the Turkish proverb that "He who sleeps on the floor will not fall out of bed." In sum, I despise almost all furniture as monstrous, heavy, space-greedy, expensive, and pretentious. Most beds and chairs make me think of crutches and surgical appliances, and while these things have merciful uses for the aged and infirm, anyone who is healthy and under sixty, especially a child, can do without them.[7]

It was also in this room that I was trapped, with the very best of intentions, into having my appendix removed by Mister (the British make it a pundonor not to refer to surgeons as Doctor) Russell Howard, Fellow of the Royal College of Surgeons, with the assistance of Doctors Tallent and Graham Hodgson (anaesthetist), and with the collaboration of my astonishing Aunt Gertrude, my mother's younger sister, who was a trained nurse at the London Hospital. Auntie Gertie was a pretty, vivacious tomboy who saved my life a few days after birth by discovering that I had an infected navel, and by watching me constantly through the cure. Before the operation she rubbed my belly (which she called my Little Mary) with some sort of iodine solution, and when I revived from the anaesthetic I beheld her in full nurse's uniform

---

[7] In some book of Victorian *curiosa* I have even seen a photograph of a special appliance, of carefully polished and elaborately shaped wood, that was supposed to be a sort of flattened-out chaise or support for the purpose of sexual intercourse, and one can imagine it being used by such a couple as is portrayed in Lautrec's *Divan Japonais*. She trussed in black, and he in his opera hat, with his amber-headed cane, and monocle, disdainfully fingering the menu.

like a guardian angel, and I was so turned on by the mixture of chloroform and ether which Dr. Hodgson had used that I found I could dream any dream I wanted to dream.

I had no sexual feeling for Gertrude Buchan. I can't even remember her figure—only her face and her style—but it simply has to go on the record— IN LOVING MEMORY—that this woman not only saved my life but was also the constant companion of my childhood, and had the incredible patience to listen attentively to the interminable tales which I made up on the spur of the moment. It is unbelievable how my adult relations tolerated me, for I talked and spun out stories incessantly, and when there was no one to listen I told them to myself. For several years (it must have been from four to eight) I elaborated, with illustrations, a serial-story about an island kingdom in the middle of the Pacific, most incongruously named Bath Bian Street, a name which I think echoed the sound of railway officials calling out the names of stations.

With the accompanying drawings you will see that these islanders were stickmen with varying types of heads. The inhabitants of Bath Bian Street itself had spoon-shaped heads, and were beneficently and heroically ruled by King Eecky, with the help of his Chief of Staff Forky, and his Generals Tocky and Bicky. The religion of the island consisted in the worship of a deceased little girl named Hiery, in whose honor they had built an immense temple with two mile-high towers known as the Hieress. Their repulsive enemies, on a neighboring island, were the Blacklanders, whose elongated heads fell back from their necks, and who tied their hair in buns. Their king was Guzzy-and-Seat, so named from the style of his walk, which was slightly to lower his seat, or bottom, after each step and thus proceed with the rhythm "Guzzy-and-Seat, Guzzy-and-Seat, Guzzy-and-Seat..." (As a child I was very conscious of people's walking rhythms—gliding, stomping, bouncing, or tripping—and used to make up ditties to describe them. The headmaster of King's School, Canterbury, in his black gown and mortarboard, went "Damson, damson, damson, damson.")

Perhaps it was this propensity for storytelling, combined with my mother's ill health and my father's necessity to take long trips all over the country in the cause of Monsieur Bibendum, that compelled them to get rid of me as often as possible—and I don't blame them! They employed four

Eecky, King of the Island
of Bath Bian Street.

Guzzy-and-Seat, King of Blackland.

Forky

Tocky

Bicky

(Lieutenants of Eecky)

Blacklander, with extreme dolicocephalous
head, and hair in bun.

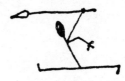

Bath Bian Street soldier, on the run.

An islander of Little Blownose,
allies of Bath Bian Street.

The Princess Hiery—always drawn
from behind, because of inability to make
a sufficiently beautiful face.

BATH BIAN STREET REPULSES AN INVASION OF THE BLACKLANDERS.

nannies or governesses to cushion themselves against me between birth and the age of seven-and-a-half, at which point I was sent off to a boarding school for instruction in laughing and grief, in militarism and regimented music, in bibliolatry and bad ritual, in cricket, soccer, and rugby, in preliminary accounting, banking, and surveying (known as arithmetic, algebra, and geometry), and in subtle, but not really overt, homosexuality. It was a school for aristocrats, attended by relatives of the Royal Family, of the Imperial House of Russia, of the Rajas of India, and sons of industrial tycoons. There was even a boy who had been buggered by an Arabian prince. And my parents knocked themselves out financially to send me to this amazing institution.

CHAPTER TWO

TANTUM RELIGIO

I was brought up in a culture that for more than a thousand years had been smothered in and diseased with religion. On at least the pretext of religious zeal it had initiated the Crusades, the Holy Inquisition, the Puritan Revolution, the Thirty Years War, and the subjugation and cultural destruction of India, Africa, China, and the native civilizations of North and South America. Diseases are not, of course, entirely bad. The finest incense in the world—aloeswood—is made from a diseased part of the tree, and pearls are a sickness of oysters. Thus there are esoteric or underground aspects of Judaism, Christianity, and Islam which, though usually persecuted, are of surpassing interest. But in their exoteric and official aspects they are a repression of all ecstasies except those of righteous indignation, violence, and military pomp. "Those who take the sword shall perish by the sword" but, on the other hand, "I came not to bring peace but a sword," so "Let not your left hand know what your right hand doeth." On the whole, therefore, I am ashamed of this culture and have done my best to tame it with more peaceful and convivial principles derived, for the most part, from Hindu, Buddhist, and Taoist philosophy.

I said "on the whole," and therefore not entirely. For my life has been an attempt to reconcile what are supposed to be opposites, and my name "Alan" means "harmony" in Celtic and "hound" in Anglo-Saxon. Accordingly, my existence is, and has been, a paradox, or better, a coincidence of opposites. On the one hand I am a shameless egotist. I like to talk, entertain, and hold the center of the stage, and can congratulate myself that I have done this to a considerable extent—by writing widely read books, by appearing on radio and television, and by speaking before enormous audiences. On the other hand I realize quite clearly that the ego named Alan Watts is an illusion, a social institution, a fabrication of words and symbols without the slightest substantial reality; that it will be utterly forgotten within five hundred years (if our species lasts that long), and that my physical organism will shortly pass off into dust and ashes. And I have no illusions that some sort of proprietary and individual soul, spook, or ghost will outlast it.

Nevertheless, I know too that this temporary pattern, this process, is a function, a doing, a *karma*, of all that is and of the "which than which there is no whicher" in just the same way as the sun, the galaxy, or, shall we be bold to say, Jesus Christ or Gautama the Buddha. How can I say this without offense—without seeming proud, haughty, and pretentious? I simply, and even humbly, know that I am The Eternal, even though such supremely enlightened people as Jesus, Buddha, Kabir, Sri Ramakrishna, Hakuin, and Sri Ramana Maharshi may have manifested this knowledge in a more forceful and authoritative style. I would be affecting the most dishonest false modesty if I did not acknowledge this, and yet the idea of my coming on as a messiah or great guru just breaks me up with laughter.

Because, at the same time, I am an unrepentant sensualist. I am an immoderate lover of women and the delights of sexuality, of the greatest French, Chinese, and Japanese cuisine, of wines and spiritous drinks, of smoking cigars and pipes, of gardens, forests, and oceans, of jewels and paintings, of colorful clothes, and of finely bound and printed books. If I were extremely rich I would collect incunabula and rare editions, Japanese swords, Tibetan jewelry, Persian miniatures, Celtic illuminated manuscripts, Chinese paintings and calligraphies, embroideries and textiles from India, images of Buddhas, Oriental carpets, Navajo necklaces, Limoges enamels, and venerable wines from France. Yet there have been two or three times in my life when I have had to abandon almost all possessions and go it alone, and thus I have also an attraction to being a no-strings-attached Taoist wanderer in the mountains, "cloud-hidden, whereabouts unknown." And, when the mood suits me, I also like to practice Buddhist meditation in the Zen or Tibetan *ʒog-chen* style, which is simply sitting quietly or walking rhythmically without thoughts or verbalizations in your head.

Sitting quietly, doing nothing,
Spring comes and grass grows by itself.

Or the Western version:

Sometimes I sits and thinks,
But mostly I just sits.

My wife, looking over my shoulder, has just suggested that this is the real meaning of the doctrine of the Immaculate Conception—to be clean of concepts, and thus to be in that state of awareness which yogis call *nirvikalpa samadhi*, and it struck us that if this news got around it would completely subvert and transform the Catholic Church.

For the Church is the world's most talkative institution, and the Church of England, in which I was most firmly brought up, is, of course, a branch of the Catholic Church—though politically and economically separated from the See of Rome.[1] But these impoverished Christians do nothing in their religious observances except chatter. They tell God what he ought and ought not to do, and inform him of things of which he is already well aware, such as that they are miserable sinners, and proceed then to admonish one another to feel guilt and regret about abominable behavior which they have not the least intention of changing. If God were the sort of being most Christians suppose him to be, he would be beside himself with boredom listening to their whinings and flatteries, their redundant requests and admonitions, not to mention the asinine poems set to indifferent tunes which are solemnly addressed to him as hymns.

---

[1] But recently I took my wife's niece, Kathleen, to Mass at Westminster Cathedral, the Roman Catholic headquarters of England, and the service, uttered in English instead of Latin, was almost indistinguishable from the same service—celebrated a little way east— at Westminster Abbey. It was beautifully done, and the sermon was a brief and highly intelligent drawing of analogy between the order of God and the order of vegetation. But the Catholic Church has lost its magic by celebrating the mass in the vernacular instead of Latin. As Clare Booth Luce said to me a few days later, it is no longer possible to practice contemplative prayer at Mass. However, things being what they are, there is no longer the least reason why the Church of England and the Church of Rome should be at odds.

This was why I was always attracted to the old style of Roman Catholicism, wherein you could steal into church unnoticed and listen to a perfectly unintelligible service in splendid Gregorian chant. The whole thing was music, and God was not bored. But, alas, my mother, though not fanatical about it, was a Protestant of the Low Church persuasion, and took me off on Sundays to Christ Church for the didactic services of Morning Prayer or Ante-Communion, in English, where the scholarly and gentle vicar, Mr. Lightfoot, would discourse upon the Bible. He wore a neatly trimmed beard and looked like Jesus, and once presented me with a copy of the New Testament in Greek, though it should be noted that my mother brought about my real downfall by giving me the same scriptures in Chinese. The translation is atrocious, by Chinese literary standards, but that little green book seeded my lifelong interest in Chinese writing and in what Chinese sages and poets had to say about life.

However, when my mother was indisposed, Miss Gussy next door would take me to the ten-o'clock celebration of Choral Communion at Saint Nicholas's, where Canon Dawson and his curate, Mr. Horner, were getting away with something which resembled—as nearly as possible under the laws of the Church of England—a Solemn High Mass. No incense, but genuflections, the Sanctus bell, and a marvelously mantric and unintelligible way of reciting the prayers, so that Elizabethan English might just as well be Sanskrit.

Now, from a child's point of view religious services—at least as conducted by most Christians—are perfectly weird, especially when everyone lines up in pews so as to give the church the appearance of an enormous omnibus, with organ music instead of the sound of the engine. At Christ Church, established and built by the *nouveaux riches* of the Victorian era, the pews were actually rented and bore the name of the family in frilly goldish frames. There were also plush kneeling-hassocks, some of which were also boxes for containing prayer books and hymnals. In front of us were the pews of the Travers-Haweses and the Balmeses, and the hassock-box of the Balmeses contained one of those horrendous Bibles like spaniels, with leather bindings which flop over the edge of the book. Those were the days when women wore immense hats with ostrich feathers, coiled up their hair into buns like cow-pats, and would come to the church-bus in glovely garments of solid grey tweed which smothered them from neck to ankle. I once turned physically sick at the sight of them, and had to be taken out of church.

Walking down Old Hill to Christ Church one would encounter freaky characters like Miss Frieze and her sister, known as Piggyligs and Doffles, faded and overblown brunette beauties under vast black hats, struggling up with their black walking sticks. There were also foppish gentlemen who affected pince-nez spectacles and wore straw hats or boaters attached to their lapels with black silk cords, and with all this straw, string, wire, and tweed—plus their formally jerky manner of hat-doffing, speech, and gait—seemed like mechanisms rather than men. But there was, too, a fabulous Mr. Dunn (who probably paid the bills for Christ Church) owning an immense mansion and estate adjacent to the church, who was stout, prosperous, and avuncular, wore a top hat and double-breasted waistcoat with gold watch chain across the belly, and with his sisters, put on delightful parties for children—especially at Christmas, when they had a tree at least twenty feet high under the glass dome of the central hall of their house. After church he would often quietly slip me half-a-crown for kicks.

But I could not make out why such pleasant people espoused such a fearsome and boring religion. There was especially the case of my mother's brother, Harry Buchan, and his veritably saintly wife, Auntie Et (Ethel), who never complained about anything, nor spoke an ill word of anyone, never read a book, but cultivated a splendid garden and wrote inscriptions in "poker-work" (writing calligraphy with a hot iron point on wood) with such sentiments as

> The kiss of the sun for pardon,
> The song of the bird for mirth;
> You're nearer God's heart in a garden
> Than anywhere else on earth.

Uncle Harry ran an institution in Bromley, just west of Chislehurst, known as the PSA or "Pleasant Sunday Afternoon." This was a Protestant, interdenominational, hearty hymn-singing fest held at three o'clock on Sunday afternoons, with Bible-reading and an address by Uncle Harry or some visiting speaker. I even addressed the assembly myself on the subject of religion and music, with my uncle's daughter, Joyce Buchan (who, ruddy and joyous as her name implied, was my closest childhood girl friend), playing the piano to illustrate my points, using one of Beethoven's sonatas. At the PSA one was greeted by effusive little men with warm handshakes, and everyone was welcome, welcome, O so welcome.

Yet Uncle Harry, bowler-hatted and black-booted, genial and generous to a fault, was also managing director of Wood's (of Queen Victoria Street in the City), which sold and produced the most glorious tobacco, cigars, and cigarettes in London. And dear Uncle Harry, pious Bibleman that he was, got me hooked on smoking tobacco at the age of thirteen when, at Christmas, he presented me with a package of small cigars. At that time, it should be remembered, smoking tobacco in school was regarded as burning incense to the Devil, and was punished by merciless floggings; and now they are doing it all over again with marijuana which, though less harmful to the organism than tobacco, incurs still more dreadful penalties. But Uncle Harry's tobacco shop was a warm, woodsily odoriferous place, from which the Worshipful and Honorable Companies of Goldsmiths, Saddlers, Merchant Tailors, and Vintners bought tobacco for their superb dinners—Eton cigarettes, made of Yenidje leaf from Asia Minor and hand-rolled like fat joints, and Villa y Villar cigars from the high hills of Cuba. On the counter there were also huge crocks of different types of pipe tobacco from which you could select your own mix, with the counsel of Uncle Harry himself or his impeccably courteous salesmen. The American parallel would be Dunhill's cedar room in New York, where they have lockers of cigars bearing the names of the Duke of Windsor, the Marx Brothers, Winston Churchill, and other celebrities.

We customarily visited Uncle Harry on Sunday evenings, for high tea, consisting of such things as a scrumptious Scotch bread called bannock, not unlike the Italian *panettone*, beef-steak-and-kidney pudding under a crust of suet, scones with globs of butter and jam, disastrous boiled cabbage or cauliflower, and treacle-tart, which is made by putting Lyle's Golden Syrup in a pie shell and baking it. Beyond that, Uncle Harry's idea of an evening's entertainment was for everyone to gather about the piano and sing hymns. And this brings me to an important point, for my childhood and adolescent life was—as by background music in a movie—haunted by hymns. I have thought of composing a book entitled *Hymns Haunting and Horrible*, bound in dark blue cloth, embossed with the mullion-forms of a Gothic church window, and the lettering in gold Olde English type, containing versical and musical parodies of these preposterously infantile ecclesiastical ditties. They are not like Hindu or Buddhist mantras, which are simply hummed for the contemplation of their sound, nor even like Alleluias in Gregorian chant. They are wretched bombastic, moralistic, and maudlin nursery rhymes, even though the choirs of King's College, Cambridge, and the Chapel Royal of London can sing some of them with the voices of angels.

Yet my attitude to these hymns is weirdly ambivalent, for they go on echoing in the dome of my skull. Just a few of them are, indeed, musically superb: *Veni creator, Coelites plaudant, Veni Emmanuel,* and those composed by Bach and Handel. But there are others which I fondle in my mind as the tongue strays over a hole in a tooth. They recall the vast, deserted darkness of Canterbury Cathedral when we all went into a small chapel in the south transept for Evensong, where a dwarf pumped the organ, and our diminutive chaplain with a big head, "Titch" Mayne, conducted the service, and we sang to a stately and triumphant melody:

> Give praise then for all them
> Who sought and here found Him,
> Whose journey is ended,
> Whose perils are past.
> They believed in the Light,
> And its glory is round them,
> For the clouds of earth's sorrows
> Have lifted at last.

And those tunes have far-off resonant names, like England's Lane, Kilmarnock, and Saffron Walden, Splendor Paternae and Woodbird, Regent Square and Saint Osyth, Monks' Gate and Down Ampney—names evoking very ancient Romanesque churchs in tiny, mysterious villages with venerable beech trees, or the ghosts of Benedictine fathers chanting Compline at nightfall in adoration of perpetual light, or solemn celebrations of Victorian pomp and circumstance in the musty hush of Westminster Abbey.

Not only did we sing hymns in church and at Uncle Harry's on Sunday nights: my father sang them to me as lullabies; we sang them morning and evening in school. I recollect a breakfast in the home of some Baptist missionaries back from China, where, while the breakfast got cold, everyone sang a hymn, read around the table a verse from some passage of scripture, and then knelt down at their chairs for interminable prayers. At the time, I didn't seriously object. I was impressed, terrified, comforted, and interested by this weird religion, as well as fascinated by tales of magic and adventure in The Bible, a volume which I was taught to regard as a sacred charm against evil and misfortune, as many Catholics regard the Blessed Sacrament.

My mother and father had the good taste to belong to the Church of England, as also did Uncle Harry, though he flirted with "chapel" people such as Presbyterians, Methodists, and Baptists who had a strange genius for worshipping God in buildings that looked like obscene mixtures of churches and factories—all entirely devoid of color, except for a peculiarly appalling yellow glass in the windows that was supposed, quite falsely, to give the impression of sunlight on cloudy days. But the Church of England, being the established religion of the land, is ruled by the King or Queen, and thus derives from the *shekinah* or radiance of their majesty a certain dignified splendor. To belong to the Church of England is to feel quite definitely connected with the Royal House, and with a hierarchy which eventually leads up to God in a clear and orderly manner. This peculiar experience is also available to the Japanese, through Shinto, whose style is oddly reminiscent of Anglican ritual; but most Americans know nothing of it, and are therefore lacking in public morale and true *esprit de corps*. This may or may not be a good thing, and I am simply pointing it out.

The style of the Church of England is heraldic. Just look at Westminster Abbey or the Chapel of Saint George at Windsor, with its elegant fan-vaulting and display of proud banners, and at once you are reminded of the noble Norman-French-English formulae of heraldry—"three lions passant regardant gules on a field or"—and this summons up associations with the knights of King Arthur and the High Quest of the Holy Grail. To me, the central shrine of this religion is the corona of Canterbury Cathedral, a high circular structure at the far east end of the building, where stands the austere stone throne of Saint Augustine, who brought the Catholic faith to England in A.D. 595. All around this corona are tall narrow windows of stained glass, predominantly blue—as good as anything in Chartres—which, with their colors reflecting on the pale grey stone, give the whole place a sense of light and lofty airiness, jeweled transparency and peace. It was in this shrine that I once heard Sir Adrian Boult conduct the Good Friday music from *Parsifal*, and though I am not much of an admirer of Wagner, his mastery of the orchestra was such that the Grail itself seemed to be present. But what secretly amuses me is that an empty throne was the original symbol of the Buddha, of the prince who abandoned kingship and the quest for power.[2]

Once I saw this throne occupied, when I, as a boy of thirteen, carried the long red train of his Grace Cosmo Gordon Lang at his enthronement as Archbishop of Canterbury, amid an immense assembly of bishops, canons, priests, professors, and government officials. Ironically, it was this same Archbishop who—for quite the wrong reason—kicked Edward VIII off the throne of England, because he had chosen to marry a divorced woman. British politics, with all its pomp and circumstance, is a game of musical chairs. Americans play the same game without the music.

So then, I was partially enchanted by the splendor and dignity of this royal religion, by the Victorian dong-dong of Big Ben's clock at Westminster, by the triumphant bells of Canterbury's high towers, by the stately and pompously didactic music of that hymn "The Church's one foundation," and by the grandeur of singing the psalm "I will lift up mine eyes unto the hills" to the ringing Anglican chant that usually goes with it—though I can't really get all this across, for relatively few people who read books can sight-read musical notation.

But there was something wrong. The sermons of the clergy—bleated or sonorously boomed for lack of electronic public-address systems—conveyed

---

[2] The Japanese artist Saburo Hasegawa once rather slyly remarked to me, "You must always remember that one of the main differences between Buddhism and Christianity is that Jesus was the son of a carpenter, and Buddha the son of a king."

nothing beyond the emotional energies of their funny voices, which all of us used to mock and mimic. So, too, we would parody the hymns, such as the doggerel

> Through the night of doubt and sorrow,
>   Onward goes the pilgrim band,
> Singing songs of expectation,
>   Marching to the promised land

as—with all the names referring to the school staff—

> Life presents a dreary picture,
>   Dull and empty as the tomb,
> Little Mo's in bed with stricture,
>   Judy's got a fallen womb.

> Butler now through masturbation
>   Never laughs and seldom smiles,
> Ralph has found an occupation
>   Crushing ice for Buckley's piles.

Thus one of the main reasons for the obsolescence of the Church of England and, for that matter, for the collapse of the British Empire, is that the children could not bring themselves to take it seriously. Canon Bickersteth had a voice so wobbly and up-and-downish in is tonality that he almost gave us hysterics, although laughing in church was most definitely not permitted. Canon Gardner had a magnificent and formidable rumble, especially when reading biblical denunciations of the Amalekites, Midianites, Hivites, and Perizzites. Canon Crum, a sweet and holy man, frail, ascetic, and archetypally priestly in appearance, would bleat his sermons—from which I remember only the phrase, "It is, as the Americans say, monkeying with the buzz saw, monkeying with the buzz saw!" Canon Jenkins, a very learned theologian, who awarded me first prize in Divinity for a highly unorthodox essay, used to declaim sermons, prayers, and scriptures in something close to a shriek, whereas Canon Helmore muttered everything as if he had a perpetually stuffed-up nose.

The Archbishop himself had an impeccably aristocratic, sonorous voice, but I cannot remember a single thing he ever said, except that he was an extremely witty and accomplished after-dinner speaker. The Dean (when I first went to Canterbury in 1928) was G. K. A. Bell, subsequently Bishop of Chichester, of whom, or of one of his more ancient predecessors in that office, it is written:

> There was a young lady of Chichester
> Whose beauty made saints in their niches stir.
>> One morning at mass,
>> The curves of her ass
> Made the Bishop of Chichester's britches stir.

But it is true that Bishop Bell made the famous remark that the clergy are like manure—excellent when spread all over the country while doing their work, but when gathered together in a heap they stink.

He was later succeeded by the notorious Red Dean Hewlett Johnson (imagine a very tall and baldpated George Washington), who talked through his teeth, kept clearing his throat, but lived to trouble the Church until well over ninety. He, and in later years Father Grieg Taber of that scandalously high church of Saint Mary the Virgin, New York, taught me the fundamentals of ecclesiastical ritual, a matter upon which I consider myself something of an authority. I have even served as master of ceremonies at a pontifical Solemn High Mass, celebrated from the throne. As a High Churchman he reformed the style of services in the Cathedral and, among other things, taught us how to process in the right way—not marching and swaying in close order, but gently strolling, about two yards from each other. I was once among a small group of boys whom he invited to dinner in his splendid mansion, where he told us of his adventures in China and, without the slightest self-consciousness, explained the delights of his own way of life. For example, he slept in a camp bed in the open air on top of the Deanery tower—withdrawing to the stairway portico when it rained—and worked standing at a high desk in his white-paneled library, where he would also take his breakfast of fruit and health-food-type cereals.

However, the most beneficent and lovable of all these Canterbury clergy was Canon Trelawney Ashton-Gwatkin, rector of the bucolic parish of Bishopsbourne, a little south of town and approached through a spacious estate with a red Georgian manor, acres of grass, and trees so spaced that they grew to their full and natural size, sometimes as thick as leaves with multitudes of chortling birds. I would regularly bicycle out to his place for lunch on Sundays in the company of the two admirable Ford-Kelsey brothers who had introduced me to him, to arrive at this tiny village in the hills with its venerable church and sumptuous rectory. For the good Canon was obviously wealthy. He and his very gentle, solicitous, and prettily scrawny wife maintained separate libraries, so crammed with books and fine editions and incunabula that they were piled on every table.

This robust and affable cleric would receive us in his library, arrayed in soutane with a wide satin sash, and topped with a Canterbury cap, which is a sort of soft biretta, indicating that he was an extremely High Churchman of the Sarum (or Salisbury) rite.[3] He would treat us to amiable conversation over sherry, and then lead us to his Elizabethan dining room where maid and butler would serve us with the only real food in the whole area, including a magnificent purée of chestnuts, buttered and browned. Once, during luncheon, the conversation turned to the virtues of *pâté de foie gras*, and the Canon's wife allowed that she had scruples about eating a delicacy which involved so much unkindness to geese. I, having recently returned from France, had to admit that I liked it very much, whereupon the Canon remarked, "I see you and I belong to the bad old school."

When lunch was over the butler would bring to each place a crystal ashtray containing a fat Balkan Sobranie cigarette, than which—besides Uncle Harry's Etons (no more to be had)—there is no whicher. Be it remembered that we three boys were all in our teens at this time. So I continue to marvel

---

[3] If Sarum = Salisbury, then figure out this one:

There was a young fellow of Salisbury,
A notorious halisbury-scalisbury.
He went about Hampshire
Without any pampshire,
Till the vicar compelled him to walisbury.

Americans please note that Salisbury (where there is a great cathedral with a high, thin spire) is pronounced "Sawlsbury," and that the county of Hampshire is abbreviated as "Hants."

and reflect on the mystery of this wonderful old priest, whose largesse was as big as his nose, because at that time he startled me into the realization that a very holy man could at the same time be worldly and sensuous, and I have continued to follow his example.

A special treat at these luncheons was the occasional presence of his son, Frank Ashton-Gwatkin, chief of the economics division of the Foreign Office, and formerly attached to the British Embassy in Japan. Under the pseudonym John Paris he wrote *Sayonara* and *Kimono*, two rather hard-boiled and realistic novels about that country. Noting my interest in the Far East, he gave me two *kakemono*, or hanging-scroll paintings, of chrysanthemums, and an old Japanese dictionary—not a word of English in it—explaining how to count the strokes of *kanji*, or Chinese ideographs, and classify them by their radicals. Frank—perpetually amused and yet detached in manner—was a superb example of what the culture of England can produce, a man truly urbane in the kindly and civilized sense of the word. Years later he took me to lunch at his London club, Brooks', and introduced me to the pleasure of eating the eggs of seagulls. Why, with the swarms of seagulls around San Francisco, don't we have them here? They have bright orange yolks, brownish-green and speckled shells, and don't taste fishy—as one might expect—and are served in most of the superior clubs and restaurants of London, such as Simpson's and Bentley's. In one of the last letters I had from Frank he gave thanks to God for having had the privilege of living in the Edwardian age, before World War I, and expressed his ideal of life in a phrase from Montaigne which may be difficult to translate: *une certaine gaieté d'esprit.*

A particular lightness, joyousness, and exuberance of mind and attitude? The opposite of Germanic *Sturm und Drang*, of that high seriousness which has so afflicted us all—and especially our more prosperous kings, priests, premiers, and presidents—and which I am simply incapable of understanding. A priest once quoted to me the Roman saying that a religion is dead when the priests laugh at each other across the altar. I *always* laugh at the altar, be it Christian, Hindu, or Buddhist, because real religion is the transformation of anxiety into laughter.

But this *gaieté d'esprit* was entirely lacking in the religious atmosphere of my childhood, although I found it later in the Christianity of G. K. Chesterton, Hilaire Belloc, William Temple, Dom Gregory Dix, and Dom Aelred Graham. Throughout my schooling the religious indoctrination was grim and maudlin, though retaining fascination because it had something to do with the basic mysteries of existence. As I attained puberty I had to escape from it, and therefore took refuge in Buddhism. *Buddham saranam gacchami.* I had to get out from under the monstrously oppressive God the Father—nothing like my own father, who never used violence against me, and who constantly backed me up, consorted with me, helped me, and even followed me in my spiritual adventures. He went so far as to become treasurer of the Buddhist Lodge of London, after I joined it at the age of fifteen. I wouldn't even call him "Father." He was always a friendly fellow named Daddy.

But at Canterbury I had to undergo the rites of puberty, which consisted in being confirmed or initiated into the mysteries of the Church of England—mysteries which had altogether ceased to exist, apart from vague and gravely dreadful warnings against masturbation, homosexuality, and playing around with girls. We were given the impression that masturbation would result in syphilis, epilepsy, insanity, acne, pimples on the crotch, and the Great Siberian Itch—not to mention death, judgment, and everlasting damnation. I still wonder what kind of game was going on, because all our preceptors had once been lusty adolescents themselves, and, deprived as we were of women, almost everyone masturbated regularly at night. I felt as if I were in some madhouse where most of the rules were self-contradictory.

Misinformation about sex seemed to be the *ne plus ultra* of initiation into the Church—that is, as conveyed to a boy of fourteen. When aroused, go and dangle your balls in cold water—of which there was plenty, and in winter the jug in my cubicle in the school dormitory was coated with ice. Otherwise, there was a tremendous verbal build-up for the rite of Confirmation. We were given the whole history of the Church and of the Apostolic Succession, and told that the bishop, by virtue of his direct descent from Jesus Christ, would at the moment of laying his hands upon our heads confer upon us some mysterious power that would enable us to be Good, and that thereafter we would be admitted to the rite of Holy Communion (which the boys called "Co-muggers") and that this would make us even Gooder.

It was a letdown that when the moment came, the confirming bishop was not the Archbishop himself, but his suffragan, and when he laid his hands on my head absolutely nothing happened. When I first received the Holy Communion there was nothing interesting about it except the taste of the port, though everyone walked back from the altar rail looking like the cat that swallowed the canary. There was no joy, no camaraderie or conviviality, no sense of being turned-on, but only an intense and solitary seriousness. Everyone in his own private box with God, apologizing for having masturbated, fornicated, or adulterated. (One of the boys, lacking all sexual education, understood the commandment "Thou shalt not commit adultery" as "Thou shalt not kick the poultry," a much more sensible admonition.)

Believe it or not, in our formal prayers we actually gave thanks to God for King Henry VIII, who endowed the school with funds plundered from the adjoining Benedictine monastery—now in ruins—and, while boasting the title *Fidei Defensor* (as if God needed any defense), married six wives of whom he had two ritually murdered. He also composed ecclesiastical music.[4] Most of us boys took all this "English History" of formal beheadings at the Tower of London and glorious wars and burnings at the stake and the naval prowess of that elegant pirate, Sir Francis Drake,[5] as a matter of course or even of grandeur.

But, for myself, I had no heart for this "Onward Christian Soldiers" approach to life. It was thus that at the age of fifteen, as a scholar supported by

---

[4] There is still, I think, a convent in Fond du Lac, Wisconsin, where around the table of a former bishop's library stand six chairs bearing the images of Henry VIII's wives. The said bishop, upon hearing that a Christian Science Church had been established in town, drove up before it in his horse-drawn landau with footmen, stood up therein, took out his *Rituale*, and solemnly pronounced a curse upon the place. Next day it burned down.

[5] It is said that once, when he held a Spanish captain for ransom, he presented him with bottles of perfume, and entertained him in his cabin to a stately dinner served on gold plate, while listening to a string trio playing Renaissance music. Sir Francis was, apparently, no slouch in his ideas of how to live aboard ship.

the foundation of Canterbury Cathedral, the heart of the Church of England, I formally declared myself to be a Buddhist. As is coming to be
known, Buddhism is not really a religion—a way of obedience to someone
else's rules, a *regula vitae*—but a method for clarifying and liberating one's
state of consciousness. I had found myself in agreement with Lucretius that
Tantum religio potuit suadere malorum: that too much religion is apt to sway
us into evils.

CHAPTER THREE

I GO TO THE BUDDHA FOR REFUGE

Speaking as of today, I do not consider it intellectually respectable to be a partisan in matters of religion. I see religion as I see such other basic fascinations as art and science, in which there is room for many different approaches, styles, techniques, and opinions. Thus I am not formally a committed member of any creed or sect and hold no particular religious view or doctrine as absolute. I deplore missionary zeal, and consider exclusive dedication to and advocacy of any particular religion, as either the best or the only true way, an almost irreligious arrogance. Yet my work and my life are fully concerned with religion, and the mystery of being is my supreme fascination, though, as a shameless mystic, I am more interested in religion as feeling and experience than as conception and theory.

The concerns of ethics and morality occupy a subordinate, though still important, place in my preoccupations, since it has long seemed to me that basic religion is beyond good and evil—indeed, beyond any choice between things which may be regarded as opposites. All such opposites define one another mutually in such a way that there can be no final choice between them. To be is, or implies, not to be, and what interests me is the field, the continuum, in which these opposites are poles. Supralogical experiences of this continuum have arisen in the human mind in all times and places, and will doubtless continue to arise no matter what creeds or opinions prevail, and no matter what forms of reasoning may be used to dub them meaningless or mad. To me they are as natural and perennial as anything else—such as electricity—which cannot be defined but which is nevertheless most definitely felt.

When it comes to the forms and styles of religion, I have, of course, purely personal tastes and prejudices—as in art and music. Prayer, for example, is alien to me, but as I have said, I love to meditate either informally or in the way of Zen, or of Tibetan *ʒog-chen*, or in the manner of mantra yoga, which employs the contemplation of sound, produced by the voice or by such instruments as gongs. Thus at the mountain cottage where I am now writing, I have installed a gonglike bell made from a large oxygen tank and set into vibration by a swinging trunk of eucalyptus wood, suspended on ropes, and it sounds like those immense bronze bells of the Buddhist temples in Japan, which hum along the ground instead of clanging out through the sky. It reminds me of the great bell of Nanzenji in Kyoto, to which I have often listened at four in the morning—when the monks begin meditation—sounding about once every minute.

If I am asked to define my personal tastes in religion I must say that they lie between Mahayana Buddhism and Taoism, with a certain leaning toward Vedanta and Catholicism, or rather the Orthodox Church of Eastern Europe. The Russian Cathedral in Paris is, for me, one of the most joyous shrines in the world for its combination of gold-glorious ritual, angelic *a capella* music, and dignified informality. In the middle of a two-and-a-half-hour morning liturgy you can go out for a smoke or to the vodka and caviar shop across the street, and come back refreshed for declaring the glory of God, kissing an icon, holding a candle, or just wandering about among friends in the standing congregation. But I am still more at home in the serene and nonmilitant atmosphere of such Buddhist sanctuaries as Koya-san and Chion-in where the deep and sonorous chant is measured by the easy pulse of a wooden drum, where pines and maples stand beyond the open screens, and the smoke of aloeswood hangs in the air.

For me, this rich and venerable tradition of Mahayana Buddhism, touched with the nature-wisdom of Taoism, has seemed one of the most civilizing and humanizing and generally amiable movements in all history. Its humane and compassionate attitudes, its tolerance of many views, and its incomparable expressions in architecture, sculpture, painting, and literature arise—most paradoxically for Westerners—from *prajña*, a way of experiencing ultimate reality so unencumbered with concepts and propositions that it is called *sunya*, the Void, like a flawless diamond or crystal in which the universes come and go as shifting reflections. All this is so strange to my Church of England origins in the hills of Kent that, short of the difficult hypothesis of reincarnation, it is hard to explain.

I have also a curious affinity for Japan, such that when I go there everything of their old-fashioned culture seems oddly familiar, and they laugh at me for strolling about in a kimono (which is still worn by old gentlemen and poets) because they, in their business suits, cannot understand why a foreigner should affect this archaic yet supremely comfortable form of dress. When I was last in Kamakura, looking at the Daibutsu, I overheard a rather pleasant bluestocking-type American woman explaining to a group of tourists that I was probably some sort of priest, for today there is a considerable number of Caucasian Buddhist clerics. But the kimono is a marvelously practical garment, especially with its huge pocket-sleeves, and for sitting on the floor in the Japanese manner. I have one made of heavy black cotton, and remember sitting in perfect comfort on a chilly morning at the Zen temple of Eiheiji, wrapped in this garment, whereas the Japanese girl next to me—clad only in slacks and a flimsy sweater—was shivering and sneezing.

At present it is still difficult for an American citizen to visit China, but I have a feeling that the old ways of China would have the same familiarity as those of Japan. I feel at ease with the food, religion, clothing, art, and literature of both these countries. For years I have made a casual study of Chinese ideographic writing, and have practiced their calligraphy with brush and incensed ink, though I make no claim to be a master of that art. I don't know whether this is a case of reincarnation, or of childhood memories of my mother's modest collection of Oriental art, or of my father's readings from Kipling.

But, at about the age of eleven, I was reading the thrillers of Sax Rohmer and Edgar Wallace concerning Dr. Fu Manchu and other sophisticated Chinese villains, nurturing a secret admiration for these gentlemen because of their opposition to the suet-pudding heroism of our own culture, and because of their refined and mysterious style of life. While other boys dreamed of becoming generals, cowboys, mountain climbers, explorers, and engineers, I wanted to be a Chinese villain. I wanted servants carrying knives in their sleeves, appearing or vanishing without the slightest sound. I wanted a house with secret doors and passages, with Coromandel screens, with ancient scrolls, with ivory and lacquer boxes of exotic poisons, with exquisite brands of tea, with delicate blue porcelain, with jade idols and joss-sticks, and with sonorous gongs. So at this time I began to collect chinoiserie and nipponery to decorate my bedroom, until finally my mother—as if to say, "No more of this cheap stuff"—fitted me out with the most splendid embroideries and hangings, including a Japanese *kakemono* (since mysteriously lost) of two herons watching a flight of tumbling sparrows.

It appeared to me, not knowing why, that most of the decor and furnishing in English homes was in hideous taste—the featureless chintz curtains and covers for bulbous chairs, the monstrous mahogany lathe-worked racks which people kept in their entrance halls or narthexides for mounting bowler hats, mackintoshes, and umbrellas, the sickening wallpaper imprinted with identical mass-produced roses in columns divided by black lines, the boring oil paintings of ancestors or gloomy rural landscapes in pretentious gold frames, and, above all, the washstands in bedrooms with their abominably designed basins and water-jugs. And their chamber-pots! I am sure there must be collectors and historians of chamber-pots, or thunder-mugs, which look like enormous teacups with handles, sat upon during the soft stage of their manufacture. No ceramic object in the world is more inept and absurd. They were sometimes provided with the willow-pattern design, and I remember one that was chocolate brown ornamented with thistle leaves, in relief, colored verdigris.

And then there were those interminable houses of red brick, all the same—which are still to be seen in North London and Philadelphia—with lace-curtained windows and an inevitable bamboo table supporting a brass pot wherein grows that most miserable of all vegetables, the aspidistra, with its elongated spear-shaped, dark green, and dustily shiny leaves. No flowers. Aspidistras must have made a major contribution to driving Englishmen out of England in search of frangipani, orchids, and golden-shower trees. I have had nightmares of being lost in one of England's industrial, mass-produced suburbs, zoned "residential" like the equally deplorable rows of uniform ticky-tacky homes erected by Mr. Doelger under the constant fog of southwestern San Francisco. Not a shop, not a pub, not a bus stop, not a restaurant for miles and miles. Only seemingly empty dormitories, isolated even at night, with nothing but the dull-blue television screen showing through their darkened windows. In the United States you may not even take a walk in such areas without being stopped by the police on suspicion of being a thief or vagrant, that is, for not subscribing to the club of General Motors, since all the best thieves approach their objectives in a Cadillac. If you want to walk, take a dog with you, giving you the excuse that you are exercising your dog. Or put on shorts and a T-shirt and go "jogging": a style of flat-footed running which jolts the bones, jangles the nerves, and is supposed to turn you into a real man.

My parents had the good taste to buy a cottage on a rural lane, with bushes of wild roses, honeysuckle, and belladonna plants under the shade of sycamore and copper beech trees. My mother would have no truck with the usual suburban decor—except upstairs. From her sensitivity to Oriental design, lilt, and color she became a master embroidress, and later worked with Charles Johnson, architect and designer, in a project to remodel the chapel of Saint Hugh's School. He was the brother of the two headmasters of the school, the Reverend Frederick Johnson (the only preacher in the area who could hold my interest) and Mr. Alfred Johnson (a brilliant teacher of literature and music).

But Charles was out of another world. He was reputed to be vaguely insane, to have read books on mysticism, to have taken obscure drugs, and thus to have to be constantly accompanied by a male nurse disguised as a butler and chauffeur. He had lived for many years in Mexico, presumably as a remittance man, but returned to England during the last days of my schooling at Saint Hugh's to build a delightful Spanish-Mexican house on the outskirts of the school grounds. He was a plump, grey-haired, fastidious, and urbane fellow, utterly removed from the crickety-militaristic atmosphere of his brothers' school. He introduced me to a proper way of drinking tea—unmilked, weak, and with a thin slice of lemon, as distinct from the frightful English practice of drinking it so strong that a spoon will stand up in it, and polluted with milk and sugar.

Charles collaborated with my mother in making the reredos and altar cloths for our school chapel in High Renaissance style, and I had the privilege of watching this meticulous work and giving occasional assistance. He worked at the general designing and wood carving, and my mother at the appliqué and embroidery panels, which comprised not only icons of Saint Augustine and Saint Hugh, but also fleurs-de-lys, ferns, and bluebirds, all on a green and gold background. Charles could give me more education in five minutes than his brothers in five years—simply by his attitude and his pleasure in his work—and this is saying a great deal, because Alfred was in many ways the ideal schoolmaster. But Charles wasn't trying to *teach*; he was simply following his own weird and allowing me to watch while my mother worked along with him.

His sister, Elvira, was a handsome, witty, and equally sophisticated woman married to my principal childhood guru, Francis Croshaw, who was likewise reputed to be crazy, and as born of a mentally "tainted" ancestry—the story being that his father, a wealthy baron of Chislehurst, had once ordered five grand pianos to be delivered on the same day. Their son, Ivan, who in those days was in a somewhat compulsively scientistic frame of mind, was nevertheless one of my constant companions. He went to the same school, Saint Hugh's, and we shared a delight in fabricating nonsense, in which his mother Elvira would frequently join. We bandied such burbles as

Iheeyeeic Paragua
Married a jaguar
Who came from Aconcagua,
And said, "O what a fag you are."
You may telephone from here.

At breakfast, his father would give names to all the eggs—Pleen, Sondom, Paradiddle, and Transom—and ask us to take our choice.

Elvira was known to her friends as Vera and to her son as Pom (Poor Old Mother). Some mother. She controlled us simply by casting an influence. I never saw her punish her son, nor lose her temper. Her secret was a phenomenal sense of humor which somehow concentrated itself on the tip of a rather long and amusingly pointed nose, from which she would suffuse the atmosphere with her particular kind of giggles. On the important social art of facial composure, she explained that to maintain a reserved and dignified appearance you should make your whole face say "Brush," and that if you wanted to appear genial and friendly you should make it say "Beesom," with a big smile. Pom's atmosphere was also glamourous, though not exactly in the sexy sense of the word for she was handsome and stylish rather than pretty, and her style was Continental and Parisian. She spoke exquisite French, and intrigued me with her cosmopolitan tastes in the arts and in her ordering of the household. Bedrooms, for example, were places for lounging and reading, not utilitarian compartments for the hygienic duty of sleep. I cannot remember any adult with whom I felt so completely at ease, and she, if anyone, is responsible for my adoption of what is sometimes called an un-English style of life. For me she became the archetypal representative of relaxed, urbane society seasoned with wit and fantasy—which is what I would like to be understood by the word "civilization."

Francis Croshaw was a vague and wealthy man of uncertain behavior. He would take off for London for the day in his two-seater Chrysler and not return for a week, explaining that it had suddenly occurred to him to visit Wales. He smoked black stogie cigars from Burma—with which he always kept me plentifully supplied—the kind that are open at both ends, nubbly in texture, and burn with a blue flame and hiss. He would wander about in a decrepit Moorish dressing gown known as the "Moorish piecey," and carry a dog whip though he had no dog. He would sit in his car on sunny afternoons reading paperbound French novels. He had two homes, the first a spacious tapestried house near Chislehurst, and the second a pleasant clapboard bungalow with verandas, by the sand dunes and the sea just to the south of Rye— a city of cottage-shops on a solitary hill, topped with an ancient church in which we once listened to the rector talking about God's purpose for the world, for you, and for me, without ever saying exactly what it was.

The first thing that Francis Croshaw did for me was to release me from the boiled-beef culture of England and let me realize that I was at least a European. In 1929 he took me with his family to France, via Jersey, sat me down in a café in Saint-Malo, and bought me my first drink. He, by the way, drank immense quantities of wine—much of it Moulin à Vent—and would toss down a whole glass, and then, with a haughty sniff, gaze up into the air in a gesture of total detachment from things of this earth. He carried a red Moroccan wallet, as I myself do to this day, and one of those carved and brightly colored Mexican walking sticks.

Saint-Malo was then a solidly walled medieval city, centered about a plaza filled with open-air cafés. The very moment we stepped off the boat from Jersey I felt a vivacious, sunny human atmosphere that was quite new to me and luminously exhilarating. Within an hour we were eating melons, artichokes, *pâté maison*, and *coq au vin* at the Hotel Chateaubriand, and it suddenly dawned upon me that eating could be an art. He took us to Mont Saint-Michel, to the horse races, to a sumptuous restaurant on the beach at Dinard, to Saint-Jacut where we drank an intoxicating bitter cider looking like orange juice—and then on to Bordeaux, where we dined at the Chapon Fin, starting out with *oeufs en gelée*, topped with truffles and based on *pâté de fois gras*. We then went to the sandy and pine forested country of the Landes, by the Bay of Biscay, to stay at the Basque-style Hôtel du Lac at Hossegor, just North of Capbreton, which afforded us at least two weeks on an all-out gourmet binge. He took us to a bullfight in Bayonne, to the casino at Biarritz, and then on to a small village in the Pyrenees, Saar, where people were assembling from all the surrounding villages to watch a game of pelota. A party arrived in a pick-up truck, parked in the plaza, and brought out a large basket of bread, bottles of wine, and cheese, around which they all joined hands and danced; with a solo funnyman wearing a short black cloak, who capered about them and, with his cloak rising into the air, became an animated mushroom. Francis exclaimed, "Just look at that! You couldn't possibly see such a sight in England." *Certaine gaieté d'esprit.*

I came back from this adventure feeling like an adult. From then on the curriculum, the sports, and the ideals of King's School, Canterbury, seemed, with some few exceptions, to be futile, infantile, and irrelevant. And then one day in Goulden's bookshop I came upon Lafcadio Hearn's *Glimpses of Unfamiliar Japan*. I bought it because it comprised a chapter on ghosts, imagining that Japanese ghosts would be the ultimate in refined horror, whereas they turned out to be rather amiable. But the book contained a description of his house and garden in Matsue (which I have since visited four times), and this, with all his poetical discourse on the various kinds of frogs, insects, and plants, and the art of giving the illusion of a wide landscape in a small space, made the glowing tinder of my interest in Oriental culture suddenly light the fire. I was aesthetically fascinated with a certain clarity, transparency, and spaciousness in Chinese and Japanese art. It seemed to float, whereas most Western art seemed chunky, cluttered, vaguely delineated, dark, and heavy. Apart from illuminated manuscripts, stained glass, and Italian "primitives" it was full of shadows and coarse-looking people, and, as I later discovered, there are no shadows in nature: everything is colored, because the whole material world is basically composed of light.

Quite recently I have looked over many reproductions of Far Eastern masterpieces to identify and put into words the particular view of nature which so captured my imagination. The characteristic first reaction of Westerners to such works is to call them "fantastic" or "stylized," and they see the roofs more curly, the rocks more jagged, and the eyes more slanted than they actually are. In looking at Chinese writing they see

Yet by the time I was twelve it was precisely the fantastic and outlandish which appealed to me, though as I became familiar with these styles they became almost more "natural" than even the photographic treatments of the West. For one thing, the brush gives a clear and fluid line, neither hard nor scratchy, and there is always enough background space to give full definition to the figure, which in turn is so positioned and related to the space that empty paper comes alive without having to be painted in as water, sky, or mist. This is the Mahayanist and Taoist feeling for pregnant emptiness. For another, these artists paint nature for itself, as its own subject, and not to moralize, illustrate a point, or serve as a background for human affairs, so that birds and grasses are given a marvelous purposelessness and freedom from human plots and schemes. This was the way I felt when I could go off alone and sit by a stream, and not have my ears boxed, bent, and battered with arguments and admonitions, or be doctored with doctrine.

Yes, I have been close to ecstasy in the Uffizi Gallery in Florence, and have had my "prurient interests" thoroughly aroused by Renoir's girls, have basked in Cezanne's landscapes, have delighted in Braque's amazing understanding of space, and laughed with Picasso. But the miniatures and arabesques of Persia, the textiles of India, and the painting, calligraphy, and sculpture of China and Japan make me feel—in my mother's words—jazzy inside. Even when they use brown—the color of decay which is not in the spectrum—they make it luminous. I can say only that, from my point of view, the Chinese and Japanese masters have a clear, uncluttered, lightsome, and gently windswept view of nature, which so enchanted me that I had to find out what philosophy, feeling, or experience lay behind it.

So then came the second thing that Francis Croshaw did for me. He had an enormous library, and, realizing my interest in the Orient in general and Buddhism in particular, began lending me books and engaging me in discussions which went on far into the night—mostly at his bungalow near Rye—drinking Moulin à Vent and smoking his dynamic stogies. This kind of discourse with an intelligent and colorful adult, in a free-and-easy atmosphere, is worth more than any amount of formal education. He lent me Edmond Holmes's masterly book, *The Creed of Buddha*, which happened to contain a yellow pamphlet, written by a certain Christmas Humphreys, about Buddhism, and the work of the Buddhist Lodge in London. I was also reading Lafcadio Hearn's *Gleanings in Buddha-Fields*, where I found an essay on *nirvana* which gave me such a convincingly different view of the universe from the one I had inherited that I turned my back on all I had been taught to believe as authority. That did it. I wrote to the Buddhist Lodge, became a member, subscribed to their magazine *Buddhism in England*, which is now called *The Middle Way*, and shortly sought out Christmas Humphreys who, after Francis, was to become my second most important teacher. And I shall not forget the awed and almost respectful way in which Patrick Leigh Fermor said to me, "Do you really mean that you have renounced belief in the Father, the Son, and the Holy Ghost?"

As I have said, I simply couldn't get along with the Christian God. He was a bombastic bore, and not at all the sort of fellow you would want to entertain for dinner, because you would be sitting on the edge of your chair listening to his subtle attempts to undermine your existence and to probe the unauthentic nature of your life. He was like the school chaplain who took you aside for a VERY SERIOUS TALK. He had no *gaieté d'esprit*, no charm, no lilt, no laughter, and no sensual delight in the world of nature which he had supposedly created. At least, this was the version of that God conveyed to me by my preceptors, who were busily preoccupied in keeping virile young men off the labor market and from sowing their oats to the begetting of unfamilial bastards.

It was thus an immense relief to find out that millions of people outside Europe and the Near East didn't have this notion of the ultimate reality. The ground of it all was, instead, something variously known as the Universal Mind, the Tao, the Brahman, Shinnyo, *alaya-vijñana*, or Buddha-nature, wherewith one's own self and being is ultimately identical for always and always, though my preceptors derided such notions as being woolly and vague and, above all, damnably pantheistic. My theological preceptors dubbed it immoral and illogical, and the scientistic and atheistical ones deemed it sentimental and meaningless nonsense. Francis's brother-in-law, John Johnson, a musician who had won some prize for finishing Schubert's *Unfinished Symphony*, and who was a devout atheist, used to look over my shoulder and roar with contemptuous laughter at the exotic terminology of the books I was reading, which was merely the old British way of putting down anything foreign—as they called Köln Cologne, Padova Padua, and Boulogne Boolone. Any Sanskrit or Chinese word would just break him up, but he was a most unhappy and frustrated man.[1]

I kept wondering and wondering what was the hang-up of the British, and of Europeans in general, about being definite and precise regarding the nature of either the deity or the nondeity. They had fought battles over

---

[1] I noticed in school that the muscular, athletic boys had an extreme and uncomfortable resistance to the correct pronunciation of French. They would grunt and mumble over their textbooks, absolutely refuse to articulate the French *r*, and seemed to feel that speaking French properly was effeminate.

the problem of whether God the Son, the Second Person of the Trinity, was *homoousios* or *homoiousios*, of the same substance or of similar substance with the Father. They slaughtered women and children and laid fields waste in verbal quarrels about transubstantiationism and antitransubstantiationism, as to whether, at Mass, the bread and wine became the veritable body and blood of Christ—whether they were, rather, consubstantiated in such manner that the Lord's body and blood became spiritually present—or whether the recelebration of the Lord's Last Supper was no more than a symbolic reminiscence. As an unabashed pantheist I am naturally a full-blooded transubstantiationist, knowing full well that the ground wheat of bread and the crushed grapes of wine are the body and blood of Christ, the Anointed One, or olive-oiled man who is so slippery that he has no hang-ups. But I'm not going to go to war about it, nor sizzle the testicles of those who don't agree with me by planting them on bonfires.

I regard my more remote European forefathers who engaged in these quarrels as utterly insane. They were hopelessly confused and hypnotized by their languages, by the crude linear symbolisms wherewith they sought to make "sense" of the world. Contrariwise, such an articulate, amusing, and reasonable atheist as Bertrand Russell was also hypnotized with words—with endless talk about talk—with making, as the French say, *précises* about this and that—all of which is an intellectual game of chess having very little to do with the realities of nature—until it came, of course, to his truly heroic and responsible protests against sexual proprietism and atomic bombs, for which he was barred from Columbia University and thrown into jail in England.

Notions of God, of the ultimate reality or the ground of being, must necessarily be vague—for the simple reason that, just as we cannot bite our teeth, we cannot make the energy that we ourselves *are* a precisely defined object. Verbal definitions of God in the form of creeds, dogmas, and doctrines are far more dangerous idols that statues made of wood, stone, or gold, because they have the deceptive appearance of being more "spiritual," and because a creedally formulated God has been *reduced* to words, and is no longer experienced immediately, like clear water or blue sky. This is why Christians have lost all magical powers except those of a false anointment, or antichrist: petroleum, powering a technology which is fouling the whole human nest.

I am not trying to frighten the millionaires who control Standard Oil and the liquid wealth of Texas with visions of revolution and the gallows; I am only suggesting that they might be kinder to themselves. People do not generally realize that those who govern states and great corporations are not really in control of these monstrous organizations of human action. They are like the drivers of runaway trucks which will disintegrate if brought to a sudden stop, yet cannot be slowed because they are carrying emergency supplies to a scene of disaster. But it is not happiness to cultivate ulcers and heart disease while amassing millions of paper dollars and covering the world with smog and greasy grime. One of my missions in life, if I have any, is to show very rich and powerful people how to use their imaginations and enjoy themselves through being disabused of the notion that money and prestige have, in themselves, material reality. Love of money and imagination in spending it seem to be mutually exclusive. Furthermore, it could almost be stated as an equation: money = anxiety. Though a man of imagination, taste, and culture, Francis Croshaw lived in horror, not of death, but of the process of dying, and he was fascinated by that extreme interpretation of Buddha's doctrine which defines the very process of life as agony and the release as a method of absolute and final suicide. I was still in school when he was found dead on the path below his bedroom, and no one ever knew whether he had jumped, or whether he had stumbled over the sill in trying to open a jammed window.

His place as guru was taken by Christmas Humphreys and his fey, Celtic wife, Aileen, who ran the Buddhist Lodge from their flat in one of the long residential streets of Pimlico in Southwest London—a dreary street of high houses pressed together, identical and drab—where they had made a hideaway with a bright fire, Persian rugs, incense, golden Buddhas, and a library of magical books which promised me the most arcane secrets of the universe. Christmas and Aileen, who shall hereafter be identified by their nicknames Toby and Puck, gave me an education which no money could possibly buy, and the depth of my gratitude to them is immeasurable. Even though I now remonstrate, mildly, against some of Toby's interpretations of Buddhism, I shall love him always as the man who really set my imagination going and put me on my whole way of life.

It must be understood that Toby and Puck were, first of all, Theosophists, disciples of that incredible and mysterious Russian lady Helena Petrovna Blavatsky, who founded the Theosophical Society in—of all places—New York City in 1875, thereafter moving off to Madras and London. Her story was that, as a young woman, she had gone into Central Asia and Tibet to become the student of supreme gurus Koot Hoomi and Maurya (which are not Tibetan names, and whose alleged photographs look like versions of Jesus), who thereafter wrote her constant letters by psychokinetic precipitation or telepathic amanuensis in a distinctly Russian style of handwriting. Madame Blavatsky's voluminous works reveal only the most fragmentary knowledge of Tibetan Buddhism, but she was a masterly creator of metaphysical and occult science fiction, as well as being a delightful, uninhibited, and outspoken old lady who spat and swore and rolled her own cigarettes. Perhaps she was a charlatan, but she did a beautiful job of it, and persuaded a goodly number of British aristocrats to consider the *Upanishads*, the *Yoga Sutra*, the *Bhagavad-Gita*, and the Buddhist *Tripitaka*. Those persuaded found them much more interesting and profound than the Bible, especially the Bible interpreted by run-of-the-mill Catholic and Protestant clergy at the end of the nineteenth century.

Thus it was through the work of Blavatsky that these traditions were delivered to Toby when he was a student at Cambridge, in company with psychiatrist Henry Dicks, and Ronald Nicholson, who later became the *sadhu* Sri Krishna Prem. They joined the Cambridge branch of the Theosophical Society, and Toby subsequently founded—in London—an independent Buddhist Lodge of the Society, of which he remains president and chief guru to this day, though there is no longer any formal connection with the Theosophists. He is a tall, slender, and limber fellow with big ears, and a clear authoritative voice—always tempered to make it even more so—in which he speaks the best King's English. He is now a Queen's Counselor and judge at the Old Bailey, and it would be hard to imagine a more fair-minded and lovingly cynical jurist.

He and Puck, silversmith with white witch in attendance, maintained an establishment that was full of mystery. It wasn't just the Oriental art and the smell of pine or sandalwood incense. It was also that, on and off, they were visited by enigmatic and astonishing people such as Tai-hsü (patriarch of Chinese Buddhism), Nicholas Roerich (Russian artist and Buddhist), G. P. Malalasekera (Buddhist scholar and diplomat of Ceylon, who is probably the most reasonable man in the world), Alice Bailey (an updated Blavatsky), and, above all, Daisetsu Teitaro Suzuki, unofficial lay master of Zen Buddhism, humorous offbeat scholar, and about the most gentle and enlightened person I have ever known; for he combined the most complex learning with utter simplicity. He was versed in Japanese, English, Chinese, Sanskrit, Tibetan, French, Pali, and German, but while attending a meeting of the Buddhist Lodge he would play with a kitten, looking right into its Buddha-nature.

Toby introduced me to the writings of Suzuki in 1930, though I didn't meet the man himself until he came to London in 1936 for the World Congress of Faiths, at which time I had become the editor of *Buddhism in England*. Suzuki fascinated me because he told endless *mondo*, or Zen stories, in which people who asked "What is the basic principle of Buddhism?" were given such answers as "The cypress tree in the garden" or "Three pounds of flax," and thereupon attained instant enlightenment and liberation from the problems of birth-and-death, instead of having to practice intense concentration on the neuropsychic centers (or *chakras*) in their spinal cords throughout fifteen incarnations. At this time (1930) I was also reading Swami Vivekananda's *Raja Yoga*, and making preliminary experiments in *pranayama*, or control of the breath, so as to discover that what is at once voluntary and involuntary, what you do and what happens to you, is all one process, all *karma* of which the real meaning is not cause-and-effect but simply doing, action, or energy. When something "happens" to you, be it tragic or comic, hideous or delightful, the Hindus and Buddhists say it's your *karma*—which doesn't mean punishment or reward, as if someone were keeping books on you, but simply your own doing.

I was thus moving from the ideal of Christian love to that of Buddhist wisdom, from *agape* to *bodhi*. I didn't like Christian love as I saw it exemplified in the lives of those who preached it. They were always going to war with other people to save them. They believed that suffering was "good for you" and considered flogging their children an act of mercy. Formerly, they had even burned heretics at the stake in a desperate attempt to save them from their own fantasies of everlasting damnation. Indeed, there were people around me, such as Aunts Gertrude and Ethel, who really lived Christian love; but they never preached it. Trying, then, to put myself back into an adolescent's point of view, it seemed to me that those who preached it didn't have it. They were solemn bombasts who, as might have been expected, ended up with the atomic bomb. "O how great a thing it is when the Lord putteth into the hands of the righteous invincible might."

I watched the antics of the Salvation Army—beating drums, blowing bugles, putting their girls' heads into ridiculous bonnets, and praying into their visored hats. They actually took them off and talked into them! Imagine the chaplains of an organization known as the Church Army wearing both surplices and military caps! Indeed, an enormous amount of anthropological research might be done concerning our bizarre hat rituals; of donning and doffing them according to the presence of ladies, or of God; of their being formally removed as a token of sincerity; of Quakers insisting that they remain hatted in church and court; of ladies' heads having to be covered in church lest the angels be tempted by the loveliness of their hair; and of the amazing case (about 1935) in which a British magistrate reluctantly permitted a female witness to be hatless in court if she felt this would not detract from the sincerity of her oath. For myself, I never cover my head except in circumstances of extreme cold, wet, or danger, for which I have a fur cap, a hooded jacket, and a tough plastic helmet. The very word "hat" is gauche and unpoetical.

"Can any man by taking thought (i.e., by being anxious) add a cubit to his stature?" Well, they try—by donning hats: top hats, heraldic helmets, busbys, turbans, stetsons, birettas, crowns, and monumentally pretentious miters (not to mention juridical wigs and academic mortarboards)—and then go on to frantically emotional debates, not only as to when and when not to don or doff these structures, but also as to whether whatever hair grows beneath them should be long or short, tonsured or completely shaved. Yet such people maintain asylums, or psychiatric prisons, for others deemed to be insane.

All this would have been amusing and delightful if done in a spirit of fun, but a Salvation Army officer praying into his hat was terribly and dreadfully serious, in a private box with God. He was most secretly apologizing and most humbly asking forgiveness for his natural inclination to debonnet one of his evangelical sisters, slide her out of her black-and-red serge uniform, and roll with her in the hay. I remember a blond and frail-looking boy, who was about to become a theological student, kneeling beside me in chapel and whimpering the prayers in such a voice that I realized he was completely intimidated by the universe, and had crossed his neurological wires in such a way as to interpret his jitters as a most passionate love of God.

For me, then, the Christian scene had beauty—as in the corona of Canterbury, Gregorian chant, Solemn High Mass, and rooks in the trees beyond Canon Dawson's rectory—but it had no depth. I wanted to plumb and understand *being* itself, the very heart and ground of the universe, not to control it, but simply to wonder at it, for I was—and still am—amazed at my own existence. Buddhist bells sounded deeper than Christian bells, and their chanting was more relaxed—and upon lower tones. OM MANI PADME HUM ran in my brain as something much more interesting than "O come let us sing unto the Lord," and very definitely more fascinating than the clickety-clickety insectual rhythms of scientific precisionists. I knew that the Buddha had taken a dim view of wenching and boozing, but he never called it *sin*— as damnable offense against ultimate reality. It was just one's own way of delaying *nirvana*—if that was what you wanted to do.

Although I was later to read Eckhart, Saint Thomas, Saint Teresa, and most of the great Christian mystics, the style of Christianity offered to us children contained no hint of mystical experience. We were told only that Jesus, and Jesus alone, was one with God, and that some prophets and saints had occasionally talked with God. But it was all talk—no vision, no feeling, no sensation, except of a certain awe and military grandeur. We were, after all, being trained as officers for the troops of the British Empire.

So I went the Wrong Way, and espoused one of the major religions of the peoples ruled by that Empire. While wandering around with Ivan Croshaw in London's flea market in Camden Town, I picked up an exquisite brass image of the Buddha from Burma, for a mere fourteen shillings, and a secondhand copy of Vivekananda's *Raja Yoga*. I followed Vivekananda's instructions in my dormitory cubicle at night, looking out to the Bell Harry Tower of Canterbury Cathedral under moonlight. Some months later I was mercifully afflicted with influenza, and was enabled to retreat for several weeks to the school hospital where I could continue this work more intensively, attended by a charming and perfectly civilized nurse, and surrounded with a garden of roses. The hospital—or rather nursing home—was mysteriously called Saint Non's, and I wish I could remember the name of the lovely and sophisticated woman who ran it, for she was simply of another—and superior—class than most of the people running the school. With the special exception of Alec Macdonald, our housemaster, who went out of his way to visit me during this period and lend me extraordinary books which were not at all like the "classics" one was supposed to study in class—the tedious histories of Caesar, Livy, Xenophon, and Tacitus, or the dreary dramas of Corneille and Racine.

One awesome and amazing thing about the British—especially those of the Church of England—is that they *know* they are in the right, so much so that they can tolerate almost any kind of eccentricity, so long as the eccentric stays in his place and does not attempt to force himself upon them. They provide restricted areas, such as Hyde Park Corner, where you may stand upon a wooden soapbox and publicly denounce the government, the Royal Family, the Church, and God Himself, while the police simply stroll around and chuckle. They have been accustomed to joke—especially during such times as U.S. Prohibition—that they got rid of most of their intolerant people by pushing them off to America. Thus when I declared myself a Buddhist the school authorities at Canterbury not only showed no offense but positively encouraged me. For here at last was someone showing an intelligent interest in religion. Norman Birley, historian and enlightened headmaster, sent me and one other boy (who was so called to the ministry that he illicitly smoked a tobacco named Parson's Pleasure) to represent the school at a conference on religion, held over a weekend at Hayward's Heath in Surrey, and presided over by no less a parson than William Temple, then Archbishop of York and later Archbishop of Canterbury.

I was in his presence—and what a presence—for three days, during which he held an almost nonstop bull session with some fifty boys. He was immensely stout, and reputed to be a formidable trencherman. He had a belly-laugh which could be heard for miles. It rang out like church bells bewitched by elves. It undulated the air so as to make weak leaves fall from the trees. There was never such a laugh in all Christendom. Anyone who has read his *Nature, Man, and God* and the volume of his collected letters knows that he was also a superb philosopher-theologian and a veritable archetype of courtesy. Late at night, when just a few of us were sitting with him smoking our pipes and discussing the doctrine of Divine Grace, he told us a real secret—and this was the first time, so far as I was concerned, that an official of the Church had said anything interesting or important. He said, "When I was a boy in school I used to be set the task of composing poetry in Latin, which was, as you know, rather difficult. However, I was working by candlelight, and whenever I got 'stuck' and couldn't find the right phrase, I would pull off a stick of wax from the side of the candle and push it back, gently, into the flame. And then the phrase would simply come to me."

The next day he told us a story about Sir Walford Davies, who was then Master of the King's Musick. He had been present on an occasion when Sir Walford was instructing an untrained choral group in hymn-singing. He started then out with some familiar hymn which they bellowed forth with gusto to impress the Archbishop, and the musical effect was terrible. But there was also present a small professional choir, and Sir Walford asked them to go through several verses of a completely unfamiliar hymn so that everyone could memorize the tune. "Now," he said, "we're all going to sing this new hymn. But one thing is absolutely important: you must not *try* to sing it. Just think of the tune and let it sing itself." The result was such a marked improvement that he turned to the Archbishop and said, "Isn't that also good theology?" That was how I learned to breathe.

But on holidays from school I was sitting at the feet of Toby Humphreys, listening greedily to everything he and Puck had to say about Buddhism, Theosophy, and life in general; loving especially the occasions when there was no meeting of the Buddhist Lodge and I could be with them alone, or with a few of their fascinating friends—explorers, psychiatrists, doctors, and such romantic Russian singers as Vladimir Rosing and Olga Alexeeva, who, for some reason that is still not quite clear to me, gave me a permanent interest in the world of Russian exiles, in their music, food, drink, religion, and general life-style. I was being enchanted by the music of Tchaikovsky, Borodin, Glazunov, and Rimsky-Korsakov, and Toby and I were such avid fans of the ballet that we had opera cloaks made for ourselves and attended the ballet at Covent Garden with ivory-handled black canes and white gloves. Toby had become my elder brother, and was giving me the education I would not be able to find in any university.

Meanwhile (this was when I was about seventeen), I was still reading Suzuki on Zen and trying to practice some form of Buddhist yoga, *ʐa-ʐen*, or *satipatthana*—and simply couldn't make up my mind which specific method to follow, or exactly what state of mind or consciousness was *satori*, *samadhi*, *moksha*, or true enlightenment. Aside from Toby, who wasn't playing the guru role, for we were just fellow seekers, I had no spiritual master. I was a shaman, on my own in a religious jungle. When, at Canterbury, I had become the head-boy, or captain, of my house, The Grange, I had the privilege of going off by myself to study and meditate in an ancient Elizabethan room, where one could light a fire and stay up until late at night. It was in the autumn of 1932—windy, with fallen leaves skittering along roads and fields— and I was trying desperately to work out this problem: What is THE EXPERIENCE which these Oriental masters are talking about? The different ideas of it which I had in mind seemed to be approaching me like little dogs wanting to be petted, and suddenly I shouted at all of them to go away. I annihilated and bawled out every theory and concept of what should be my properly spiritual state of mind, or of what should be meant by ME. And instantly my weight vanished. I owned nothing. All hang-ups disappeared. I walked on air. Thereupon I composed a *haiku*:

All forgotten and set aside—
    Wind scattering leaves
        Over the fields.

CHAPTER FOUR

ON BEING HALF-MISEDUCATED

The title above is taken from George Bernard Shaw, as a description of education in England, and its American parallel would be Paul Goodman's title *Growing Up Absurd*. For we must now backtrack and look at another side of my peculiar story. Strictly speaking, I cannot regard myself as a well-educated person. I have not read Homer in Greek, nor do I understand Hebrew. In Latin I never mastered the style of Tacitus. In French I can read most technical works, but not idiomatic novels. German is beyond me, though I can often get the sense of it when spoken aloud. I have a large vocabulary in Sanskrit, but no syntax. I can write and read ancient Chinese, but do not speak it. I can get by with spoken Japanese for purposes of ordering food in a restaurant or giving directions for a taxi, but I have never bothered to find out how the language really works and thus cannot maintain an intelligent conversation. I let them do the work, for every educated Japanese has had at least seven years of English; but most are ashamed to speak it unless mildly drunk. (D. T. Suzuki, as a young man, taught English in Japan, but told me that when he first came to the West he found the spoken language there entirely different from what he had been teaching.)

I have concentrated rather thoroughly on the English language for, as Bernard Shaw also said, no man can truly master any other language than his own. However, when it comes to English literature, I am really an ignoramus. I have read most of Shakespeare and all ten volumes of S. R. Gardiner's *History of England from the Accession of James I to the Outbreak of the Great Civil War, 1603–1642*; but I know almost nothing of Spenser, Boswell, Coleridge, Dryden, Thackeray, Hardy, the various people whose names began Ford Madox, or of Dreiser, Thomas Wolfe, or Carl Sandburg. I could go on with this catalogue of ignorance forever, but do not wish to be boring. Nevertheless I have now a library of at least four thousand volumes, some of which, such as the *Encyclopaedia Britannica*, I have not read entirely; though I can tell you from memory the alphabetical indices of all volumes of its great Eleventh Edition from A TO AND to VET TO ZYM.

This may be the moment to interpose a story about my much-admired friend Aldous Huxley. It is said that he had read the entire *Encyclopaedia*, but at random. He would, for example, look up the article on the letter P, then go off to a party at which he would gently move the conversation to this subject and then give an extremely learned, and invariably witty, discourse on the history of this letter. Once, when he was visiting Gerald Heard's coeducational monastery at Trabuco in Southern California, the gas stoves went out of order—whereupon Huxley went into the kitchen, gave a lecture on the whole history and engineering of gas stoves, but was unable to correct the trouble. He was a much, much more literate man than I; but, when his tutor at Balliol College, Oxford, suggested that he consider the career of a professor of English literature, he remarked in his extraordinarily lilting voice, "I have never felt that literature was something to be *studied*, but rather something to be *enjoyed*."

I was first sent off to *study* things at the kindergarten school of Saint Nicholas, next door to the church of Saint Nicholas, and managed—unbelievably—by a pretty brunette named Miss Nicholas. She was (and I think still is, for I visited her in 1958) an exceptionally warmhearted person, though I once became furious at her for making me the "It" in a game of General Post—similar to Blind Man's Bluff—in which I was blindfolded and supposed to capture other children moving from points identified as, say, Birmingham to Bristol. For some reason, blindfolding offended me so deeply that the next day I presented her with a set of drawings which showed Buckingham Palace on fire, King George V lying dead with an arrow in his heart, and knights in armor with flaming eyes saying, "How dared you do that to Alan?" These drawings had such an electric effect that she displayed them before the whole school and gave me a public lecture on my abysmal wickedness.

The kindergarten division of the school was run by Miss Nicholas and

her sister, Doris. They taught us to read by the old method of learning the
sounds of the letters, which I had already found out from my mother, and to
make scrawny paintings of flowers right in the middle of the sheet of paper,
so that we discovered no sense of space or lively background. Doris taught
us elementary French, which included collective chanting of the alphabet to
its giggly climax—*u, vé, double-vé, iks, ygrec, ʒed*—especially with the lilt
put into it by a plump and cheeky boy named John Bennett, with whom I
had a peculiar affinity for the unintentional disruption of classes by mutually
arising chuckles at any and every stray element of nonsense that struck our
funny-bones. For such pleasure in nonsense, I, and millions of other children so inclined, have been considered silly, frivolous, and wanting in seriousness. But we have a secret forever closed to stuffy, sober, and serious
people. I am still incapable of understanding such people. Do they have a
secret closed to me?

The school overlooked the village green, set about with flowering chestnut trees and elms. Across and to the west was the Crown Inn, done in fake
Tudor with stucco and wooden beams. Behind and to its left was a secluded
estate entirely surrounded with a wall of dark red brick, old and mossy.
When classwork became too arid and abstract to hold my interest, I would
gaze out into this more real and lively world and wander mentally into the
down-sloping gardens behind the houses opposite—one of which was a paradise dedicated to Saint Francis—and then on down the gravel road to
Cheesman's farm, where Birdcage Walk—a bush-enclosed footpath—descended to the grassy embankment of the Southern Railway. By curling my
left hand so that thumb and index finger touched, I could see an imaginary
replica of that path, where my palm was the ground and my fingers the over-
arching shrubbery.

By such means I escaped from the misery of Miss E.—stout, bespec-
tacled, red-haired, and ugly—who compelled us to memorize multiplication
tables and thus permanently ruined my interest in arithmetic and calculation, though not in the more philosophical aspects of mathematics. This
wretched woman would whack us on the legs with a ruler for not being able
to recite—instantly—the uninteresting fact that $12 \times 9 = 108$. In a world of
flowers, birds, butterflies, clouds, stars, music, friendly boys, and lovely girls,

I did not want to waste my consciousness on such textureless, tasteless, and colorless figurations. If you need them you can always look up multiplication tables in a book, or use a slide rule or an adding machine. But that was considered cheating.

So many would-be students of astronomy have lost interest when bogged down in the mathematical analysis of spectra, because the doubtlessly informative calculations of the science screened out its poetry. I wonder, therefore, whether minds fully conditioned to look at the stars through mathematical screens may not have blinded themselves to other aspects of the science. They look at the world through lattices whose mullions block the view of interconnections between the objects and patterns which they are designed to measure. Seeing it thus, they are Venetian blind.

From Saint Nicholas I went on to Saint Hugh's, Bickley, a boarding school for boys aged seven to thirteen, immediately to the west of Chislehurst. The building was a huge and even ornate mansion of Victorian times, done in red-brick Gothic, to which was attached a single-story annex of wood, roofed with corrugated iron, for classrooms, gymnasium, and chapel. Along the south side of the main building ran a splendid, spacious terrace looking down upon a lawn encircled with noble trees, including an ilex, two horse chestnuts, and a venerable cedar. The lawn was large enough to serve as the main cricket field, whereon the height of prowess was to hit a ball right over the lofty school building. Beyond the circle of trees were a garden, a rifle range, and two huge playing fields. The physical environment—apart from the ticky-tacky classrooms—was gorgeous, but the intellectual, moral, and spiritual environment was . . . well, I can only call it weird.

My first lesson, given at night in a six-bed dormitory by the other occupants, was in the vocabulary of scatology and sexual anatomy, with a brief introduction to buttock fetishism. The next morning seven-year-olds were consigned to the class supervised by Miss Elsie Good, a precise and serious lady with a sharply pointed nose, who instructed us in English, French, Latin, Arithmetic, History, Geography, and Holy Scripture. I suppose all this was, as my mother called it, "good grounding," but the whole process was carried out under such duress that only exceptionally gifted Englishmen survive it and retain any lifelong fascination with arts and letters. I now suspect that all the necessary rudiments of these subjects can be mastered in a single year when one is sixteen or seventeen, or sooner if one feels so inclined. I was most certainly "motivated" to study literature, philosophy, religion, Oriental culture, painting, and graphic arts when I was fourteen.

Miss Elsie's sister, Elizabeth Good, dark-haired, plump, and pretty as she was, had a dual personality, the dark side of which emerged when attempting to teach us to play the piano. Much as I love music, she gave me a permanent block against reading notation and instrumental playing. She would balance a rubber eraser on each hand to be sure that you learned "correct posture," and hit your fingers with a pencil if you played a wrong note. And the "music" consisted of ridiculous exercises in playing scales and moronic "pieces for children" by some totally uninspired composer named Czerny. Even then this gave me the suspicion that there is something basically wrong with Western musical notation, and with the whole idea of playing music by reading from marks on paper—a method seldom used in Asia. I wanted to learn by ear, or at least to turn the score on its side, to the right, so that the notes would be aligned with my hands. Many years later I was happy to find that these objections were shared by one of the most brilliant scientists in the world, Gregory Bateson, who was brought up under the same system, and found himself almost paralyzed in trying to read music. But somewhere around 1948 I was cured of these inhibitions by Oswald Jonas, a fabulous musicologist who then taught in Chicago and had been trained in Vienna under Schenker. He started out by getting my arms perfectly relaxed and then simply dropping my hands at random on the keys, saying, "Just take it easy. Imagine that you are Lao-tzu. Now all you have to do is to get your fingers on the right notes. There is enough weight in your arms so that you do not have to *hit* the keys, like Horowitz and Wanda Landowska."[1] He then went on to explain that I should play as slowly as was comfortable and simply keep the rhythm, and that if I played a wrong note, just to forget it and go on. But that was not the way of Miss Good: you had to go back and play

---

[1] Recently I watched Rubinstein, in London, using this same technique of weight rather than force. When he wanted to produce an immensely sonorous chord he would simply rise from his seat and put the weight of his whole body on the keys.

it over and over again, so that the whole sense of flowing melody and rhythm was destroyed.

The notorious and ritualized brutality of British schools of the traditional upper-class type has been sufficiently described by such writers as Charles Dickens, Hugh Walpole, Somerset Maugham, and Aldous Huxley that I need not go into it—save to say that as a senior prefect, or monitor, at King's School, Canterbury, I had the nerve to admonish the headmaster to cease and desist from the custom of flogging because of its sexual complications. The French call it *le vice anglais*. Though I find pleasure in gently smacking the bottom of a comely girl, I have no pleasure whatsoever in hitting someone full tilt with an enormous cane so as to bruise him or her for days and draw blood. But British erotic literature, especially of the late Victorian era, abounds with scenes of utterly merciless whippings—especially upon girls—with everything from horsewhips to barbed wire. But my advice to the headmaster was in vain, and his immediate successor was a fervent believer in flogging—as I learned long after from an alumnus of a later generation whom I met by chance in Kyoto. At Saint Hugh's I could not escape this treatment, but at Canterbury, where it was vastly more brutal, I managed by sheer guile and skullduggery to avoid it altogether—only to learn the curious fact that a man who uses brains against brawn is, by the brawny, considered a sneak, a cheater, and a coward—almost a criminal. Nevertheless, I have continued thus far to use such brains as I may have against the periodic convulsions and emotional eruptions of brawny people. Once I was so baffled and frustrated by this school that I attempted to run away, more as a protest than as a serious attempt to be out of it—for the seemingly dreadful alternative, vaguely threatened, was the public County School for boys of the lower classes, where I would learn to say "ain't" instead of "isn't." The immediate cause for my protest was the furious rejection of a Latin exercise which I had most carefully written in Gothic script with a decorated initial capital, imagining that the teacher would be relieved of monotony and entertained by something resembling a medieval manuscript. But he reacted as to an insult, and this struck me as so irrational that I felt myself given over to the care of maniacal bullies. Doubtless the poor fellow was so illiterate as never to have seen such a manuscript. I, however, felt that a serious attempt to make a work of graphic art had been treated as a prank, and that the judgment and taste of my preceptors was no longer to be trusted. Then, as later in life, people seemed to be telling me that the things I can do well are irrelevant.

What, in retrospect, astonishes me is that in these schools we learned nothing, except the English language, which was of much relevance to life— although there was a very pleasant Captain Walpole who taught me how to swim and who cured warts on the feet. And there was also a particularly amusing Mr. Mintoft who taught basic physics and electronics, a tall lanky man who never took the system seriously and was always poking subtle fun at Mr. Sladen, a former member of the Secret Service who taught Holy Scripture with earnest verve, occasionally appeared in Bedouin garb, gave us extracurricular lectures on such odd matters as deciphering codes, and had a military voice that could be heard for miles. He taught me how to put platoons through ritual drills so that I developed a voice of command like a marine sergeant.

There was also a humorous and very well-intentioned Mr. Lines at Saint Hugh's who taught mathematics and French with utterly disastrous results. All mathematics really comes down to the formula "If, then"—but I had the greatest difficulty, especially in algebra, in understanding how they got from "if" to "then." I could always understand the geometry of Euclid, but this turned out to be a method of formal logic which has completely confused the human race because we are always trying to straighten things out or put them in boxes, whereas the world so geometered is naturally wiggly. But in algebra we would be confronted with statements like:

$$a(b^2 + a^3) - 3c.4d[x + 2y(a + b)^2 + c] = p - q,$$
From which it is obvious that $f/x = p - a^2$.

If you presumed to ask *why* it was obvious, you were denounced as an idiot or smitten on the behind with the large wooden compass used for the blackboard.

The English method of teaching French was permanently bamboozled by a certain Monsieur Ahn who, at the turn of the century, submitted to a London publisher a book of lessons which he had written as a parody on the English approach to French. The publishers scratched their heads and decided that, since hardly anyone would see the humor of it, they would issue it as a serious textbook. It is thus that generations of English schoolchildren have memorized such nonsense as:

Avez-vous le parapluie de ma tante?
Non, mai j'ai la plume de mon oncle.

And then, because everything was based on an artificial system of grammar, we received the weird information that there were six words ending in –*ou* which were pluralized by the addition of *x*:

Bijoux, cailloux, choux, genoux, hiboux, joujoux, poux.
Jewels, stones, cabbages, knees, owls, toys, lice.

This led on to such exercises as translating into French:

Do you have some pretty jewels?
No, but I have given water to the owls.

It was thus that we arrived in France with an amazing vocabulary concerning umbrellas, pens, owls, lice, blackboards, desks, benches, tables, and chairs, but incapable of ordering in a restaurant or understanding what French people were saying.

The study of history was basically propaganda for the British Empire and the Protestant religion according to the persuasion of the (Low) Church of England. It was largely a memorization of dates of kings, battles, revolutions, executions, assassinations, plots, and councils, and of short lists of the alleged causes of various wars—a succession of "good things" and "bad things," which led up to the glorious present, with George V and Queen Mary on top of the world and, coming up, that nice and gallant boy— Edward, Prince of Wales. It was almost exclusively a slanted political history. American history was practically ignored as being too short for serious consideration, although in one term at Canterbury we did read a brief account of the Civil War. But we learned nothing of the histories of art, science, agriculture, and architecture, and it was only through my parents that I found Marjorie and C. H. B. Quennell's delightful *A History of Everyday Things in England*, with its clear and luminous drawings of costumes, buildings, and technical implements.

I had two extraordinary teachers in Latin: the first, at Saint Hugh's, a blond and extremely athletic young man, Mr. Lemon, who when we made mistakes used to turn us over his lap and spank us in such a comic style that no one resented it, at the same time shouting out the correct form of translation. Once when he was spanking a boy for not remembering the nature of an "ablative of respect," another member of the class exclaimed, "But, sir, that's an ablative of disrespect!"—for which he was at once given a good mark, much treasured because for lack of fourteen such prizes per week one was ritually whipped on Saturday mornings by Mr. Alfred Johnson.

The second of my extraordinary Latin teachers was at Canterbury, a formidable Mr. Goss, who wore a red toupee, and, although he instructed us in the absolutely boring histories of Livy, nevertheless introduced us to the poetry of Virgil and the stately prose of Cicero. In retrospect I realize that he was a considerable scholar, who started off my interest in etymology and word-play, later to be reinforced by reading Joyce and Ananda K. Coomaraswamy. Boring as Livy may be, Mr. Goss's lectures were invariably interesting, especially when he went into the historical problems of pronouncing Greek and introduced us to Sophocles with the *Antigone*.

But the main preoccupation of these schools was Sport. The American *Who's Who* does not, like the British, have a section under which celebrities list their recreations. Under this category Bernard Shaw wrote, "Anything but sport." Sport consisted mainly of cricket, soccer, rugger (American: football, though less violent), and track racing. I detested cricket. For one reason, I do not have binocular vision and thus cannot be quite sure of the correct position of a moving ball. For another, merely fielding for hours on a summer afternoon was a total waste of time. At Saint Hugh's I made the school team for rugger, but lost interest at Canterbury and went instead for fencing and rowing. We were not taught soccer properly and used too much force. Anyone who saw the victory of the Brazilian team for the World Cup of 1970 will realize that, by superb footwork, they literally danced their way to triumph, and, though apparently disorganized in the formal disposition of their team, could make rapidly interchanging passes with infallible accuracy. *Certaine gaieté d'esprit.*

On the whole I dislike formal games—bridge, chess, Monopoly, and even Japanese *go*. Yes, it is all right to play poker on a large table covered with bright green felt with a convivial company drinking beer. But, on the whole, formal games are a way of getting together with other people without ever meeting them. Whether they be intellectual games like chess or brawny games like wrestling, I see no point in finding my identity through competition with others. I regard others who excel in sports, arts, or sciences as my own admired delegates or limbs, without the least tinge of jealousy, and realize that I, in turn, am one of their limbs. Since about 1926, when I got into serious trouble for the childish prank of squirting acetylene liquid at the plump older sister of one of my boy companions—which did her no injury—I have known that beyond and beneath the superficial personality of "Alan Watts" there is an eternal and invulnerable center which Hindus would call the *atman*. This is not a center in the geometrical sense of the word, not a fixed and rigid point. It is T. S. Eliot's "still point of the turning world," and yet it is also Saint Bonaventure's "circle whose center is everywhere and whose circumference is nowhere." I do not know whether this is a virtue or not, for I do not keep accounts on such matters. But I feel no need to prove myself by defeating others. Yet it is strange that I first found this out by being made to feel intensely guilty for perpetrating a practical joke, and finding a center in myself untouched by the feeling.

Meanwhile, Ronald Macfarlane joined me in my distaste for organized sports and games. Instead, we roved and zoomed over the commons of Chislehurst on our bicycles, carrying air rifles, and followed by his friendly elkhound, Taxel. We considered ourselves as quite apart from the common throng of nice boys who played cricket or tennis, whom we regarded as dismal squares, doomed to a future of office work in London. All such boys seemed to have a certain haughtiness and facial expression whereby they could be recognized instantly: they raised their eyebrows and looked down their noses at us. At roll call they said "Hah" instead of "Here." At another extreme there were low-class, ill-spoken, non-U, and tough-egg boys who dropped their aitches, and we also stayed away from them. Both categories seemed to be equally lacking in imagination, in any capacity for fantasy or interest in the exotic. This is perhaps why the subtopias of England are so drab, slovenly, and even squalid. Ronald and I saw ourselves as free-floating adventurers, somewhat like Japanese *ronin*, and it may be of current interest that in all these exploits we were never troubled by officious policemen. On weekdays the commons were virtually deserted, and thus we had vast areas of wild land at our disposal.

I left Saint Hugh's for King's School, Canterbury, in 1928—a year of economic depression—by winning a scholarship. In the last days at Saint Hugh's I began to realize that the headmaster, Alfred Johnson, was not so bad after all. He had black hair and a nose like a vulture's beak, but also a resonant and stately voice (nonparsonic) and a true passion for music, especially for Wagner. He taught us to sing the principal arias and choruses from the *Meistersinger*, one of Schubert's Masses, Mendelssohn's *Lobegesang*, and Brahms's *Requiem*. And with evenings of listening to records of symphony and opera in his study he simply wiped out my problematic attitude to music imparted by the piano lessons of Miss Good. I glimpsed that he and his family—Charles Johnson, Elvira and Francis Croshaw—were in some curious way European rather than insularly British. They had French and German vibrations which, at that time, gave them an aura of the magic of far-off places—of Paris and Munich, Cannes and Biarritz, Florence and Venice.

I went to Saint Hugh's in times that were economically harsh for my father, and realizing this, Alfred Johnson was kind enough to cut the fees. Nevertheless, the financial burden on my parents was heavy, as also during the years at Canterbury. In retrospect I wonder what this schooling did for me, and whether it was worth my parents' efforts. Perhaps it made me a gentleman, in the class sense of the word, and put me in a position to consort with people higher on the social ladder. Yet my father did not attend such schools, and in speech, manner, and culture he is the very archetype of what the British call a gentleman—and genuinely so. There is no false note in him. It is useless to "if" about things like this for, after all, the pattern of my school years included Francis Croshaw, Christmas Humphreys, and all manner of interesting "side effects." I am inclined to believe that these schools are

justified more by the eccentrics who resist the system than by the conform-
ists who come out as the system intends.

It is now becoming obvious that the same may be said of almost *all*
schools, and of universities as well. They are production lines turning out
stereotyped personnel and consumers for the industrial machine—a machine
which is more and more subservient, not to human needs, but to the abstract
purposes of technological expansion for its own sake, of the money game,
and of competition for the hollow rewards of status. And the markets are
flooded with things which I, and others who have come to their senses, do not
want to buy. In my own school days the stereotypes were a little different, but
no one can resist a stern system designed to produce preconceived "character" without suffering a few wounds. To compensate for lack of real success
along the lines laid down for me I came out of the process with an ego larger
than I needed, and was as clumsy among "normals" as one whose clothes
are too big for him.

It is perhaps idle to wonder what, from my present point of view, would
have been an ideal education. If I could provide such a curriculum for my
own children, they, in their turn, might find it all a bore. But the fantasy of
what I would have liked to learn as a child may be revealing, since I feel
unequipped by education for problems that lie outside the cloistered, literary domain in which I am competent and at home. Looking back, then, I
would have arranged for myself to be taught survival techniques for both
natural and urban wildernesses. I would want to have been instructed in self-
hypnosis, in *aikido* (the esoteric and purely self-defensive style of judo), in
elementary medicine, in sexual hygiene, in vegetable gardening, in astronomy, navigation, and sailing; in cookery and clothesmaking, in metalwork
and carpentry, in drawing and painting, in printing and typography, in
botany and biology, in optics and acoustics, in semantics and psychology,
in mysticism and yoga, in electronics and mathematical fantasy, in drama
and dancing, in singing and in playing an instrument by ear; in wandering,
in advanced daydreaming, in prestidigitation, in techniques of escape from
bondage, in disguise, in conversation with birds and beasts, in ventriloquism,
in French and German conversation, in planetary history, in morphology,

and in classical Chinese.[2] Actually, the main thing left out of my education was a proper love for my own body, because one feared to cherish anything so obviously mortal and prone to sickness.

King's School, Canterbury, is reputed to be the oldest Public School in England, and is believed to have been founded by Saint Augustine of Canterbury shortly after A.D. 595. I went there in the autumn of 1928, when Randall Davidson was about to retire as Archbishop and Norman Pellew Birley had just become headmaster. Although Canterbury was then a somewhat squalid city, the precincts of the Cathedral, which included the school, were literally a garden enclosed—walled and gated on all sides, the east wall being the original bastioned wall of the city. Almost every building was of pale grey stone, and the architecture Romanesque (Norman) and every variety of Gothic, though there were some modern stone buildings, tiled with slate, made so as not to clash too abruptly with the ancient.

The whole atmosphere was strangely light and airy, full of the sound of bells and the cries of jackdaws floating around the great Bell Harry Tower of the Cathedral, and when March came in like a lion the air swept through the buildings, slamming doors and rattling shutters, and seeming to cleanse the place of human meanness. The magic of these surroundings was naturally enhanced by contrast with the tedious disciplines of ritual learning (all real education being extracurricular); by the working out of pecking orders; by having to dress like dowdy dandies—in speckled straw hats, or boaters, with blue and white ribbons, in starched wing collars with black ties, and in black

---

[2] This is a serious proposal, for Chinese is, for us, a far better language for "mind-training" than Latin or Greek because it is the most highly evolved and sophisticated language least like our own. Thus the patterns of thought upon which it is based bring out, by contrast, the implicit and largely unrecognized patterns of thought which underlie our own tongue—as that "events," represented by verbs, must be set in motion by "things," represented by nouns. Furthermore, anything said in English may be said in half the time in Chinese, while German and Japanese take twice the time. Some form of written Chinese would also be a marvelous language for computers, because it can be read at high speed, and because each character, or ideogram, is a nonlinear *Gestalt*, or configuration.

jackets with Oxford-grey trousers; and by a diet of boiled beef, boiled cabbage, boiled onions, boiled carrots, boiled potatoes, and slabs of near-stale
bread, all of which we were allowed to supplement with our own jams and
pickles. Thus the real eating was also extracurricular.

Underneath the arches which supported a spending medieval hall with
stained glass and carved and canopied wooden thrones was the Tuck Shop,
run by kind and patient Mrs. Benn, where we ruined our teeth with chocolate bars, barley sugar, butterscotch, toffee, marshmallow in chocolate, and
ice cream sodas. Aside from this, we all owned or shared Primus stoves for
the frying of sausages and eggs, for concocting Welsh rarebit, and for preparing what then seemed a splendid curry by the following recipe:

> 2 large onions
> 6 saveloys (American: small hot dogs)
> 1 handful raisins
> Salt and pepper
> Curry powder
> Margarine or cooking oil

> Slice onions and fry until rings have separated and are lightly
> browned. Add saveloys, cut into half-inch sections. While they are
> being stirred and browned, throw in the raisins. Season lightly with
> salt and pepper, and add a heaping tablespoon of curry powder.
> Sprinkle with somewhat less than a gill of water, stir all together,
> cover the pan, and simmer until the smell is irresistible.

Immediately opposite the school gate was a teashop with a rhomboid
door—the whole being a most ancient house carefully preserved in mid-
collapse—and here we could guzzle after classes on coffee, hot buttered
scones, and nut cake with mocha icing. It was also possible to bicycle sufficiently beyond the city limits to escape surveillance and pop into country
pubs, the best being some two miles beyond the fortified West Gate; a friendly
place where no questions were asked, and which supplied a dark Kentish
ale known as Gardner's Old Strong. This was a favorite resort of senior pre-
fects, especially on Sundays after Morning Prayer in the Cathedral. So often
I wonder why, instead of drinking in pubs, Americans put up with dark and

lugubrious saloons, glimmering with the phosphorescent light of jukeboxes. Presumably, so as to be invisible to their guilty consciences.

Probably the most important adult I met at Canterbury was Alec Macdonald, housemaster of The Grange. He had been a pilot in the air force during World War I, but was actually a true man of peace and culture. He had strangely dark eyes and always looked at you unwaveringly and directly. He maintained a spacious study carpeted in royal blue and surrounded with books on white shelves, mostly French and German classics. Although he could not sing a note or play an instrument, he was a fervent lover of music and used to play records of Bach, Mozart, and Beethoven to us while entertaining small groups to afternoon tea. He worked out a system of musical notation similar to the Hindu and showed us how Mozart's *Jupiter* Symphony could be represented graphically by a wavering and prancing line. Alec Macdonald always conveyed something extracurricular—a civilized, urbane culture outside the boring routines of school. Alas—from my point of view—he married Felicity Hardcastle, the Archdeacon's daughter, and disappeared for parts unknown, so that I have entirely lost contact with this inspired teacher of music and literature.

He was succeeded in office by R. S. Stanier, a stocky Calvinist, who debated stoutly and intelligently with my Buddhist views, and taught me inadvertently but interestingly all the fallacies of Western logic. I liked him so much that, for a while, I imitated his handwriting—so well that I could forge permissions for other boys to go out on the town after hours. He gave us fascinating lectures on Milton's *Paradise Lost* and on Plato's *Republic* in Greek, and challenged us to think deeply about the basic philosophical problems involved. He was a confirmed fatalist and predestinarian who, supporting capital punishment, believed that people could be "cured by death." The only point he missed was that to be inevitably compelled by God is to be one with God, and that in this way, determinism becomes freedom.

Then there was a genial and scholarly little Welshman, William Moses Williams, a real master of Latin and Greek, who, again inadvertently, taught me the art of public speaking. We had a school debating society which got down to really basic problems, and Mr. Williams would arrive as a principal speaker, at the last moment, knowing neither the subject of the debate nor which side he was supposed to take. He would thereupon deliver a perfectly lucid and logically ordered speech, with items one, two, and three, straight off the top of his head, and from him I learned not only the art of talking spontaneously without notes, but also the dangerous truth that you can pitch a good argument for any cause whatsoever.

In these debates, held in that ancient room with stained-glass shields on the windows, and a canopied throne for the chairman, we spoke much of war and peace. I took the pacifist side and, in passing, derided the weekly antics of the obsolete Officers' Training Corps, which required interminable polishing of brass buttons and putting a drab green paste on canvas belts. If the thing had been realistic, we should have been learning how to drive tanks, fly planes, operate machine guns, practice karate, and strangle people noiselessly with piano wire. With such training there would have been no "heroic retreat" at Dunkirk. Furthermore, these military antics, held every Thursday afternoon, were canceled if it rained. Imagine an army unable to function in the rain! The whole ritual was so detested that almost everyone hoped it would rain, and we used to command a gracious but much-persecuted Egyptian boy—a Mohammedan named Kasimoff—to prostrate himself and pray for rain every Thursday morning. It often worked.

One other scholarly man must be mentioned, Mr. Edgerton-Jones, teacher of history and political science, who lisped, and once made the cogent remark that "A shchoolmashter is a man among shildren, and a shild among men." We had a system wherein one finished general education at the age of fifteen. Thereafter one specialized in a particular subject in preparation for the 'varsity, which meant Oxford or Cambridge. Because I respected Mr. Edgerton-Jones and his principal student, Peter Scott, an urbane intellectual-athlete who was then head-boy of the school (and also practiced yoga), I chose modern history, and was aiming at a scholarship at Trinity College, Oxford. We worked in the school library instead of the classrooms, and gathered there every so often for highly intelligent tutorial seminars with Mr. Edgerton-Jones. But I lost interest. I wanted to study Oriental philosophy, for which there were no facilities either at the school or, in those days, at Oxford—not, at least, for undergraduates. I failed to get a scholarship at Trinity because, as I was told later, I wrote the essay examination on Courage in the style of Nietzsche, having just read his *Zarathustra*. Some theologically occidented examiner must have been offended. So I never went to college, and had to go it on my own—with Toby Humphreys, Geoffrey (Nigel) Watkins, Alan L. Watts (*sic*), Dmitrije Mitrinović, and others as my preceptors.

The mores of Canterbury involved the deplorable principle that one should not form friendships with boys of a lower class, grade, or age than one's own. I fought this system with fury because the only really interesting boy in the House was Patrick Leigh Fermor, an Irish lad about one year younger than myself, a romantic, a fine poet, a born adventurer, a splendid actor, and a gallant lover of women who, in sheer desperation, used to flirt with a dowdy blonde—one of the kitchenmaids—and who was gifted with an Arthurian and medieval imagination. We took bicycle rides and long walks together to visit ancient churches and pubs. We luxuriated in the landscape of eastern Kent, its circles of beech trees, its cedars, its rose gardens, and hop-fields. When utterly oppressed by the social system of the school, we would sneak off to Canterbury Cathedral—which, because of its colossal sanctity, could never be made out-of-bounds—to study the stained-glass windows, to explore the Anglo-Saxon crypt, or to read books in the serene and secluded garden adjoining the Cathedral library. Patrick, as an adventurer of extreme courage, was constantly being flogged for his pranks and exploits—in other words, for having a creative imagination—and finally, as I have said, suffered the ultimate disgrace of being expelled from the school for the peccadillo of taking a walk with Miss Lamar, a comely brunette who was daughter of a local greengrocer. A year or two later he took a ship across the Channel and walked to Constantinople, pausing awhile in Vienna to earn some money by making portrait-sketches on a plaza. On the way back he visited the monks of Mount Athos, which he discovered to be an elaborate homosexual organization, and then spent a year as the lover of a Rumanian princess. During World War II he slipped quietly into the German headquarters in Crete and—almost singlehanded—captured the General Staff.

Today Patrick is a highly respected prose-poet, published by my friend John Grey Murray, who now heads the venerable firm in London which once published the works of Byron. The oddity is that King's School, Canterbury, founded by Saint Augustine and endowed by Henry VIII, cannot claim the honor of one of its most imaginative alumni. He lives somewhere on a Greek island. The point is, I think, that England has a climate so dismal, an educational system so antiquated, a social system so rigid, a diet so lugubrious, and business operation so boring and conducted in such miserable surroundings that it shoots off its more sensitive sons to other places. This may, indeed, be a positive virtue, for I cannot find it in my heart to have any hatred for the land in which I was born. But Patrick had an energy and individuality which the oldest Public School in England could not tolerate, the real trouble being that he liked women and did something about it, and this was like the sin against the Holy Ghost.

I would not go so far as to say, with Kenneth Rexroth, that English public schools are positively seminaries for sodomy, buggery, pederasty, and sadomasochism. But monastically separated from girls as we were, a good deal of this kind of thing went on, and my first serious love affair was with a younger boy. We did nothing about it physically except hold hands, and as soon as I could escape from school I sought the company of girls, but found it strangely difficult to consummate any relationship until the age of twenty-two. There were scared, and I was afraid of rejection.

Less adventurous than Patrick, but equally romantic, poetic, and raven's-blooded, was Richard Weeks—as still river, running at great depth. In countenance he was always serene and absorbed and, as he walked, somehow gave the illusion that his fair-haired head was far out in front of his neck. In the library, walking on the hills, and wandering through the precincts, we passed hours discussing poetry, philosophy, religion, and, above all, magic, for which Richard had a particular inclination. He explained that to create a wonder-working wand one must arise very early in the morning, go out to some woodland, and cut a stick of hazel. Thereafter it had to be seasoned, carved, and polished so as to be an expression of one's will and skill. After leaving school he went along with me for a while in the study of Buddhism, but, increasingly attracted to ritual magic, he discovered and joined a secret group in London which practiced that art with high seriousness. However, some months later he awoke in the night to find himself being watched by a Presence of unfathomable malice and horror, a tangible darkness, a black light. He converted at once to the Roman Catholic Church. But when, after many years, I met him again on a recent visit to London, I found that he had become a Sufi, and that his head was back on his neck.

I left King's School a term before the end of the academic year. Although I was a senior prefect, captain of my house, member of the Sixth Form, and had the pleasure of holding adult discourse with several scholarly teachers, I had had enough of this juvenile atmosphere. I was writing articles for the journal of the Buddhist Lodge. I had published a booklet on Zen, which is happily out of print. I had no use for going to the university. I was reading Suzuki, Keyserling, Nietzsche, Vivekananda, Lao-tzu, the *Upanishads*, Feuchtwanger, Bergson, Blavatsky, the *Bhagavad-Gita*, Lafcadio Hearn, Anatole France, Havelock Ellis, Bernard Shaw, the *Diamond Sutra*, Dwight Goddard (if anyone remembers him), Robert Graves, and Carl Jung—all the literature which was "oddball" and screened out of the curriculum. I was seventeen, and all set to go.

CHAPTER FIVE

MY OWN UNIVERSITY

No literate, inquisitive, and imaginative person needs to go to college unless in need of a union card, or degree, as a certified physician, lawyer, or teacher, or unless he requires access to certain heavy and expensive equipment for scientific research which he himself cannot afford, such as a cyclotron. In 1932 my father could not afford to send me to Oxford without a scholarship, and I did not really want to go there. But he did something much better. He gave me a temporary job in his office until I could find my feet, and this consisted in raising funds for the London hospitals. Otherwise, he went for long walks with me on weekends through the hills of Kent, during which we discussed all the basic problems of life, admired haystacks, views of the Weald (the central forest of Kent), and ancient churches and mansions—including Sir Winston Churchill's house at Westerham. We drank beer and ate excellent bread and cheese—the tart and solid Cheddar, and sometimes the blue Cheshire—at village pubs. Almost invariably he accompanied me to sessions at the Buddhist Lodge, and soon became the institution's treasurer. He is a serene, quiet man who never says anything unless it is really worth saying, and I cannot imagine a more companionable father.

His own father, Thomas Roberts Watts, was a princely man who sported an Van Dyke beard, looked like Edward VII, dressed with jaunty elegance, was a great architectural photographer, and was private secretary to Sir John Pound—at one time Lord Mayor of London. He wore a gold ring in the form of a snake, thrice coiled around the finger, with rubies for eyes, and gave me a silver Buddha from Thailand. He died instantaneously in 1936 in the midst of photographing the abbey at Bath.

Thus, with my father's unfailing support and encouragement, I designed my own "higher education." I chose Toby Humphreys as my chief preceptor, and he, in turn, introduced me to Nigel Watkins and his aged father, John. Nigel runs the most magical bookshop in the world, and is the most unobtrusively enlightened person I have ever known. The shop is on a secluded place named Cecil Court at the south end of Charing Cross Road, close to the National Gallery and the Coliseum. He sells books on Oriental philosophy, magic, astrology, Masonry, meditation, Christian mysticism, alchemy, herbal medicine, and every occult and far-out subject under the sun. But he himself has, if you will take his own advice, perfect discrimination in what one should read, for he knows that much of this literature is superstitious trash. His father, John M. Watkins, was a disciple of Blavatsky and a close friend of the Gnostic scholar G.R.S. Mead. He was almost blind when I knew him, but he advised me carefully as to what I should read of the principal texts of Hindu philosophy. Nigel not only became my bibliographer on Buddhism, comparative religion, and mysticism, but also my most trusted adviser on the various gurus, pandits, and psychotherapists then flourishing in London.

He remains so to this day, and his shop likewise remains one of the world's most important centers of what I must call "metaphysical gossip." Imagine the bookish counterpart of a warehouse which deals in Chinese ink and jade, Indian incense, Turkish tobacco, Lebanese hashish, Tibetan jewelry, Persian carpets, Japanese implements for the tea ceremony, Buddhist gongs and rosaries, and—as an international center for information about what is going on in the whole "occult subculture" all over the world—managed by a modest fellow who knows exactly where it's at. In the Watkins bookshop one would expect, at any moment, to come across a Mahatma or a high Lama visiting England on a secret mission to feel out potential initiates for the Great White Lodge, and who might arrange for you to be whisked off to an unknown sanctuary in Bhutan.

Nigel is worth at least twenty academically accredited professors. Instead of giving lectures and holding seminars, he simply tells you what to read. That is his business and, *pace* McLuhan, reading is still the fastest way of absorbing information, although to comprehend mysticism you must also follow some type of *sadhana*, or discipline in nonverbal perception—except that you have to do it without seeking any result in the future. You have to stop competing, justifying yourself, and just be/not-be. This requires that you stop, look, and listen, abandon thoughts and theories, and feel directly whatever it is that is going on without asking questions—i.e., for translations into words of what is going on. Nigel achieves all this without the least fuss. He never tries to convert anyone to a system. He is what the Japanese would call a *buji-nin*: a man without affectations, who has also compassion and clarity of mind. He is also no grizzly ascetic. Whenever we go to London he takes us to lunch at a most cheerful pub just around the corner, stuffs us with veal-and-ham pie, and drowns us in beer.

One day in 1934 he told me that he had another customer named Alan Watts, and that, just for the fun of it, we should meet.[1] Whereupon he introduced me to a bright-eyed, light-hearted, breezy man about twelve years older than myself, who was going with an exquisite paramour, later his wife, named June. This nominal alter ego became a most valuable ally and teacher. He told me all the things about sex I had never been taught at home or in school. He introduced me to Freud, to Adler, and to psychoanalysis, and went on to inform me that he had a guru named Dmitrije Mitrinović, from Yugoslavia, who was very probably a high initiate into the mysteries of the universe.

Mitrinović lived in Bloomsbury, close to the British Museum. He was a stout Slavonic man with a completely shaved head, black winglike eyebrows, and entrancing eyes. On the street he wore extremely formal clothes—an exalted bowler hat (a sort of cross between a bowler and top hat like the one used by Winston Churchill), cutaway morning coat, and striped trousers. He carried a walking stick with an amber handle, always paid his bills with crisp white five-pound notes, which in those days looked like legal documents, and smoked very fat Virginia cigarettes. He also drank formidable amounts of whiskey. But he resembled Gurdjieff and was a great magician and "rascal-guru." He was surrounded by devoted disciples and adoring

---

[1] And there is at least a third Alan Watts, who lives on Hayling Island in Hampshire, and writes fascinating books on sailing and meteorology.

women and lived, semisecretly, in a sanctum sanctorum so as to give one the impression that it was an immense privilege to be invited there. And it was. I loved him and feared him, for my Buddhist and Theosophical friends were of the opinion that he was a black magician. He used to take us to dinner in the Hungarian, Greek, and Russian restaurants of Soho, order six different dishes, and mix them all up. At home he wore loose robes, sat on his bed, and regaled us with conversations, some of which I cannot repeat because I promised him not to reveal them. But one night he gave us a discourse on an essay from Manly Hall's *Lectures on Ancient Philosophy* (Los Angeles, 1929), in which he explained the complementation of the principle of unity and the principle of differentiation in the universe, using for the latter the image of the sharp form of a fox's face. He showed me that acute differences positively manifest unity, and that you cannot conceive the one without the other. This was the philosophy that I have subsequently called "goeswithness," and which the Japanese call *ji-ji-mu-ge*—the mutual interdependence of all things and events. Thus the sharp form of a particular fox's face necessarily implied the existence of galaxy M 81.

Both Gurdjieff and Mitrinović came into a scene which had already been set by H. P. Blavatsky, who had claimed to be in touch with a universal fraternity of gurus or Masters of Wisdom, adepts in mysticism and occultism maintaining lonely and secret monasteries in the Himalayas, the Andes, and other remote parts of the world. The cult of the Masters had been further spread abroad by the adventure stories of Talbot Mundy (in particular his novels *Om* and *Ramsden*) and by the composer Cyril Scott, anonymous author of *The Initiate—by His Pupil* and *The Initiate in the New World*. It was said that on rare occasions a Master would leave sanctuary and appear in the everyday world, as had happened in the instances of the Buddha, Lao-tzu, Jesus, and obscure individuals who had not founded great religions. The fraternity was, furthermore, of incalculable antiquity. It had been at work in the lost civilizations of Atlantis and Lemuria, and kept its records, written on indestructible paper in the secret language of Senzar, in great underground libraries hewn out of the mountains. Wittingly or unwittingly, Gurdjieff, Ouspensky, Aleister Crowley, and Mitrinović, as well as Yogananda, Meher Baba, Alice Bailey, Paul Brunton, and even Krishnamurti, had the aura of this legend attached to them. And of those whose lives and techniques did not correspond to what one would expect of a saint, it was said that they "moved in a mysterious way" and must not be judged by commons standards, or that they had to have some small human failings to remain incarnate in a physical body.

Certainly the atmosphere of Mitrinović fascinated me—his humor, the power of his eyes and voice, his secretive and night-owl habits, his oracular way of writing (under the pseudonym M. M. Cosmoi), and his exotic tastes in art and literature. I was delighted to find that he possessed the rare and superb French translation of Lao-tzu, published by Stanislas Julien, S.J., in 1848.

Mitrinović invariably began his activities late at night, and would arrive among his disciples about 11:00 P.M. To me this was utterly frustrating, for the last train for Chislehurst left just before midnight from Charing Cross Station, and this circumstance ruined most of my love affairs and interesting encounters, for I could not then afford a *pied-à-terre* in London, and realized that my parents were vaguely anxious about what I was doing. But once he kept me up until 3:00 A.M. and then sent me home in a chauffeur-driven limousine.

The historical importance of Mitrinović was that he tried to save Europe from Nazism and economic insanity. With the aid of C. B. Purdom, editor of *Everyman* and disciple of Meher Baba; David Davies, an eloquent Welshman; the aristocratic Colonel Delahaye, Watson Thomson, and Winifred Gordon-Fraser, he created—in the years between 1933 and 1936—the New Britain movement, which put forth its views in such widely circulated magazines as *New Britain* and *The Eleventh Hour*, for which I wrote reviews of books. I may be mistaken, but I am not aware that this movement has been properly chronicled, and it should most certainly "go down in history."

Mitrinović's work began in the milieu of a group, located at 55 Gower Street in Bloomsbury, which was studying the psychotherapeutic techniques of Alfred Adler and Trigant Burrow, author of *The Social Basis of Consciousness* (1927) and *Phyloanalysis* (1933) in which he contended that the ego-personality was a socially implanted fiction and not a psychophysical entity. On this ground Mitrinović developed the method of "personal alliance," which is doubtless one of the principal origins of what we would now call the "T group" or "encounter group," a no-holds-barred mutual psychoanalysis, though the meetings were not then, as sometimes now, held by both sexes in the nude. My nominal alter ego, Alan L. Watts, Gilbert Mayo, a charming physicist, and a psychoanalyst whose name escapes me constituted one of these groups, and, for some months, we resolutely destroyed and rebuilt each other's personalities. One of my train-spoiled romances was with the nannie who looked after Gilbert's children, a brunette Danish girl—Hilda—who would kiss and hug like a mink, until I had to go off and catch the 11:55 to Chislehurst.

The New Britain movement proposed four basic changes in the social order. The first was Social Credit, based on the economic philosophies of Major Douglas, Ezra Pound, and Frederick Soddy, who had realized that money was an abstraction, a mere measure of such real wealth as land, food, and clothing. They suggested that, in a technological society, there should be a national dividend paying people for the work done on their behalf by machinery, since there would otherwise be an economic slump with manufacturers unable to move their goods off the shelf. This view is still held today by Buckminster Fuller and Robert Theobald. The trouble is that it transfers the power of issuing credit from the bankers to the State.

The second was Guild Socialism, which means roughly that workers should be stockholders in the corporations which employ them so that there is no longer any class of expendable people who are mere "hands." The third was Rudolph Steiner's idea of the Threefold State, comprising a political assembly elected by region, an economic assembly elected by guilds or unions, and a cultural assembly elected by universities and learned societies, all regulated and dominated by a senate appointed by the various assemblies. People have, of course, forgotten that a republic—such as the United States was intended to be—is quite different from a mobocracy ruled by referendum. It was not without reason that we had a College of Electors for the presidency, since most people have neither knowledge nor real interest in high politics, no acquaintance with the men contending for presidency, and are easily swayed by skillfully contrived propaganda. We had it in mind that, for

England, the reigning monarch should be Chairman of the Senate and thus have something more important to do than laying the foundation stones of hospitals and viewing the races at Ascot.

The fourth basic change was to press for immediate federation of all the nations of Europe—a system now, at last, muddling into being with the Common Market and the relaxation of passport and customs inspections at the borders. When we last drove into Switzerland a policeman simply looked into the car and told us to move along. But when Hitler came into power in 1934, Mitrinović said, "Stop him now!" The New Britain movement invoked the governments of England and France to use force, if necessary, to prevent his refortification of the Rhineland in defiance of the Treaty of Versailles, and it would have worked. As Lao-tzu suggested, eliminate problems at their beginning, when they are weak. But all this was to no avail, and I decided to drop out of politics.

My work with Mitrinović involved meetings, bull sessions, public lectures, and even selling our magazines on Piccadilly Circus. I worked at book reviewing, proofreading, typography, and make-up, both with *The Eleventh Hour* and the Buddhist Lodge's journal, and thus gained a training in graphic arts in case I should ever be deprived of some more "exalted" profession. I changed my style of handwriting to the Italian Chancery Script, which, somewhat informally, I use to this day, and made a careful study of the typographical techniques of Eric Gill, who designed such classic type-faces as Perpetua, Times Roman, and Gill Sans-serif (which seems to be oddly unavailable in the United States).

During all these exhilarating adventures with Mitrinović and his disciples, my chief mentor remained Toby Humphreys. I don't always agree with him, since his Buddhism is mixed up with Blavatsky and crypto-Protestantism, and my mother commented that he ran meetings of the Buddhist Lodge like an old-time Sunday school. But he is a man of immense generosity and compassion, and through his taste in Oriental art and literature, radiates an atmosphere of warm mystery. He took me to the Japanese *budokwai* in London, where we practiced judo and *kendo* (fencing), as well as a certain Japanese equivalent of the *t'ai-chi* known as *ju-no-kata*, a slow motion judo which demonstrates its fundamental principles. Though I never became a true expert in these arts, such practices taught me how to use my feet, how to dance, and above all, how to generate energy by following the line of least resistance. Together we made an intensive study of the rambling and enigmatic writings of D. T. Suzuki on Zen Buddhism, which I had the impudence to clarify and popularize in a small book entitled *The Spirit of Zen*, written in one month of evenings when I was twenty years old.

At this point my father put me in touch with the head of his fund-raising operation, Robert Holland-Martin, Chairman of the Board of Directors of Martin's Bank, whose signature I could forge to perfection but made no use thereof. He was a big, heavy, husky man who used to run through the streets of London on his way to appointments, and knew all the short-cuts through that wiggly town. This was in 1936 when the Royal Academy of Arts, in collaboration with the Chinese government, put on an absolutely sensational exhibition of Chinese art, the center of which was a standing sculpture of the Buddha sixty feet high. Holland-Martin presented me with an official pass to this display, which I visited day after day, trying to understand and absorb the mood beneath Chinese art forms.

My self-constructed university next comprised the psychiatrist Eric Graham Howe, who then maintained consulting rooms on Harley Street and cozy living quarters in the mews behind, where I had lunch with him one day, consisting simply of a superb baked potato covered in butter. For some reason it is impossible to find such potatoes in America, though they still exist in England and France. I was not his patient. He was simply a genial, dignified, and reassuring doctor who let me in on his mind. He had then written *I and Me* and *War Dance*, and was working on the principle that has always fascinated me—that the course of gravity is the way of energy. Once a week he hosted an intimate discussion group attended by Professor Richard Arman Gregory, astronomer of the University of London, a dark and angular intellectual with a nose as penetrating as his mind; Philip Metman, a Dutch psychiatrist, more-or-less Jungian, who seemed to understand everything about dreams and symbolism; Prince Leopold von Loewenstein, a fascinatingly detached and unselfconscious aristocrat; and finally, Frederic Spiegelberg, a refugee from Hitler, Orientalist and philosopher (now a professor emeritus of Stanford University), one of the most interesting, because interested, men I have ever known—a mountain of mirrors—who, with his *ewig weibliche* wife, Rosalie, now looking no older than on the day when I first met her, still adorns San Francisco with his tall and gracious presence and infinitely inquiring mind.

Since we are not doing things in strictly chronological order, this may be the point to discuss Spiegelberg. Several years ago the students of Stanford voted him the best teacher on the faculty, which must have enraged his colleagues because you cannot maintain proper status in an American university without cultivated mediocrity. You must be academically "sound," which is to be preposterously and phenomenally dull. Once I had a professor who was teaching me the New Testament in Greek. When one of Jesus' more enigmatic sayings was about to come up I would figure out some five different interpretations and bet that he would choose the most uninteresting. It worked invariably.

But though Spiegelberg may not be fully up to scratch as a writer, in English, he is a fabulous teacher because of his way of being able to communicate his own enthusiasm for the subject. He believes, for example, that the difference between the physical body and the subtle body is that the former is the way others see and define you, and the latter the way in which you feel your own existence. This he used to illustrate in class with a sequence from the *Corky* comic strip in which the boy watching the stunts of an airplane grows his neck longer and longer and is finally tied up in knots. He also used an advertisement for some cure for "the morning after" in which a distorted photograph shows a man with a hugely enlarged pate. Spiegelberg is like the people of Athens whom Saint Paul described as "always in search of some new thing," but not so much to pacify his own anxiety as to entertain himself and others. He has the finest collection of Tibetan wood-block prints in America. He has inspired generations of Stanford students with his lectures on Indian, Tibetan, and Chinese philosophy, including my son-in-law's brother, the sculptor Oliver Andrews; the exquisite Betty Bass, or La Jolla, who is a considerable authority on Tibetan painting; and Michael Murphy, who, with my own former student, Richard Price, founded the Esalen Institute at Big Sur.

When I first met Spiegelberg he wore a hat with an exceedingly wide

brim, spoke English with a delicate German accent which always suggests a
sense of authority and high culture, and was propagating the theory that the
highest form of religion was to transcend religion. He called it the religion
of nonreligion. I call it atheism in the name of God; that is, the realization that
ordinary everyday life and consciousness is what the Hindus call *satchit-
ananda*, and which I translate as "the which than which there is no whicher."
Flowers, cats, and butterflies attend no church, have no illusions of history
and destiny, and do not require laws, parliaments, and policemen to maintain
their lives. Never have I heard a clergyman preach on that passage of the
Sermon on the Mount which begins, "Consider the lilies of the field, how
they grow," and I have heard sermons galore; good philosophy for Jesus—
who was the Boss's Son in any case and didn't really have to worry—but
impossible for us practical people engaged in the work of the world. Spiegelberg and I have always regarded ideas and conceptions of God, as well as
compulsive and scheduled notions of the "right way" of spiritual culture,
as forms of idolatry more confusing than any amount of material images and
icons. No sensible person ever confused a crucifix or an image of the Buddha with the divinity itself, and as for techniques of spiritual development,
"The ways to the One are as many as the lives of men."

Before Spiegelberg came to England he had studied with Jung, Zimmer,
and Hauer, had acquired a considerable knowledge of Sanskrit, and knew
much of Tibetan iconography. I published his first essay on "The Religion
of Non-Religion" in the journal of the Buddhist Lodge, and we later issued
an expanded version as a pamphlet. He left for America in 1937, and I followed him a year later. He taught at Columbia and Union Theological Seminary until about 1945, and then went to Stanford. I followed him again when,
in 1951, he designed the American Academy of Asian Studies in San Francisco, and invited me to join the faculty. In other words, he got me to the
place at which my interior compass was aimed. What is more, he introduced
me to two astonishing artists, Gordon Onslow-Ford and Jean (Yanko) Varda,
who shall be discussed at a later point and for whom God shall be thanked
through all the endless ages of ages.

One afternoon in 1936 Eric Graham Howe called me and said, "This is
tremendously important. Cancel any plans you have for this evening and

come to my place." I knew that Krishnamurti was in London at the time, and suspected that Eric had invited him to our group. So it turned out. I had read the lectures and dialogues of this celebrated Indian sage, but never met him. Jiddu Krishnamurti was, and still is, one of the most elegant men in the world. He wears clothes from Saville Row and used to zoom about the country in Alfa-Romeo and Mercedes-Benz sports cars. By courtesy of wealthy aristocrats he is supported palatially in Ojai, California; in Gstaad, Switzerland; or in London. He doesn't drink booze, eat meat, or, as he told Rom Landau, have any genital sex life because he is polymorphously erotic and gets the ecstasy through every nerve-end on his skin.

Just after World War I, Annie Besant, then president of the Theosophical Society in Madras, proclaimed him avatar, incarnation of the Christ, and Savior of the World. In his honor she founded the Order of the Star in the East, which had offices all over the world, and he was given a castle in the Netherlands, Schloss Erde, at Ommen, and a stadium in Australia. But supposing that Krishnamurti was indeed the *jagad-guru*, the world teacher, how would he have responded to such adulation? He would have done exactly what he did, which was—in 1928—to dissolve the Order of the Star, and to proclaim that he was not a guru and acknowledged no disciples. Nevertheless, this incredibly gracious man goes on giving lectures and is surrounded with nondisciples.

That evening he made the following points, which are still the main themes of his dialectic teaching: *Why*—and again why—do you want to know whether there is a God, whether there is life after death, or what method you should follow to become enlightened, liberated, or realized? Could it be that you identify yourself with a merely abstract ego based on nothing but memories? That therefore you are not alive and aware in the eternal present, and thus worry interminably about your future? Furthermore, don't you realize that when you accept someone as a spiritual teacher, you do so by your *own* authority and choice? You yourself license the Bible, the Koran, or the *Bhagavad-Gita* as infallible. Wake up! . . . and, without putting it into words, watch what is, now. You thus realize that there is no "feeler" apart from feelings, and no granular, billiard-ball "self" confronting the universe. Krishnaji liberates people and then adamantly refuses both thanks and adoration, except to say, in reply to the offer, "You may give me a Mercedes-Benz if it will really make you happy." I hope saying this will not embarrass him, but such a man has my boundless admiration.

Many people say that he is an iconoclast, anarchist, and negator and has nothing positive or helpful to say or offer. He is actually a spiritual window cleaner who takes our pictures of the sun off the glass so that we can see the real thing. In 1953 I had a long heart-to-heart conversation with him in the Ojai Valley, behind Santa Barbara, with its stately cypresses and orchards of oranges beneath the towering and holy presence of Mount Topa-topa. We discussed the art of meditation. Was I practicing yoga? If so, why? I replied that this was my problem: I could not do any systematic or formal meditation because I had pondered too long his own reiterations of the point that methodical spiritual disciplines are merely highbrow ways of exalting the ego. Aiming at unselfishness is the most insidious form of selfishness.

Thereupon Krishnaji picked up two cushions from the couch and said, "Look. On the one hand there must be the understanding that there is nothing, nothing, nothing, absolutely nothing that you can do to improve, transform, or better yourself. If you understand this completely you will realize that there is no such entity as 'you.'" He then moved his hands from the first cushion to the second, and went on, "Then, if you have totally abandoned this ambition, you will be in the state of true meditation which comes over you spontaneously in wave after wave after wave of amazing light and bliss." Why did he continue to use the word "you"? Merely because he was speaking English and was therefore conforming to the grammatical rule that a verb must have a subject, and that processes are mysteriously initiated by pronouns and nouns.

Going back to that year of true grace in my life, 1936, there was held— at the University of London—the World Congress of Faiths, sponsored by Sir Francis Younghusband, who was an incarnation of all the positive virtues of the British Empire—Kipling's spiritual ideal. He was a short, stocky, and warmly gruff little man with a bristling moustache who was a devotee of the Himalayas and had led the first British expedition into Lhasa; a basically friendly exploit, just to be sure that Tibet would not fall into the hands of the Russians or the Chinese. Sir Francis assembled for the Congress a cluster of holy men and scholars, such as the Russian Orthodox lay theologian Nicolas

Berdyaev, Hindu philosopher Radhakrishnan, Islamic theologian Yusuf Ali, that splendidly reasonable Buddhist G. P. Malalasekera, Jewish philosopher and statesman Lord Samuel, Rom Landau, authority on modern cult-religions, Sir Dennison Ross, scholar of Persian literature, and finally D. T. Suzuki, who completely "stole the scene."

This was when I first met this naive intellectual—wisely foolish, gently disciplined, and simply profound. Suzuki has been accused of "popularizing" Zen—beginning with three huge volumes with notes in Chinese, a translation of the difficult *Lankavatara Sutra*, and a commentary on the Sanskrit terminology of the same text. The American sinological fraternity, as represented by the fanatically pedantic *Journal of the American Oriental Society*, regarded him as a dilettante. The uptight school of Western Zen Buddhists, who seem to believe that Zen is essentially sitting on your ass for interminable hours (as do also some of the Japanese), accused him of giving insufficient emphasis to harsh discipline in the course of attaining *satori*. Even Mitrinović derided him as a sentimentalist.

Suzuki himself would not regard this as necessary, but the time has come for someone to defend him like the swordsman Miyamoto Musashi, and smash his critics to pieces with a wooden oar against their finely tempered steels. I am not, at present, going to undertake this task, but no one who actually knew the man could possibly question the profundity of his spiritual insight—and I use this phrase advisedly although it is a little trite. For the last time I saw him, in Kamakura, he emphasized the earthiness of Buddhism and his fascination in exploring the inmost depths of his own mind. Suzuki never worried. His *apsara*-secretary, Mihoko Okamura, told me that when tossed about on a stormy plane ride he would simply sink into his seat and enter into *samadhi*, or perhaps go to sleep. No one was ever quite sure which it was.

Actually, the mood or atmosphere of Suzuki was more Taoist then Zen Buddhist. He didn't have the skin-headed military zip that is characteristic of so many Zen monks, nor their obedient seriousness. For my feeling, that was good riddance. I do not like this attitude, although I have found so many of these *unsui*, or cloud-watermen, most kind and friendly. But it is not generally realized that, today, most Zen monasteries in Japan are principally boarding schools for the sons of priests, and that all church schools, whether

Buddhist, Catholic, or Protestant, are run on the same lines: with drill and
the big stick. It is simply ludicrous for adult Westerners, sincerely interested
in Zen practice, to imitate these adolescent rituals which were designed for
boys with only the most nominal interest in Zen.[2]

In such ways they make some sort of camaraderie with their legal and
military brothers:

Laws that never shall be broken
        For our guidance he hath made—
and again:

Stand up, stand up for Jesus,
        Ye soldiers of the cross;
Lift high his royal banner,
        It must not suffer loss:
From vict'ry unto vict'ry
        His army shall he lead
Till ev'ry foe is vanquished
        And Christ is Lord indeed.

But I simply cannot understand this rigidly fixed, adamantine, and un-
moving image of the spiritual dimension. To worship the Rock of Ages, or
ein'feste Burg is to bow down to images of stone. More to the point is Isa-
iah's image, "For he is like a refiner's fire," or Jesus' comparison of the Spirit
to "the wind that bloweth where it listeth," or, in speaking to the woman of
Samaria, to "the water which, if you will drink, you shall never thirst." Even
the "diamond" image of Mahayana Buddhism is actually an electronic-looking

---

[2] It might also be remarked that Catholic methods of meditation such as the Ignatian and the
Salesian, with their proximate and remote considerations, their beginnings, middles, ends,
and final resolutions, were designed for adolescent ignoramuses who knew nothing of orderly thinking, and had been sent off to monasteries by pious parents. To some extent the
history of religious monachism is a history of the compulsive masochism of persons dis-
inclined to the compulsive sadism of military service, or the devious intrigue of law and
commerce. Thus it used to be customary in eighteenth-century England to send one's first
son into the law, one's second into the armed forces, and one's third into the clergy—
whether or not he had the slightest interest in religion—and in those days enthusiasm for
anything, especially religion, was deemed extremely bad form.

device (the *dorje*) representing a lightning flash or thunderbolt. Buddhists commonly used the image of space, which cannot be grasped or pinned down, and Lao-tzu frequently illustrated the Tao with the flow and dynamics of water.

Suzuki's feeling for the basic reality of Zen was definitely elusive, and the moment you thought you had finally grasped his point he would slip from your grasp like wet soap, thereby showing that Zen itself is neither a formulable idea or concept, but something like dancing or the movement of a ball on a mountain stream. But neither is it mere chaos, just as the flow-patterns in flame and water are animated designs of superb complexity, which the Chinese call *li*, the markings in jade or the grain in wood. He was, in fact, highly critical of traditional Zen as practiced in Japan, and once remarked that the best thing for Zen would be for all the monasteries to be burned down, splendid architectural monuments though they might be. So far as I know he practiced *ʒa-ʒen*, or formal sitting meditation, only occasionally, as I do myself, when the mood is on me. I prefer the more active Zen of walking meditation, archery, *t'ai-chi* exercises, mantra-chanting, practicing Chinese calligraphy, tea ceremony, swimming, and cooking. Too much *ʒa-ʒen* is apt to turn one into a stone Buddha. In the words of Hui-neng, the Sixth Patriarch:

A living man who sits and does not lie down;
A dead man who lies down and does not sit!
After all these are just dirty skeletons.

For Zen, as Suzuki exemplified it, was spontaneously intelligent living, without calculation, and without rigid conceptual distinctions between self and other, knower and known. He used the force of gravity as a sailor uses the wind.

In connection with the Congress, Suzuki was invited to deliver one of the major papers at the University of London—a masterly argument to the effect that Buddhism, especially in its Mahayana form, was not a rejection and escape from life, but on the contrary, total acceptance of all its vicissitudes, and compassion for all sentient beings; a mastery of *samsara*—the world of birth-and-death—by a kind of spiritual judo. I, aged twenty-one, was given the honor of being chief discussant after this paper, and it fitted in so perfectly with all that I was learning from Yukio Tani and Setsu Koizumi at the *bu-dokwai*, and also from the writings and lectures of Carl Gustav Jung, who was in London about the same time, though I did not meet him personally until 1958. In the meantime I attended every lecture and seminar that Suzuki gave, and became so deeply involved in the work of the Congress that I was appointed to its council and later to its executive committee.

I was still working occasionally with Mitrinović, but was losing interest because I had found what I had really been looking for, a girl friend. Also, I was increasingly absorbed in the work of the Congress and in editing the journal of the Buddhist Lodge, and I had come to realize that Mitrinović himself was beginning to foresee the failure of his political ideals. It was clear by then that Hitler had Europe intimidated and was about to go on a military rampage which he would undoubtedly win if the (then) reluctant Americans did not intervene. One afternoon two of Mitrinović's henchmen, Harry Rutherford and John Harker, rushed over to my office in the City to say that it was of the utmost importance to cancel any plans I might have for the evening and meet them at our usual rendezvous, a pub on the corner of Tottenham Court Road and New Oxford Street. We gulped down a single beer and boarded a taxi for 33 Bloomsbury Street, which was then Mitrinović's inner sanctum.

I found him sitting at the head of his bed like a plump Buddha, clad in a loose robe, smoking a fat Churchman's Number One cigarette, with a glass of straight Johnny Walker on the table beside him. After some amiable preliminaries in which he apologized for being "a bit whiskey," he said, "Alan Watts, I love you but I do not like you. Nevertheless, I am going to invite you to join an eternal and secret fellowship which will watch you, guard you, and keep track of you wherever you may go in the world. We call it the Wild Woodbines, named after the cheapest cigarette in England. Every member is to carry a package, and the sign of recognition is to produce your package and say, 'Have one of mine.' Now if you are inclined to enter into this masonry you must confer with the Jehovah which is in your heart of hearts, and answer me yes or no." After a suitable pause, in which I realized how much I admired Mitrinović and how many close friends I had in his following, I said, "Yes, I will."

"So then," he went on, "I am going to tell you a mystery which you must never, never reveal to others. It will unlock for you the meanings of all kinds of ancient symbolisms." In good faith I cannot go into the details of what he told me, save that it described a mandala of eight different flowers, each with a particular sexual symbolism. As a matter of fact, I have forgotten most of the details, just as all good father-confessors have a way of forgetting what they are not supposed to disclose. This done, he produced a tiny package of Woodbines, saying, "Have one of mine!" And as I accepted, all the other members in the room rushed up and embraced me.

With the institution of the Woodbines, Mitrinović effectively went out of politics. We concentrated on intimate *carpe diem* parties, boys and girls in the group began to get married off, and my real interests reverted to the work of the Buddhist Lodge and the psychological explorations of Eric Graham Howe, with constant visits to my bibliographical adviser, Nigel Watkins. I wrote another somewhat immature book, *The Legacy of Asia and Western Man*, which John Murray published, and which attempted to summarize what I had learned in my self-made university. It was later published by the University of Chicago, but I think it is for the best that it has long been out of print. I was trying to amalgamate Buddhism, Vedanta, Taoism, Jungian psychology, and Christian mysticism, and as the *Church Times* said of it, "This witty and perverse little book. . . ."

A second meeting of the Congress was held at Balliol College, Oxford, in the summer of 1937, where I shared quarters with Baron Hans Hasso von Veltheim, a former zeppelin commander turned ardent disciple of Rudolph Steiner, a big, boisterous, humorous, and warmhearted fellow who was, I am afraid, subsequently liquidated by the Nazis, for whom he had no sympathy and whom he regarded as vulgar and tempestuous rabble. After the war I tried to trace him through my friend Edward Groth, who was then American Consul in Hamburg, but no record could be found of him, not even at his ancestral home, Schloss Ostrau at Halle-Saale. I cannot remember all the details of the enthralling bull sessions we held late into the nights, about Steiner's horticultural methods, about women ("English women, cows! American women, zoomph!"), about metaphysics, reincarnation, and parapsychology. One afternoon a special service was being held for the Congress at the chapel of Christ Church College. But as we strode down the street so as to get there at least by the First Lesson, he said, "Do not worry; kings are always late!"

The preacher was a canon of Christ Church, celebrated for such abominable handwriting that he could not read it himself. He peered at his notes and began, "You who are frivolous, of course." Slight pause, and then more slowly, "You who are frivolous... of course.... Ahem! You who are followers of Christ."

At this Congress I also had long conversations in bad French—the only language we had in common—with the Catholic lay theologian Ernesto Buonaiuti, a courteous and inquiring young scholar who walked round and round the quadrangle with me, picking my brains as to the true nature of Buddhism, and on his part displayed an understanding of Catholicism so profound as to amaze me.

The remainder of my self-designed university course was chiefly concerned with such highly important subjects as music, dancing, and loving, owing to the advent in London of a highly satisfactory American girl who had come to London to study piano with George Woodhouse (whose philosophy of music fitted exactly with my own philosophy of life). He explained melody by analogy with the flow of water, and showed that finesse of touch was not simply striking a key but letting the finger fall upon it with the same sense of "follow-through" as in striking a golf ball. Although this young lady did manage to get me to memorize a Scarlatti sonata, I was never good at anything except vocal music, and unfortunately I tried to imitate the "clickety-clickety-click" style of Wanda Landowska, who played with fingers like steel springs and sometimes made the harpsichord sound like a nasal hurdy-gurdy. Otherwise, we went constantly to opera and ballet at Covent Garden and Sadlers' Wells, to Cortot playing Chopin, to Solomon playing Beethoven's piano concerti with his bright-eyed verve, to the violin wizardry of the Hungarian Jelly d'Aranyi', and, above all, to the Beethoven sonatas (including the *Diabelli Variations*) of Artur Schnabel, who sounded like an archangel playing upon an instrument of crystal.

She had also studied the hula in Hawaii, and showed me that there was much more to dancing than formal stepping, prancing, and turning: there was also swinging, that essential wriggling of the pelvis which allows the rhythm to pass through the whole body from the head to the feet, a gesture deemed by stuffy and proper persons to be lewd and lascivious. But for me there is no true dancing without it. Watch the Hindus: they sway glidingly like plants under gently moving water, and the stiff *mudra*-gestures of their fingers and the occasional stamping of their bangled feet simply bring out the serpentine rippling of the rest of their bodies. They even dance with their eyes.

It should now be said that this vivacious and talented young woman was Eleanor Everett, daughter of a genial but fearsome red-haired Chicago attorney, Edward Warren Everett, and of Ruth Fuller Everett who, after her husband's death, married a Zen master and is thus better known as Ruth Fuller Sasaki; a woman of extremely high culture and a will of steel, which I suppose she had to cultivate in self-defense against her husband. He had suffered from infantile paralysis and was so derided by his peers for having to hobble about in leg irons that he practically took a vow of hatred against the human race, in fulfillment of which he because a lightweight boxing champion, a master tennis player who seemed to have such an intuitive knowledge of where the ball would be returned that he never had to run, and a corporation lawyer universally feared for his demolitional venom in cross-examination.

Until her marriage with Sokei-an Sasaki, Ruth was something of a social climber—not too offensively—but for a woman of spiritual and aesthetic resources such as hers, she seemed unduly impressed with the industrial captains and kings of Chicago and their especially feather-headed wives. Several years before, Ruth had come under the influence of a phenomenal rascal-master (like Gurdjieff, Mitrinović, and Aleister Crowley) who maintained an *ashram*-cum-zoo at the Clarkstown Country Club at Nyack on the Hudson. This was Pierre Bernard, known to the press as "Oom the Omnipotent," teacher of Tantric and *hatha* yoga, and whose disciples included members of the highest New York society. Pierre's wife, De Vries, was a graciously handsome woman who could go through the most astonishing *hatha*-yoga contortions I have ever seen, although Virginia Denison of Los Angeles comes a close second. Pierre was formerly in the circus business in

San Francisco, picked up his yoga from a traveling Hindu, and moved to New York. He would test out his applicants for discipleship by sitting with his feet on the desk, wearing a baseball cap on the back of his head, puffing and chewing at a big cigar in one corner of his mouth, and spitting as near to their feet as possible. If they could pass this barrier—and it also helped to be well-heeled financially—they had the pleasure of knowing a man as well-versed in the ways of the world as of the spirit.[3]

It was during her work at Nyack that Ruth became acquainted with Zen Buddhism, and decided then and there to take off for Japan and study it at first hand. Eleanor accompanied her, and, on their reaching Kyoto, D. T. Suzuki introduced them to Nanshinken, the great old master or *roshi* of Nanzenji, a monastery which I have visited many times and which, apart from Rengejoin (a Shingon temple on Mount Koya), remains my favorite of all such places. The whole is done in T'ang-style architecture, with hefty wooden pillars interspersed with screens and supporting enormous roofs of curved interlocking blueish-green tiles, the whole with ridges and surfaces very gently curved inward. The monastery, which comprises a nirvanic rock, sand, and moss garden by Kobori Enshu, nestles into a forested hillside of pines, maples, and cryptomerias. My present wife and I once spent an afternoon upon that hillside, sitting on the steps of an ancient tomb, having taken a small amount of LSD-25. We served each other the tea ceremony and looked down upon those ancient roofs through the pines. We understood why Japanese artists painted screens of backgrounds of gold leaf, for light seemed to shine out from the scene rather than upon it. An architectural anomaly of the place, though not at all unattractive, is that the precincts are traversed at the east end by a brick, Roman-style aqueduct, where water flowing into Kyoto from Lake Biwa is constantly followed by birds and little boys, and one or two old men sit fishing. For reasons which I will try to explain later, we also acquired a vivid understanding of the *ji-ji-mu-ge* principle: that all things and events are mutually interpenetrating and interdependent.

---

[3] There is an old and virtually unobtainable book, *In Re Fifth Veda*, which sets forth Pierre Bernard's philosophy. There might be a copy in the New York Public Library or the Library of Congress, but it would be worth reprinting in paperback.

Nanshinken took a great liking to Eleanor. She could, of course, do *za-zen* in full-lotus posture like the rest, but *his* idea of Zen teaching for a girl of fifteen was to sit with her on the veranda looking at picture magazines of those enormously fat *sumo* wrestlers, and pick out suitable husbands for her.

It was thus that when Ruth came to London with Eleanor they immediately visited the Buddhist Lodge, where Ruth discoursed on her experiences in Japan (she had a curious way of looking up at a distant corner of the ceiling while talking), and it took me just about a week to fall hopelessly in love with her daughter. Shortly thereafter, Ruth left for the States—knowing full well that she was leaving Eleanor to my tender mercies—with the comment, "He's all right, but he'll never set the Thames on fire." It must be understood that were I to meet myself today as I was then, I would be horrified. I affected a moustache and a black Homburg hat in the style of Sir Anthony Eden, wore black formal clothes with striped trousers, a silver-grey tie, and carried a neatly rolled umbrella with chamois gloves and a briefcase. Eleanor began, subtly, to change all this; first by buying me colorful striped ties and suggesting that I come out in more relaxed and informal clothing, such as a green tweed jacket with a matching felt hat that sported a brilliant feather in the band.

Now it must be understood that throughout all the activities of my private university I had been in search of erotic feminine companionship. Contrary to its avowed intentions, the monastic regimen of boys' boarding schools imbues most male adolescents with a flaming lust for women which, like all good and lively things, can be overdone—especially insofar as one imagines that sexual ecstasy is, above all else, the principal delight which women have to offer. But I came out of school like the monk from Siberia, who of fasting had grown wearier and wearier. I naively supposed that girls had the same longings as boys, and that nothing would be more natural, simple, and mutually agreeable than for the bee and the flower to confer this ecstasy upon one another. But it took me four years to run into any such situation, for I had not realized to what a degree sex is used as a bait and a prize in amazingly complex social games. Furthermore, girls of my own age and set seemed to be content and satisfactorily excited by purely titillatory sex, and could keep one dangling in foreplay for so many months that the relationship soured, and came to be all retch and no vomit.

Beyond this, young people who have responded properly to social conditioning are all fishing for marriage partners. Even I took it for granted that every mature person should aspire to become the father or mother of a family, and remained a firm believer in this obsolete institution until I was forty-five. But at twenty I was so far from being able to support a wife, let alone children, that I saw no prospect of being in an economic position to marry until I was at least thirty—that is, unless I let my vocation become no more than a hobby and went to work simply for money. And it was quite obvious to me that World War II would come up long before then.

In the meantime should I be continent? Over the years it has become my firm opinion that sexual activity (even if only through masturbation) is "requisite and necessary, as well for the body as for the soul"; for men and women alike. It stimulates your glands, exercises your pelvis, thrills your nerves, brings mind and body together as one, and culminates in an ecstasy in which there is neither past nor future nor separation between self and other. We need that as we need vitamins, proteins, water, and air.

This, again, is only my own opinion, but I have the strong impression that religious celibates who actually refrain entirely from sex (as do some of the swamis and yogis of modern India) become sentimental, sour, and greedy for power.[4] The married Tibetan lamas and Zen priests I have known seem to have a far greater "spiritual presence," including a *roshi* or Zen master who, on one occasion, made it with his lady friend sixteen times in twenty-four hours. I often wonder whether those religious people who would find these remarks deeply offensive have ever really asked themselves just exactly what is wrong with that affectionate and warmly communicative feeling called lust, especially in the context of intense rapport with another person. They must surely have their neural wires crossed in such a way that they get the "disgust" signal along with the "lust" signal, perhaps because the organs of sex are also those of urination.

Before Eleanor appeared on the scene I had been in love with Betty and

---

[4] Some of the most effective Christian celibates are, of course, homosexual, and—despite the fulminations of Saint Paul—justify themselves by the arcane and underground tradition that Jesus had a homosexual relationship with the "beloved disciple," John.

Greta, both of whom I had met in Mitrinović's circle. Betty was light and slight, but not thin, and had a spring in her walk. What first attracted me to her was her performance of the song "There Was an Old Farmer Who Had an Old Sow," with all the whistles and grunts that go with it. I still have a set of her architectural drawings—pillars and gargoyles from some ancient church in Hampshire—for she aspired to be an architect, but lacked interest in the drearily mathematical aspects of the art. She was literate and witty—I can still hear her laugh—and was always ready to kiss and cuddle (up to a point), but the poor girl had four disadvantages: chronic bronchitis, an anxious mother, a crabby grandmother, and eventual conversion to one of the few religions I specifically detest—Frank Buchman's Oxford Group Movement, now known as Moral Rearmament. She thus taught me that it is not so much the girl herself as what goes with her, and that you must always be careful to discover a person's religion. For everyone has a religion, whether admitted or not, because it is impossible to be human without having some basic assumptions (or intuitions) about existence and the good life.

I met Greta at a party of the Wild Woodbines—an ultra-blond, soft-faced Swede, with the pale blue eyes and high culture so characteristic of her people —but I never understood her game. She aroused me right from the start by dancing, not cheek-to-cheek, but leg-to-leg, and she had legs that still return in dreams. I pursued her for many months and our outings included an evening with Puck and Toby at Covent Garden for the Russian Ballet; all of us in full regalia with cloaks and ebony canes and satins and jewels, jostling at the great bar with princes, rajas, duchesses, marquises, counts, viscounts, barons, bankers, eminent journalists, novelists, actors, and artists, and a select company of wizards, sages, and gurus in disguise. But Greta seemed to have a phantom lover. Nobody, not even her brother, knew who he was. She and her brother shared a flat in Notting Hill, and he would have known. Though Greta was frustratingly elusive, her immense and athletic brother, Douglas, became a good friend. One summer we rented a long two-man rowing boat with a pull-down awning, and rowed up the Thames from Marlowe to Oxford and back. By night we had simply to tie up at the bank, pull down the awning, light lamps, and set the Primus stove going for dinner. For lunch we stopped at riverside pubs for beer and crusty bread with real, nonprocessed Cheddar

or Cheshire cheese. Best of these pubs was the Beetle and Wedge at Mouls-
ford (which I later frequented with Eleanor), where they served a dark and
alarmingly potent cider from Somerset. It should be explained that a "beetle"
is also a type of mallet and, in this context, is not to be confused with an insect or a musician. Returning, we rowed down Henley Reach by night, lustily
singing the "Volga Boatmen" in imitation Russian.

Douglas was an uncomplicated, easy-going, and humorous fellow—
with the priceless gift of being comfortably silent—also shared by my father, who can puff away at his pipe and look into the fire for a whole evening,
without saying a word. It's like the best kind of Quaker meeting, perfect
companionship without talk. I do not have much to say about Douglas, but
that has to be taken as a compliment. Our friendship was on the nonverbal
level. It was in terms of action, and we had no need to give wordy expression to the mutual enjoyment of willows on the bank, the peculiar smell of
the river (which is rotten, but in the same way as fine cheese), starting the
day's unhurried journey at dawn, and pulling in at twilight when the water
is pale and iridescent, and the moon primrose yellow.

As to what "went with" Eleanor, there was her amazingly interesting—
if sometimes difficult—mother who gave me a start in life that might otherwise have been hard to find, as well as an education in the ways of Buddhism
of which I shall have much more to say. Eleanor, too, was more or less a Buddhist so that we were without conflict in that basic dimension of religion
which, as I have said, is inevitably present in human relations.

We regularly attended meetings of the Buddhist Lodge together, and
worked at their meditation sessions. At that time I was practicing the method
of holding one's consciousness in the present moment, being—as Krishnamurti puts it—choicelessly aware of what is, or—as Gurdjieff expressed it—
in a state of constant self-remembering. This was also in line with George
Woodhouse's idea of mind flowing with melody, for if the attention lags or
overanticipates, the melody is lost, and it is the same with dancing. It should
be the same with the rhythms of life. Do this, and you actually feel yourself
one process with the whole energy.

One evening, when Eleanor and I were walking home from a meditation
session, I began to discuss the method of concentration on the eternal present.

Whereupon she said, "Why try to concentrate on it? What else *is* there to be aware of? Your memories are all in the present, just as much as the trees over there. Your thoughts about the future are also in the present, and anyhow I just love to think about the future. The present is just a constant flow, like the Tao, and there's simply no way of getting out of it." With that remark my whole sense of weight vanished. You could have knocked me down with a feather. I realized that when the Hindus said *Tat tvam asi*, "You ARE That," they meant just what they said. For a whole week thereafter I simply floated, remembering Spiegelberg's telling me of the Six Precepts of Tilopa:

> No thought, no reflection, no analysis,
> No cultivation, no intention,
> Let it settle itself.

This was doubtless a premature *satori*, for I was unable to resist the temptation to write, think, and intellectualize about it. Yet when I am in my right mind I still know that this is the true way of life, at least for me. Conscious thought, reflection, analysis, cultivation, and intention are simply using the mind's radar or scanning beam for purposes which the mind as a whole can do of itself, and on its own, with far more intelligence and less effort. Every month it becomes increasingly obvious what this surgical style of thinking as applied in technology is doing to the planet. We call it Progress, but not one person in a hundred thousand has any clear conception of the actual state of life and society to which he would like to progress. We know only what we hate and would like to abolish, and do not realize that Jesus was jesting ironically when he said, "If thine eye offend thee, pluck it out."

I am perpetually grateful to Eleanor for that chance remark, even though we have gone our separate ways since 1949. However, when in 1937 we decided formally to get married, her family invited us both to come to Chicago for Christmas, so—I suppose—that they could all look me over. We left from Southampton on the *Bremen*, and simply gorged ourselves on the fabulous cuisine. There was in particular a white wine named Oesterreicher Hölle Riesling Spätlese, vintage 1927, such as I have never tasted since. On arrival we zoomed through the canyons of New York and boarded the Commodore Vanderbilt for the night ride to Chicago. As is seldom the case in

England, all the towns and villages were festooned with colored lights for Christmas. The fields were gleaming with snow under the moon, and all night there was that far-off sound of the old-fashioned American steam-engine whistle with its suggestion of vast spaces and distances. We stopped at places with outlandish names like Poughkeepsie, Schenectady, Ashtabula, and Toledo, and when in the morning we went by the steelworks at Gary and saw an immense parking lot filled with sleek-looking cars, I asked Eleanor, "Why, who are all these big shots gathered here?" "Ha!" she laughed. "Those are just the cars of the steelworkers."

At La Salle Station we were met by Warren, Eleanor's father, by Ruth, and by Ishmael, their ingenious Philippine chauffeur and servant. Although Warren was at the time bad-tempered and sick because of arteriosclerosis, we formed an instant friendship—perhaps because we both thoroughly enjoyed such vices as we held in common: smoking cigars, telling ribald stories, thumbing through girlie magazines, and my drawing him out to reminisce about his career. On Christmas Day we were gifted and feasted like kings, and Ishmael served the tenderest and most succulent turkey I have yet eaten—except one I made myself—boned, stuffed with chestnuts and sweetbreads, and rolled into the form of a *poupeton*. But just as he was starting to cook it, Ruth went into the kitchen and found him carefully studying the *Boston Cook Book*, whereupon he had to confess that he had never cooked a turkey before.

There is a saying that "God gives us our relations, but let us thank him we can choose our friends." Aside from Ruth, Eleanor's artist cousin Walker Everett, and her picturesquely problematic uncle David Fuller—a frustrated actor—the rest of the family connections seemed to me pompous and vapid. But it was otherwise with Eleanor's own friends—sassy and bawdy Suzie Budge, her genial and gutsy boy friend Fred Baker, sisters Gwen and Valerie, Edward Johnson, a bright-eyed Don Juan insurance man, and the fey Teresina Rowell (now Havens), daughter of the Hinsdale Congregational minister. I keep in touch with Joe and Teresina Havens to this day, for they are a couple of saints who have done the most remarkable work in imaginative education.

We returned to England, again on the *Bremen*. The crossing was stormy, but it was fun to do the Viennese waltz on a rolling dance floor to the music of a Bavarian oom-pah-pah band. I once got sick, not, I think, because of the rolling ship, but because a young German professor with whom I frequently played chess insisted on filling me up with enormous amounts of Benedictine.

For reasons which I still cannot quite understand, Eleanor and I were married on April 2, 1938, at the Parish Church (of England) in Earl's Court. After all we were both Buddhists. So was her mother, and at that time my father was treasurer of the Buddhist Lodge. But someone got the idea that a Buddhist wedding would not be socially *de rigueur*, and this had, above all, to be a wedding plus reception in high style. I was most dictatorial about the music and insisted that instead of that corny "Here Comes the Bride," the music for her entry be taken from the *Meistersinger* overture, and that the processional exit be accompanied by the theme of the last movement of Beethoven's Ninth. Ironically, during the taking of the vows, the organist played (very softly) a melody from Tchaikovsky which was later made into the popular song, "Will this be moon love, nothing but moon love?"

But I will not dwell further on this wedding. When I was chaplain at Northwestern University it was my fate to solemnize socialite marriages galore, and though a college chaplain has little opportunity to conduct funerals, I much preferred them. At weddings people were insufferably bumptious and puffed-up, but at funerals they were human and real, and the ceremonies were decent and in order, provided that one could make the "morticians" stay out of the act.

We moved into an almost palatial duplex on the west side of Courtfield Gardens, carpeted from wall to wall in dark purple, curtained with yellow Chinese damask, and set about with Elizabethan and Jacobean furniture. But not for long. I was listening to the ravings of Hitler on the radio. I knew that the French government was in its usual state of chaotic indecision, and that the Maginot line was no defense against air-borne troops. I knew that the British forces were prepared for World War I, but as yet in no condition to handle the type of conflict that this was going to be. I knew also that at this juncture there was no immediate prospect of American intervention, without which the defeat of Germany would be even more impossible than in 1918. Having read much of the new technologies of warfare, I expected Hitler's *Blitzkrieg* to use biological and chemical warfare to the full, and in every way to be so much worse than it actually was that I foresaw the collapse of England and France in a matter of weeks. To stay and fight seemed valorous, but entirely futile. Furthermore, I was in no position to fight usefully, for when it comes to basic slugging I am about as serviceable as a violin for hammering nails. In warfare the role of the intellectual is to plot and scheme, to spy, decipher codes, write propaganda, or "fight dirty" like a guerrilla or commando. But so far as the official Britain of 1938 was concerned, I had no intellectual qualifications, no university education, no knowledge of German, and no training in the sciences. I had even failed the theoretical part of the Certificate A examination for the Officers' Training Corps, which, incidentally, gave me some qualms about the strategic intelligence of the examiners. For several years I had taken a strong pacifist position, but, under these particular circumstances, it seemed as futile to bear witness as a pacifist as to join the ordinary ranks. When you are standing on top of a collapsing skyscraper there is nothing for it but to take to wings, if you can find them. I was lucky.

My luck was not only that Eleanor and I had the "wings" to go to America, but also that my country had as little need for me in war as in peace. One could perhaps say that my interests and abilities were so odd that they were of no economic value or intellectual interest to the community at large. Quite aside from the war, there was, as I have said, no prospect whatsoever of making a living at my particular trade in England, and to this very day my works are little known in my homeland even though publishers have done their best to sell them. In this connection, then, I must quote a section from my favorite philosopher, the Chinese Taoist Chuang-tzu:

> The area of Ching-shih in the state of Sung grows fine catalpas, cypresses, and mulberries. But those of more than one or two spans in girth are cut down for monkey-perches; those of three or four for ridgepoles, and those of seven or eight for the solid sides of coffins for the wealthy. Thus they do not attain the normal term of their lives, and fall in mid-career to the axe. This is the danger of being useful.

In sacrifices of purgation one does not use bulls with white foreheads, pigs with large snouts, nor men with piles as offerings to the river. This has been revealed to the soothsayers, and such creatures are therefore held inauspicious [for sacrifice]. The sage, however, would regard them as highly auspicious.

Then there was a hunchback named Su. His chin touched his navel. His shoulders were above his head. His pigtail pointed to the sky. His innards were upside-down, and his thighs were against his ribs. By tailoring and laundering he made enough to live, and by winnowing grain he produced enough to feed ten. But when the authorities conscripted soldiers he stood in the crowd waving them off, and when a work-party was pressed into service he was passed up as an invalid. Yet when they doled out grain for the needy, he got three full measures as well as ten bundles of firewood. If a weird body helps a man live out his full term, how much greater would be the use of a weird character! (*Chuang-tzu*, 4)

Often I wonder if I could be a consistent pacifist, since it seems to me that massive nonresistance against any enemy whom one cannot easily defeat would, in the long run, be more effective and less destructive than the insane wars which industrial societies must fight. It is hard enough to rule one's own people, and much harder a foreign nation, and it might be well if those who yearn to rule should be allowed to try. Furthermore, one has only to consider the loss of individual liberty in the United States over the past fifty years to see that in resisting tyranny one must become tyrannical—especially with the use of highly centralized military systems.

On the other hand, whereas Gandhi's nonviolence worked against the uneasy conscience of the British in India, one could easily imagine that, especially in an overpopulated world, a ruthlessly efficient military organization would simply get rid of submissive populations by refined techniques of genocide, so that even Hunchback Su would be classified as "substandard human material for recycling." Under such circumstances I feel that my emotions might well get the better of my pacific ideals, and that out of sheer animal fury I would be working with the underground resistance.

An idea that occasionally gnaws at me is that the monstrous horrors of mass warfare, and the rapidly rising cost of ever more questionable "victories," are due largely to bad strategy—culminating in nuclear devices which are not weapons at all but simply engines for planetary suicide. One might even suggest that, in developing such techniques, the generals have so neglected their proper craft as to merit prompt and dishonorable discharge. For we have reached the point where military machines protect no one but themselves. Civilian populations are left open to saturation bombing while their "protectors" work from underground fortresses or from ships in the sky far above the nuclear blasts. The point is that we are still at the primitive level of slamming one another with brute force because the military mind takes more pride in muscle than in cunning. And when we get to real cunning, as between more or less evenly matched powers, the computers will tell us— if we don't realize it first—that amicable settlement of our differences will be so vastly cheaper and easier for all concerned that no one will be able to imagine why we didn't think of that before. The energy and treasure which Germany and Japan alone put into World War II, and which the United States has squandered in Vietnam, could have gone a long way towards ending poverty over the whole earth. Would that have been peace without honor?

CHAPTER SIX

DAWN IN THE WESTERN SKY

O n a clear day one should look west to see the dawn. On the Pacific
Coast, a little south of Big Sur, is a spot known as Willow Creek where
a rivulet pours out of the mountains into the ocean. I was there early one
morning as a thin white fog was lifting to show the western sky full of light
from the rising sun—a sky far and deep, a luminously blue transparency
with a few flat-bottomed clouds hanging over but beyond the horizon. Into
such a sky the minds expands without actually seeking or visualizing anything beyond, such as the South Sea Islands or the China Coast. Simultaneously one goes out and stays put. The view is from *here*, and in Hawaii it is
still the night; yet such a sky is like the green mist of buds breaking in a spring
woodland, when it is almost a pity to think of it turning into the thick foliage of summer. As the Zen master Dōgen put it, the spring does not become the summer: there is spring, and then there is summer. Likewise
firewood does not become ashes, nor the living body the corpse. This is how
reality appears to one who knows that only the present is real.

That was also the sky I saw crossing the Atlantic to New York, and again
between Steamboat Springs in Colorado and the Wasatch Mountains in Utah.
So, too, in the Ojai Valley in California as I crawled out of a sleeping bag
amid orange, loquat, and grapefruit trees, to see against that sky a white
Spanish house on a hill, set about with tapered cypresses. Something happens
in the solar plexus which is not exactly the thrill of hope but the feeling (to
change Wordsworth's words a little), "Good is it now to be alive, and to be
young is very heaven." I must still be young, for the same feeling comes

early in the morning when I look down Frank Valley from the sundeck of this cottage to the green ridge which hides the Pacific.

In the same way, one should look east to see the sunset. Those red, gold, and purple skies have become clichés of postcard photography, and I turn rather to the indigo blue of approaching night with a few stars overcoming their shyness, and go gentle into that good night. This is the best time to see the towers of Manhattan, in autumn (when I first lived there), immediately after sunset: thousands of bright rectangles in rows and high columns, a mosaic of gold tiles on a ground of deep yet brilliant blue. There they call it the witching hour. The exhilaration of leaving the office for the first cocktail of the evening, heedless of the hangover next morning. Watch it from the south end of Central Park where layer upon layer of hotel rooms, with lights just turned on, are floated skywards with parties gathering and dinners being prepared.

Eleanor and I moved into an apartment adjoining Ruth's on a high floor of the Park Crescent Hotel at Eighty-seventh Street and Riverside Drive, overlooking the Hudson, and in the heart of Jewry—with refugees swarming in from Germany. Close to us, on Broadway, was the delicatessen and restaurant of the Tip Toe Inn for the gourmandise of kosher dills, smoked sturgeon, cheese cake, lox, gefilte fish, and borscht. The drugstore nearby was selling excellent steaks for forty-five cents, and the soda jerk would make up sundaes of my own composition—vanilla ice cream globbed with butterscotch, ringed with maraschino cherries, and topped with whipped cream and chopped nuts. (Forgive me, but I was only twenty-three!) In the shops, they spelled my name "Watz." In the streets, leggy, olive-skinned girls with mink and silver-fox furs, purple orchids, and forelocks rolled up above brows as was then the fashion; mamas wheeling plump babies galore with lacy bonnets in shiny black buggies; bearded rabbis, who would have looked venerable and holy in skullcaps, going about in black felt hats set straight on the head, despite Christopher Morley's admonition that a halo should always be worn over one ear; a crate the size of a hut dumped on the sidewalk, bearing the rough inscription "Zeitlin, Leipzig." The time came when not some but most of our best friends were Jews—and I still don't know what a Jew is.

On November 14, 1938, Eleanor gave birth to Joan. We installed her in a cot in our bedroom where she seemed to be protected by some invisible fairy. Perhaps the bell on her rattle reminded me of Tinker Bell, but that corner of the room was happily enchanted. Joan burbled and bubbled and, within a year, developed a lilting language of her own that sounded like a mixture of Hopi, Japanese, and Malayan. Her water call was "Iggoo-iggoo-iggoo-iggum!" When this turned into English she asked us to "Shup de light" or "Ope de light" when she wanted the electricity turned off or on.

Joan was the first of seven children, and there are now five grandchildren. By all the standards of this society I have been a terrible father, with a few disastrous attempts to be a "good" one, for the simple reason that I have no patience with the abstract notion of "the child" which our culture imposes on small people; with the toys and games they are supposed to enjoy, with the books they are supposed to read, with the mannerisms they are supposed to assume, and with the schools in which they become lowest-common-denominator images of each other. I am completely at ease with the infant who still enjoys nonsense and plays spontaneously at unprogrammed games, and then again with the adolescent who is calling the brainwashing into question. But the Disneyland "world of childhood" is an itsy-bitsy, cutie-pied, plastic hoax; a world populated by frustrated brats trying to make out why they are not treated as human beings. If your wife buys this abstraction, little can be done about it, for you are torn between being straight with the children and propitiating a wife who has the moral support of most of her friends and neighbors, not to mention the school system and the child-befuddling industry. If my children have found me distant and aloof, this is the explanation.

At the time we came to New York, Ruth was studying with the local Zen master, Sokei-an Sasaki, who maintained a small temple in a walk-up on West Seventy-fourth Street; just one large room with a shrine that could be closed off with folding doors, and a small kitchen. Here he lived in extreme simplicity with his Maltese cat, Chaka. He represented the Rinzai school of Zen, as distinct from the Soto, and taught with a curious mixture of orthodox and unorthodox methods. Since he was the only Zen master available and, indeed, the only one I had ever met, I asked at once if he would accept me as a student, although in Asia it is often the custom to shop around for a teacher with whom one feels a special rapport. He accepted me, with the odd observation that "a person with a good brain" could get well into Zen within three

or four years—odd, because I was under the impression that Zen involved
something far more than "brains" in the usual intellectual sense of the word.
However, I worked along with him for several weeks, contrary to my lone-
wolf inclination to find my own way. I found that he was using the Hakuin
method of handling *koan*, or Zen problems, such as "What is the sound of
one hand?" This method was devised by a great Japanese master of the
seventeenth century and is quite formal, since every *koan* has to be answered
in a specific way—which seemed to be hunting for a needle in a haystack. For
myself, I preferred the informal approach of Hakuin's contemporary Bankei,
and of such ancient Chinese masters as Hui-neng, Shen-hui, and Matsu
whose methods followed no codified system. It was strange that, while using
the Hakuin method, Sokei-an gave no instruction in *ʒa-ʒen*, or sitting in meditation, nor were sessions for *ʒa-ʒen* held in his temple. His teaching was
confined to *sanʒen*, the private interview for presenting one's view of the
assigned *koan*, and to lectures. I learned about *ʒa-ʒen* from Ruth, even though
she herself was not seriously practicing it at this time.[1]

I decided, therefore, to change my approach and study with Sokei-an without his knowing it. I wanted to observe a Zen master in his personal everyday
life, and for this I had ample opportunity, since he visited us often at the hotel,

---

[1] I am assuming that most of my readers have at least some basic information about Zen. For
those who do not, it should be said that Zen—or, in Chinese, Ch'an—Buddhism is a school
which arose in China between the sixth and eighth centuries, and passed on to Japan
in the twelfth. It continues, in its own way, the general practice of Buddhism, which is to
free the mind from its habitual confusion of words, ideas, and concepts with reality, and
from all those emotional disturbances and entanglements which flow from this confusion.
Thus the ego, time, the body, life, and death are all viewed as concepts having neither more
nor less reality than abstract numbers or measures, such as inches or ounces. The Zen
school holds that this freedom has to be found by an intuitive leap rather than a gradual and
cumulative process of learning, although this leap may not be possible until one has tried
through long periods of meditation to let the mind settle into calm clarity, silencing the
perpetual chatter in the skull. The *koan* are based on anecdotes about the question-
and-answer teaching of the old masters, and are problems designed to tease one out
of thinking. Zen monks (or, rather, seminarists) were prolific artists, poets, architects,
and gardeners, and left a strong mark on Chinese and Japanese culture. Zen training has
always been open to both men and women, and is now available at at least six centers in the
United States.

and accompanied us to restaurants and for drives about the countryside. Most of our discussions took place in Ruth's apartment, where she had assembled a considerable library and sundry works of Oriental art, for which she had infallibly good taste. Later it came out for all to see in her house-cum-temple at 124 East Sixty-fifth Street and her reconstruction of the Ryosen-an temple in Kyoto. In these early days he was working with Ruth on a translation of the *Sutra of Perfect Awakening*, which, along with his other translations, has not yet been published because Ruth was an excessive perfectionist and voluminous footnoter, having in mind the dubious objective of impressing the more dreary pandits of the American Oriental Society, the in-group of academic Orientalists who, as librarians, philological nit-pickers, and scholarly drudges, dissolve all creative interest into acidulated pedantry. She was, however, much more than a mere "Englisher" of these translations, for in the course of time she went quite deeply into T'ang Chinese, and her own translations of Zen poems and anecdotes are models of accuracy and clarity.

Sokei-an was just over sixty when I met him, a gentle, stocky man with hair closely shaved, and head shaped like a short watermelon as is characteristic of the men of Kyushu. (Many of them have Dutch blood.) He came to America with his teacher, Sokatsu Shaku, before World War I, and for some years wandered and worked as a farm laborer in the Northwest. In New York he came on at first as an artist and short-story writer (under his secular name Shigetsu Sasaki)—very much the bohemian, with long swirling hair, the original Dharma bum of America. He was an accomplished woodcarver, and the wooden slab on which he worked used to hang in the Sixty-fifth Street temple—indistinguishable from an interesting abstract painting. When he began to teach Zen he was still, as I understand, more the artist than the priest, but in the course of time he shaved his head and "sobered up." Yet not really. For Ruth was often apologizing for him and telling us not to take him too literally or too seriously when, for example, he would say that Zen is to realize that life is simply nonsense, without meaning other than itself or future purpose beyond itself. The trick was to dig the nonsense, for—as Tibetans say—you can tell the true yogi by his laugh.

One evening he was giving a formal lecture on the *Sutra of Perfect Awakening*, dressed in robes of brown and gold brocade and seated in his chair of estate at a small table-altar with candles and incense. He would pause from time to time, and drop powdered sandalwood or aloeswood on the hot brick of charcoal in the *koro*, or incense brazier. He came to a passage where the sutra spoke of the importance of living without purpose, and, true to his accent, commented: "In Buddhism pahposeressness is fundamentar'. No pahpose anywhere in rife itser'f. When you drop fart you do not say, 'At nine o'crock I drop fart.' It just happen." The audience, accustomed to Christian decorum on such occasions, stuffed their handkerchiefs in their mouths.

He never fidgeted nor showed the nervous politeness of ordinary Japanese, but moved slowly and easily, with relaxed but complete attention to whatever was going on. In going over a Chinese text he would say the words to himself in a whispered chant, and likewise mutter through a menu until settling for "broir'd bruefish." He loved to reminisce about his childhood in Japan, his training under Sokatsu Shaku, and his adventures in New York during the Depression, many of which he wrote up as short stories (in Japanese) somewhat in the style of de Maupassant. At this time he and Ruth had just fallen in love, and we were the fascinated witnesses of their mutually fructifying relationship—she drawing out his bottomless knowledge of Buddhism, and he breaking down her rigidities with ribald tales that made her blush and giggle. Whenever she was peeved at him he would accuse her of looking like a lantern fish, and make the skin of her slightly jowly face so itchy that she had to laugh.

One evening he gave us a lesson on using the *I Ching*, or *Book of Changes*.[2] He interpreted the oracular hexagrams not by consulting the text

---

[2] Reputedly the most ancient of all Chinese classics, the *I Ching* (pronounced *Ee Jing*) is a commentary on sixty-four hexagrams, each composed of six lines, positive or negative in value, and consisting therefore of any two of eight possible trigrams. The eight trigrams represent the basic life-principles of heaven and earth, fire and water, mountain and lake, thunder and wind. As in throwing dice, various methods are used to select a hexagram at random—in answer to a specific question or to determine the general character of the total pattern of events as centered in the here and now—on the assumption that the random casting will of necessity be in accord with it, or symptomatic of it. The *I Ching* presupposes a philosophy of nature based on polar vision of the universe; an "electrical" system in which a single energy manifests itself through two mutually arising poles, the *yang* (+) and the yin (-).

but by going directly to the component trigrams and showing their relationship. Thus, on casting one for the general situation of the time, he came up with mountain over thunder and his interpretation was quite different from that given by the book itself, for he saw the image of a volcano about to erupt—and this was 1939. He then explained that hexagrams could be found by other means than casting. Using the bowl of flowers on the table he derived a hexagram from their grouping and discussed the state of mind of the person who had arranged them.

By studying a Latin translation of the *I Ching* Leibniz invented the binary number system whereby all numbers can be represented by combinations of 0 and 1, which is the system now used by digital computers and by means of which we can code, on magnetic tape, information of almost any kind, including pictures in color, and by using lasers we can also transmit solid images. The nervous system works on a similar principle, and experimenters (including myself) with such psychedelic chemicals as LSD-25 have been able to detect a structure of this type in all percepts and concepts. The universe appears as an intricate dynamism of balanced opposites, mutually interdependent, and in such faultless harmony that one could well be scared of it. For the harmony cannot be broken and "anything goes." In the words given to the saintly Dame Julian of Norwich, "Sin is behovable [permissible], but all shall be well, and all shall be well, and all manner of thing shall be well."

Much of what I learned from Sokei-an and Ruth has so become part of me that I cannot now sort it out. If I have overstressed the wayward elements of Sokei-an's personality, it is only because I felt that he was basically in the same team as I; that he bridged the spiritual and the earthy, and that he was as humorously earthy as he was spiritually awakened.

When war broke out with Japan, a cantankerous attorney in the Department of Justice saw to it that he was interned as a dangerous enemy alien, although he had had nothing to do with political matters. He was sent off to a concentration camp when only recently recovered from an operation for hemorrhoids, and put in a hut from which he had to walk some fifty muddy yards to the nearest latrine. However, the major in charge of the camp tried to make things as easy for him as possible, and in gratitude Sokei-an carved

him a cane in the form of a dragon. But when anything aroused Ruth's dan-
der, she was not to be stopped. She acquired the services of Hugo Pollock, a
redoubtable lawyer, and had him released just as soon as the schedule of hear-
ings would permit. The star witness for Sokei-an was George Fowler, one of
his students (later a professor of history at the University of Pittsburgh),
who as a commander in the navy appeared in splendid white uniform—tall,
lean, and grey-haired—and between him and Hugo Pollock the government's case was demolished. Shortly afterwards, Ruth and Sokei-an were
married. But the concentration camp had ruined his health. He died in 1945
with the parting words, "Sokei-an will never die."

During all this time my own concern was to find my vocation in the
United States. For reasons already explained, taking a job was something I
would do only in desperation, and therefore I began to do just what I am
doing today, writing, lecturing, and conducting seminars in the European
sense of that word—i.e., informal conferences for small groups, with ample
opportunity for discussion. In search of students I discovered that the New
York equivalent of Watkins's was the Gateway Bookshop on East Sixtieth
Street, run by Bill and Mary Gorham with the assistance of Ted Roberts. In
London I had lectured before the Jungian Analytical Psychology Club, and
accordingly sought out the sister institution in New York to which I was
most helpfully recommended by Frederic Spiegelberg, then teaching at
Union Theological Seminary. Bill and Mary gave me a mailing list of suit-
able prospects, and the club invited me to present a lecture which they sub-
sequently published in mimeograph. It was called "The Psychology of
Acceptance," which I went on to expand into my first American book *The
Meaning of Happiness*, subtitled "The Quest for Freedom of the Spirit in
Modern Psychology and in the Wisdom of the East."

It must have been about this time that I was "looked over" by a formidable and elderly lady who had some connection with Eleanor's family. During the conversation she turned to me like Lady Bracknell, with metaphorical
lorgnettes in hand, saying, "And what, young man, are *you* planning to do for
a living?" I must have mumbled that my interests lay in the direction of philosophy. "Phee*lo*sophy!" she exclaimed. "Why you can't make a living out of
phee*lo*sophy!" The clouded crystal ball. But *then* I almost believed her.

I started out with a series of seminars on Oriental philosophy for which I had five students: Charles G. Taylor, a Jungian analyst and homeopathic physician; Lillian Baker, assistant to Alexis Carrel at the Rockefeller Institute; Florence Harrison, teacher of singing; and Eva Lewis Smith and Elizabeth Tyson, social workers. We began in a furnished apartment, Bauhaus style, on West Seventy-seventh Street, overlooking the Natural History Museum, and graduated to the sixteenth floor of 435 East Fifty-seventh Street, between First Avenue and Sutton Place, when our own furniture arrived from London. There I conducted seminars several times a week, and the number of students grew to respectable proportions.

It was there also that, during the fall of 1939, I wrote *The Meaning of Happiness* with the original intention of calling it *The Anatomy of Happiness* in line with Burton's *Anatomy of Melancholy*; but though this would have been a better title my friends felt that happiness was amorphous and should not be treated anatomically. "Happiness" was not the right word anyhow, for what I really meant was enlightenment, mystical experience, or cosmic consciousness, though this resembles happiness in the sense that it cannot be attained at will like mere pleasure. But, if so, what is the function of yoga, of Zen meditation, of Christian contemplative prayer, and of psychotherapy? For all these disciplines seem to be systematic ways of self-realization, of transforming consciousness so as to see clearly that the separate and alienated ego is an illusion distracting us from knowing that there is no self other than the eternal ground of all being.

In my own funny and immature way I knew this to be so, but the followers of all the systems seemed to be trying to talk me out of it. I was too young. I hadn't suffered enough. I hadn't worked with a guru and been through all the stages of initiation. I hadn't sat for hours, days, and years in meditation. I hadn't even been psychoanalyzed. Furthermore, it was surely neurotic for so young a man to be interested in such things. Worse still, my style of life showed no evidence of genuine God-consciousness, for it was obvious that I thoroughly enjoyed the pleasures of good food, of smoking and drinking and sex, and that I was immoderately infatuated with the sound of my own voice. Yet as I looked around at the people who claimed, explicitly or by implication, to have gone through the ropes and to have attained (or to be just about to attain) the genuine article, it seemed evident that they were all human, and often all too human. Sokei-an made no bones about it, and once said that if he had any ideal at all it was just to be a complete human being.

In *The Meaning of Happiness* I tried to work out my position vis-à-vis these criticisms from the system-followers. Going by a system is often, though not necessarily, an elaborate and subtle ego-trip in which people inflate their egos by trying to destroy them, stressing the superhuman difficulty of the task. It can so easily be mere postponement of realization to the tomorrow which never comes, with the mock humility of, "I'm not ready yet. I don't deserve it. Perhaps, if I work as hard as the great sages of old, I can get it in twenty years or in my next incarnation." But what if this is just self-punishment and spiritual masochism—lying, as it were, on a bed of nails to assure oneself of "authentic" existence? Mortification of the ego is an attempt to get rid of what doesn't exist, or—which comes to the same thing—of the feeling that it exists. Do we *feel* the ego? Do we hear ourselves listening? Are we conscious on purpose, knowing just exactly how to produce awareness?

You may wish to ask where the flowers come from,
But even the God of Spring doesn't know.

My point was, and has continued to be, that the Big Realization for which all these systems strive is not a future attainment but a present fact, that this now-moment is eternity, and that one must see it now or never. For right now this problematic ego cannot be found. It seems to exist only when we forget that the past is nothing but a present memory, a shadow, a trace; the illusion that a cigarette whirled in the dark is an actual circle of fire. It says here, in the *Upanishads*, "*Tat tvam asi*—you *are* THAT!" What could be more clear? But I found that when people hear this they burst into storms of words, raise all imaginable questions, and find every possible excuse for attending to everything except now. Perhaps I have been too patient, for in book after book I have answered these questions. What happens to now when you die? If we live in the present, who will plant crops for the winter? What will become of progress? Won't this turn us into morons? Surely you are leaving out the unconscious and all its ancient archetypes? If I am Buddha at this moment, what is the difference between a Gautama and an ordinary, ignorant person? Well, isn't this just living life as it comes? How does it differ from plain pantheism? It might have been better if I had simply remained silent, or shouted "BANG!"

In the words of an old Chinese Zen master, "If you want to see into it, see into it directly. When you begin to think about it, it is altogether missed."

Thus the philosophical people wanted to know just exactly what I *meant* by the eternal now, and why it should be of any significance. If they were told that it meant nothing because it was not a word, and signified nothing because it was not a sign, they would shrug their shoulders and change the subject, because all they really wanted was a construct of words. When the academically schooled philosopher asks for a meaning he asks only for another set of signs, and so *ad infinitum*. What *is* meaning as distinct from what *has* meaning never enters into his game. All such philosophers should play Vish. Each player is given a copy of the same dictionary. A referee draws a word from a hat, and immediately the players look it up, take a key word from the definition and look that up, and so on. The first player to get back to the original word calls out "Vish!" (vicious circle), and the referee checks his steps to be sure they are legitimate.

Another kind of sign-seekers are the people fascinated with psychic powers, believing that all genuine mystics must also be magicians who can remember their past lives, foretell the future, read other people's thoughts, heal diseases, and travel about in their astral bodies. Though I am open to the possibility of such powers I have never seen them exercised (excepting a man who walked on fire and the phenomena of hypnosis), and it has always struck me that most of the magical feats reported are trivial. The wizards make high scores on ESP cards, read questions in sealed envelopes, cause vases to fall off shelves, project pictures on films by mental concentration, or materialize flowers, jewels, and other baubles out of the air. No one so materializes tons of rice for starving Indians, and of all the prominent astrologers only one or two predicted the actual outbreak of World War II.

Over the years I went into this problem carefully with both Sokei-an and Ruth, and others who had sound firsthand knowledge of Zen in Japan.

All have stated that the great Zen masters of today neither practice nor give instruction in such wizardry. Zen has its own way of understanding the *siddhi*, or supernormal powers of a Buddha. There are, for example, *koan* which request miracles, such as "Stop the ship on the distant ocean." In the Hakuin system this is answered by rocking gently from side to side and imitating a ship furling sail. But when a joke is explained, one laughs only from the throat. In the mid-fifties, after she had worked at Zen in Japan for nearly ten years, Ruth wrote me that the last word of Zen on the miraculous was the verse of P'ang-yun:

> Miraculous power and marvelous activity—
> Drawing water and hewing wood!

When *The Meaning of Happiness* was almost finished, Eva Lewis Smith brought Eugene Exman, the religion editor of Harper and Brothers, to a seminar. Why didn't I put some of this into a book? Dear Mr. Exman, you shall have the manuscript in a few days. He took it immediately and it appeared in May 1940 just as Hitler moved into France and no one wanted to read about happiness and mysticism. John Haynes Holmes blessed it extravagantly in the *New York Times*, and the *Dallas Morning News* took two columns to say that it was a highly esoteric work for Brahmins only, and that the mountain had labored and brought forth a mouse. *Asia* magazine bought two articles from me and seminar attendance went up. Harper's took me on as an outside manuscript reader. But perhaps the best thing was a letter from a certain Jim Corsa, who described himself as a penniless hermit living on Captiva Island off the coast of Florida. Would I be so kind as to send him a copy in return for a collection of sea shells? Shells were once used for money, so I sent it, and shortly received a box of true miracles recently washed up on the same beach from which Anne Morrow Lindbergh received her *Gift from the Sea*.

There was, then, still the question of how I should make my way in America, for I could not depend on Ruth's generosity indefinitely. Ruth wondered if I shouldn't get a Ph.D., and go into teaching, so I went to talk this over with Marguerite Block, who was then editing the Columbia *Review of Religion*. This cheerful white-haired, beady-eyed woman was a member of the Analytical Psychology Club and an authority of Swedenborg, who had been the subject of her doctoral dissertation. No—she said—it wasn't worth it. I simply wouldn't waste your time with all that picayune, myopic-minded, long-drawn-out, mole-eyed academic ritual. Just write a long and learned article on some new wrinkle in comparative religion and we'll publish it in the *Review*. That should do instead.

Now I had, as I have said, been fascinated by the seeming conflict between those who held that the mystical experience required a supreme effort of will, and those who held that such effort was simply an exhibition of egocentric pride which could only postpone the experience and push it away. There was a parallel in Christianity between the Pelagians, who held salvation to be the result of good works, and the Augustinians (including Luther), who held that it came solely by faith. There were likewise the psychotherapists who said, "Pull yourself together!" and those who said, "Accept yourself as you are." There was also a much less well-known parallel in Mahayana Buddhism between the adherents of *jiriki* (self-power) and *tariki* (other-power)—between, so to speak, the willful meditators of Zen and the faithful devotees of Jodo Shinshu, the latter holding that the human will is so perverse that liberation can come only by faith in the loving power of Amitabha (Japanese: Amida), the transcendental Buddha of Boundless Light.

Suzuki had let fall some interesting hints on a solution to the problem, which he discussed at a later date in his *Mysticism: Christian and Buddhist* (New York, 1957), and these I explored further by comparing the relevant texts of the two schools. I saw that the two could be reconciled if their overt differences could be understood in a deeper and more experiential (as distinct from theoretical) way. It could be assumed, on the one hand, that the method of Zen was a *reductio ad absurdum*—a fierce exercise of ego and will to bring about the certainty of their nonexistence and futility. The *koan* are not solved unless you work at them with all your might until you are simply forced to give up, and the answer comes of itself. On the other hand, it could be assumed that Amitabha need not be considered as "other" in the theistic sense, but simply as that true or real Self, which, like the heart or the brain, is other than the ego and the will. Amitabha would then be the equivalent of the Tao in the dialogue where Joshu asks his teacher Nansen, "What is the Tao?"

Nansen replies, "Ordinary mind is Tao." "How does one get into accord with it?" "If you try to accord, you deviate." As is said in the *Ch'ung-yung*, "The Tao is that from which nothing deviates. That from which you can deviate is not the Tao,"—which adds an extra flip to Nansen. Perhaps the followers of Zen might still criticize the Jodo Shinshu people for giving up their ego-power (*jiriki*) without full conviction as to its futility. But they, in turn, would come back and say that the attainment of full conviction still involved the vestiges of personal pride. It could further be argued that there is a lot of pride in thinking, "I am not as proud as you are." But such argument is a vicious circle or an infinite regression, and when we get into such arguments it should be clear that we are trying to bite our teeth.

So I wrote all this up at length, and it was published as "The Problem of Faith and Works in Buddhism," which appeared in the May 1941 *Review of Religion*. For me, this work had momentous consequences, because I saw that if you substituted "Christ" for "Amitabha," Zen, Jodo Shinshu, and Christianity were all approaching the same point by different routes. It might thus be possible to develop a deeper and more intelligible form of Christianity which would, however, have to bypass that religion's imperialistic claims to be the one true and perfect revelation. At the same time, Christianity would be strengthened in being seen as a form of the common religious experience of mankind. It would have more validity by being less of an oddity.

In the meantime, there had been changes in Eleanor's inner life, and we lived together so closely and were, perhaps, so overdependent on one another that our crises were mutual, if different in form. She began to have periods of black depression during which she felt the universe was a malignant trap or torture mechanism, designed to give hope in order to crush it. One might say that such depressions were the natural result of living with me and my rooted disinclination to be "just like everyone else," for every now and then Eleanor upheld to me the ideal of living like a couple in her hometown of Hinsdale, Illinois—a Mr. and Mrs. Seaman. For the Seamans were a happy, conventional pair with a bonny brood who—as Eleanor described them— lived in a cute little house with white flouncy drapes and New England colonial furniture; the convex mirror, gold-framed with eagle; the cabinet with glass door and thin mullions, repository of china dogs, silver cruets, a small bust of Lincoln, the last of a set of green-and-gold wineglasses, a model farmhouse in a glass ball (made to snow when jiggled), and an Easter egg of permanent icing with a peephole at one end, garlanded with pink leaves. No green idols, no curiously inlaid teakwood cabinets, no Buddhist gongs, no thigh-bone trumpets from Tibet, no cups made from human skulls, no carpets from Isphahan.

Eleanor's basic trouble was that, like so many people of wealth, she worried passionately about money. She had comfortable holdings in stocks but, as a good old-fashioned Republican, used only the dividends, yet went so far as to turn them all over to me in the hope that this would make me feel more like a man and head-of-a-house. In those days I, too, was a good Republican and left everything just as it was. Despite the psychiatric ministrations of Charlie Taylor, the depressions kept coming. She was overweight, for we all ate too much. After an evening seminar we would go out to the Sutton, an unpretentious restaurant on First Avenue, where I would order a full-course dinner with broiled mackerel and a steak on the side. Charlie put Eleanor on a three-week diet of lettuce and lamb chops, at the end of which everything tasted of wet string and she had gained three pounds. Not that this original lanky Yankee with long hollow cheeks and white hair was a bad doctor. He cured Eleanor of a chronic eczema by taking salt out of her diet, instantly fixed a click in her jaw with two tiny pills, and by the same homeopathy pulled me swiftly out of pneumonia. We loved him and were probably too close for effective psychiatry. He would talk to us until late at night about Jung's ideas and about his experiences in medicine, centering around his conversion from the fashionably mechanical to the organic approach to his art. "Yes," he said, "in those days I had a swell office on Park Avenue and made lots of money. I had four partners and all the right gadgets, and there we were, all set and ready for the torpedo to come through."

One day Eleanor was out shopping on Fifth Avenue and dropped into Saint Patrick's Cathedral for a rest. Suddenly she was confronted with a completely vivid vision of Christ, so much so that she could describe every detail of his dress, though I do not remember that the figure said anything. Visions are, of course, unnerving; especially when Christ appears to a Buddhist, and especially when you have had no more exposure to Christianity than singing occasionally in the choir at Grace Episcopal Church in Hinsdale. I have often wondered what *I* would do if I had a vision of Christ. I think I would ask him to turn down that supernatural light a bit so that we could have a good talk, for I don't think it's playing quite fair to go around impressing people with visions which might well be hallucinations. I have once seen a "ghost"—an elderly Frenchman with a bald head and a goatee, resting his chin on his arm as he read a book at the dining table. The book was real, but the rest was a composite of objects around the fireplace as reflected in the window.

But Eleanor was beside herself to get professional advice on this vision, and to this day I cannot imagine what such advice might have been. There was a simple old lady who saw Christ every time she received Communion, but said nothing of it because she supposed that this was a regular part of the service and that everyone else saw him as well. There was also a young girl who, during instruction for Confirmation by a very holy old nun, asked whether one had to believe that the Virgin Mary was visited by a real angel, white robe and all. The nun thought it over for a moment, and answered, "Well, my dear, I am sure he would have to have been wearing something."

Eleanor sought out one of the priests at Saint Patrick's under the naive but common impression that Catholic priests, with all their seven years' training, are immensely learned in theological and supernatural matters. But nothing can be more embarrassing to a solid Irish cleric than a young woman suffering from visions. You can't get clinical about visions and test their veracity by going into every detail of feature, hair style, and clothing, as if there were an authentic portrait of Christ in the secret files of the Vatican. If you are honest there is not much more to say than, "So you had a vision." The apparition was too startlingly real to be explained away as one of Dr. Charlie's Jungian archetypes. Eleanor was looking for the sort of person whom Aleister Crowley had aspired to be: an occult psychiatrist familiar with the full methodology of magic, with astral pathology, necromancy, angelology, demonology, and mystical analysis.

However, the vision coincided with my own growing realization that Christianity might be understood as a form of that mystical and perennial philosophy which has appeared in almost all times and places. One could go behind the screen of literal dogma to the inner meaning of symbols, to the level at which Eckhart and Shankara, Saint Teresa and Ramakrishna, Saint Dionysius and Nagarjuna are talking the same language. Furthermore, it struck me that I was on the way to becoming a misfit and an oddity in Western society—a twenty-six-year-old guru who might make a living only by the ignominious ruse of persuading wealthy old ladies that I was a reincarnation of Padmasambhava or the Master Koot Hoomi. This can be done by giving the impression, allowing rumors to spread, and claiming nothing overtly. Just look knowing when funny coincidences happen, and you acquire a reputation for working miracles. Given the reputation, the actual miracles follow, because people believe in you. When it doesn't work you lament about their lack of faith, or explain that their progressed moon was in square to Neptune. Your successes will be remembered and your failures forgotten because so many people hope against hope for a real wonder-working Master, and you will end up by believing your own hoax.[3]

Besides, I thought I should find some way of fitting in with the traditions of Western culture, of going along with—if not blindly following—the ways and customs of the world in which I was living. Because, then, there was no doubt of my paramount interest in religion, what if I should fit myself into the Western design of life by taking the role of a Christian minister? I did not then realize that within ten to fifteen years from this time

---

[3] I have often considered doing an article called "Books I Shall Never Write," to give away some ideas to younger authors. One would be a novel, similar to Thomas Mann's *Confessions of Felix Krüll*, which would be the autobiography of such a trickster who comes to believe in his own hoax. Thereafter he gets up the nerve to proceed as a magus with full self-confidence, employing all the techniques of hypnosis to acquire the curiously effective power of mass support. Collective illusions are immensely persuasive, and when one considers how many supposed "facts"—such as the reality of the past and the solidity of matter—are illusions, the art of the trickster begins to take on serious metaphysical implications. If what we call the real world of things and events is a collective projection upon a cosmic Rorschach blot, the trickster could become a creative and even beneficent artist, suggesting that we project things in a different way. Has anyone yet written a thorough study of fashions in belief, not only in religion and metaphysics, but also in science, medicine, and history?

(1940–1941) the ministerial role would—at least to the intelligent young—
seem ineffectual and obsolete, and even out of the stream of Western culture. I could not foresee that by the mid-1950s the intellectual community
would see nothing especially crackpot in one's being a Buddhist; that
Indian, Chinese, and especially Japanese influences would be streaming into
America; that theologians would be discussing the death of God and the
possibilities of "religionless" Christianity; or—to go further—that eminent
scientists would be questioning both the fundamental premises and the practical applications of science, and pointing out the catastrophic consequences
of the Western project for the conquest of nature, and that, therefore, a basic
revision of our idea of the universe as a created artifact or mechanism would
be in order. But back then I thought I was going into something as perenni-
ally useful as if I were to become a doctor, though without the intention of
adhering slavishly to the American Medical Association's party line.

Naturally, I discussed my idea with a number of friends and noticed that,
almost instantly, they took a curious attitude to me which should have
warned me of the unreal and unnatural position which ministers hold in our
culture. One of my first discussions was with Robert E. Hume, a professor
at Union Theological Seminary, Indologist, and translator of the *Upanishads*,
whom I had met some years before at the World Congress of Faiths. He was
almost startled at the notion. He seemed to see it as a discontinuity. How *very*
interesting, how really remarkable that I—Alan Watts—should be contemplating this momentous STEP. He would be fascinated to know in just what
ways I had come to feel that Buddhism was insufficient. Ruth assumed an
artificially patronizing attitude as well, how nice that you dear children have
at least found a belief that really means something for you. Eugene Exman,
who, as religion editor of Harper's, had probably had his fill of ministers,
urged me not to bother with the entanglements of ordination but to join the
Quakers. But somehow I could not see myself as a Quaker, because for all
the undoubted merits of the Society of Friends, they struck me as almost op-
pressively serious and concerned—as if the good life required a personal
style suggestive of perpetual straining from constipation. My students had
mixed feelings. I had discussed Buddhism as a key to the inner meaning of
Christianity in seminars, and many of them, especially those with Jungian

inclinations, had no difficulty in seeing Christian symbols as archetypes of the collective unconscious which is common to mankind as a whole. Others felt instinctively uncomfortable with Christianity, for, although they could grasp the rationale of my explanations, they could not stand the atmosphere of church and churchy people.

With a few exceptions, our personal friends—those with whom we went dancing and drinking and partying—were astonished. They knew Eleanor as an earthy girl with a rich belly-laugh, and me as a fathomless source of bawdy limericks with a propensity for outlandish dancing and the kind of chanting which, today, brings calls from the police, the citizenry supposing that the Apaches—in full war paint—are in their midst. The coincidence of opposites involved in the possibility of such persons being also a minister and a minister's wife was beyond belief. Were we about to repent our sins and become godly, righteous, and sober?

The apparent anomaly of the whole situation was not unconnected with the problem of what brand of Christianity I should use. Being married I could not become a Roman Catholic priest, quite aside from my objection to a denomination which puts the virtue of obedience higher than the virtue of charity. As for standard Protestant—Presbyterian, Methodist, Congregational, and Baptist—it would afflict me with its folksy lack of color. It simply had to be Episcopal—the awkward denominational label for the American branch of the Anglican Communion, which, as is not so well known by outsiders, is the most liberal form of Christianity. For within the charitable embrace of this Communion you can be a Rococo Catholic, a stately High Churchman, a virtual Presbyterian, a Marxist, and even a Theosophist—just so long as you keep loosely to the Book of Common Prayer in the conduct of services, and take care not to play around openly with any of the ladies on the altar guild. If you want to take full advantage of this liberality and adopt one of the more far-out positions, it helps to be rich so that you can thumb your nose at "lay popes"—prosperous businessmen who want the church to be as solid and respectable as a funeral parlor.

Accordingly, Eleanor and I began an investigation of the Episcopal churches of Manhattan, beginning with Saint Bartholomew's, Park Avenue, a most pleasing Byzantine monument where they were offering, however,

only a very desultory Morning Prayer as the principal service. I asked a curate—a tall, serious, and athletic young man—whether they had Choral
Communion on the first Sunday of the month, and he replied with a somewhat shocked expression, "Oh no, we never have anything like that!" Next
we tried Saint James, Madison Avenue, then under the dispensation of the
Reverend Dr. James Donegan—later Bishop of New York. Again, Morning
Prayer, but not quite so desultory. Incidentally, Morning Prayer is an elision
of the monastic offices of Matins and Lauds, and it seems a little strange that
Protestant-minded Anglicans should prefer a monastic service to the Eu-
charist.

After a few more unrewarding tries we discovered an invisible church on
West Forty-sixth Street, a long, lofty French Gothic structure entirely hidden by adjoining buildings, its entrance unseen until you are right up to it.
Through this Gothic hole in the wall you pass into a high and indeterminate
vastness, where the distance is blurred by a mist of frankincense hanging
over clusters of votive lights, where almost all daylight is shut out, and where,
wide and high, a polychromatic altar looks down upon the sanctuary from the
far end. No, it was not Roman Catholic. The notice on the door had said
plainly:

CHURCH OF SAINT MARY THE VIRGIN
(Episcopal)

This was Palm Sunday, 1941, and what we were to witness was the entire ritual drama of the Blessing of the Palms, the Entry into Jerusalem, the chanting of the Passion, and Solemn High Mass, all celebrated before this great
altar in a wide, theaterlike sanctuary. The music was Gregorian and poly-
phonic; the organ was no textureless, fluty, Victorian diapason, but one of the
good snarly classic type; and the choir, hidden in a gallery at the back, was
faultlessly directed by a genius named Ernest White. Furthermore, these
people understood ritual. Their movements were natural and unhurried.
They genuflected with ease and grace—none of your hurried Romish
bomps—and in procession they neither marched like soldiers nor waddled
like ducks. They just walked as if they had already arrived.

The following Thursday (Maundy Thursday) we went back in the evening, taking along our friend Adolph Teichert, from California, just for the music. Adolph was one of our feistier friends—likewise a devotee of limericks—a tall, blond, and bird-like pianist, then studying with Wanda Landowska. What we witnessed was a strange contrast to Palm Sunday—the Office of Tenebrae—an interminable chanting of psalms, without accompaniment, interspersed with verses from *The Lamentations of Jeremiah* by Palestrina. After the first hour the chanting became hypnotic. One by one they extinguished the brown candles on a stand before the altar, and gradually the church went into darkness—with only one candle left burning on the stand, and this they carried out behind the altar and sang the *Benedictus.* There was a loud thump. The candle was returned, and everyone left the church. All of us, including Adolph, were affected. There was undoubted magic in that church.

Now it seemed natural to me to be exuberant about religion, just as it also seemed natural and contradictory to be religious and at the same time to be exuberant about life, to go about our loving and eating and drinking with the innocent splendor of the flowers doing likewise. If one is going to have church and ritual of any kind, why not live it up? If I put on vestments of brocade, light candles, burn incense, and intone mysterious chants, I do not do it to fool people or to flatter God. I do it out of simple delight and fascination for the color, the stately dance, and the sense of mystery—not of the kind of mystery which can be revealed or explained, but the kind of mystery which God must be to himself. Mystery, mystic—the Greek *rueiv*—the finger on the lips; mum's the word; do not spoil it with an explanation. I was not really interested in what rites and ceremonies symbolized, and still less in future results they might be supposed to achieve.

If I were to be a priest I would be sincere, but not serious. For religion and ritual alike must be conducted with a light and easy touch, with unhurried and unpompous naturalness. But, as I was to discover, Americans (and Protestants in general) lack the light touch in both religion and sex, for both aggravate their sense of guilt. This is perhaps because their religions are so exclusively concerned with morality that they lack metaphysical depth and any interest in self-knowledge deeper than the personal and psychological level. Thus there was always the question, "Why do you have to perform these strange ceremonies? Do they make you any better than those of us who do without them? Do they have some special meaning, and, if so, wouldn't it be easier just to explain it in simple language?" Why does one listen to birds? Why dance? Why watch clouds, or hear the sound of rain? I can only reply, "Please stop looking for wordy answers. To understand ritual—or, for that matter, chopping firewood—do it as if it were happening all by itself, without seeking any result or benefit."[4]

Here again, as in so many other matters of personal preference, my choice of a religious vehicle was part and parcel of my inability to understand dullness as a virtue. There are, as I found, dull Anglo-Catholics who rationalize their ceremonies by legalistic regard for ancient rubrics, and make each movement of a finger according to Fortescue (the ecclesiastical equivalent of Hoyle), as if the rite would fail if a sign of the cross were made in the wrong place. To this day it remains beyond my comprehension why so many people who are neither sick nor starving cultivate drabness as a way of life, and feel embarrassed for those who come out in vermilion trousers or dance in the streets.

I did not, then, consider myself as being converted to Christianity in the sense that I was abandoning Buddhism and Taoism. To tell the truth, I never warmed up to the personality of Jesus as it comes down to us through history and tradition, art and doctrine, and the Gospels never appealed to me so deeply as the *Tao Te Ching* or the *Chuang-tzu* book. It was simply that the Anglican Communion seemed to be the most appropriate context for doing what was in me to do, in Western society.

---

[4] This might well be a reasonable interpretation of the *ex opere operato* doctrine, whereby the validity of a sacrament, such as the Mass, depends on the carrying out of the rite itself and not on the moral character, spiritual development, or personal intention of the individual priest. Of course, for "not I, but Christ [who] liveth in me" does and is the action, just as it is Amitabha who says *Namu Amida Butsu*. The "result" of the sacrament is transcending the ego, which, because it is essentially a social fiction, cannot seek or attain this result.

CHAPTER SEVEN

THE SUNWISE TURN

I look back on all this from the place at which, all along, I have been aiming, for this cottage in which I am writing, hidden in a high grove of eucalyptus trees, is almost as far west as the West goes. Late this afternoon a fresh wind from the Pacific was dispersing the misty rain and the clouds, and the low sun was turning those giant trees with their long flame-shaped leaves into green fire. Yet at any point on the Earth there is as much west of you as there is east. Though I might be considered by some to have reached a goal, I have discovered along the way that at every position in the whole hierarchy of beings there is as much above as below, and thus that there are standpoints from which every position is as much a failure as it is a success. I think often of the Hermetic inscription on the *Tabula Smaragdina*:

> Heaven above, heaven below;
> Stars above, stars below;
> All that is over, under shall show.
>   Happy who reads the riddle.

For deliverance from life lived as a vicious circle—the Buddhist *samsara*—is to realize that sorrow is not to be escaped by going up, or, for that matter, west.

In going back over one's past one remembers all too much foolishness. Yet how can I forgive anyone else if I don't forgive myself? And how can I believe that now, as I have become and matured, I am no longer a fool? If "judge not that you be not judged" means anything, it means that we must look at human affairs, including our own, as we look at nature.

In the scene of spring there is nothing inferior, nothing superior;
Flowering branches grow naturally, some short, some long.

Our deeds, our feelings, our thoughts, and our sensations just happen of
themselves, as the rain falls and the water flows along the valley. I am neither
a passive and helpless witness to whom they happen, nor an active doer and
thinker who causes and controls them. "I" is simply the idea of myself, a
thought among thoughts. Taken seriously it gives the illusion of being something apart from nature, a subject reviewing objects. But if the subject is an
illusion, the objects are no longer mere objects. Inside the skull and the skin
as well as outside, there is simply the stream flowing along of itself. The
bones flow too, and their inner texture has the same patterns as moving liquid. In nature there are neither masters nor slaves.

From the beginning, I saw the Church as a way rather than a destination,
and it so happened, for me, that the Church was in Chicago and the destination in California; concerning which I had a fantasy, a dream, which somehow came true. I wanted to be in a place where there were mountains and
aromatic trees—pine, redwood, and eucalyptus—where lemons would flourish, and where I would be close to the ocean. I wanted to see the white houses
of the Mediterranean and the unpainted wooden houses of mountain forests,
all something like the Basque country of Southwest France which I had visited in 1929. On the sides of those mountains and under those trees I dreamed
of some sort of retreat or *ashram* where I would undertake a work involving
the study, practice, and teaching of a way of life both natural and spiritual,
a place where I could find the delight of sharing and clarifying my basic
intuition: that here and now, without any artificial striving and straining, the
flow of life in man is inseparably one with the Tao, the flow of the universe
—call it God, Brahman, the Divine Ground, or what you will. This dream
may seem foolish and sentimental, and not to be reckoning with drab poverty,
with slums, ghettos, and prisons, with napalmed babies and atomic bombs,
and with all those things which now seem far more real than lemons in the
sun and aromatic trees.

The sowers of this dream were old friends of Eleanor's family, Blanche
and Russell Matthias, whom I had first met in London. Originally from

Chicago, Russell had made a fortune in the lumber business and had retired at forty, to become an ardent conservationist. Clean-cut and impeccably dressed, he relished the good things of life with what can only be called luxurious asceticism. There was no clutter or display of excessive possessions, but almost everything he owned was of the finest quality, imaginative in taste (including a narwhal's tusk), and kept in uncrowded order. Blanche was of the same aesthetic persuasion—light and slight with bright dark eyes and white hair worn with bangs and tied at the nape with a black velvet bow, George Washington style—undeniably beautiful even in aging. She was also a close friend of Krishnamurti and an avid reader of his writing. They traveled constantly and seemed to turn up everywhere—at the Savoy in London, the Savoy-Plaza in New York, the Drake in Chicago, and the Fairmont in San Francisco—yet always carried with them an atmosphere of California, where they had made their headquarters. At Christmas, for example, Russell would always have ornamental bunches of redwood branches flown in from Bohemians' Grove on the Russian River, and, in some odd way, their style of life evoked the rocks and cypresses of the Carmel coastland (obviously painted on the Pacific mists by Sesshu), the blue crystal skies of the Southwestern desert country, with mountains floating beyond the orange trees and date palms, and the high valleys of the Sierra Nevada with sequoias and sugar pines sounding in the wind like lost waves in search of forgotten shores.

That, they said, is where you must go. That is the best of America. In my mind's eye I could see Krishnamurti walking alone through the orange groves of Ojai under the vast mass of Topa-topa and, in flat contradiction of all that he taught, wanted to be in his situation in my own way. What a mix-up! For I felt that I understood him quite clearly, and knew very well that all attempts to avoid conflict by accepting beliefs, following authorities, and trying to change one's own consciousness were the vicious circle of an illusion attempting to get rid of an illusion. Yet on the one hand I was about to play a sacerdotal role, and on the other I felt that Krishnamurti was not so much an authority as one who took the words out of my mouth: a strong ally who awakened responsive chords in me by the freshness of a way of thinking that was quite outside the usual ruts of moral and spiritual teaching.

This would not have been possible if I had believed in a religion, as belief is generally understood. I was not really concerned as to the literal historicity of the Virgin Birth or the Resurrection, but could see that the *idea* of God becoming incarnate at a particular place and time was a sort of blessing on particularity. As Spinoza put it, "The more we know of particular things, the more we know of God." The Church's insistence on literal historicity was itself symbolic. Although the creeds state that the risen Christ is sitting in heaven at the right hand of God the Father, no theologian in his senses thinks that God the Father has a corporeal hand, and the statement is always taken as figurative. Because, then, the creeds do not specify the types of language in which their statements are made—whether literal or symbolic, factual or analogic—you are free to make your own judgment.

It was thus that whatever Krishnamurti represented in me always lay beyond the Church. He is a purist in his avoidance of doctrine, ritual, symbolism, and specific methods of meditation, as well as all reference to the traditional literatures of mysticism, even though, as Aldous Huxley once said, "No one else reminds me so much of the Buddha." At which Jano chipped in, "Why, did you know the Buddha?" "No," he said, "but what else can one say?" But I am not such a purist, for I think of religion as something to be used—like a set of tools—rather than followed. Tools can easily run away with you, especially magical tools. But I am not prepared to argue that the *Upanishads* and the *Bhagavad-Gita*, the *Tao Te Ching* and the New Testament, the *Dhammapada* and the *Lankavatara Sutra*, Canterbury Cathedral and the Kamakura Daibutsu, or the Shingon Fire Ceremony and the Mass should simply be ditched. If so, we would have to consign the greater part of pre-Renaissance and Oriental art to the morgue, and read nothing but travelogues and mystery stories. My mind runs to such things as a solemn and reverent ceremony for burning a copy of the Bible, to be held annually on the Feast of Pentecost. And the person who burns it must have read it.

It was through Blanche and Russell that we met Adolph Teichert III, scion of the Sacramento family which undertakes vast projects of construction (including, alas, superhighways) in California, and his then girl friend, Anne Greene, whose father, Charles Sumner Greene, was the Buddhist architect who tried to preserve Carmel-by-the-Sea from suburbanization.

Like Adolph, she was a pianist and whereas he was fabulous on technique, she had the grace of interpretation. I remember her rendering of some Beethoven *Écossaises* one afternoon at the apartment of her patroness, Anna Clark, widow of Senator William Clark of Montana and heiress of the millions of Anaconda Copper. Poor Anna was as deaf as Beethoven himself and gave the impression of being, so to speak, expensively unhappy, going about New York in one of those chauffeur-freezer Rolls-Royces under the warmth of a sable lap-robe. She also had the loveliest Mexican necklace of ancient jade beads interspersed with groups of pearls.

Anne Greene was a tall, angular brunette, full of laughs which seemed to originate on the tip of her nose. For some reason we called her Anya Ban.anya. She eventually drifted away from Adolph and married another of our friends, Ted Roberts, a Welshman from Pennsylvania, who was then working at the Gateway Bookshop. In those days, Theos Bernard—the nephew of Oom the Omnipotent, Pierre—had returned from Tibet in the guise of a lama, married the singer and millionairess Ganna Walska, and set up an *ashram* in Santa Barbara. I shall remember Ted as the dust-begrimed packer of the hundreds of volumes which Theos ordered from the Gateway for the *ashram* library: all concerned with what, for want of a better name, must be called These Things, as in asking, "Are you interested in these things?" This comprises everything from the esoterica of Vajrayana Buddhism, Taoism, Zen, Vedanta, and Sufism, through Theosophy, Christian Mysticism, Astrology, Psychic Research, and Magic, to New Thought, Jungianism, Hypnotism, and Psychoanalysis. Ted and Anne, however, were more earthy than all that, and disappeared at last into the wilds of the Northwest. But Adolph was swept as by music into Anglo-Catholicism, became a sparkling organist, and in the end withdrew to Sacramento to mind the family business.

How to sort out the details of the multitudinous encounters in which Eleanor and I were involved? The parties, the different apartments, the country houses, the restaurants and night-spots, the loft on West Fourteenth Street where we learned folk dancing . . . it all breaks into a colorful sea of interesting faces. In all this Adolph was a constant—as a rollicking, generous, bawdy, limerick-chanting, intelligent, argumentative, and sometimes drunken companion, who puzzled me because he had so much wealth and didn't seem to know what to do with it. Charlie Taylor must have analyzed him to the utmost archetype, but he seemed at last to find peace in playing for the Church and, still later, in marriage to an elegant Scotch girl from Nova Scotia.

A curious reason for gratitude to Adolph was not just that he was at times startlingly generous, but that he knew my weak spots. He knew, that is to say, the moments in which I was covering up loss of nerve, in which I said something silly because I was tongue-tied, and he knew some of the secret places of my conscience: that ambivalent faculty which is sometimes the voice of sanity but mostly the echo of parental qualms and social conditioning. On the important occasions when I have followed conscience in the latter sense, I have invariably done something absurd, and in a spirit of blind righteousness. Somehow Adolph, intentionally or otherwise, helped me to see that one must never attempt to use expiation for the exorcism of guilt. It may heal your own wounds, but it shows no real consideration for those you have injured, and they, as often as not, wish fervently that you would simply go away and not give any more trouble. Again and again I have found that, for me, deep relationships of this kind are possible only with people who can let their hair down, and I could hardly be offended or overawed by the ribald inventor of a laxative called Jumbo-Dump, for which he recited side-splitting radio advertisements with dead-pan folksy testimonials from such reassuring nonentities as Mrs. Beulah Stitch of Centerville, Iowa.

But an apparently spotless holy man seemed to be so identified with a consistent role that any basic personal relationship was difficult. It was thus with that serene, lovable, and gently humorous priest Grieg Taber, the Father Rector of Saint Mary the Virgin, a bald-pated owl who took his religion with the simplicity of a wise child. Indeed, Father Taber was so committed to his faith that he disapproved of any formal discussion or questioning of its principles which might in some way imply that it was not entirely true. For him, religion was total obedience and intense devotion without either fanaticism or offensive zeal. He was so much the model priest that he was almost difficult to believe. At the same time he was refreshingly indifferent to fascination with the politics and gossip of the Anglo-Catholic in-group, which, as a militant minority in the Episcopal Church, finds its favorite sport in one-upping the Protestant majority. (Did you know that

Father Smith, at Saint James's, wore a chasuble last Sunday, and that at Saint Christopher's they are getting away with singing the *Kyrie* in Greek? What's the story on Father Jones? He was doing such a great job at Ascension, but I heard something about his resigning and becoming chaplain to the sisters at East Hampton.) I did not realize at the time that by going in with the Anglo-Catholics I had been politically astute in easing my way into holy orders, for as a minority on the make they welcomed almost anyone who would help in the discomfiture of the "Prots."

It is a good general rule for any layman who delights in Catholic worship to stay out of Church politics and to shun familiarity with the clergy. But with Father Taber this was no problem. He was still an archetype, even when you came to know him quite well. In seminary courses on pastoral theology one is always advised to maintain a certain aloofness from one's flock, and to avoid becoming the hub of any favored inner circle of disciples. Personal friends are best chosen from outside the parish. My own experience has been quite different. My best students stop studying with me and become personal friends. Surely, this is just as it should be, for why keep coming around when you've got the message? Furthermore, if religion is a medicine, addiction to it should be discouraged. Physicians try to get rid of their patients, but clergymen want to keep them coming. When Jesus healed people he sent them about their business and told them to keep their mouths shut.

But from watching Father Taber and his various curates, Arnold Craven and John Bruce in particular, I rapidly absorbed all the details of conducting Mass according to the Anglicized ritual of the Roman liturgy, which then followed the old secretive and sacerdotal style, with the priest facing away from the people and saying the canon *mystikōs* in a barely audible voice. These details included the complex hand gestures (*mudra*) made over the sacred elements—a mysterious performance which gave the more superstitious Protestants of Wales the notion that Romish priests put a live crab on the altar, and had to keep it from running away. It was also *de rigueur* to celebrate with a certain reverent rapidity and casualness, possibly to bring home the point that the mystery of transubstantiation had nothing to do with personal emotion or feeling, but came to pass simply by the rite itself. The Church is so often right for the wrong reasons—or should one say rather that it sometimes gets to the point despite its clumsy theology? A Tibetan spins a prayer wheel and a Japanese says the *Nembutsu* without feeling any need to force an act of faith or even to think about what he is doing, for all things have the Buddha-nature or are of "one Suchness" whether you know it or not. More than this is "putting legs on a snake."

The immediate tactical problem was to get my foot in the Church door, for, at least on paper, the requirements for becoming a postulant for holy orders seemed formidable. On reading the Canon Law of the Church, it appeared that one must be an undoubted square, cube, or event tesseract, and Dean Fosbrooke of General Theological Seminary in New York, whom I consulted, wove a festoon of red tape. I had no bachelor's degree. Yes, I had published a book on philosophy and psychology which—ahem—he had not of course seen, but what was important about Christian theology was *history*. I was only twenty-six, really too young to be a priest, and certainly I should spend some time making up my academic background. It seemed useless to tell him that I had read history voluminously, including the history of law and the history of historiography, and was properly qualified to be bored with it. However, my clerical friends advised me to forget Dean Fosbrooke: the thing was to find a bishop who would take a risk on me as a suitable candidate. Bishop Manning of New York, although a High Churchman, was a terrible stickler for the formalities; the Bishops of New Jersey, Connecticut, and Massachusetts were Protty; so it might be better to try a real sharp "spike" like Bishop Conkling of Chicago—"spike" being jocular in-language for an enthusiastic Anglo-Catholic, presumably in reference to the spikes of ecclesiastical candlesticks.

Chicago? Why, of course, for the Rector of Hinsdale, Richard Lee, was an old friend of Eleanor's, a cheerful, easy-going Broad Churchman who would surely be delighted that one of his former choir members was contributing a husband to the ministry. The combined influence of Doctor Lee and Father Taber opened Bishop Conkling's door, and we hopped on the Commodore Vanderbilt express for Chicago to see him. Again, in the pit of my stomach, the curious thrill of moving with the sunwise turn, to the West.

The Right Reverend Doctor Wallace Edmonds Conkling turned out to be quite a surprise, for as a rule bishops are selected for the same reasons as college presidents. They must be good fund-raisers and administrators, should give the appearance of the discreetly successful man of business, should be large in bulk, and have a fine memory for faces and names. Plus Wallace, who signed himself "+Wallace, Bishop of Chicago," was a warm iron hand in a velvet glove. He was certainly an administrator and, with prematurely snow-white hair, certainly patriarchal. He was also big. But he was also a mystic, of the *bhakti* or devotional type, and a sophisticated man of culture. He was, moreover, colorful, and went about in scarlet cassock and skullcap with a gold pectoral cross, as befitted the Diocesan of so great a See as Chicago. His *bhakti* approach lent a faintly androgynous style to his manner of speech and gesture, such as is always seen in the figures of Bodhisattvas, and he was undoubtedly a splendid pastor to most of his clergy. In fact he was too good to be a bishop and, for reasons of nasty holier-than-thou diocesan politics, he was eventually goaded into resigning. When Bishop James Pike was, in a somewhat similar way, squeezed out of the Diocese of California one found oneself scratching one's head to think of a great bishop of the Episcopal Church.

Bishop Conkling sent me out to the Northwestern campus in Evanston to see Bishop McElwain, who was then Dean of Seabury-Western Theological Seminary, awkwardly so named as an equally awkward amalgamation of the High Church Western Seminary of Chicago and the Low Church Seabury Divinity School of Minnesota. Here was a very short, perky, white-haired little man with an honest twinkle in his eyes and a rich, kind voice. Everyone loved his sermons, but you came out remembering only that voice and little or nothing of what he said—although once, during a class on the Greek New Testament, he said something rather deep for a bishop: "The mystery of the Cross is the heart of the universe." Bishop McElwain (pronounced Macclewain) conducted these classes, as well as a weekly meditation, in the quiet of a splendid and almost unused library devoted to the literature and antiquities of the ancient Near East, of the Hebrews, Chaldeans, Assyrians, Persians, and Egyptians. He also went through the whole Old Testament with us in a way that was as memorable as his sermons were forgettable, for he was a considerable scholar of Hebrew.

He hummed and hawed a little over my lack of credentials, but then said,

"Perhaps we could enroll you as a Special Student, that is, as one who will not be a candidate for the Bachelor of Divinity degree. Tell you what, why don't you send me a list of everything you've read on religion, history, and so forth, and I'll ask the faculty if this will do instead of the usual requirements." I sent him an honest bibliography—four pages in single-spaced typewriting—and that did the trick. Eleanor and I packed up our furniture in New York, and on the white rectangle left where there had been a Japanese screen I painted a large mural of the Tree of Life, attended by a stag and a unicorn.

Which reminds me that in those days I was an enthusiastic painter and calligrapher (in the Western Renaissance style). I worked in watercolor, ink, and tempera—never in oils—and was usually inclined to the jewel-like style of illuminated manuscripts and Persian miniatures, though I must have done hundreds of erotic drawings for raunchy friends. Paradoxically and typically, I also made icons, using the technique of putting varnish over watercolor to make it glow. The only one of these efforts to have been "seen" publicly was a painting of the Resurrection in my book *Easter—Its Story and Meaning*, a potboiler published by Henry Schuman in 1950. The work is identified as "Modern Indian—artist unknown." It is an indifferent mixture of the Persian miniature and one of Kay Nielsen's fantastic illustrations for fairy tales, for I was moved at one time to do a series of illustrations for the New Testament, in the obviously psychedelic style of the Persians and the Mughals, to displace the usual depressing Sunday-school style. I was tired of seeing Christ and his disciples dressed as Arabs against the arid background of modern Palestine, and wanted a Bible with the flavor of the *Arabian Nights*, where Jerusalem would look like the City of Brass and the Mount of Olives like Aladdin's garden of jewels. But I am not visually inventive. I am a copyist, and as time went on I contented myself with typographical design and Chinese calligraphy.

We rented a house in Evanston at Clinton Place, at the north end of the town and close to Lake Michigan, and once more boarded the Commodore Vanderbilt with Joan and our Negro maid, the beautiful Nettie. Like almost every house into which one moves, its interior was painted institutional buff, but this one had been expensively "antiqued" along the moldings to give an appearance of grime deposited by smog or of tobacco-stained teeth. We covered it all in pale green. This move dropped us right into the middle of Midwestern upper-middle-class suburbia, which has much the same values as its British equivalent, and from which I had been escaping most of my life. But now that I was deliberately going square, it was necessary for me to learn to act in style with this milieu, even if only for brief periods. Accordingly we watched football at Dyke Stadium, attended church socials and dances, bought life insurance, and sponsored poker parties for our friends and neighbors.

But the best poker parties were held next door at the home of Ernst Liegl, who was then first flutist with the Chicago Symphony, a true magician with the instrument, for whom music had become detestable. These parties were attended by other members of the Symphony, and all seemed to regard their art as a business, to be undertaken at stated hours and forgotten. This was partly because, at the time, the Symphony had an unpopular conductor, and partly because of the politics of professional music. The public may not realize that the psychological harmonization of a symphony orchestra is quite as important as—and indeed inseparable from—its musical competence, and these men spoke in glowing terms of conductors who could achieve it, of Pierre Monteux, Eugene Goossens, and Sir Adrian Boult. I felt, moreover, that this business attitude to music had something to do with a mentality of which Chicago is the spiritual center. In essence it is that everything done to earn a living must be regarded as a chore.

Of Chicago I can say only what Chesterton said of Pimlico (that dismal district of London near Victoria Station): "Take anything desperate—Pimlico for instance." Chicago has Lake Michigan. It has the noble and spacious "front" which extends for a few miles north of the Art Institute, and is now disfigured by a decapitated obelisk which might have been taken from an engraving of the Tower of Babel in a family Bible: the megamonstrous John Hancock Building. Otherwise it is a business-district slum where people are blown about like dust and wastepaper in the winds of both nature and commerce. On the Near North Side there are some warm and welcoming holes in which one can take shelter—the Cape Cod Room at the Drake, and Don the Beachcomber's, which, cornily Hawaiian as it may be, sustained us for nine years with excellent Chinese food washed down with navy grog and Kona coffee served with slices of lemon peel and flaming rum, and beguiled our spirits with the sounds and smells of lovelier climates.

It is often said that no one lives in Chicago except to make money, save those who have been captured there by the accident of birth. Now making money just for the sake of making money is a game, like bridge, in which people can find extreme pleasure and which can occupy almost all their waking hours. But one of the rules of the game is that you must pretend not to enjoy it. It must most definitely be classified as *work*; as that which you *have* to do as a duty to your family and community, and which therefore affords many businessmen the best possible excuse for staying away from home and from their wives. The nemesis of this attitude is that it flows over into the so-called leisure or nonwork areas of life in such a way that playing with children, giving attention to one's wife, exercising on the golf course, and purchasing certain luxuries (which are largely symbolic) also become duties. Survival itself becomes a duty and even a drag, for the pretense of not enjoying the game gets under the skin and tightens the muscles which repress joyous and sensuous emotion. To some extent this may be a penance for the exploitation of poverty, but, as should be well understood by this time, penances do nothing to correct evil: they are simply payoffs which allow business as usual.

It is thus that most businessmen work in environments, such as the average office, which are unpardonably ugly. I was astonished, in coming to America, to find that even doctors had offices—as distinct from consulting rooms, which were often pleasant libraries set about with works of art, with a surgery set off behind. Only quite rarely do people involved in the money game know what to do with money when they make it. They make ritual gifts to charity, religion, and the arts, but their beatific vision is crisp green paper in the hand, and this wholly abstract, inedible, and spiritual satisfaction far surpasses harems of fair women, wide lands and forests, gorgeous palaces and solemn temples, silks and furs, and even reasonably palatable food. By and large, no one is poorer in real wealth than a man of business. For he is a very strict ascetic.

In this atmosphere the arts and literature also become serious business instead of simple delight. Paintings and works of sculpture are bought and sold as investments, Picassos and Pollocks having ups and downs like shares in General Dynamics. William Earle, a professor of philosophy at Northwestern, pointed out that his up-to-date colleagues would not even dream of lying awake at night pondering vast problems of the universe. Instead, they arrive with briefcases at their offices, punctually at 9:00 A.M., and "do philosophy" (as they say) until 5:00 P.M., whereafter they return home to martinis, dinner, and television just as if they were accountants.[1] Performing musicians must join a trade union managed by goons who can barely whistle. My son-in-law, Joel Andrews the harpist, once showed me a bulletin from his union which consisted mainly of insulting directives to members, indicating how much they would be fined for this or that infringement of union rules.

There must be some connection between the commercialization of life and the separation of religion from mysticism and magic. It is, of course, well known that the lords spiritual and temporal of the feudal system gradually lost their power to the bankers and merchants during the centuries following the Reformation, and it is understandable that this new ruling class would want the Church to have no power of its own, but to be subservient to the mysticism and asceticism of money. Throughout my experience in the Episcopal Church I found that Anglo-Catholic trends were almost invariably opposed by "lay popes" in the form of prosperous businessmen on the vestry; "conservatives" with very short historical memories. It is thus that, in the late 1960s, the Anglo-Catholics began to make common cause with the Social Gospelers in opposition to racial intolerance and the Vietnam War, and wherever this happened, the big money was withdrawn from the Church.

Thus the religion of Seabury-Western had only a slight glimmer of the numinosity of Saint Mary the Virgin, for the simple reason that the clergy didn't really believe in it and, furthermore, were so impressed with the virtue of honesty that they lacked the nerve to put it across with sheer drama. But

---

[1] "Notes on the Death of a Culture," in Maurice Stein et al., eds., *Identity and Anxiety* (Glencoe, Ill.: Free Press, 1960).

being impressed with honesty really meant being impressed, however reluctantly, with the nineteenth-century mythology of objective realism which
became twentieth-century common sense. Their apologetics were preoccupied with feeble defenses against the Freudian view of religion as infantile
fantasy in the face of what Weston La Barre (himself a Freudian) has called
"the objectionable objective world": the world of geological and astronomical mindlessness in which living organisms are seen as alien flukes, as figs
upon thistles.

Almost all churches in the Middle West were as arid as mortuary chapels,
as if they were memorials to a dead religion. Seabury-Western was itself a
new structure in the ubiquitous Tudor Gothic style, though the lofty, long,
and narrow chapel with its high, thin spire harked back a little to the Per-
pendicular. By 1950 it had some of the best stained glass in the country, but
when I first saw it, it was a colorless alley lined with oak choir stalls where
the black-gowned seminarists sat in somber rows to chant the psalms of
Matins and Evensong—young men from Minnesota and Nebraska, Indiana
and Texas, Wyoming and Kansas, whose future lay in small towns with
churches where the Gothic arch was simulated in dark varnished wood.

Finding myself in a graduate school without ever having been to
college, I was somewhat in awe of the scholastic requirements, but after a
couple of weeks I was amazed to find myself getting A's on most papers, and
though my Greek was certainly rusty it was the best in the class. I soon found
I could get by with one night's formal study a week, and spend the rest of my
time reading what I pleased from the two libraries of the Seminary and the
library of Northwestern University. After one year of this I asked permission, which was given, to work on a tutorial basis without required attendance
at any class, and thereupon I "hit the books" with gusto for the sheer joy of
having two years without anything else to do. I read Harnack's *History of
Dogma* to find out whether Early Christianity had any forgotten secrets, and,
for the same reason, combed through Patristics, reading Clement and Origen,
the remains of the Gnostic writings, Saint Athanasius, Saint Irenaeus, Saint
Gregory Nazianzus, Saint John of Damascus, and the apocryphal literature
excluded from the New Testament. Then I went heavily into Russian theology—Solovyev, Berdyaev, Bulgakov, and the Hesychasts—and thereafter

became fascinated with the architectural magnificence of Saint Thomas Aquinas and his modern interpreters, Jacques Maritain and Étienne Gilson.

There followed mystical and ascetic theology: almost all the classics from Saint Dionysius to Leon Bloy, as well as the historians and commentators, Bremond, Underhill, von Hügel, Inge, Dom Cuthbert Butler, Dom John Chapman, and Garrigou-Lagrange. In the course of this I went scrounging in the basement of the Seminary library and discovered, thick in dust and scraps of decayed leather, the complete collection of Migne's edition of the Greek and Latin Fathers, and from this extricated the Greek text of Saint Dionysius's *Theologia Mystica* as well as the Latin translation by John Scotus Erigena. Later, under the critical eye of Father Elmer Templeton, the instructor in Greek, I worked this into English to find a Christian equivalent to the negative theology of Nagarjuna and Shankara.[2]

I had come upon Saint Dionysius by reading Aldous Huxley's *Grey Eminence*, in which there was considerable discussion of the almost vanished tradition of negative or apophatic mysticism in Christianity. This is the approach to God by "unknowing" (*agnosia*), that is, by silence of the mind and being simply at the disposal of God without holding any image or concept of God. Here, transcending its own symbols, Christianity came to the same place as Mahayana Buddhism and all the great traditions of contemplative mysticism. But with the Renaissance and Counter-Reformation it faded out in the growing popularity of Christocentric devotional mysticism, an affective and discursive form of "meditation" making great use of the visual imagination which interpreted Saint Paul's "pray without ceasing" as chattering to Jesus all the time, mostly about how horribly one has sinned.

It was at this time that I first met Huxley in person, and through him, I became aware of the British Mystical Expatriates of Southern California, to wit Huxley himself, Gerald Heard, Felix Greene, and Christopher Isherwood.

---

[2] This was published (with a very indifferent Introduction by myself) as *The Theologia Mystica of Saint Dionysius*, by the Holy Cross Press, West Park, New York, in 1944. It included also two of his Epistles. I have now reissued it with a new Introduction, since, deriving from Plotinus, Porphyry, and probably Asian sources, it remains the seminal work behind medieval Christian mysticism (Sausalito, Calif.: S.C.P., Inc., 1972).

They were all more or less associated with Swami Prabhavananda and the Vedanta Society of Hollywood and with Gerald Heard's *ashram* at Trabuco Canyon in the Santa Ana Mountains. Huxley and Heard in particular were developing a synthesis of Christian and Oriental mysticism such as I too had in mind, except that, at the time, their approach was to my mind too spiritual, and leaned towards an asceticism which sought final liberation from the body and the physical world. I, on the other hand, felt that the Christian stress on incarnation, on the Word made Flesh, implied a resolution of the spirit-matter dualism close to the position of Zen where

> This very earth is the Pure Land,
> And this very body the Body of Buddha.

I met Huxley during the 1943 Easter vacation, when we were visiting Ruth in New York, and there was the original cerebrotonic ectomorph of W. S. Sheldon's human typology, the tall, skinny intellectual—but with the difference that Huxley was a lot more than brains. Despite his reputation for cold, mordant wit, he was actually a kind, sensitive, and even sensuous man whose wit expressed genuine astonishment at the wondrous enormities of human folly. To get its full flavor you had to hear the essential which books can never convey, the sound of his lilting, aristocratic King's English, with its tone of gentle, scholarly detachment and benevolent amusement. He was such a magnificent conversationalist that once, while I was having lunch with him in a San Francisco restaurant, all those at the adjoining tables fell silent to listen to him. It was difficult for me to be with him for much more than half an hour without starting to imitate the rhythm of his speech. At this first meeting he was on the subject of fashions in medicine, for Aldous was always "on" something, usually the current preoccupations of his reading and writing. He was saying how curious and really alarming it was that fashions in medicine almost changed with the seasons, and it wasn't just in small points of detail. Why, not so long ago all kinds of people were undergoing complete removal of the large intestine, a really very expensive operation. The only trouble was that they had to go to the lavatory as often as birds. But now this whole treatment has been completely forgotten, and they are doing things like muddling up the prefrontal lobes of the brain by inserting an ice pick through the eye socket.

During all this study I was trying to get my inner being over the conflict of atmospheres between Buddhism and Christianity. There was little difficulty about intellectual reconciliation. The problem for so gregarious a person as myself was to be in constant company with people whose emotions were colored Christian. Belief in the forgiveness of sins seems to aggravate rather than assuage the sense of guilt, and the more these people repented and confessed, the more they were embarrassed to go creeping to Jesus again and again for his pardon. They felt simply terrible about drawing so heavily on the merits of the Cross, infinite as they might be, and idealized being good children in their paternalistic universe. But taking such as attitude to God seemed, for myself, maudlin, stupid, and out of character. I found myself simply incapable of taking any idol (that is, formulated idea) of God seriously, and felt it utterly silly to speak of God as "He." "She" might have corrected the balance, but so far as I was concerned God was "It" or "That."

Yet this, I suggested to myself in other people's words, may show a lack of ability to establish interpersonal relationships. "Doc" Kramer, our gritty-voiced and warmhearted professor of theology, spoke often of relating to God as to another person, to a Buberish "Thou" as distinct from a cold and neuter "It." Here there is some truth, for as I write this story it strikes me that I am better at describing ideas, events, and scenes than people, and seem to have little memory for dialogue—which explains why I have never been a novelist. But, putting it all in another way, I could say that this is for the same reason that I do not like to pick flowers. A flower goeswith a plant which goeswith a natural environment, and I see people as flowerings of their environments and not as separate objects. Thus warfare is like cutting off the tops of weeds, and saturation or nuclear bombing like wiping out whole gardens to create wastelands which upset the ecology of such cultivated areas as remain. Convention compels the novelist to "pick" people, because he writes in a culture where people feel basically disconnected from earth and sky.

Thus if a flower had a God it would not be a transcendental flower but a field—moreover a field as discussed in physics, an integrated pattern of energy, a field which would not only be flowering, but also earthing, raining, shining, birding, worming, and beeing. A sensitive flower would, through its roots and membranes, feel out into this entire pattern and so discover itself as a particular exultation of the whole field.

Now highly intelligent and sophisticated theologians are more influenced in their emotions by symbols than by ideas. The same is true of scientists who think in terms of quanta and physical fields, but feel in terms of machinery, in the nonorganic symbolism of steel, wire, and glass. I saw that if Christianity were to cease being ecologically poisonous there would have to be a shift of emphasis in its symbolism. It would have to tone down its patriarchal, political, and urban imagery; all such archetypes as the kingdom of God, the court of heaven, the legions of angels, the New Jerusalem, the armor of righteousness, and the dungeons of damnation. Instead, its organic and vegetative symbolism must come to the fore: the Body of Christ, the New Eden, the Rose Garden of our Lady, the Vine and its branches, the Water of eternal life, the Bread from heaven, the Tree of the Cross, and all the imagery of the Song of Songs. This, of course, would involve a shift to immanentism and even pantheism, which is the very devil to theologians in their black worsted suits and hard collars, their book-lined studies, and their hard stone churches. It would be like grass growing in the cracks of the altar steps, and the straight planks of the Cross giving forth branches and twisting into the shape of a tree.

Throughout my seminary and ministerial career I was always suspected of pantheism, but with a gift for semantic dexterity I could not be pinned down by people with one-track minds whose thinking was restricted to the linear order of the Book, with its one-way strings of words. For example, my own "pantheistic" view cannot be stated as a proposition, but must be felt as an experience. If one asserts that the universe is God, and by "the universe" means an ordered collection of separate things, then I am certainly no pantheist because I do not hold this conception of the universe. As I see it, every distinct or separate thing is a merely conceptual entity, isolated from the total field of the universe strictly for purposes of using a certain kind of language or method of charting the field. You cannot be a formal or propositional pantheist if you see that the chart is not the field, if you understand that a separate thing is real only in a system of abstractions. It is not physically or naturally real, for just as there cannot be necks without heads and trunks, there cannot be flowers without environmental fields. The field flows into the flower, and what we call the "thing"—flower—is a wiggle in the flow, while the flow itself, the energy of the universe, admits of no definition. The word "God" is more of an exclamation than a proper name. It expresses astonishment, reverence, and even love for our reality. If you want to put a human face on it, that will do—if you do not take it literally—since we know nothing higher or more mysterious than people, and an energy-field which peoples can hardly be less intelligent than people. Certainly events happen in the field which seem absolutely horrible, but faith is the gamble that there is some way of understanding or at least accepting them. I do not see what other attitude a sane person can take.

CHAPTER EIGHT

PARADOX PRIEST

And so it came about that on Ascension Day, 1945, I was ordained a priest, and formally exercised this priesthood for five years. It would not be quite true to say that those years have left a bad taste in my mouth, for I am simply reconciled to the fact that I make mistakes, and can be particularly foolish when attempting to do "the right thing." But I was simply "not myself" in the role of a Christian priest; that is, a praying and preaching priest in the Christian atmosphere of preoccupation with sin and with niceties of doctrine and belief. Yet there is another sense in which I seem to be a priest by nature and have priestly functions thrust upon me. Even today, personal friends ask me to name their children, celebrate their marriages, and bury their dead, because I have a feeling for ritual magic. To be precise, I am not so much a priest as a shaman. The difference is that whereas a priest is a duly ordained corporate officer and caste member in an agrarian culture, a shaman is a loner who gets his thing from the wilds, and is usually found in hunting cultures. Priests follow traditions but shamans originate them, though truly original traditions stem from the origins of nature and thus have much in common. The shaman follows his own weird, or destiny, and is thus considered a "weird" fellow, in the sense of transcending social convention. He is "out of this world" or otherworldly, and is credited with magical powers because he represents the uncanny and gets along in life without going by the usual rules and traveling by the beaten path. It is thus that when I am "successful," conventional people ascribe it to pure luck.

I chose priesthood because it was the only formal role of Western society into which, at that time, I could even begin to fit, not being qualified for

tinker, tailor, soldier, sailor, doctor, lawyer, merchant, or chief. But is was an
ill-fitting suit of clothes, not only for a shaman but also for a bohemian—
that is, one who loves color and exuberance, keeps irregular hours, would
rather be free than rich, dislikes working for a boss, and has his own code of
sexual morals. But this way of life is possible only for the successful and in-
depen-dent artist, craftsman, or author.

The economics of priesthood, or ministry, are such that most priests are
assigned to parishes as the rectors, vicars, or curates of churches which serve
particular areas. In the United States one serves not only a particular area
but also a particular subculture, and in this respect the Episcopal Church
gathers most of its membership from Americans of British descent who belong to the white-collar bourgeoisie. For original Americans or Americans
of African, Oriental, or other European descent it has, not self-supporting
parishes, but missions financed by the Church at large to recruit souls for
Christ among foreigners and heathens. A young priest without connections
is usually assigned to a mission, but if he is genteel and well-spoken he may
be taken on as a curate, or assistant, to the rector of a more affluent urban or
suburban parish. If you are bored with the description of this situation, you
will understand how much more I was bored with the actual prospect.

But from the beginning, I had no intention of getting involved in this
kind of ministry. My hope was to be able to set up a relaxed retreat-house
for contemplative religion, and I asked Bishop Conkling simply to let me
loose on Chicago as a priest-at-large, ostensibly to wangle intelligent and
wealthy people into the Church, but actually to initiate some sort of mechanism or process whereby the mystical approach to religion could become
available through the Church.

For this, the format of the parish church, whether Episcopal, Roman
Catholic, Methodist, or Presbyterian, is quite unsuitable. The principal function of these institutions is to hold services, and services—apart from certain
magical ways of celebrating the Mass—are not conducive to mysticism.
Neighborhood church religion is all talk—petitionary prayers and exhorta-
tory sermons—plus a certain amount of indifferent musical entertainment.
To practice meditation or contemplation in church you must gather together
an entirely new congregation, which was just what I had in mind, realizing

that what I had to contribute might be of little interest to standard Episcopalians. A priest friend of mine has tried to get his congregation into the right mood for Mass through some preliminary aids to stilling the mind, such as watching the breath and giving up compulsive thinking, only to find that his people were as disconcerted at his mention of such things as if he were advising them on playing golf or purchasing underwear. When Christians go to church they leave their bodies at the door.

The priest-at-large idea was too unconventional for the Bishop, but the next best thing was the ailing mission to the Evanston campus of Northwestern University. I suggested, therefore, that I move my family into Canterbury House, the Church's center for the University, next door to the Seminary, and see what I could do to prevent such professors as Bergen Evans and Paul Schillp from destroying the faith of good Episcopalian Alpha Delts and Pi Phis. Despite the run-down condition of the house and the miserable stipend, the situation gave me all the advantages of the academic environment and a congregation of young people whose religious ideas and attitudes were not yet firmly embalmed.

Adolph Teichert gave us the funds for redecorating the house, and Eleanor and I went to work with surgical masks over our mouths to remove a two-year accumulation of dust, garbage, and general filth from the premises. Within a month Eleanor, who had admirable taste and imagination in such matters, transformed 2046 Sheridan Road into a modestly palatial residence enclosing a small, baroquelike chapel dedicated to Saint Thomas-à-Becket of Canterbury. Beyond this, we had the use of the great Seminary chapel for Sundays, and there, over the five years of my chaplaincy, we wrought a magical liturgy which attracted not only undergraduate students from the University, but also members of the faculty, seminarists, stray adults in search of a religion, and deviates from the local Episcopalian parishes.

With the aid of volunteer choirmasters from the Northwestern School of Music (notably the then budding composer Carlton Gamer), we trained a small ensemble of men and women students to sing Gregorian chant and Renaissance polyphony, and a group of acolytes to assist at the Mass according to a stately Anglican version of the Western rite as it was followed before the questionable reforms of the Aggiornamento. We included also the dramatic rituals of Palm Sunday and the Vigil of Easter, holding the latter at midnight. We banned all corny hymns, and I never let a sermon run longer than fifteen minutes. I told the students that a celebration of Mass was indeed a celebration—a joining with the Cherubim and Seraphim, the Archangels and Angels, in the celestial whoopee of their eternal dance about the Center of the Universe—and that we wanted no skeletons at the banquet coming merely out of a sense of guilt or duty. I tried to exorcise their idea of God as a Victorian paterfamilias, saying instead that Creator and creation were an outpouring of reckless and ecstatic love, to be seen in Christ "as poor, but making many rich; as having nothing, but possessing all things," a love which had no other object than to share its own delight, and which (as Saint Athanasius put it) had in Christ become man that man might become God.

So we manifested a center of joyous worship, using the best resources of the Christian tradition. But the Dean of the Seminary, then Alden Kelley, with long experience of work with college students, warned me that our standards of worship were too high, and that our students would feel let down when they returned to their local parishes. He felt I should prepare them to take their places in the Church as it is, not in the Church as it could or might be. And then the mother of one of our students came to me saying, "Don't you realize, Father Watts, that you are just a decoy? The religion you are giving these young people is not the religion of Saint Luke's and Saint Mark's here in town, and from what I can see it isn't the religion of the Episcopal Church anywhere. They're going to feel very lost when they leave Northwestern."

It was more than what went on in church that would make the ordinary Episcopalian community seem relatively dull. Canterbury House was the scene of an almost perpetual bull session, involving students, seminarists, and members of the University faculty. I gave individual courses of "theological instruction" to anyone seeking it, and to every candidate for Confirmation (or adult initiation to the Church). Eleanor contrived Sunday afternoon tea-parties for the elegant young women from the sororities and their "beaus," parties which lingered on into the cocktail hour and became decidedly merrier than anything ordinarily foreseen in the prospect of tea at the vicarage. Sunday evenings were set aside for seminars, or informal lectures with discussion, which went on far into the night or dissolved into entertainments where Gloria Love—an angular and handsome lass with a genius for giving a false impression of total incompetence—would split our sides with zany improvisations on the piano. She had perfect pitch and could play by ear anything she had ever heard.

Somehow I seem to "collect" people with an itchy and even diabolical sense of humor. In this category there was, first, Richard Adams, then an ensign in the navy, later a seminarist and priest, and now a professor of the history of religions. Whenever we meet, Richard and I are unable to suppress ribald laughter concerning some permanent and always unstated joke. Neither of us know quite what it is, except that it is very deep and metaphysical, and has something to do with getting away with murder in heaven, and revolves about the flip point where *yang* turns unexpectedly into *yin*. This sense of humor has always prevented him from becoming a success as a clergyman, since there is no knowing when it will burst forth. He may well have carried out his threat to preach a sermon by hanging a biretta with a set of clockwork false teeth over the pulpit. In those days he was known as the Sorcerer's Apprentice, for he has a peculiar imagination for ritual, myth, and symbol, dreams the most Jungian dreams, and paints icons, and was therefore my chief liturgical assistant. He carried the thurible for incense at Mass, and, as we arrived at the altar in a cloud of smoke to the accompaniment of some angelic medieval hymn, neither of us could stop laughing; just as we were about to confess to God Almighty, Blessed Mary Ever-Virgin, Blessed Michael the Archangel, Blessed John the Baptist, the Holy Apostles Peter and Paul, and all saints, that we had sinned exceedingly in thought, word, and deed by our own most grievous faults.

Next there were John Gouldin and his mischievous girl friend, Jacqueline Baxter, both from the School of Speech, he an actor, singer, and stage-manager, and she a dancer. John was—and is to this day—a master of surprise transformations of junk, a trickster, and a showman whose verve and dexterity have never been properly rewarded. On Thursday nights—when people put out their junk for collection next morning—the three of us would cruise the streets in Eleanor's enormous black Packard sedan, I—then bearded and looking like Jesus in clericals—driving, and John eagle-eyeing the sidewalks and darting from the car whenever he spotted an abandoned saucepan to be turned into a clock or a cast-off doll to be sprayed with gold and made into an image of Shiva. Once he carried an air rifle on such an excursion and so loudly demolished a large street light that I had to swoop around the nearest corner and speed from the scene. He adorned the living room of Canterbury House with an astrolabe comprising a circle of plate glass engraved with the signs of the Zodiac centered around a copper sun, and suspended in a wide metal ring. He acquired cavalry sabers, ground off their sharp edges, and welded ball bearings to the points so that we could practice fencing. We gathered aluminum floats for fishnets from the Lake Michigan beach, stuffed them with match-heads, and exploded them. One night he arrived with a large helium-filled balloon, to which we attached a thin wire and a wad of Kotex soaked in gasoline, and set a flame floating far out over the lake so that people called the police to report flying saucers. He also sang in the choir.

And Jacqueline would do trick-dancing for us, or go limp and challenge the strongest man in the room to pick her up, which was impossible. This lithe, blond, elfin girl with a soft squeaky voice and pointed ears on her astral body had unsuspected depths. I keep a file, labeled SATORI, of letters from people who have written to me about their mystical experiences, and this, from Jacquie, goes back to September 1950 when she had been giving a sympathetic ear to a friend who had lost her husband:

> The oddest thing has happened: in my feeble attempts to help her, so many things have fallen into place for me. Oh, I do wish you were here to talk to; these things look so pretentious on paper. But, hang it, I have never felt so excited, and yet so calm, in my life. I have the same problems I've always had, and yet I can accept them. All of a sudden, I *expect* nothing. I *have* everything, and even if I lose all I have I still have *everything*! Do I sound positively crazy? . . . I'm at a loss to explain to her or even to you what I feel: that there is no God outside her letting things happen, but she herself who is making the trouble, and that God isn't *any thing*—he just is.
>
> I am verbally out of my element. . . . What do you SAY to a person when you want to convey so much more than, "This is the way

things are; in everything you see a beauty of a sort; that God is," and not in any soupy sort of way that sounds sentimental and soothing, because it isn't that way, and she wouldn't accept it that way, and neither would I. It has something to do with every minute being something of its own—enough in itself—although it might even be a very unhappy minute.

Well you probably think I'm loony?

And I probably am.

But, damn it all, it's the best looniness I've ever known!

I forget how I replied, but I should have quoted the following from the Zen Buddhist *T'an-ching*:

> In this moment there is nothing which comes to be. In this moment there is nothing which ceases to be. Thus there is no birth-and-death to be brought to an end. Wherefore the absolute tranquillity is this present moment. Though it is at this moment, there is no limit to this moment, and herein is eternal delight.

Then there was Emerson Harris—a vast, fair-haired, and handsome version of Mr. Punch, recently a sergeant in the marines who had been in the worst fighting on Guadalcanal, and now did valiant battle with the militant logical positivists who were taking over the department of philosophy. I once dreamed that he and I were flying about in a large room with our arms outstretched to imitate airplanes in combat, and going "Rat-tat-tat-tat-tat" at each other like children—the point being that we would have done just that if we could. He was that way. As I remember he was then courting one of our notable beauties, Margaret Jacobson, who later married James West, who was involved with my present wife's brother-in-law at OECD in Paris, who introduced my wife to Mary Holley Hicks, who went to college with Janice Chase, who once went with one of my wife's former boy friends and then married Benjamin Weininger, a noted psychiatrist with whom I became friendly, long before I met my wife, because of our mutual interest in Krishnamurti—and my wife has been threatening for years to write a novel called *The Net* which will show how everyone and everything is related to everyone and everything else.

Some of these students, like Richard Adams, were so, shall I say, beguiled by these activities that they went on to become priests, and if I did not feel that everyone is responsible for his own *karma*, I might reproach myself for leading them up a blind alley. But there was, for example, Robert Platman, a scholarly musician with a real gift for theological and philosophical thinking, who is now one of the most intelligent clergymen to be found and maintains an exquisite church on Long Island. There was also the colorful Robert Morse, whom everyone loved despite the enormous holes in his nonmatching socks, a huge dark fellow whose irrepressible and perfectly unmalicious humor so infuriated the more pompous spirits at the Seminary that he was denied the privilege of carrying the processional cross. Nevertheless, he became chaplain at the University of California at Berkeley, and his subsequent success as a priest derives from the fact that he is one of the few people who genuinely feels that God is exuberant love.

As I try to reconstruct and explain what I was doing in those days, I realize that many of my present friends and readers will feel that I temporarily lost my wits. It would be truer to say that I was trying to find them, for there were many respects in which I was still intellectually and emotionally confused, in ways that no longer trouble me. Despite all that I knew of Oriental philosophy, and despite some very real glimpses of mystical vision, I was still overly impressed with the spiritual authority of the Western and Christian traditions, and was trying desperately to come to terms with my own cultural history. Wide reading in theology had shown me that Christian belief was by no means the shallow mythology that I had supposed it to be when, as a boy of fifteen, I had abandoned it for Buddhism. Though by no means disposed to do a complete about-face and recant my Buddhist sympathies, I felt for a time that I could almost completely accept the Christianity of, say, Étienne Gilson or Evelyn Underhill. The fellowship of the Seminary and of other clergy had also had its persuasive effect, so that when I was ordained I was far more disposed to being a Christian than when I had first considered the ministry as a way of life.

I had even gone so far as attempting to use Christian forms of devotion and mental prayer in my own interior life, reciting the Divine Office from the Breviary, going to confession, and following the spiritual direction of Alan

Whittemore, a saint and religious genius who was then Superior of the Order
of the Holy Cross, a community of Anglican monks at West Park on the
banks of the Hudson. This tall, athletic, and joyously open-hearted man was
a full-blooded mystic who could not only sense the presence of God in every
flicker of light and sound, but had also reached the deep state of contemplative prayer where one feels God in the very feeling of not feeling him, the
state of the "divine darkness" or the "cloud of unknowing." He let me read
his extraordinary spiritual journal, a manuscript which—if still extant—
should be published forthwith, since it contains some of the finest mystical
writing in the Christian tradition.

Yet while I could participate with delight in the formal ritual of the liturgy,
the Christian style of the interior life went completely against the grain. At
Mass one could chant the words with one's lips, ignore their sense, and keep
one's mind on the presence of God. But personal talking and praying to God
in so many words just isn't in my nature. I feel it as a clumsy encumbrance
which not only puts God at a distance but also treats him as another person
or creature, however exalted and holy, and distracts one from the realization
that "God is nearer to you than you are to yourself."

Personal prayer simply got in the way of my fundamental mystical feeling that God is what there is and all that there is. It is obviously difficult
to feel this if you suppose that the universe is a work of pottery, wherein the
Divine Will has given form and order to some gross and basic stuff known
as matter. But any such stuff has escaped the detection of scientists as much as
spirit, since all scientific descriptions of the world are in terms of form and
structure, process and pattern, and never in terms (could they be found) of
any primordial, unstructured, inert, and stupid sludge—which would,
of course, be something quite other than God. Yet the ghosts of material and
spiritual stuffs or substances still haunt our common sense, and these obsolete metaphors from ceramics and metallurgy render it hard to see that there
is no such *thing*, no such definable object, as reality. We cannot classify what is
common to all possible classes, and yet we know very well that it is there!
And it has been obvious to me, for as long as I can remember, that whatever
it is, I am that, and whatever I am is also what stars and galaxies, space and
energy are.

My whole work in religion and philosophy has been to convey this feeling to others, and to show that our apparent separateness from what there is and all that there is arises, in the main, from our failure to notice space as a vital reality, which is just as important as the negative pole in an electric circuit. Although this feeling has not protected me from a vast amount of folly and confusion, just as it would not restore sight to a blind man, it has nevertheless delivered me from basic, existential anxiety. It is simply that I think people would be much happier and more at home in this world if they felt as I do, that I have no other self than this whole universe. I am not controlling it volitionally any more than I am controlling my autonomic nervous system, and at the same time it is not befalling or happening to any separate me as its observant victim. There is simply the whole process happening of itself, spontaneously, and with every pair of eyes it takes a fresh look at itself. This happening is what I call God, and what it is essentially is beyond all possible conception. I feel it most intensely in a stillness of mind where words and ideas are not running around in my brain.

But this sort of contemplation is virtually impossible while you are apologizing to Jesus, or God the Father, for your sins, asking him not to spank you, and telling him how great and glorious he is. More and more, all this struck me as jurisprudence rather than religion, and today it simply amazes me that for so many centuries the spiritual discipline of millions of ordinary Christians has never, except by chance, involved interior or mystical silence. It seems that even Quakers still go on thinking during their silent meetings. One can, of course, induce a form of this silence by saying a short prayer— such as the *Kyrie eleison*—over and over again until the words become meaningless sound and yet exclude other thoughts, a method used by the Hesychast mystics of the Eastern Orthodox Church. But Western Christians, Protestants especially, think of this as the vain repetitions of the heathen, who "think they will be heard for their much speaking," not realizing that vain repetition more aptly describes their own endlessly talkative devotions.

Yet, as I have said, the Christian tradition was so impressive, so hallowed with archaic authority, so confident of itself, and so grand with patriarchal personages that it got under my skin. I had to try it, even though I felt like a fool, and even though I imagined that feeling like a fool might be good for me by way of inculcating a proper humility. The vanity of self-deprecation runs one through some very weird mazes. Thus to get down on my knees and pray, especially when alone, is just plain icky. I wouldn't want people to do this to me if I were God the Father, for—as a matter of history—kings required their subjects to kneel at court so that they would be off their feet and unable to run or fight. Does God need to be on his guard? Must the citizens of heaven, like the courtiers of the Japanese shoguns, wear immensely long pantaloons in which they can only hobble? I could be accused of being unwilling to surrender my pride, but I prefer honest-to-God pride to the whining obsequiousness of deliberate self-humiliation. There is a significant difference here: the Christian kneels in prayer before his Lord and King, whereas the Buddhist sits in meditation along with the sitting image of the Buddha.

Thus, after a few years of experiment with prayer, of trying quite earnestly to get into a Christian frame of mind under the dangerous assumption that it might be good for me, I went back to meditation—especially walking meditation, which I have always preferred to long periods of sitting. For one reason, when walking there is no need for others to know that you are meditating and thus to feel guilty or embarrassed for not doing likewise. For another, the self-consciousness of sitting in a special way, of having a special time or place for the practice, does not obtrude itself. Thus I could go out for a walk, under the pretext of taking the air, or pace the floor, seeming to be thinking out a book or a sermon, and yet be absorbed in mystical silence of the mind. And, oddly enough, at the time it didn't really occur to me that I was practicing meditation, so that I have always considered myself rather lazy and haphazard in respect of this discipline. I didn't think of myself as doing an exercise, but simply as exploring a state of consciousness out of sheer interest. A Christian writer has said that the monk prays best who does not know that he is praying.

It was only natural then, that I began—in a round-about way—to speak about meditation to the students in my congregation and to the seminarists from next door who, sensing that I had an odd and interesting attitude to religion, used to come over to talk shop with me. This, in effect, made me an unofficial and subversive member of the theological faculty. At this time

I discovered an extraordinary little book by a seventeenth-century Jesuit, J. P. de Caussade's *Abandonment of the Divine Providence*, in which he insisted that the presence of the moment—the eternal now—should be regarded as the presence of God.

> If we knew how to greet each moment as the manifestation of the divine will, we would find in it all the heart could desire. . . . The present moment is always filled with infinite treasures: it contains more than you are capable of receiving. . . . The divine will is an abyss, of which the present moment is the entrance; plunge fearlessly therein and you will find it more boundless than your desire.[1]

This was exactly what I had discovered in Buddhist meditation years before, and have described in a previous chapter. But now I had the authority of a most orthodox Catholic for saying it out loud, and making excellent sense of the place in the Sermon on the Mount where Jesus speaks of taking no thought for the morrow, "no thought" being the literal equivalent of *wu-nien* in Zen Buddhism, and of what I have called mystical silence in which one is simply aware of what *is*, here and now, without verbal or ideational comment.

Used as they are to ideas of changing or transforming thought, feeling, action, or will, Christians hardly ever consider changing consciousness itself, but assume that the usual feeling of "I" is our sensation of the soul and not a socially sanctioned hallucination. But intelligent Christians welcome, and are indeed hungry for, some deeper dimension of religious experience than emotional uplift, and thus it was not long before I found myself conducting retreats and being sought out for spiritual counsel by people from all over the country. For at the same time I was writing on these matters in the *Holy Cross Magazine* and, in 1947, published *Behold the Spirit*, subtitled "A Study in the Necessity of Mystical Religion,"[2] a modestly scholarly book which moved the faculty of the Seminary to award me a master's degree in theology.

---

[1] J. P. de Caussade, *Abandonment to the Divine Providence*, trans. Ella McMahon (New York, 1887), 2. 10, pp. 79–81.
[2] Originally published by Pantheon Books, New York, this book was reissued by that publisher in 1971.

In fact, *Behold the Spirit* was not narrowly confined to mysticism. It was a miniature *summa*, containing my total view of Christian theology at the time—of doctrine, ethics, and liturgy, as well as the special domains of ascetic and mystical theology—and I was bending over backward to speak from within the Christian tradition and to use theologically acceptable language. Compared with most of my other works, it is, therefore, a very *serious* book written for people who are, so to speak, tush about religion and speak of it gravely in a lowered voice. Bernard Iddings Bell, who was then my opposite number at the University of Chicago, hailed it as one of the century's most important books on religion, and it seemed that I was on my way to fame as a theologian. Requests for lectures and retreats took me to New York, Boston, Dallas, Pittsburgh, and San Francisco, and the reception was, on the whole, so warm that I might have ended up as a bishop, were it not that I found my role as a clergyman increasingly embarrassing.

For one thing, I had gone back to the Buddhist practice of the interior life, and I was also keeping up my studies of Oriental philosophy, reading the works of Ananda Coomaraswamy and René Guénon, in particular because these two authors had some sympathy for medieval Catholic theology and mysticism as a form of the *philosophia perennis*—along with Vedanta, Sufism, Taoism, and Mahayana Buddhism. I was, therefore, less and less impressed with the authority of the Christian tradition, especially in those respects in which it diverged from the others. I began to see the imperious claims of the Church as fatal weaknesses which made it more freakish than unique. The insistence on Jesus as the one and only historical avatar or incarnation of God, the urge to proselytize, and the passionate adherence to such improbabilities as corporal resurrection should, in my judgment, have gone the way of worshipping relics and burning heretics.

In retrospect I see that if I had persisted, I would have seemed more orthodox than Bishops James Pike and John Robinson, let alone the "death of God" theologians, and it would have been easy to show that there was excellent historical precedent for giving certain biblical tales a nonliteral interpretation. Furthermore, as I have said, neither the scriptures nor the creeds specify the type of language they are speaking, whether literal and historical, allegorical, mythical, or analogical. If it is not to be supposed that the ascended Christ sits quite literally at the right hand of the Father, must we still give literal sense to the dogmas of the Virgin Birth and the bodily Resurrection? It struck me, moreover, that to treat such doctrines as mythic images made them all the more interesting, for what, other than the mere shock of the thing as a manifestation of power, is so edifying and inspiring about a case of human parthenogenesis and revivification of a corpse? The interest of power, including miraculous power, is not in its simple existence but in what is done with it, and Christian ideas of the final miracle—heaven—have never shown any great imagination. There is something even puerile in debates between members of different faiths as to the validity and superiority of their various signs and wonders.

If strictly theological problems had been the only concern, I could have worked on as a priest, and might have persuaded many Christians to grow up and see their religion in a global context. *Beyond Theology* might even have been selected by the Presiding Bishop as his annual Book for Lent! But the more serious problem was that in taking the role of priest I was, willy-nilly, saying things about myself that I did not want to say. The clerical garb and title imply the claim to be better and holier than other people, and one is simply assumed to be on the make for converts, and to consider oneself as an officer of the one and only valid religion. People are automatically afraid of being themselves in a clergyman's presence, and because of this many priests affect a superficial worldliness to be able to get along with layfolk. These automatic suppositions about the clerical role underlie the humor of ecclesiastical anecdotes about the lovable foibles of priests, foibles that would pass without comment in ordinary people. Thus Father Whittemore would re-gale us with tales about his brother monks: how Father Huntington, the founder of the Order, would—in public conveyances—extract a large black bottle from his robes and take a swig from it, and how that extremely holy contemplative and stern novice-master, Father Hughson, would put on his spectacles and gloat over a box of chocolate candies which he had confis-cated from one of the novices, having just given them a lecture implying that it was a venial sin even to lick a postage stamp between meals.

But the major social assumption about the clergy is that their sex life is either nil or very strictly monogamous, because the Church continues to give the impression that sexual sins are by far the naughtiest—so that such phrases as "living in sin" or "a virtuous woman" have a purely sexual connotation. Furthermore, conservative churchmen have utterly unrealistic ideas on the permanence and sanctity of marriage, and preachments on conjugal chastity come strangely when they are from the lips of men whom one knows to be active homosexuals. For sex, like truth, will out, and in this respect the clergy are just like other people. You may be sure that those who lay down a hard line of sexual rectitude are talking mainly to themselves. You may also be sure that celibate clergy with fine taste in ritual, vestments, and music are, for the most part, homosexually inclined if not active, and in my book this is not against them, so long as they do not preach chastity to those who prefer women.

Now I have what might be called a temperamental incapacity to understand conventional sexual mores. I can see no association of sex, per se, with dirt—unless, perhaps, one takes the flea's-eye view of sex often found in our new full-color pornographic magazines. Perhaps that is most people's view. Perhaps the idea of its being dirty is just what arouses them. I can see no good reason for regarding anyone as my exclusive sexual property, or being so regarded myself, just as no one else is my exclusive property for dining, walking, talking, or working together. What two human beings do together in private, by mutual consent, is as little other people's business as anything can be, though if they have accidents—such as pregnancy or disease—as a consequence, they must together be as responsible as if they had had an accident while driving, and although it is hard to know which of the two adventures is the riskier, people seldom get killed by intercourse.

My own sexual mores are largely principles of style and taste concerning how and with whom I should participate in the most intimate pleasure that people can give to each other. By nature, I enjoy such pleasure only with the feminine sex, and only if it is equally pleasurable to my partner. Thus the Augustinian saying, *Omne animal post coitum triste est*, is true for me only if I fail to delight her. Otherwise, I could crow. For this reason I have never employed a prostitute, imagining most of them to be difficult to please. I do not believe that I should be passionately in love with my partner—though it is the best of pleasures under such circumstances—and still less, married. For there is a special and humanizing delight in erotic friendships with no strings attached. If marriages are holy and made in heaven, the proverb still applies that God gives us our relations, and let us thank him we can choose our friends. My life would be much, much poorer were it not for certain particular women with whom I have most happily and congenially committed adultery, and the value of such friendships is not to be measured by the calendar. There are women to whom I am permanently grateful for but one or two embraces, and I have every reason to believe that they feel the same way towards me, for our sexual communion was the natural culmination of our admiration for one another as people.

And what a person is includes the so-called physical body, which is not simply a given chunk of flesh and bones, statically considered, but the way it moves, its rhythms, its voice, and its perfume. For the body is as much a streaming pattern of energy as a flame. Indeed, I hesitate in speaking of the body as "it." Nobody likes to be treated as an it, to have shapely breasts, chest, shoulders, neck, hips, bottom, genitals, or legs considered as if they were external appendages that might go with just any body. For all that, they are nonetheless admirable, and one must not feel treated as an it if fondled in certain particular places. To a discerning and sensitive eye, a bottom shows character as clearly as a face, for the whole organism is manifested in every one of its features. Yet, as of today (1972), I am vaguely aware of a growing prissiness among intelligent women as a, nevertheless, understandable reaction against being treated as lust dolls. But if you disown your body, and think of yourself and want to be appreciated purely as your soul or character, your body does indeed become a doll, a mere vehicle in which the abstract "you" goes around.

Men's attitude to women invariably reflects their attitude to nature as a whole, and thus I have often said that if the tacit goals of technological progress were realized, if all events were predictable, and all natural phenomena perfectly controlled, life would be like having intercourse with a plastic doll. You cannot have an experience called "self" without an experience called "other." This is why the two are really one, which is both self and other and yet neither, as may be realized in the climax of sexual love.

As for marriage, there is nothing wrong with it except the legal institution.

The natural event of a man and woman living in constant companionship, with or without children, is an admirable arrangement which works to the degree one does not insist that it *must* work, and does not treat one's partner as property. Another being regarded as property is automatically a doll. Whenever I perform a ceremony of marriage for personal friends, I give some such discourse as this:

"What I am about to say may at first sound depressing and even cynical, but I think you will not find it so in practice. There are three things I would have you bear in mind. The first is that as you now behold one another, you are probably seeing each other at your best. All things disintegrate in time, and as the years go by you will tend to get worse rather than better. Do not, therefore, go into marriage with projects for improving each other. Growth may happen, but it cannot be forced. The second has to do with emotional honesty. Never pretend to a love which you do not actually feel, for love is not ours to command. For the same reason, do not require love from your partner as a duty, for love given in this spirit doesn't ring true, and gives no pleasure to the other. The third is that you do not cling to one another as to commit mutual strangulation. You are not each other's chattels, and you must so trust your partner as to allow full freedom to be the being that he and she is. If you observe these things your marriage will have surer ground than can be afforded by any formal contract or promise, however solemn and legally binding."

A couple that would object to this discourse should not marry.

My first marriage came to an end from neglect of the third of these precepts, and my second from mutual neglect of the first. In the summer of 1949 I was writing *The Supreme Identity* in an attempt to put Christian theology and Indian philosophy into a constructive relationship, and at the same time Canterbury House was a buzz of activity, with seminarists, professors, students, clergy, and wandering seekers from all over. I was also being invited, more and more, to give lectures and conduct retreats away from home. Inevitably, the problems of sex and marriage came into these discussions, and Eleanor was increasingly disturbed by my libertarian views. Under the circumstances she acted with great tact and consideration, for in the autumn she simply feigned sickness as a result of the pressure of work, and went to live with her mother in New York. A little later she went quietly to Nevada and, without fanfare, had our marriage annulled for the interesting reason that, if I believed in free love, I could only have contracted a monogamous marriage under false pretenses. I made no contest, and handed back the capital assets she had made over to me.

In ecclesiastical circles gossip flies faster than elsewhere, and it was not long before Bishop Conkling heard of this interesting legal decision, and wanted to know whether I was indeed a believer in free love. About the same time I had been giving a series of lectures at Saint Ignatius's Church in New York, which is—if possible—higher and more Rococo-Catholic than Saint Mary the Virgin, and my work had just come to the attention of Douglas Auchincloss, who was then the religion editor of *Time*. He sent a photographer to cover my lectures at Saint Ignatius's—a thorough and enthusiastic fellow who insisted on posing me, garbed in lacy surplice, in front of the high altar which there resembles something between Milan Cathedral and a soda fountain. As I surveyed the background I involuntarily expressed the qualm, "I say, isn't this too terribly churchy?" To which the photographer replied, "But it's what you *believe* in, isn't it?" Obviously I didn't.

This was, then, the final straw in the slow process of realizing that I would have to go it alone and work outside the sphere of organized religion. Upon returning to Evanston (this was June 1950) I found the Bishop's letter of inquiry, to which I responded with a careful letter of resignation, the substance of which I later circulated among my friends in the form which appears in the appendix to this chapter. Thereafter I disappeared from Northwestern to the seclusion of a farmhouse in Millbrook, New York, near the desultory town of Poughkeepsie, where, during the six months following, I wrote a book appropriately called *The Wisdom of Insecurity*. Readers will note the strong influence of Krishnamurti in this work, for I had been rereading him thoroughly so as to recognize that it wasn't just that I didn't believe in the Anglo-Catholic religion (as taught), but that I didn't believe in believing. I saw belief as the antithesis of faith, as anxiety rather than trust, as holding on rather than letting go—and any form to which one clings becomes an idol.

To keep the custody of my two children, Joan and Ann, I married again.

Previously I had discovered that Bishop Conkling was such a stickler for what A. P. Herbert had called "Holy Deadlock" that he would permit no remarriage so long as I remained in the Church. The lady was Dorothy DeWitt, a graduate student in mathematics, who had been my most devoted helper at Northwestern, and I imagined—erroneously, as it turned out—that her extraordinary good sense about practical matters would rub off on me. It took a long time to realize that our aspirations for each other were absolutely incompatible: I would never become what she wanted me to be, and she would never become what I wanted her to be. Despite what I was writing about the futility of trying to lift oneself up by one's own bootstraps, both of us still seemed to believe (she more than I) in the potency of effort and willpower in the process of psychological transformation.

I should have known by then that self-improvement is a dangerous form of vanity. By the age of thirty-five one's character is firmly formed, and has to be regarded as an instrument to be used rather than changed. When you try to be other than what you are, you give people expectations that are most unlikely to be fulfilled. To avoid being a serious disappointment to others you must accept and respect your own limitations. The difficulty of being humble, and even kind, is that it often requires that you be frankly selfish, that you discover your real feelings and follow them as if they were holy scripture.

This should be easy. As a Zen master has said, "Act as you will. Go on as you feel. This is the incomparable way." Rabelais's *Fay ce que vouldras*. But it took me ten more years to get up the nerve to do it, during which time I strove to be a good family man, to everyone's immense disappointment. Our ideas of what we should be have generally about as much relation to what we are as the grid plan of streets to the hills of San Francisco, to which it should be added that there is an equal lack of correspondence between what we really feel and what we think we feel. Thus, when those who speak of civilization as a "thin veneer" over barbarism attempt to be spontaneous or, as in wartime, to abandon convention, they do indeed behave like barbarians—as if it were a duty. Responsiveness to the subtle motions of inner feeling is as much an art as sailing, and is entirely untaught in schools. Surely, if our neurologists are the first to admit that they do not understand the brain, isn't it possible that the brain—and the nervous system as a whole—is wiser than the conscious intellect? For conscious intellect is only a fragmentary use of the brain, bound to the cumbersome process of linear thinking, which cannot—without long deliberation—synthesize more than a few variables. But the brain regulates thousands of bodily processes at a time without having to think about them, and this—not one's personality—is the self.

This began to dawn on me, albeit dimly, when I met Lancelot Law Whyte at the University of Chicago shortly before my resignation. I had just read his *Next Development in Man*, and we were both invited to take part in the University's radio forum, the Round Table of the Air. This gentle, modest, and twinkly-eyed Englishman is difficult to classify. A freelance theoretical biophysicist with interests in mathematics, psychology, anthropology, and history will do for a try. But I would put him with Gregory Bateson, Joseph Needham, and John Lilly as one of the most intellectually stimulating scientists I have known. Every time I have seen him he has given me a radically important new idea, and it was he who first showed me, from the scientific viewpoint, the disparity between linear thinking and the multidimensional, organic patterning of the physical world, and pointed out what he termed "the European dissociation" of the conscious ego from the total nervous system.

Through him I saw that the main difficulty of Western religion was its linearity—its one-way-street version of history, and its obsessive verbosity, as if the will of God could be expressed in the strung-out form of statements and commands—so curiously unlike the patterns and organic forms of nature. I could see why religion becomes demonically destructive when it goes by the book and tries to make the dancing order of nature conform to the marching order of law, and force this essentially wiggly universe to toe the straight and narrow line. This is why the world's most terrible idol has been the Holy Bible. This also explains why I had always felt a strange difference of style between things churchly and things natural, for it struck me that the God worshipped in Church could no more have designed nature than Euclid could have written *Finnegans Wake*. Small wonder, then, that I came out buffeted and bruised from the experiment of trying to straighten out my wiggly nature to pass the narrow postern of Saint Peter's Gate.

APPENDIX

From Alan W. Watts, Thornecrest Farmhouse, Millbrook, N.Y.

My dear Friends:

After long and careful thought I have had to take a step which will perhaps be most disturbing to many of you, though to others it may come as no surprise. I have come to the conclusion that I cannot remain in either the ministry or the communion of the Episcopal Church.

In retrospect, I believe that I entered the ministry under the influence of a tendency which has become rather widespread—a tendency to seek refuge from the confusion of our times by giving in to a kind of nostalgia. In a world where all the traditions in which men have found security are crumbling, the mind seeks peace and sanity in an attempt to return to a former state of faith. It envies the inner calm and certitude of an earlier age, where men could put absolute and childlike trust in the authority of the Church, and in the ordered beauty of an ancient doctrine.

Undoubtedly the form of Christian doctrine and worship contains the most profound truth, but I am afraid that the attempt to maintain and revive it is an ineffectual resistance to inevitable change. For so many people, the forms no longer convey their meaning, and the language they speak is both archaic and cumbersome. Others *want* to believe, and try to convince themselves that they do so, but their faith has that hollow self-consciousness so characteristic of the modern convert, since the mind is acting a role untrue to its inmost state. You cannot imitate faith, and when forms of belief, like all other finite things, begin to die, the effort to revive them is imitation. It doesn't ring true. But the forms perish, not only because they are mortal, but also because the Spirit within them is breaking them as a bird breaks from its shell.

We are living in a time of disintegration and iconoclasm which the Hindus call Kali Yuga. It hurts and frightens us, but is not essentially evil. It is rather a universal Passion in which man cries, "My God, my God, why hast thou forsaken me?" But it is the prelude to a Resurrection, because spiritual growth depends upon ceasing to cling to any form of life for security. Forms are not contrary to the Spirit, but it is their nature to die; their transiency is their very life, and a permanent form would be a monstrosity—a finite thing aping God.

The Spirit uses forms, and reveals itself through them, for which reason they are both wonderful and necessary. But they are not exempt from the simplest law of life—that, like every other living thing, to grasp them is to strangle and kill them. To preserve them in death is to cling to corruption.

He who is, for Christians, *the* form of God, the "express image of his Person," did not forget to warn us: "It is expedient for you that I go away, for if I go not away the Paraclete cannot come unto you." After his Resurrection the same warning was given to Saint Mary Magdalene: "Do not cling to me!" The tragedy of the Church is that in trying to love form, it has denied its whole nature by attempting to make it absolute. The image and the words of Christ himself have been corrupted in the very act of giving them permanent and absolute authority. He has been made into an idol which must be destroyed in his own Name.

I do not want anything that I say here to hurt the Church. For the Church is people—people whom I have learned to love. For that very love I cannot be a party to their hurting themselves and others by seeking security from forms which, if understood aright, are crying, "Do not cling to us!" Out of very gratitude for all that the Church has done for me, I must be honest, and say what I see to be true.

Insofar as the Church is committed to a desire for and a clinging to authority, permanence, spiritual safety, and absolute guides of conduct, it is clinging to its own death. By such means, belief in God, the hope of immortality, and the quest for salvation, become only escapes from the inner emptiness and insecurity which most of us feel in the depths of our being when confronted with the loneliness, the transiency, and the uncertainty of human life. But that inner emptiness is not a void to be filled with comforts; it is a window to be looked through. It is not an evil that life—our own life—flows, changes, and passes away. It is a revelation to prevent us from clinging to ourselves, for whoever lets go of himself finds God. The state of eternal life and oneness with God comes to pass—like a miracle—only when we release our grasp on every kind of spiritual security. To cling to security is only to cling to one-self, and perish of strangulation.

It would be a silly kind of pride to pretend that we can surren-der this passion for safety just by trying. It is not effort that breaks the vicious circle of self-strangulation; it is an awareness and un-derstanding of its complete futility. To be aware of this futility is to look through the emptiness within—that window into heaven which affords the vision of God.

Much of this has a familiar ring to the Christian. "Whosoever would save his soul shall lose it." But I have found that you cannot make the point clear within the Church as it exists without running into contradictions at every step. The liturgy is cluttered beyond hope with sentiments, prayers, and hymns conceived in the state of anxious grasping to forms. And that is by no means all.

During the past years I have continued my studies of the spiri-tual teachings of the Orient, alongside with Catholic theology, and, though I have sometimes doubted it, I am now fully persuaded that the Church's claim to be the best of all ways to God is not only a mistake, but also a symptom of anxiety. Obviously, one who has found a great truth is eager to share it with others. But to insist—often in ignorance of other revelations—that one's own is supreme argues a certain inferiority complex characteristic of all imperi-alisms. "Methinks thou dost protest too much." This claim to su-premacy is, for me, the chiefest sign of how deeply the Church is committed to this self-strangulation, this anxiety for certainty, and I cannot support the proselytism in which it issues.

It has been my privilege to know priests of the Church who are men of wonderful humility. But, whether they intend it or not, their assumption of that office usually becomes, in the eyes of laymen and the general public, a claim to spiritual authority and moral superiority. Beyond doubt there are priests who speak with true authority and who are morally superior. But to claim such gifts vitiates them, even when the claim is tacit or derivative, and is a stumbling-block to those who mistakenly cling to authority in their quest for security. For true authority says, "Let go. You will only find God if you do not try to possess him." I must, then, do what lies in my power to renounce event tacit claim to superiority, whether spiritual or moral. For one reason, such a claim would be untrue. For another, the expectation that every clergyman be a moral exemplar is an aspect of that unfortunate moral self-consciousness which has so long afflicted the Western world.

The best Christian thought has always seen that only Pharisaism comes through trying to be good. For sanctity is less in wanting to be moral than in loving God and other men. But the moralism which condemns a man for not loving is simply adding strength to that sense of fear and insecurity which prevents him from loving. You may help him to live neither by condemning nor consoling, but by encouraging him to understand and accept the fear and insecurity which he feels. Yet one who tries to suggest this healing acceptance of fear within the framework of the Church is again beset by contradictions, since in all its official formularies and utterances the Church is either threatening with penalties or consoling with promises. The result is to exploit and aggravate man's fear, to foster a simulated love which is fear in disguise—fear running away from itself—for love will no more grow from such blind fear than the grape from the thorn.

The unhappy effects of this moralism appear quite devastatingly in the realm of marriage and of the love between man and woman, as I have discovered from my own hard experience. This is one of those emotionally charged subjects whereon those who disagree accuse one another of the wildest excesses, as if there were no alternative but to be either a puritan or a libertine. Because of this "emotional charge" it is almost impossible to get churchmen to face the subject frankly, or to approach it without laws and attitudes manifesting, not love, but possessiveness and fear. Despite all the work that has recently been done upon them, the Church's laws of marriage, because of the spirit underlying them, remain as inadequate to deal with its problems as a crowbar for unraveling fine thread. For when, in fear, we try to make the relationship of love absolute, we make it, not divine, but merely inhuman.

We are now in the strange and, indeed, scandalous position that a conjugal relationship not in accord with the Church's law is, with few exceptions, the sole effective reason for excommunications. Some have said that this is because such relations are the special "sin of our age," but in fact they are no more so than pride, heresy, hatred, slander, and greed, which flourish as habitually as ever. But there is slight chance of their affecting one's "communicant status" in the Church.

I am not pointing out this anomaly as one of those who

Compound for sins they're most inclined to
By damning those they have no mind to.

I am citing it as a glaring example of the confusion to which all self-conscious moralism leads. For, despite all fine words to the contrary, the Church's attitude to marriage, as to so many other things, issues not from love but from a desire for security. In this the Church is not peculiar. The same attitude, though it assumes other forms, is popular, to say the least. Obviously a man who marries a woman (or vice versa) for security does not love her. If he does love her, no law is necessary to protect such love. Indeed, a "love" which hedges itself about with absolutist laws is merely a relationship in which husband and wife cling to one another in such a way that their self-strangulation is mutual. Such a marriage becomes only a "holy deadlock" which is certainly no beneficial atmosphere for the children whom much of this security-legislation is supposed to protect.

Let us be frank, and admit that all this legislation is not for love or spirituality, but for the protection of a necessary social institution which, however, it protects none too well. If, as is inevitable, there must be laws governing marriage, let it be stated plainly that their function is more political and social than spiritual, and let it not be assumed that marriages based on fallible human choice are "made in heaven." "Those whom God hath joined," those united in the spirit of love rather than possessiveness, expect no guarantees and ask no protection.

Am I, in all that has been said here, demanding of the Church a spiritual perfection which cannot be forced—falling into the old heresy of antinomianism, which expects all Christians to be so completely in the Spirit that they need no law? I ask no such thing. Nothing is further from my mind and my meaning than to condemn the Church for falling short of an ideal. My departure from the Church is not a moral protest; it is simply that, seeing what I see, I cannot do otherwise. I take no credit for it. My viewpoint is not one of moral judgment and condemnation, but of simple inability to conform to a rule of life based on what I see to be illusions.

What I see is what life has shown me: that in fear I cling to myself, and that such clinging is quite futile. I have found that trying to stop this self-strangulation through discipline, belief in God, prayer, resort to authority, and all the rest, is likewise futile. Trying not to be self, trying to realize an ideal, is simply the original selfishness in another form. Worship as an expression of joy or thanksgiving I can understand. But spiritual exercises or moral disciplines undertaken to raise oneself by one's own spiritual bootstraps are absurd, for they are based on the illusion that the "I" who would improve is different from the "me" who must be improved. And to ask for the grace to be so improved is merely an indirect form of the same thing.

The more clearly I see this, the less choice I have in the matter: I cannot go on doing it. The more I am aware of the futility of myself trying not to be selfish, of the contradiction of myself even desiring or asking not to be selfish, or to love where I do not love, I have no choice but to stop it. At a yet deeper level, the more I see the futility of myself clinging to myself, I have no choice but to stop clinging. In this choiceless bondage one is miraculously free. For where the actual possibility of "I" loving "me" is seen to be an illusion, the vicious circle is broken, and there remains only that outflowing love which is called God.

Much more remains to be said, but in this brief space I can do no more than sketch the point of view on which I must act. But I do want to warn any of you who might want to follow my example and leave the Church likewise. You cannot act rightly by imitating the actions of another. This is to act without understanding, and where there is no understanding the vicious circle goes on. I have no wish to lead a "movement" away from the Church. If any leave, let them do so on their own account, not from choice, but because they feel they "should," but only if understanding makes it clear that, for them, there is no other alternative.

I expect, now, to devote most of my time to writing and lecturing, not because I wish to make converts, but because I love this work more than any other, because it enables me to live and take care of my family, and because I believe I have something to say which is worth saying.

Faithfully yours,

Alan W. Watts
August 1950

For the record, some correspondence following from this letter may be of interest.

From Canon Bernard Iddings Bell

Dear Alan:

It is difficult to answer your letter of the 11th August, or to comment on the printed apologia that came with it. There is, on the one hand, danger of my being so moved by compassion that I fail to speak my mind honestly and, on the other hand, a possibility that what I say in all sincerity may serve only to wound a man who has lately been through hell.

I think about all I can do is to tell you, both how sorry I am that you have been tortured and also how much I regret that you have circulated so weak a defense. I do not doubt your intended honesty, but the apologia reads painfully like rationalization. It reads, indeed, like *hasty* rationalization, incomplete in your own eyes. I find some comfort in thinking it incomplete and that you will see things in different and clearer focus later on.

Meanwhile, you have burned your bridges. I hope that you will not find life, in consequence, as barren in older age as did another friend of mine who was deposed, after a not too different experience, the late Albert Jay Nock. It is not easy, not possible, to undo spiritual commitments. You are a priest forever—and a priest inhibited. You think you can wipe out your ordination, restore that which was before your ordination, start all over. You can't. Life is not like that. What has been, still is.

I remain your friend, but I see no good in our seeing one another, nor in correspondence, at least for as long as you are able to persuade yourself you are content. If ever this becomes no longer possible, call on me and count on an understanding response.

Ever faithfully yours,

B. I.

University of Chicago, August 30, 1950

To which I replied:

My dear B. I.:

I have delayed to answer your letter because you did not wish correspondence. At the same time I do not wish to slight the spirit in which you wrote by being dumb, because I appreciate both your kindness and your frankness very much indeed.

One has to speak of "giving up the priesthood" as an accommodation to convention and Canon Law. I know that I am a priest forever, and have no thought whatever of going back to a former state, or making a fresh start. As you say, such things are simply impossible.

But at the altar it was one of my functions to break the Body of Christ that his life might be spilled into the world. I find the successors of Christ unwilling that this should happen, having tried to turn him who is Life, and God incarnate, into a Rock, which is a dead thing. It is, then, the logical fulfillment of my priesthood that I must break the Body of Christ in act as well as in symbol. I understand this not only as risking my own body, but also as breaking, and breaking with, the use of Christ as a means of spiritual safety.

One may embrace this kind of insecurity as a gesture of adolescent bravado. One may also embrace it, because, having seen the futility of other courses, there is nothing else to do. As a result I feel my priesthood to be uninhibited rather than, as formerly, inhibited.

My vision is not infallible, but we may both have the joy of knowing that, if I am right and you are wrong, or vice versa, neither of us can dim the glory of God , save by being untrue to the light as we see it. And even then it shines in spite of our darkness.

Most sincerely yours,
Alan
Millbrook, New York, October 1, 1950

FROM DR. E. STANLEY JONES

My dear Mr. Watts:

I have your letter of August 12 with the enclosure which I have read with the deepest interest.

I followed you in much that you said in this explanation about your leaving the church until I came to one sentence which gave me a big question mark: "During the past years I have continued

my studies of the spiritual teachings of the Orient." You further
state: "I am now fully persuaded that the Church's claim to be the
best of all ways to God is not only a mistake, but also a symptom
of anxiety."

I do not know that we said that the church is the best of all ways
to God. I thought we emphasized that Christ was the way to God
and that the church was helpful in getting us to God to the degree
that it followed Christ.

When you say that one of the things that led you to leave the
church was this study of the spiritual teachings of the Orient, I wonder if you mean that you had to have something from the Orient to
piece out Christ. I have decided after many years of contact with
the Orient and its faiths that in Christ we do not have a religion but
a gospel. There are many religions. There is but one gospel. Religions are man's search for God; the gospel is God's search for man.
I can take much from the Oriental religions in the way of interpreting Christ, but I find nothing in them that adds to him one iota. In
him I believe we have seen the complete revelation of God and life
and destiny.

If you hold steady at the center, then I can sympathize with you
in your judgment of the church. But if you are trying to add to the
center and making Christ more complete through Oriental faiths,
then I feel that you have missed your step and are bound to end up
in a syncretism, and syncretism always ends in a paralysis.

"Eclecticisms pick and choose; syncretisms combine; but only
life assimilates." Jesus, being Life, assimilates from every culture
and faith things akin to his life and teaching. But it is a different
thing after he has taken it up into his purpose and remolded it according to the laws of his nature.

My conclusion is this: I can get light on the interpretation of
Christ from other faiths and cultures and can use their techniques in
my interpretation of him. But when it comes to him, I do not have
to add to him one iota from anywhere. He stands as the one perfect

possession of the Christian church. Because the Christian church has this treasure in a very earthen vessel, I stay with the church.

Again thanking you for your letter and assuring you of my best wishes,

> Sincerely, your brother,
> E. Stanley Jones
> New York, New York, August 23, 1950

And to this I answered:

My dear Dr. Stanley Jones:

Thank you so much for your interesting letter of August 23.

I don't think we need argue about the relationship between Christ and the Church, although if the latter word is used in any true sense at all it means the Body of Christ, for which reason the Church must, in its highest sense, mean the extension of Christ and Christ's action in the world.

It is, I think, clear to me why you say that Christ is a gospel, and represents, or rather, *is* God's search for man. Yet it has become very clear to me indeed that Christ is not the only incarnation of this gospel. I don't know that he "needs" any interpretation from outside. I only know that the identical theme of "God's search for man" is the essence of the Hindu doctrine (and likewise fact) of the Avatars, and the Buddhist Bodhisattvas. For me they are all incarnations of "the only-begotten Son." If this is syncretism, I do not see how it can be helped, for I must acknowledge a truth where I see it.

Such an interpretation of the Avatar and the Bodhisattva may seem strange, when it is the common opinion in the West that Vedanta and Buddhism are religions of "self-help." But I am convinced that this interpretation is profoundly erroneous—a conviction which I was glad to find confirmed in Dr. Coomaraswamy's *Hinduism and Buddhism*, to cite but one other example of the same view. For there are many.

I agree with you that "Jesus is Life." And for that very reason I cannot set him up as an example, an authority, or anything to which one can cling for spiritual security. To me, this is an attempt to make life into death, to shut the wind of the Spirit in a box. Thus, to use your own analogy, it makes no difference whether the Church "possessing" Christ is a vessel of earth or of gold. The moment Christ is "possessed" he is lost; the moment the vessel holds him instead of pouring him out, it holds only stagnant water.

This is perhaps an unfamiliar point of view, because we think it right and natural to make an example and authority of what is highest and best. But it is less of a truism than it sounds to say that to the extent we make Christ our ideal, he becomes unreal—a future dream instead of a present actuality. To me, all idealism, all setting-apart-as-an-example, is simply postponement; it is pushing the reality which is Christ to the elsewhere and the tomorrow. If he *is* risen; if he *is* the Truth and the Life, he must be immediately here and now. To set him up in any special way is then to "gild the lily" and so destroy it.

In other words: if Christ is really God's search for man, God, to have effectively "come down to earth," must be discoverable here in this very place and moment. But the emulation of the "Jesus of history" obscures that truth. It concerns itself so much with what happened two thousand years ago that it misses the point, confusing the pointing finger with the truth. "Why seek ye the living among the dead? He is not here, but is risen." The disciples sought him at the tomb; we seek him in the tradition of the Church or the record of the Bible—or in the future, which is merely the past projected ahead. They are all tombs, and "he is not here."

I wonder if the latter part of my printed letter makes it clear why idealism is simply postponement, and following an example, self-deception. We are so conditioned into thinking the other way that this involves something of a Copernican revolution of thought. Were it clear, I don't think there could be any question of following either the Christ or the Buddha or Krishna or Lao-tzu or all four together. The problem would disappear as a case of asking the wrong question.

With very best wishes, most sincerely yours,
Alan Watts
Millbrook, New York, August 29, 1950

From Professor Theodore M. Greene

Dear Mr. Watts:

I have read your printed letter with great care and I want to tell you how deeply it has moved me. I do think I understand your position and I am very sure you have taken the right and courageous step. As a layman in the church I have been in doubt again and again as to whether my proper course should be to remain in the church and, in all humility, try to fight its multiple failures and abuses, or whether I should leave it and join the vast army of the unchurched. Rightly or wrongly I still feel that I should take the first course and that is what I am doing, although with great misgivings at times. Meanwhile, you have a tremendous contribution to make as a scholar and teacher from your new vantage point. I do hope that things will work out in such a way that you can put forth your best efforts where they will be most effective. If I can, by any chance, be of any possible service to you I hope you will call on me. Believe me, it is heart-warming to know that you have taken so difficult a step in so fine a spirit.

Most cordially yours,
Theodore M. Greene
Yale University, October 10, 1950

From the Right Reverend Wallace E. Conkling, Bishop of Chicago

My dear Alan:

Though your letter grieves me yet it is not a surprise. I do not believe there is any need for comment on your position. When an

individual moves as far as you have from the group, words have
little avail. Sometimes the individual proves to be a leader and to
have a genius for truth; more often he shows himself in a much less
complimentary position. . . .

[Some technical details omitted.]

I am grateful for all you tried to do for good in your ministry
and I commend you to the justice and mercy of God.

Sincerely yours,
+Wallace E. Conkling, The Bishop of Chicago
Chicago, Illinois, July 5, 1950

In his position, could any response have been more courteous and charitable?

CHAPTER NINE

INTERLUDE

The six months I spent at Thornecrest Farmhouse in Millbrook were an interlude between two careers: priest at Northwestern University and teacher at the American Academy of Asian Studies in San Francisco, and thereafter philosopher-at-large, free-lance, gyrovagus, unaffiliated. Sometimes, half in jest, I call myself a philosophical entertainer, because I have some difficulty in taking myself and my work *seriously*—or perhaps the right word is "pompously." For this reason, halfway through the job, I find it somewhat embarrassing to be writing so much about myself, that is about the personality "Alan Watts," because all personality is a big act and a "put-on." As often pointed out, the very word "person" meant the actor's mask in Graeco-Roman drama, and I wear many masks, seeing that "all the world's a stage" and that I love to act. For this reason, people sometimes wonder if I ever show my true and natural self, and whether I am even in touch with it.

When I first came to the United States I used to dress rather formally, in the British style, to wear a hat, and to carry gloves and a silver-topped cane. I did not affect my way of speaking, save to Americanize it rather slightly and quite deliberately, for I have always been aware of my own voice as a pianist is aware of his fingers. Basically, I speak the same English as my father (and mother) and he, and his father, spoke it in just the same way as King George V. I realized, however, that to Americans I appeared affected, distant, and a little haughty. Thus the United States immigration officer at Montreal gruffed at me, "Whaddya carry a cane for? You sick?" "Not at all," I replied. "It's just for swank." It must be understood that to cultured Englishmen and Europeans there is nothing unnatural in developing a certain personal style, with even a touch of swagger, provided one does it with humor and avoids making a caricature of oneself. The motto of Winchester School is "Manners Makyth Man."

But to most Americans the high style of British speech and manners seems blatantly put-on and offensive, as if anyone who speaks with a lilt and says, "Oah, it's reahlly *aw*fully nice to be in Ameddica," were assuming airs and graces, and a refinement to which he is not entitled. For in America, which in declaring its independence also disclaimed royalty, even the top brass are obliged to appear unaristocratic, casual, folksy, and natural, and it took me some time to realize that this was just as much an affectation as British urbanity. In Europe men were unequal, and no attempt was made to conceal it. In America men are unequal—and women more so—and it simply must not be admitted, despite all our fury at Marx's vision of a classless society. This subject is very strictly taboo, and there is no way of discussing it without giving offense to those who insist on maintaining the status quo.

While, then, the situation of Amerindians and Africans remains what it is, this affectation of equality and folksy naturalness seems particularly hollow. I am still disturbed by the artificial and meaningless intimacy of the facile use of first names, so prevalent in California, and resent being addressed as "Al" by a post-office clerk. Might it be argued that, to present a natural personality, I should come on like a Hopi? Or would it be better, as is momentarily the fad among many young people, to wear grubby denims and go by a first name only? If you are aware of your own behavior there is no way of *not* being affected, so I have long abandoned all attempts to "act naturally." If, as at a gathering of university professors, I dress and behave like everyone else, it is purely for reasons of camouflage. In such circles it is *de rigueur* to cultivate a certain mediocrity, not only in dress and manners but also in performance, since it is very bad form indeed to be an outstanding or popular teacher.

The latest and most desperate form of artificial naturalness is the organized encounter group, where, for purposes of therapy, people are supposed to encounter each other without psychological defenses and barriers. As one would expect, many such sessions are held in the nude. But for the most part those involved simply affect various preconceptions of what natural behavior is supposed to be, such as showing hostility, sexual interest, or some form of bad manners. In such situations people will invariably say to me, "Oh come on, Alan, we haven't yet seen the real you." To which I can only reply, "Well, look. I am right here, all of me, and if you can't see me you must question your own sensitivity." The most natural, and therefore taboo, thing you can do in an encounter group is to call in question the tacit rules of the game, and so bring out people's unconscious metaphysical assumptions as to just what constitutes honesty, the real person, true feeling, artificiality, and so forth. Because such metaphysics will usually prove to be ill-digested Darwin and Freud, with a touch of Jesus, and because the assumptions are demonstrably false, the group finds itself in the agonizing situation of not knowing what it is *supposed* to do. There, I suggest, we are at last getting down to reality.

For I do not believe that there is anything special which I am supposed to be, by the standards of some outside metaphysical authority, whether Freud or Jesus or even Lao-tzu. D. T. Suzuki would sometimes sign himself *Buji-nin*, or "No special person," and when the Emperor Wu asked Bodhidharma, "Who are *you*?" he answered, "I don't know." Neither do I, for it is impossible to bring vision into clear and objective focus upon itself. Just try—and somewhere along the way you will discover that the only real "you" is the shifting and momentary totality of everything you see and feel, within and without. I do not, then, bother with the vicious circle of discovering my "real personality" or make any special attempt to act naturally. I just put on whatever personal style seems appropriate to the circumstances, or entertaining to myself or others. Others may see a consistent personality underlying all these "acts," but this must be their projection on my Rorschach blot, and this autobiography is my projection on the same. All interesting descriptions of human character are poetic, imaginative, dramatic, and fantastic, whereas all attempts at valid description are myopic, interminable, and dull. This is why the writing of history and biography is an art, not a science.

So, then, I am unashamedly in "show-biz." But so is everyone. I feel an artistic responsibility for making the show interesting, and therefore cannot settle down into a humdrum role: the plodding and cautious scholar, the earnest clergyman, the affable administrator, or the suburbanly sociable family man. This may give some people an impression of unreliability, and to those who, fearing unreliability, try to force me into a fixed role I can indeed be unreliable. Also, I find it difficult to relate to people who cannot admit to an element of the rascal in themselves. I say "an element," like a touch of spice which is by no means the whole stew. Not to admit this shows an unconsciousness of human nature and an identification of one's heart with a prefabricated behavior pattern which can make a person very unreliable indeed. If you are not aware of the rascal in yourself, you will cheat others without warning—to yourself and to them. To know this is the only good reason I can imagine for confessing one's sins, although this involves the hypocrisy of saying, "For these and all my other sins, which I do not now remember, I am heartily sorry and firmly purpose amendment." This discomfort with those who are unconscious of their *yeẓer hara*, or "wayward spirit," which, according to Hebrew theology, God himself put into the heart of Adam, sometimes gets me into trouble. In this land of the Protestant ethic, which afflicts Catholics and Jews as well, far too many people are, as Jung would have said, unaware of their shadows. I may perhaps err in being too fascinated with my own. Yet I have to go along with Radar Wenesland, a celebrated Danish physician in San Francisco who practiced in the disreputable bohemian district of North Beach, in having a dislike for living in an environment where there is no suggestion of sin.

I am therefore ill at east with people who earnestly abstain from such things as smoking, drinking, and sex, to the point of making their squeamishness militant. Obviously, there are forms and degrees in which these pleasures can be unhygienic, as also can be driving cars, climbing mountains, and nursing the sick. There are points of view from which almost everything can be seen as bad for one's health, and Jung once remarked in jest that life itself is a disease with a very bad prognosis: it lingers on for years and invariably ends with death. And in this connection I might also quote Freud, writing to Dr. Fleisch: "As to your injunction to give up smoking, I have decided not to comply. Do you think it such a good thing to live a long and miserable life?" So Freud contracted a horrible cancer of the mouth, as did Aldous Huxley, who never smoked at all. I have no wish to defend my "vices" with propaganda, making out that they are in fact virtues which others should follow. I am only saying that I distrust people who show no sign of naughtiness or self-indulgence.

My vocation in life is to wonder about at the nature of the universe. This leads me into philosophy, psychology, religion, and mysticism, not only as subjects to be discussed but also as things to be experienced, and thus I make an at least tacit claim to be a philosopher and a mystic. Some people, therefore, expect me to be their guru or messiah or exemplar, and are extremely disconcerted when they discover my "wayward spirit" or element of irreducible rascality, and say to their friends, "How could he possibly be a *genuine* mystic and be so addicted to nicotine and alcohol?" Or have occasional shudders of anxiety? Or be sexually interested in women? Or lack enthusiasm for physical exercise? Or have any need for money?

Such people have in mind an idealized vision of the mystic as a person wholly free from fear and attachment, who sees within and without, and on all sides, only the translucent forms of a single divine energy which is everlasting love and delight, as which and from which he effortlessly radiates peace, charity, and joy. What an enviable situation! We, too, would like to be one of those, but as we start to meditate and look into ourselves we find mostly a quaking and palpitating mess of anxiety which lusts and loathes, needs love and attention, and lives in terror of death putting an end to its misery. So we despise that mess, and look for ways of controlling it and putting "how the true mystic feels" in its place, not realizing that this ambition is simply one of the lusts of the quaking mess, and that this, in turn, is a natural form of the universe like rain and frost, slugs and snails, flies and disease. When the "true mystic" sees flies and disease as translucent forms of the divine, that does not abolish them. I—making no hard-and-fast distinction between inner and outer experience—see my quaking mess as a form of the divine, and that doesn't abolish it either. But at least I can live with it.

Perhaps all this is a way of saying that I see the same problems in being natural, genuine, or authentic as the saints have found in their efforts to be truly humble, contrite, and in love with God. You can't make it without faking it, for the real thing is a grace not of your own making, which comes upon some people as involuntarily as their lovely eyes or golden hair. It is thus that by grace or nature (take your choice) I am a mystic in spite of myself, remaining as much of an irreducible rascal as I am, as a standing example of God's continuing compassion for sinners or, if you will, of Buddha-nature in a dog, or of light shining in darkness. Come to think of it, in what else could it shine?

These rather self-conscious observations may help to explain the point from which I began: that I find it hard to take myself and my work seriously, even though I am dealing with what are supposed to be the most serious subjects. I am sincere but not serious, and one of my most sincere convictions is that God is not serious. Irreverent and idolatrous as it may be, it is sometimes useful to speak of God anthropomorphically, as a person. I cannot conceive any zealous earnestness or missionary dedication, much less solemnity or pomposity, in the mind of One who has created the hippopotamus, the toucan, the giraffe, and the Brazilian bell-bird. (The latter creature, about the size of a pigeon, puffs itself up into a complete sphere, opens its beak, and returns suddenly to normal shape with a high, penetrating "Dong!") And when I contemplate such ordinary creatures as pigs, chickens, ducks, lazy cats, sparrows, goldfish, and squids, I begin to have irrepressibly odd notions as to the true shapes of angels.

For this very reason I take an intense dislike to the use of humor, jocosity, or good clean fun as sugar upon some religious pill, because this is a reversal of the true situation. The outward and superficial aspect of religion should rather be ascetic and solemn, to conceal the guffaws in the inner sanctum. My feelings here have been greatly influenced, since my twenties, by the work of Gilbert Keith Chesterton—that Catholic equivalent of Hotei, the "laughing Buddha"—who, though neither a great poet nor a great theologian, had the sort of bewitched imagination from which great poetry and theology can be made. He shone as an essayist and fantast, and of all his many essays the most profound and provoking was "On Nonsense," the peculiarly British kind of nonsense represented by Edward Lear and Lewis Carroll, which is something of a much higher and subtler order than mere twaddle, gibberish, poppycock, or balderdash. So much higher, indeed, that it would take a better literary critic than I to define its precise spirit, for it has in it something waywardly ineffable, which Chesterton invoked to unravel the problem of Job.

That problem is, of course, why the righteous should suffer if God is truly just, and the deeper problem is why Job should have been satisfied with God's answer, given in a long speech at the end of the book. For God's speech is a series of riddles in the course of which he asks Job why it rains on the desert "where no man is," and whether he can bind the influences of the stars or catch a whale with a fishhook. Is it stretching things too much to believe that this is like asking

Why the sea is boiling hot,
And whether pigs have wings?

Not if Chesterton was right in feeling, as I do, that if *le rire est le propre de l'homme*, that humor is uniquely human, and that if, furthermore, man is made in God's image, then, as Chesterton suggested, we should not be surprised at the verbal similarity of cosmic and comic. One thinks of *The Divine Comedy* in which Dante likened the song of the angels to the laughter of the universe. Chesterton finished his essay by observing that those who think that faith is nonsense may have the tables turned on them when it comes back in the form that nonsense is faith.

But I part company with Chesterton so long as he must insist, as a Catholic, that man is only a creature of God, for then I cannot imagine God as laughing while children are sprayed with napalm. But what if—and only if—those children are God himself in disguise, incognito, dreaming the most horrible dream imaginable for the convulsive shock of waking up divine? In a time when we can entertain notions of the curvature of space and the paradoxes of quantum theory, might not this constitute a relatively reasonable theory of what life is about? So long as I, too, am God dreaming, and dreaming so well that it all seems vividly real, I am not, however, going to spray children with napalm, for in my half-awake state I suffer from the knowledge that I am those children, and that they feel the "quaking mess" of self-consciousness as strongly as I.

Basically, my own laughter at myself has something to do with the incongruity of such a clown being God in disguise, of the "big act" called Alan Watts being a manifestation of the infinite energy of the universe. For behind the scenes you see all the string, tacks, wire, and masking tape that prop up the show, and as I witness the universe getting away with me I wonder what other uproarious deceptions it will perpetrate. I say this mainly so that you— dear reader—possibly ashamed of your own string and wire, may have the courage to go on with your show.

During this interlude I applied myself to the art of cooking, for in cold weather the kitchen was the only tolerable room in the farmhouse—one of those archaic rural structures whose rooms are severe closetless boxes with small window-frames decaying from much painting. Dorothy and I would pore over recipes and challenge ourselves to increasingly ambitious feats of gourmetism, so that by the time Christmas came we were ready to stage a gastronomic house party which is not to be forgotten, both for the fare and the combination of guests. Why is it that in America a *charcuterie* is hardly to be found? In France every village has at least one shop for the sale of cold meats, and more especially, of sausages, galantines, and *pâtés* in crusts of pastry. Even in England the cold pork pie is to be found in most pubs, and since childhood I have been unable to resist this type of fare. We therefore prepared an ample *pâté de veau en croûte*, a long loaf-shaped pie stuffed with veal, ham, truffles, and pistachio nuts, and encased in glazed pastry lined with small French pancakes. There was also a roast turkey dressed with a parsley forcemeat that I had learned from my mother, with chestnuts added, and before being put into the oven the skin was treated with a mysterious alchemy of spices put together by one of our guests—Luisa, widow of the fabulous Ananda Coomaraswamy.

The party was somehow in his honor. Though I had never met him, I was at that time much under the influence of his writings, for he had exemplified my own vision of the complete man as both mystic and sensualist, and he had gone before me in the work of discussing Christian scholastic theology in a global context which included Hindu, Buddhist, and Islamic metaphysics and iconography, being a religious man who had transcended religions. Yet he was at the same time an antiquarian, art historian, linguist, botanist, lover, and fisherman; so gifted in the latter art that it was said that with one cast of his line into the Atlantic off the coast of Massachusetts he would hook a fish only to be found along the coasts of France. Like my present wife's father, he would fish with unbarbed hooks and give the impression that fish actually wanted him to catch them.

Much of his wisdom had rubbed off on Luisa, who helped me find my way in the maze of his writings—mostly learned articles buried in obscure journals, with the important parts further concealed, squirrel fashion, in the small print of footnotes, and sometimes footnotes on footnotes. In my own writing I have striven for lucidity and brevity, with a minimum of learned apparatus, and am therefore—especially to the academic fraternity—known as a "popularizer," which in those circles is a dirty word.[1] Coomaraswamy was deliberately obscure, being an Oriental esotericist who felt that anyone seeking his nuggets of wisdom ought to dig for them. Nevertheless, his learned arabesques with their multilingual terminology were as fascinating as a dark and dusty antique shop, crowded with Tibetan Buddhas and skull-cups, palm-leaf manuscripts in Pali, Iranian miniatures, Moorish swords and hookahs, Chinese embroideries and bronze mirrors, wooden statuary from Bali, and Japanese temple gongs. This might be a description of Coomaraswamy's own library in Cambridge, Massachusetts, where Luisa and I first met, and where the room was dominated by an inscription in the superb Roman hand-lettering of Eric Gill: EX DIVINA PULCHRITUDINE ESSE OMNIUM DERIVATUR —"The being of all things is derived from the divine beauty"—words of Saint Thomas Aquinas.

At the time, I was working with Luisa to get her a grant from the Bollingen Foundation for the editing and republication of these very articles, and in this I was assisted by Joseph Campbell, who also attended the party with his wife, the dancer Jean Erdman. Joseph had in fact saved my own life at this time by helping me to get a grant from this astonishing institution, which I regard as model and exemplar par excellence for all foundations supporting scholarship and the arts. For it was the only great foundation that would pay

---

[1] When a scholar tells me that I cannot possibly understand Indian philosophy without a full knowledge of Sanskrit, I am apt to remark, "Are you really saying that you are a poor translator?" The scholar who is not also a teacher and communicator is killing his own field of study by making it impossible for others to follow him. This is why there is so little enthusiasm for Oriental scholarship in American universities, for the field has been completely cornered by pedants. The same is true of academic philosophy, though every philosopher should follow the discipline of setting out his ideas in the plainest English. It may show him that much of his thought is nonsense.

any attention to off-beat people interested in such matters as Oriental philosophy, medieval alchemy, and Egyptian magic, and to qualify one didn't have to come dangling with degrees. Work was judged on its own merits, primarily by the director, John Barrett, whom I must describe as one of the most urbane and exquisitely cultured men of my acquaintance. Even if such epithets are a little trite, anything more exotic would give the wrong impression, for the Foundation, and Jack himself, have about them an atmosphere of relaxed though solid American respectability. The Foundation's offices are in a converted brownstone, and the pleasing shock is to find, in the midst of such assured and unostentatious elegance, an imagination which extends to illuminated manuscripts of the *Divina Commedia* and the *I Ching*. Call it a cool weird.

Bollingen is a village at the eastern end of the lake of Zurich, where C. G. Jung had his country retreat, and the Foundation was established by Paul Mellon and his late wife, Mary (Mima), who had been one of Jung's patients, so that the Foundation's purpose was to support work in all the many spheres of Jung's interests. It was then underwriting Joseph in the tremendous undertaking of editing, or rather rewriting from rough notes, the works of Jung's deceased friend Heinrich Zimmer: *Myths and Symbols in Indian Art and Civilization, Philosophies of India*, and *The Art of Indian Asia*. It should be known that the vivid and rich style of these works is more Campbell than Zimmer, notably in *The King and the Corpse* where a number of mythological tales are retold as only Joseph can tell stories. For by telling fairy tales and unlocking the mysteries of ancient religions he has enchanted generations of beautiful young women at Sarah Lawrence, even ensorceling one of them into becoming his wife. On the night of the party Dorothy was so magicked with his tales that she just about fell in love with him, and here it should be said that Joseph's gifts include an athletic physique in which masculine strength is given a slight touch of feminine grace. Furthermore, his attitude to life is tantric: an almost fearsomely joyous acceptance of all the aspects of being, such that whenever I am with him his spirit spills over into me.

All this happened when I first knew Joseph, which now seems a long time ago, since when—although he has been in New York and I in San Francisco—we have constantly compared notes and exchanged ideas, so much so that to do justice to him I would have to interrupt this book with a minor biography. Joe is simultaneously an athlete and a *jñana* yogi—a man of wonderful physique who, however, has a wisdom that does not seem to have been attained by formal meditation under any guru, or by being psychoanalyzed, or anything of that kind. He is an example, although such examples are rare, of the fact that one can understand certain deep matters of the spirit simply by understanding them. To see it "intellectually" is to see it all the way through.

This was recognized, in Joe's case, by the Indian guru (not the politician) Sri Krishna Menon. For when Joe went to see him on a visit to India and found him surrounded by students who were trying to get rid of the consciousness of *maya*, of the illusion of this everyday world, so as to experience the undifferentiated Brahman, Joe interposed a single remark. "Surely," he said to the guru, "if there is no reality except Brahman, this state of illusion is also Brahman." The guru regarded him with astonishment and said, "You are the first person to come by here who has understood that!" Whereupon he requested Joe to explain it to his students, saying that if an American could understand it why couldn't they. Yoga is sometimes the world's most elaborate way of postponing liberation.

Joe exhibits this understanding precisely in his strong individuality and in his recognition of the value both of the individual and of particular things. There is, as I have often noted, a widespread and wrong impression that anyone who sees through the illusion of the ego must become a self-effacing and anonymous personality, whereas my own feeling has always been that in order to be a real person you must know how to be a genuine fake. In other words, only those who can accept their own annihilation can have the courage to be true individuals. The rest are too tender with themselves, too scared of losing individuality. In this connection (which may not be at first obvious) Joe loves to tell of an occasion when he and Heinrich Zimmer were attending a celebration of Wesak, the Buddha's birthday. A swami was explaining that so many Westerners thought of Buddha as a weird Oriental idol with eight arms and six fingers, whereas he was in fact just a plain ordinary man like ourselves. Zimmer leaned over and whispered to Joe, "I prefer them with six fingers!"

Now this may explain the seeming paradox that Joe, who has given so

much of his life to Indic studies, has no patience with modern India. Like
Spengler, he regards most of it as a fellaheen culture of shiftless, quarrelsome, self-pitying, and fraudulently arrogant impostors. I have not been to
India, but I doubt whether any people encompassing such a vast variety of
individuals can be all that terrible. But every Western enthusiast for the spiritual wisdom of India should face the fact that most Oriental holy men are
no different from our own clergymen. Being human, they have the same
share of dogmatists, bigots, hypocrites, gossips, and ecclesiastical politicians,
so that one must regard the yellow robe with the same discrimination as the
Roman collar and the black suit. What Joe disdains is of course the failure of
India's nerve in seeing its own vision, in having the courage to accept the
plain words of the Upanishadic doctrine that there is no reality but Brahman. The difficulty is, of course, that this is a supreme act of faith which, on
the surface, seems to imply that all differentiations of value should be ignored. But it has the same unexpectedly life-giving effect as giving oneself
up for dead, as having nothing to lose, as being a meaningless undulation in
infinite space. Curiously, this total negation gives one the time, the energy,
and the freedom to be concerned with how marvelously life can be lived. Joe
feels, I think, that this should be easier for Hindus than for Christians, who,
even in their apostasy, are haunted by the longing for heaven and the terror
of hell. It is thus that Joe invariably gives me the feeling that because there
is nothing to lose there is nothing to fear, and that the illusion of having a
space of time is for living it up nobly.

It was, as I remember, through Jean—who is to dancing what Vivaldi
was to music—that we met the other member of the party, composer John
Cage, who had then become interested in the relationship of music to Zen
and was beginning to explore the melodies of silence. My principal tie with
John was that we had the same kind of humor, for he would simply bubble
with laughter whenever describing his latest plans for a musical outrage, such
as a very formal piano recital in full evening dress, complete with an assistant to turn the pages, in which, however, the score consisted entirely of rests.
The joke wasn't merely that he was getting away with murder in the hopelessly deranged world of avant-garde music, so as to constitute the master
charlatan of all, but that beyond all this and to make matters still funnier, he

had also discovered and wanted to share the meditation process of listening to silence. This is simply to close your eyes and allow your ears to resonate with whatever sounds may be happening spontaneously, making no attempt to name of identify them, just as when one listens to formal music. After a while one hears the sounds emerging, without cause or origin, from the emptiness of silence, and so becomes witness to the beginning of the universe.

John slept that night on a divan in the living room, where we kept a hamster in a cage furnished with a vicious wheel, or *bhavachakra*, wherein the benighted creature could run forever without getting anywhere. This particular wheel squeaked abominably as the hamster ran, so I told John to put the cage out in the passage if it bothered him. "Oh, not at all!" he said. "It's the most fascinating sound, and I shall use it as a lullaby." What may not be generally understood about John is that he is an extremely accomplished musician who has, however, realized that we do not know how to listen. Conventional music, as well as conventional speech, have given us prejudiced ears, so that we treat all utterances which do not follow their rules as static, or insignificant noise. There was a time when painters, and people in general, saw landscape as visual static—mere background. John is calling our attention to sonic landscape, or soundscape, which simultaneously involves a project for cleaning the ears of the musically educated public. As painters once framed "mere" landscape, John is using the ritual of the concert hall to frame silence and spontaneous sound, which we shall in due course find as beautiful as sky, hills, and forests. Imagine, then, the sonic equivalent of those places in national parks usually called Inspiration Point where tourists from Kansas exclaim at the view, "Oh, it's just like a picture!" Buddhahood is the state in which *all* sensory input is viewed in this way.

In line with Jano's project for writing *The Net*, I must explain that John, Joseph and Jean, and Jack Barrett all became my friends as the result of an aesthetic whim, derived from my interest in typography. For it was in 1945 or 1946 that I received a publisher's announcement from the new firm of Pantheon Books in New York, and was at once struck by the sophistication of its typographic layout. It may seem uncanny, but typographic style is as revealing to me as handwriting to a graphologist, and I knew at once that I would like my own books to be published by this firm. My instinct was further corroborated by their list of titles and by the physical appearance of the books themselves, and it was thus that without any introduction I had sent the manuscript of *Behold the Spirit* to Pantheon and so came to know Kurt and Helen Wolff. How could I have guessed that Helen was profoundly interested in Catholic mysticism and Oriental philosophy, an interest shared by her husband, Kurt, who in turn represented for me all the virtues of high European culture—German, French, and Italian? They evoked all those childhood feelings, which I have described, of the glamour of continental Europe, and, though their offices were as dreary as most offices, their apartment on Washington Square was in faultless taste, from the Canalettos on the walls to the design of Kurt's scratch pads by the telephone.

Helen—a woman of strikingly intelligent beauty—has a sort of motherly way of flattering one's insight without insincerity, implying that you and she are, after all, in the know and belong to an unspecified Western elite. Kurt exemplified the principle that no one speaking English as other than his mother tongue should abandon his foreign accent. For although Kurt felt unable to be himself fully in an English-speaking environment, his German accent somehow conveyed gentle humor combined with a loving concern for scholarly and aesthetic excellence. At our first meeting he produced a German edition of Rudolf Koch's *Book of Signs* to find a suitable emblem for the cover of *Behold the Spirit*, and my typographology told me again that I had found the right man. When Koch draws a plain cross, the black bold lines are slightly widened at the ends to suggest a serif without actually drawing it, so that an otherwise mechanically geometrical figure becomes alive.

Before the Nazi regime, Kurt had been an outstanding publisher in Leipzig and Munich, and came to the United States with the then unbelievable idea that there was room in this country for a publishing house with his own impeccably high standards. He might have foreseen that this is, in fact, the *only* country in which a rather esoteric philosopher, such as myself, can make an adequate living by writing and speaking alone, without employment by a university, for the simple reason that the literate public is relatively enormous. Pantheon became, furthermore, publisher to the Bollingen Foundation and thus of the marvelous Bollingen Series which includes the complete works of Jung, as well as such classics as Campbell's *Hero With a Thousand*

Faces, Zuckerkandl's *Sound and Symbol* (on music as a philosophical method), Gombrich's *Art and Illusion*, Richard Wilhelm's *I Ching*, and D. T. Suzuki's undoubted masterpiece, *Zen and Japanese Culture*—to mention but a few of their formidable array of books which are, incidentally, as fine in design as they are profound in thought.[2]

Quite aware that Kurt and Helen had provided me with a soil into which I could most happily transplant myself, I was dismayed when they left Pantheon and returned to Europe, where Kurt died in an accident. Helen has returned to New York publishing, but meanwhile another lady had become my guiding genius at Pantheon—Paula Van Doren, who subsequently and very appropriately married one of the editors of the Bollingen Series, William McGuire. After Kurt and Helen, and for an interval Kyrill Schabert, who had been an original partner with the Wolffs, I was startled to find myself with a publisher so much younger than I, although this came about much later than the time of which I am writing. It was in the early 1960s. As a young author I had been used to looking at publishers in much the same way as a student looks at senior members of his university faculty, so that when I found Pantheon in the hands of Paula and of André Schiffrin I realized, with a pleasant shock, that I was no longer a younger author. Why pleasant? Because it is of definite advantage to a philosopher to get older, and I was getting tired of meeting people who said, "Why, are you Alan Watts? That's not possible... er, I had expected someone so much more mature in years."

---

[2] The Bollingen Series in now published by Princeton University Press.

CHAPTER TEN

JOURNEY TO THE EDGE OF THE WORLD

N ot so many years ago the man-made disaster now known as Los Angeles was an area so bright with flowers that it could be spotted from far
out at sea. When I first passed through it in 1947, and then in 1951, there was
still a lingering sense of the paradise lost. Even today there are occasional
breaks in the artificial weather when, in some few nooks in the Hollywood
hills, one can imagine being in Ascona in the Ticino or some other terraced,
treed, and flowered city of Mediterranean Europe, with white walls, orange
tiles, and courtyards with wrought-iron gates. Where Gower Street curls as
it meets the hills there is a district of faded glamour that was once haunted
by pandits of the Theosophical Society, where the streets have such names
as Temple Hill Drive and Vasanta Way, and where the architecture simu-
lates the wealthier parts of Marrakesh and Fez. Here, too, is a miniature Taj
Mahal which is the temple of the Vedanta Society where, in those days,
Swami Prabhavananda discoursed with Aldous Huxley, Gerald Heard, and
Christopher Isherwood, and where young ladies clad in saris meditated
among the cypress and lemon trees.

Unbelievably, there is still here one of my most favorite places—the
home of Henry and Ruth Denison at the very top of the hill, at the end of a
road going nowhere, hanging above a reservoir-lake surrounded with pines.
They have a sundeck under a eucalyptus tree where I have slept some mem-
orably deep sleeps, and awakened very early in the morning, before sunrise,
with stars still showing through the branches. In this house I have made some
of my greatest friendships, so much so that I cannot think of it without that
curious pleasure-pain which the Japanese call *aware*—the sense of echoes in

the courtyards of the mind after the sun has left and the people have gone their ways forever.

Before the smog had overcast Pasadena, Claremont, and Riverside, and come to the very edge of Palm Springs, there was, east of Los Angeles, a country of bright blue air where mountains—such as San Giorgone and the San Jacinto Range—seemed to float in transparency on the far edges of a warm plain of citrus orchards and pepper trees. But through Blythe, Indio, Banning, and Riverside there was U.S. Highway 60 skirting the San Bernardino Range, along which we came from the East together with four hundred other migrants on the same day, to be followed by another four hundred on the next and the next—all of us frantic to get away from whatever we disliked about Iowa, Illinois, Oklahoma, and South Bend, Indiana; and yet—too many of us—carrying along the very plagues we were trying to flee, so that today most of the smaller townships of Southern California are rural slums inhabited by disappointed and embittered people with dismal and repressive religions.

But we were only passing through this area on our way to San Francisco, in response to Frederic Spiegelberg's invitation to join the newly founded American Academy of Asian Studies. We had taken the southern route to avoid the winter of February 1951, and to pause in Los Angeles to make connections. For I must confess that Los Angeles, with its notorious interest in goofy spiritualities, seemed—and turned out to be—an economic blessing for one with my own peculiar talents. One of my friends there was Floyd Ross, then professor of the history of religions at the University of Southern California, who had just written a powerful book, *Addressed to Christians*, in which he pointed out how even very liberal Protestants were still obsessed with the conceit that their version of the Gospel of Jesus Christ must necessarily be the "top religion."

Floyd fascinated me because he combined this high intellectual generosity with the reserved and cautious personal style of a minister, just a little Quakerish and concerned, and perhaps for all that a wonderfully reliable friend. Before our arrival he had arranged meetings with psychiatrist Fritz Kunkel, Zen master Nyogen Senzaki (*dharma*-brother of Sokei-an Sasaki), old friends Joe and Teresina Havens and their friend Hilde Elsberg, teacher of an indescribable art for which no one has ever found a satisfactory name, but which could be seen as an indigenous form of Western Taoism. There were also people connected with the Vedanta Society, Theosophists, "nondisciples" of Krishnamurti, and—associated with Fritz Kunkel—the bookseller Harry Hill, who maintained a shop on Wilshire Boulevard opposite the Ambassador Hotel. Through these people and all their friends, students, patients, clients, and customers, it was arranged that I give a public lecture at a mansion on the corner of Los Feliz and Vermont boulevards which had formerly been the Russian Consulate, and which was then occupied by Teresina and Joe, and Hilde.

In the course of this lecture I let drop, as merely a passing remark, that there was some analogy between the ecstasy of *samadhi*, or mystical experience, and sexual orgasm—not realizing that I had then and there made myself the cat among the pigeons. For there was then in process a great soul-searching and spiritual argument among the followers of Oriental religions which was repeating, in new terms, the ancient theological debates between those who believed in salvation by faith and those who believed in salvation by works, by grace and predestination or by free will, by relaxation and self-acceptance or by grim effort, and by world-affirmation or world-denial. As always, the root of the matter was sex: can you be an enlightened, realized, and liberated being and still engage in sexual intercourse?

The taking of sides on these matters was then, and probably still is, very complicated. Swami Prabhavananda and his Vedantists were all for asceticism and sexual abstinence, and believed strongly in the efficacy of willpower, concentration, renunciation, and specific spiritual disciplines for attaining a mystical bliss impervious to suffering. Gerald Heard was of approximately the same opinion, though he had just suffered a rude shock when the star pupils of his coeducational monastery in Trabuco Canyon had decided to get married. The Krishnamurti people were vaguely embarrassed by sex, yet held that asceticism and spiritual disciplines were fraudulent, being ways of exalting egoism by denying it. Aldous Huxley, with his infinitely curious and open mind, was wobbling on the edge of decision. The Zen contingent had no qualms about sex, but went full tilt for tough discipline in meditation, dropping hints, however, that all this was like "looking for the ox when you are riding it." The psychotherapeutic clan, as good Freudians and Jungians, were all for healthy sex and self-acceptance, with some subtle accommodations to social convention.

All these factions were somehow represented at a tea party gathered by Swami Prabhavananda, a few days after my lecture, in his apartment at the Vedanta Temple—in a room which had so many doors that it seemed like a setting for a French farce. As the guests assembled, the various doors kept opening to admit young women who identified themselves as Sister Radha, Sister Parvati, Sister Shaktidevi, Sister Indira, and Sister Anandamaya (I am just making up the names), and we were joined by Huxley, Isherwood, and many of the Swami's distinguished lay disciples. Very soon it became apparent that I had been put on the path of the razor's edge: that on the one hand, the Swami wanted to demonstrate the error of my views, and that on the other, I did not want to embarrass him in front of his disciples.

The trouble started when one of the sisters said, rather too innocently, "Oh Mr. Watts, I'd be so interested to know what you think about Krishnamurti."

"Well," I replied, "I must say that I find his work very fascinating, because I think he's one of the few people who have come to grips with such basic problems of the spiritual life as trying to make oneself unselfish."

"Yes, Krishnamurti is a very fine man," the Swami chipped in. "I don't think any of us can doubt the greatness of his character. But his teaching is very misleading. I mean, he seems to be saying that one can attain realization without any kind of yoga or spiritual method, and of course that isn't true."

"No indeed," I countered, "if in fact there is something to be attained. Your *Upanishads* say very plainly, *Tat tvam asi*, 'You *are* That,' so what is there to attain?"

"Oh no, no!" the Swami protested. "There's all the difference in the world between being merely informed, in words, that this is so and realizing it truly, between understanding it intellectually and really knowing it. It takes a great deal of work to go from one state to the other."

"But so far as I can see," I went on, "the more people consider themselves to have made progress in such work, the greater their spiritual pride. They are putting legs on a snake—congratulating themselves for bringing about, by their own efforts, a state of affairs which already *is*."

"Well, I wonder," mused Aldous, "isn't it rather curious that there has always been a school of thought in religion which attributes salvation or realization to an unmerited gift of divine grace rather than personal effort?"

"Of course," said the Swami, "there are those exceptional cases of people who seem to be born—or suddenly endowed—with realization. But we mustn't leave out of account the work that must have gone into it in their former lives."

"But that virtually cuts out the principle of grace altogether," I said. "When Christians say that something comes about by the grace of God, Hindus and Buddhists say that it is so already and always has been. The self, *atman*, is the Godhead, Brahman. It has always been so from the very beginning, so that your very *trying* to realize it is pushing it away, refusing the gift, ignoring the fact."

"But this is ridiculous," the Swami objected. "That amounts to saying that an ordinary ignorant and deluded person is just as good, or just as realized, as an advanced yogi."

"Exactly," I said. "And what advanced yogi would deny it? Doesn't he see the Brahman everywhere, and in all people, all beings?"

"You are saying," said the Swami, "that you yourself, or just any other person, can realize that you are the Brahman just as you are, without any spiritual effort or discipline at all!"

"Just so. After all, one's very not realizing is, in its turn, also the Brahman. According to your own doctrine, what else is there, what else is real other than the Brahman?"

"Oh!" he exclaimed. "There was someone who came to Sri Ramakrishna with such talk. He said, 'If that is your Brahman, I spit on it!' Don't fool me. If you were truly one with the Brahman and truly in *samadhi*, you would be beyond suffering. You would not be able to feel a pinch."

"You mean that the Brahman can't feel a pinch?"

"Of course not!"

At that moment I had one of the great temptations of my life, and resisted it. Instead, I said something like, "Well I don't think your Brahman is very sensitive," laughed, and changed the subject. Yet, in a way, I regretted it. I felt, in retrospect, that I should have honored the Swami by going the whole way, pinching him hard, and seeing what he would have done, for although he may be shrugged off by those who see him as representing the idle romanticism of Hollywood Swami-Land, he has nonetheless given thousands of people that startling and disquieting question: "Who, what, do you think you really are? Absolutely, basically, deeply within?"

But what I later found out to be the real reason for this contretemps—the question of spirituality and sexuality—never came to the surface. The blind spot for Hindus is that they never question the superstition that emission of semen is equivalent to loss of blood; a superstition I found also among boys with whom I went to school in England. They believe that "loss" of semen wastes *ojas* or psychic energy which should, instead, be pumped up the subtle *sushumna* channel in the spine to flower as a thousand-petaled lotus in the brain. Similar ideas are found among those Chinese Taoists who solve the problem by so pressing the scrotum at the moment of orgasm that the semen flows into the bladder, though one would suppose that this, from a Hindu standpoint, would be cheating. The root of the superstition is, I believe, the confusion of a symbolic and psychic anatomy with the physiological anatomy as if we, for example, were to give literal sense to such an expression as "my heart came into my mouth." I am by no means alone in believing that the symbolism of *kundalini* yoga, and of the various *chakras* or lotus-centers along the spine, refers not to physiology but to steps in a method of meditation.

For the rest, I see no more reason why a Buddha or spiritually "realized" person should abstain from sex than that he should abstain from breathing, unless, of course, it just happens that he is not interested. But because I have said this very plainly in such books as *Nature, Man and Woman* and *Erotic Spirituality*, there are—at least in the West—Buddhist, Hindu, and Theosophical circles which regard my views as immoral and dangerously misleading. Yet, having noticed how greatly such circles relish gossip and righteous indignation, should I not be happy to afford them such pleasure?

On the way from Los Angeles to San Francisco, early that March, we passed through a magical stretch of coast known to some of its older inhabitants as Gondwanaland—the remaining fringe of a lost country which is not really part of the United States. This territory runs from Monterey, at its northern end, to a point somewhere south of Big Sur and north of San

Simeon: you have to have a special feeling for the area to know just where the southern limit of the magic lies. Some say at Gorda, though others identify it as the point where the coast road, going south, leaves the wall of the Santa Lucia Range. In Monterey and Carmel the magic has almost vanished, since these towns have been too attractive for their own good; but the exact place were it begins in force is at the junction, in Carmel, of State Highway 1 and Ocean Avenue where, looking south, you first catch sight of the Santa Lucia Range. I have passed this point again and again on my way to Big Sur, and invariably my heart surges with delight at the enormous green and golden hills which—against a fog-fringed sky—loom above the lonely pines and cypresses of Point Lobos, coming straight from a Japanese screen by Sesshu.

In Big Sur, where forested mountains meet ocean with a plunging crash, scattering guano-covered rocks out to sea, we drove up the steep track to Partington Ridge in search of Henry Miller, with whom I had been in correspondence and who had written of my old friend Eric Graham Howe in *The Wisdom of the Heart*. He was, alas, away for the day, but his wife, Lepska, entertained us to breakfast—or rather brunch—and then, in what I can only describe as a bubbly-happy mood, gave us a tour of their home and of Partington Ridge. For me, this has remained an especially important moment. From the Ridge you look straight down to the Pacific a thousand feet below, and to the south, through Henry's nasturtiums and lemon trees, you see peak beyond peak dreaming away along the ocean to the blue horizon. Above you, the mountain ridge is thick with fir and redwood, and that morning it was appearing and disappearing between strands of sunlit mist. The house, half open to the outdoors, was ablaze with contemporary paintings by Schatz, Donner, Varda, and Henry himself: all of them in intense color so as to give the sense of a fiesta to the whole scene.

Lepska then took us up to the house above, Big Star Way, the home of Maud Oakes, where poet Hugh Chisholm was taking breakfast with a friend in Maud's kitchen-library-dining room, with windows commanding the whole view of the Pacific from north to south. Maud herself was away, but she was represented there by an icon of herself made of broken fragments of colored mirrors put together by her neighbor, Louisa Jenkins. I looked over her library to find it much like my own, although her principal interest was in the Amerindian cultures of the Southwest and of Guatemala. I did not then know what invigorating friends Maud and Louisa were both to become, but I knew instantly that I was in an atmosphere in which I had to belong. Yet, though I have stayed in Big Sur for long periods, I have never settled there— on the principle that to live on a mountain peak is not to see it—and thus I have always left it as an ideal location to which I might retreat in a future in- definitely postponed, visiting, in the meantime, other people's Shangri-las.

But in the mountains of the California coast I knew I had found home— somewhere, if not in Big Sur, or Santa Barbara, or Los Gatos. I was con- sulting my interior compass again to find out, now, whether I should go north or south, and the needle wavered for a long time over Big Sur although I had immediate business in San Francisco. Big Sur is marked on the map as a par- ticular village, but it is really a large territory, a substantial part of the Gond- wanaland strip, and can be said to run from the mouth of the Little Sur River on the north to the great bay of Lucia on the south, above which Camal- dolese hermits have established their monastery. For this is, indeed, mystical country. Just north of the Camaldolese is now the Esalen Institute, where you can study yoga, Gestalt therapy, *t'ai-chi* exercises, Oriental philosophy, or sensory awareness, and go lolling in sulphur springs at the ocean's edge. Ten miles inland, as the crow flies, is the Zen Buddhist monastery at Tassa- jara Springs, now probably the second largest such institution in the world. Near Carmel Highlands is the convent of the enclosed order of Carmelite nuns, permanently shut away from the world and devoted to unceasing ado- ration of the Holy Trinity. And scattered through the canyons and forests are numerous hippie-style yogis, shamans, and anchorites living in cabins, tents, and caves.

Much of the territory is a steep mountain wall traversed by a winding road that undulates from seven hundred feet above the ocean to as little as forty, and bridging densely forested canyons with hidden waterfalls. One of these falls, two miles in along a rocky river, supplies water just the right heat for a good shower, and stands on the edge of an opening in the tall redwoods where the river forms a clear, cold pool, and butterflies glide wobblingly through shafts of sunlight. This fall is little known and hard to reach, and one must hope that the secret canyon where it flows will never, never become a public park. For what is the fascination of T. S. Eliot's image of the hidden waterfall in *Four Quartets*? I have a childhood memory of walking at twilight near the village of Chiddingly in Sussex, and hearing a fall that I could not see, somewhere off in the woods, and realizing even then that it was better to keep it a mystery. Imagine the whole world stark naked under fluorescent light. And there is another Big Sur waterfall that streams thinly over a massive rock of green serpentine at least sixty feet high, so that when I first saw it I thought I had discovered the Jade Mountain.

Under the hot Pacific sun, tempered with periodical visitations of fog and winter rainstorms that seem to fall upwards, there is everywhere in Big Sur a smell of aromatic herbs and hay—sage, wild thyme, sorrel, Indian paintbrush, and acres of dangerous, fire-prone golden grass three to four feet high, amidst which one can sometimes discover rattlesnake grass with its light, fragile, and airy heads designed like the rattlesnake's tail, or like those of Japanese fish ornaments, sometimes used for earrings, made of tiny overlapping plates of metal so that the creature will wiggle.

Looking down from Partington Ridge, one realizes that the Pacific seldom has a clear horizon. For most of the year a fog bank lies some miles out to sea, against which pelicans fly high and lazily and cormorants skim low and hurriedly, like running asterisks. The fog bank tells my interior compass that this is the edge of the world. I have come far enough, and can watch the sun go down without regret, chasing it no further.

Coming to San Francisco I was plunged into a world of associations and activities so complex that I can record only outlines refreshed with occasional detail, like flowers scattered through a filigree of bare stems. For six years I was to be absorbed—for sometimes as much as fourteen hours a day—in teaching, and later in administration as well, at the American Academy of Asian Studies. At the same time I became involved with Lewis Hill, Richard Moore, and Wallace Hamilton of the Pacifica Foundation, which was then sponsoring radio station KPFA in Berkeley (having subsequently added KPFK in Los Angeles, WBAI in New York, and the much bombed KPFT in Houston, Texas) to create a style of broadcasting superior in quality and freer in speech than even the BBC in England, and without commercial advertising. Later I worked also, with Richard Moore, on San

Francisco's educational television station KQED—an equally imaginative and intelligent project, which even today is still gasping for adequate funds. I was also giving lectures and conducting seminars up and down the West Coast: in La Jolla, Los Angeles, Ojai, Santa Barbara, Big Sur, Carmel, Palo Alto, Marin County, Berkeley, and on up to Eugene and Portland in Oregon. In those six years I contrived also to write two major books, *Myth and Ritual in Christianity* and *The Way of Zen*, and a monograph called *The Way of Liberation in Zen Buddhism*. Oriental students and faculty members at the Academy gave me the opportunity to study the written form of Chinese. At the same time I was attempting to sustain the desperate social and family life of suburban Palo Alto and Mill Valley, in somewhat reluctant imitation of the style of life represented by *Sunset Magazine*—the picture windows of the ranch-type house, the outdoor barbecue, the children playing ball on the lawn, the do-it-yourself projects of tiling the bathroom and putting up shelves, and the station-wagoning of loads of sun-browned and quarrelsome papooses and brats to picnics on the beaches or marshmallow roasts in state parks.

The American Academy of Asian Studies was one of the principal roots of what later came to be known, in the early sixties, as the San Francisco Renaissance, of which one must say, like Saint Augustine when asked about the nature of time, "I know what it is, but when you ask me, I don't." I am too close to what has happened to see it in proper perspective. I know only that between, say, 1958 and 1970 a huge tide of spiritual energy in the form of poetry, music, philosophy, painting, religion, communications techniques in radio, television, and cinema, dancing, theater, and general life-style swept out of this city and its environs to affect America and the whole world, and that I have been intensely involved in it. It would be false modesty to say that I had little to do with it, and I am at once gratified and horrified to see how a younger generation has both followed and caricatured my philosophy.

But the Academy was at cross purposes with itself. There was no point in being a center of highly refined and academic Oriental studies such as already existed at the University of California in Berkeley under such celebrated scholars as Ferdinand Lessing, Murray Emmeneau, and P. A. Boodberg. There was, however, an obvious need for an institution teaching

Asian languages, arts, histories, politics, and religions at a more practical level, especially on the West Coast where the war with Japan and the oncoming jet age were slimming the Pacific to a river. One idea was, therefore, that the Academy should function as an information service for businessmen, government officials, teachers, anthropologists, sociologists, and general travelers who needed a thorough knowledge of Asia without getting bogged down in, say, doing graduate research for the compilation of a Mongolian dictionary or exhaustive studies of the primitive Haniwa statuary of Japan.

In practice, however, we had neither the funds nor the facilities to provide either type of study. We had premises, at first in the financial district of San Francisco, and later in Pacific Heights. We had a very modest library, heavily bolstered by books on loan from myself and from one of the students, Leo Johnson; a library that only began to be adequate in the fields of comparative religion and philosophy. But we had an interesting faculty. Frederic Spiegelberg, as Director of Studies, was the *de facto* mastermind of the project. From India he had invited Haridas Chaudhuri, a professor of philosophy at the University of Calcutta, and Sir C. P. Ramaswamy Aiyar, formerly Diwan of the State of Travancore and later Chancellor of the University of Banaras—a princely man, close to seventy, who somehow reminded one of the elephant god Ganesha. Then there was Judith Tyberg, learned in Sanskrit and yoga, and both she and Chaudhuri, together with Spiegelberg himself, were enthusiasts for the teachings of Sri Aurobindo Ghose—the mahatma of Pondicherry who had written the voluminous *Life Divine, Essays on the Gita*, and numerous other works including some very stilted and ponderously British-style poetry under the title *Savitri*, all of which was, for my taste, unreadable and as sober and sound as it was boring. There were also Tokwan Tada, a Japanese lama trained in Tibet, who brought with him the entire Buddhist canon in Tibetan wood-block prints, and my old friend from England, Polish-born Rom Landau, to take charge of our Islamic program. There was too, for some months, the Princess Poon Pismai Diskul of Thailand, an exquisite little lady who—years before on a visit to London—had been characterized by the British press as "the Pocket Venus," and was at this time curator of the National Library of Thailand.

The entrepreneur who gave the initial funds for this project leaned to the view that it should be an information service at the graduate level. At the time this made sense, because American universities were largely ignoring Asian studies; their offerings at the undergraduate level were almost nil, and at the graduate level were mainly preoccupied with research. Strictly speaking, we should have been a university department at the undergraduate level, but our classification as an independent graduate school awarding master's and doctor's degrees invited comparison with Harvard's Yenching Institute or London's School of Oriental and African Studies, which was absurd. Looking back, our concerns about academic status and degrees seem ridiculous, but at the time we needed accreditation to get students, and for students to have any operating funds.

But Spiegelberg and I had no real interest in this nonetheless sensible idea of an information service about Asian culture, nor was this what really concerned Chaudhuri, Aiyar, and Tyberg. We were concerned with the practical transformation of human consciousness, with the actual living out of the Hindu, Buddhist, and Taoist ways of life at the level of high mysticism: a concern repugnant to academics and contemptible to businessmen, threatening to Jews and Christians, and irrational to most scientists. Two professional fund-raisers cost us more than they raised, and the Ford Foundation shrugged us off with a shudder. Clearly, we were just another California cult trying to assume the mask of a respectable educational institution. But then—only twenty years ago—it was not as easy to see as it is today that when you make a powerful technology available to human beings with the normal form of egocentric consciousness, planetary disaster is inevitable. Moreover, the point had to be made that the egocentric predicament was not a moral fault to be corrected by willpower, but a conceptual hallucination requiring some basic alterations of common sense; a task comparable to persuading people that the earth is round rather than flat.

This was very largely the subject of discussion at the weekly colloquium of the Academy's faculty, at which Spiegelberg was the invariably provocative moderator, and which became an event increasingly attractive to San Francisco artists and intellectuals. In the course of these panel discussions I was astonished and amused to discover that Aiyar and I had both received the same education, that he in India and I in England had both been brought up on Caesar and Livy, Ovid and Virgil, Shakespeare and Scott, and were familiar with the same Latin jokes. He told me that he knew nothing of his own culture until he was over forty, since Lord Macaulay had established a system of higher education in India expressly designed to stamp out the Hindu tradition. As a result, many educated Hindus had therefore become crypto-Protestants and had religious attitudes reminiscent of Victorian England, though Aiyar himself was much too much a man of the world to take such attitudes seriously. Chaudhuri also seemed in some ways to have learned his Indian philosophy through a Western approach, but his gentle humor and learned mind made him a wonderful partner in debate, so that we could argue endlessly without losing tempers.

As I have indicated, most of these discussions revolved around the problem of self—the nature of consciousness, ego, personality, and will. Most forms of Indian philosophy, whether Hindu or Buddhist, take the view that the individual self, or *jivatman*, is in some sense an illusion. The Buddhists leave it at that, and will make no positive statement concerning the reality behind the illusion. They will say only that it is beyond all conception. Hindus, notably Vedantists, will say that the only real self is the Brahman, the Self of the Universe, but because this, too, is beyond all conception, their view does not differ essentially from that of the Buddhists, though nit-picking sectarians make much of minute verbal differences. Westerners thereupon rush to the conclusion that Indian philosophy has a negative and nihilistic attitude to the natural and physical world, failing entirely to see that this attitude applies only to certain ideas or conceptions *about* the world. No one who would go to the trouble of, say, learning the techniques of Indian music could possibly have a negative attitude to life itself.

But, invariably, our main problem was how to penetrate the illusion of the isolated, separate ego, for how can *I* accomplish this if this particular "I" is unreal? Chaudhuri, and others, would recommend methods of yoga-meditation involving intense concentration and effort, whereas I would keep coming back to the point that such efforts could only aggravate the illusion. Effort is essentially muscular, and ghosts are not dissolved by fisticuffs, even when the latter are purely imaginary.

Someone has told the story of meeting, on a train, a weird gentleman who took a bag down from the rack, opened it, extracted from his pocket a cabbage on the end of a string, and began to dangle it into the bag. Consumed with curiosity, the traveler asked what was in the bag and was told that it was a mongoose. "Well, why do you carry a mongoose?" "Alas," said the gentleman, "I am an alcoholic and suffer from delirium tremens, so that I need this mongoose to keep away the snakes." "But surely you realize that those snakes are only imaginary?" "Yes, indeed," he answered, "but so is the mongoose."

I was therefore arguing that one does not dissolve an erroneous concept, however hypnotically compelling, by an effort of will, by straining one's muscles, clenching one's jaws and fists, wrinkling one's brow, or holding one's breath against an idea. For our seeming sensation (as distinct from image) of ego is precisely the chronic muscular tension of trying to use brawn to accomplish results in the brain, which is as futile as trying to lift a plane off the runway by straining at your seat belt. An erroneous concept—as that a rainbow touches the ground at a particular spot, that a ship actually gets smaller as it moves out to sea, or that a rope stepped upon in the dark is a snake—cannot always be dissolved by verbal explanation. The error must somehow be *shown*, and then the intelligence (and I must use this word rather than "intellect") will comprehend it at once. When people say to me, "I understand what you are saying intellectually, but I don't really feel it," I am moved to reply, "No. You understand the words, but your intelligence hasn't seen the point. You have heard the joke, but you haven't laughed." And so I have been working for years to find ways of showing that we don't confront the world as isolated subjects confronting alien objects. What we experience is always ourselves, and this is a more or less intelligent "happening" which is neither voluntary nor involuntary, subjective nor objective, controlled nor uncontrolled. Methods of meditation are effective only insofar as, through failure of dogged persistence, they *show* that the ego and its willing are unreal. There ought to be a less clumsy way of seeing the point, but I have only been partially successful in finding it. Krishnamurti has the same difficulty and has been working along the same line.

Thus in these faculty colloquia, as in all my work at the Academy, in my lectures, and in my writing, I was always being accused of being a lazy fellow who had the absurd idea that transcendence of egocentricity could be achieved (by whom?) without long years of effort and discipline. You would immediately feel one with all nature, and with the universe itself, if you could understand that there is no "you" as the hard-core thinker of thoughts, feeler of feelings, and senser of sensations, and that because your body is something in the physical world, that world is not "external" to you. Thus when you listen, you do not hear anyone listening. This has nothing to do with making an effort or not making an effort; it is simply a matter of intelligence. To find this out seems to me almost more important than understanding that the world is round, that Africans are people, and that persons with opinions other than your own will not fry forever in hell. Fully to understand that the universe is ourselves must put an end to frantic panic about death and to our hostile exploitation of the planet Earth.

In working out these problems I was enormously helped by two of my students, Leo Johnson and Pierre Grimes. Leo had been haunting the University of California in Berkeley as a voracious reader and auditor of courses without the slightest interest in credits, examinations, or degrees. He was the ideal student, simply interested in knowledge. His material ambitions were minimal; he lived in extreme simplicity; such money as he had went mostly for books, which he gave away; he had a ribald, bawdy, belly-laugh attitude to life which came out at unexpected moments, and was so informed with intellectual expertise that it was a real risk to expose him to scholarly company. Let's say that he had tact but wouldn't use it. Leo impressed upon me the important idea that the ego was neither a spiritual, psychological, or biological reality but a social institution of the same order as the monogamous family, the calendar, the clock, the metric system, and the agreement to drive on the right or left of the road. He pointed out that at times such social institutions became obsolete, as in the case of Roman numerals, Ptolemaic astronomy, and the Hindu caste system, and that the "Christian ego" was now plainly inappropriate to the ecological situation into which we were moving.

Pierre Grimes came to us from Saint John's, Annapolis, where he had been nurtured on Plato, but in working with me he graduated to Nagarjuna and began very practical experiments with that great Mahayanist's philosophy. He saw that Nagarjuna's method was a dialectical process that went far beyond sophistry and intellectual acrobatics, and could be used as a very powerful instrument for what I had in mind—namely, the dissolution of erroneous concepts felt as percepts. Pierre devised an encounter group on the metaphysical level. That is to say, he worked out a situation in which the participants would probe for each other's basic assumptions, or axioms, about life, and then demonstrate that they were no more than assumptions; not truths, but arbitrary game-rules. This dialectic was as traumatic for a logical positivist as for a Hegelian, for as basic assumptions crumbled, members of the group would begin to show intense anxiety. He would then probe for still deeper assumptions underlying the anxiety until he could bring the group to a state of consciousness in which they could happily relax, and abandon the frustrating and futile project of trying to make a false hypothesis called "I," on the one hand, get mastery over another false hypothesis called "experience" or "the world," on the other. The process seemed extraordinarily therapeutic both for Pierre himself and for those who worked with him. I had feared that he would become a scornful, prickly intellectual, but he turned out to be a man of singular compassion and humor, as well as of good sense in the practical matters of life. For Pierre was a true *jñana* yogi; that is to say, one who comes to an authentic realization, or *satori*, by an intellectual rather than an emotional or physical discipline.

The colloquium was attended from time to time by an astonishing group of artists (more strictly, painters) which included Mark Tobey, Gordon Onslow-Ford, Lee Mullican, and Jean Varda. As is well known, Tobey's technique of "white writing" derived its inspiration from Chinese grass-style calligraphy, for both he and Morris Graves were painters of the Northwest strongly affected by the Far East, as was, in turn, Gordon Onslow-Ford who subsequently studied Chinese calligraphy at the Academy under Zen master Hodo Tobase to attain a real mastery of the art in a line of succession which derives from Kobo Daishi, a Buddhist priest and mystic of the ninth century. For reasons which I cannot understand, Tobey was intellectually sidetracked by a fascination with the Bahai religion, which I have studied in vain search for anything more than a collection of amiable platitudes. Yet for my taste he is a superb painter who can dance with a brush like no one else. Mullican had just finished a stint in the army which had been devoted to map-making, and the drawing of contours had led on to a style of intricate abstraction with the palette knife that glowed with the brown and gold colors of the Southwestern deserts. Sun and sand manifesting themselves as supernatural designs of ceremonial feathers.

Gordon Onslow-Ford is a shy Englishman of retiring disposition, for which reason his work is far less well known than it should be. His output is prodigious, but is very rarely shown because he does not blow his own trumpet. His work gives an impression of infinite depth and transparency, and is achieved with a calligraphy of circles, lines, and dots, sometimes in black and white, sometimes in color, resulting in arabesques of marvelously rich texture and orderly randomness. He is also a chemist of painting, and has invented an almost indestructible acrylic paint which he applies to the canvas with squeeze-bottles. He was educated at Dartmouth to become an officer in the British Navy, from which, during World War II, he resigned thirteen times to devote himself to painting—showing a contempt for patriotism which I believe only an Englishman could accomplish. Before the war he studied in Paris with the Surrealists and Cubists, and acquired a notable collection of works by Braque, Tanguy, Delvaux, Chirico, and Matta; to which he added such painters of the New World as Paalen, Mullican, Graves, and Brian Wilson.

At this time Gordon was living on Telegraph Hill in San Francisco in an apartment which, because of his collection, seemed more of an art gallery, and in which paintings were curiously hung from the top of the wall. His wife, Jacqueline, seems—quite deceptively—a little childish, though she has a scholar's knowledge of literature and the history of art, is a master of *haute cuisine*, and maintains a household in which there is not one single cheap-and-nasty object. You will look in vain in her kitchen for any trivial tool or gadget that is not of some special beauty or interest.

It was not until 1961, ten years later, that I really came to know Jean Varda, and lived with him as my shipmate for ten years (until his death) on the ferryboat S. S. *Vallejo*, which he and Gordon had just acquired for their studios, and tied up at the north end of Sausalito. This substantial craft, a side-wheeler, was built in Portland, Oregon, in 1879, and until about 1948, after the building of the Bay bridges, went back and forth between Vallejo (at

the mouth of the Sacramento River), Mare Island, and San Francisco—
owned and operated by the Southern Pacific Railroad. When I first met Gordon and Varda—or Yanko as he was known to intimates—they had just
finished converting this craft into two spacious studio-apartments, Yanko's
outrageously colorful, and Gordon's luminously austere. In those days
Waldo Point, as the area is called, had not become the American Hong
Kong—the fascinating waterfront slum that it is today—and the enormous
windows of Gordon's studio looked out to Mount Tamalpais over quiet waters, troubled only by seagulls, grebes, wild duck, terns, and pelicans. In this
studio we spent hours discussing the problems of spontaneous or instant
painting, and playing a game in which we would shuffle Chinese characters
on cards, deal them out in rows of four, five, or six, and then try to read them
off as poetry.

For Gordon was fascinated with what he called automatism, of painting undeliberatively in such a way that the movements of his brush, or
squeeze-bottle, would not manifest contrived and artificial designs but the
fundamental rhythms of the universe. He knew very well that this problem
was not to be solved by merely capricious and messy motions, and that, to
accomplish it, he had to get his spirit into a state of profound quiet and emptiness. He read, and listened to all that I had to say about the use of Chinese
calligraphy as a discipline of Taoism and Zen, and therefore went on to study
that art under Hodo Tobase and, later, Sabro Hasegawa, and acquired a far
greater mastery than I myself have attained.

Shortly, he moved out of San Francisco to Mill Valley, in the southern
part of Marin County and of the foothills of Mount Tamalpais, and frequent
visits to his home moved my interior compass decisively to this region of the
world. I moved to Mill Valley in 1953, and have lived there, and in adjoining
Sausalito, ever since. *J'y suis, j'y reste*. I can live anywhere I like, so long as
I am reasonably close to an airport, but so far as I am concerned this
is the American Mediterranean. The southern wall of Mount Tamalpais has
the same flavor as the Alpine foothills of Ticino, overlooking the islanded
Bay of San Francisco as they overlook Maggiore or Como, and Sausalito—
a steep slope of wooded and begardened villas going straight down to a colorful mess of shops and harbors—is the nearest thing in the United States to

a fishing village on the Italian Riviera. I can be seemingly lost in uninhabited hills, or wriggling lanes of shrub-hidden houses—some mere shacks, some architectural fantasies—and yet be within thirty minutes' drive of a cosmopolis which, for a hundred years, has been increasingly invaded by the cultures of China, Japan, and Italy.

Here in San Francisco and Southern Marin—I will not speak of Berkeley and Oakland—we have succeeded, more than anywhere else in the United States, in curbing the oppressive White Anglo-Saxon Protestant subculture of the nation, though our slight margin of victory requires incessant vigilance. Now it is curious that wherever there flourishes what may loosely be called a bohemian style of life, the affluent bourgeoisie are filled with envy and want to move in, so that the land values go up and the artists, writers, hippies, and other weird characters who gave the place its color can no longer afford to live there. One calls to mind London's Chelsea, the Montmartre of Paris, New York's Greenwich Village, and, in California, Monterey, Carmel, and Big Sur, as well as San Francisco's Telegraph Hill, and Sausalito itself.

At the present time, 1972, we have here on the northern fringe of Sausalito, on the shady side of my ferryboat, a formidable social crisis of this kind. An ornery, wealthy, and anarchistic Portuguese old-timer, Don Arques, owns a tract of waterfront and docks which he rents, for berthage, to a huge cluster of ferryboats, arks, barges, hulks, and houseboats which are largely inhabited by unconventional, shiftless, colorful, poetic, wayward, irresponsible, alcoholic, drug-taking drop-outs—as well as millionaires and celebrated writers and artists. Seen, especially at dawn and twilight, this is one of the most flamboyantly romantic spots on earth, where the waters are plied by Chinese junks and sailing craft with eyes on their prows and bright lateen rigs. Yet, hard by, there is a prim marina where the yachts and cruisers are all blue and white, shipshape, washed, scrubbed, slick, sterile, plastic and fiberglass uniformities. To their owners, and to the county officials, this vividly irregular waterfront slum is an eyesore and a horror, and though they do not bat an eye at acres of identical, cheap, prefabricated dormitories, they have been plotting for years to rid the area of its principal claim to color and fame.

This resulted, only recently, in a pitched naval battle wherein the police, gold-helmeted and riding coast-guard cutters, were successfully obstructed in their attempt to tow away some houseboats by a fleet of dilapidated tugs, dhows, junks, canoes, and rowboats manned by long-haired freaks, who howled, jeered, hooted, cursed, and anathematized those maternally incestuous officers for depriving people of their homes—and I am proud to say that my son Richard played an important part in the battle. It was as picturesque as a tapestry of the Armada being routed by Sir Francis Drake, and was fully covered by television. No one was injured or killed.

Two things amaze me. One is that American bureaucracies cannot tolerate those minor pockets of irregularity that are essential to a free people—little areas where building codes and bluenose laws do not apply, and where adventurous young men and women can try to live without money, and without the routines of offices and factories. The other is the failure of the affluent bourgeoisie to realize that such pockets are a huge economic asset, that the bohemian community is, so to speak, a sort of cultural manure for the perennial fertilization of zones which will, because of their presence, become particularly attractive and valuable. One of the curses of Western industrial culture is the proliferation of "nice residential areas" where no shops or small businesses are permitted, and which require, as their counterparts, business districts for unrelieved commerce, to which one must commute for several miles to ply one's trade or buy groceries—there to find parking impossible and, in transit, to clog the air with unnecessary gasoline fumes. These "nice residential areas" establish an aesthetic standard of the good life which—though millions buy it—is for me a dreary wasteland in which people are trying to divorce pleasure and leisure from work, so that the pleasure becomes vapid and the work drudgery. Unless I am to live far out in the country, give me a place where a grocery, a laundry, a smithy, and a pub are within easy walking distance.

By virtue of its hilly landscape, its redwood forests and eucalyptus groves, its wayward coastline, and its liberally bohemianized population, the peninsula of Southern Marin has attracted imaginative people from all over the world. Unless I am mistaken or bewitched, I would judge that during the past twenty years it has also become a powerful spiritual center of the nation (for reasons which I shall attempt to describe), as befits the fact that its geographical center is a mountain holy to the Indians, and named after their princess Tamalpa. Though not much more than twenty-five hundred feet high, Mount Tamalpais rises almost directly from sea level, and thus looks bigger than it is, and most of it has been set aside as a state park. Seen in the first light of dawn, even the radar domes of the air force which now crown the western summit look like the domes of a mosque, and the whole mass of hills, valleys, and canyons with their forests, groves, meadows, and giant rocks confers an atmosphere of strange beneficence.

Extraordinary people live upon it. Occasionally you may come across an order of Western *yamabushi* or Buddhist mountain-monks, with their rattling pilgrim staffs and conch-shell trumpets. There are a few true hermits, on the northern slopes, which are its most lonely and untraveled parts. There is a potter who makes fine *raku* ware for the Japanese tea ceremony. There are two importers of the rarest forms of incense from Asia. There is a psychiatrist who lives all year in a tent and uses astronomy to cure his patients by letting them see their problems from the perspective of the galaxy. There is a white (or beneficent) witch and poetess who cultivates a paradise-garden in a most unlikely spot, and who has taught countless people how to respect and cooperate with nature. There is an exuberant carpenter and house designer who leaps, dances, and screams with glee, who plays the saxophone, the oboe, and all kinds of drums, and who has centered his home about a Japanese Buddhist shrine. There is a surgeon who heals people by doing nothing. There is a teacher of dancing who, in her outdoor theater, teaches her students to leave the ground and fly. There are also mountain lions, bobcats, and deer galore, and wild goats and eagles and vultures and raccoons and rattlesnakes and gophers and two cats, named Sol and Shakti, who go for walks with people like dogs, and who respond to commands given in fake declamatory Japanese. All these and many more wizards, yogis, artists, poets, musicians, gardeners, and madmen cluster about this mountain, largely unheeded by the orderly streams of tourists who dutifully inspect the vast redwood cathedral of Muir Woods and attend the annual play given in the enormous amphitheater just below the summit.

And so I find myself far-out, living on the edge of the world—from the standpoint of the place from which I started—although I am surrounded by millions who were born here or have become so accustomed to the scene that Mill Valley is their Chislehurst and San Francisco their London. But for me this environment is still exotic, romantic, and exciting, and in some way represents the frontier at which extremes meet, where Western civilization has, by going to its logical limits, met the East. At the same time I must feel somewhat like an Amerindian: I love the country but I am not so sure of the people—or would it be kinder to say the culture? As I have said, there are, in this area, enough civilized people to keep the barbarians in their place and to permit a free, colorful, and imaginative style of life. But all about us there are enthusiasts for such as Billy Graham and Ronald Reagan, who may be very charming in private life, but who represent and exploit a vulgar multitude of Bible-bewitched prudes, bluenoses, and all-American boys who, despite the legal separation of Church and State, pay the police to be their armed clergymen.

There barbarians, obvious as they may be, are not easy to identify and classify when one tries to be precise. They are, perhaps on the whole, Protestants (and Irish Catholics are crypto-Protestants), and would be Baptists and Methodists rather than Episcopalians or Unitarians; they would be found more densely in the Southern and Middle Western states, including Southern California, than in the Northeastern and Northwestern, and would be living in rural and suburban areas rather than urban; if not an alcoholic, they will drink beer and whiskey rather than wine, but always with a vague sense of guilt, so as to become nasty-drunk rather than happy-drunk; in personal style their hair will be shorter rather than longer, their clothing and furnishings will avoid brilliance of color, and their manner of speaking will identify them instantly, though this must not be described lest they find out and try to disguise it. For these are extremely dangerous people, and what they have in common is a virulent sense of guilt, a righteous zeal to improve the world, and a tendency to dislike and bully their physical bodies. They carry with them their own minority of fellow-traveling sinners, who go for dirty sex and relentless greed for money—as distinct from wealth—and who might be described with a phrase coined by H. L. Mencken when trying to find words for a fabulously ugly building in a dismal Pennsylvania town—"a Presbyterian with a grin."

What troubles me is that I come from the same white Protestant milieu, and must therefore have, in my predisposition to life, some vestiges of this barbarism—against which, for this very reason, I may be rebelling too strongly. Nevertheless, I feel that if I were bending over backward to be careful, fair, and sober in my judgment of it I would be lending weight to the fearsome force which it exercises in shaping the policies and laws of the United States in all their righteously beneficent cruelty. True, there is a far inside point of view from which I can see Billy Graham as a Buddha getting himself into such a horrible state of consciousness that it will be all the more wonderful when he wakes up. I can see, too, that boiled onions and showers in ice-water might be good for me, but shall nonetheless resolutely avoid them.

CHAPTER ELEVEN

BEGINNING
A COUNTERCULTURE

Rudyard Kipling made the famous statement that "East is East and West is West, and never the twain shall meet." He also said that "he does not know England who only England knows," and though this might be taken to mean that untraveled Englishmen cannot realize how good it is at home, the two statements, taken together, suggest something more profound. Kipling was, as I have said, one of those channels of British colonialism through which Himalayan culture backed up into England, as were also Sir Edwin Arnold, author of *The Light of Asia*, Sir Francis Younghusband, president of the World Congress of Faiths, Sir Frederick Treves, whose book *The Other Side of the Lantern* aroused my interest in Japan along with Lafcadio Hearn, and Sir Charles Eliot, who wrote scholarly and sympathetic studies of Hinduism and Buddhism—all knights-errant who plundered Asia of far more valuable gifts than rubber, opium, and tea. The point is that cultural renewal comes about when highly differentiated cultures mix. It is as when, by triangulation, a distant position is ascertained by sighting it from two different points. Our grasp on reality is better when we look at it from the standpoints of different cultures, and the comparison brings to light aspects of one's own point of view so basic as to have been ignored.

What we were doing in San Francisco in the 1950s must, of course, be seen in the context of America's military involvements in Japan, Korea, and then Vietnam, for these exploits were bound to bring the cultures of those areas back home. My own interest in this cultural encounter was peculiar, in the sense that I was not simply a fact-seeker, like a historian or journalist, nor a missionary trying to convert Westerners to Buddhism—though I have been taken for that. No one, however, has ever accused me of being a scholarly Orientalist. I am more often considered a popularizer of Zen, Vedanta, and Taoism, who often twists the facts to suit his own views. One reason for this impression is that my style of writing does not lend itself to the tortuous course of interminable qualifications, reservations, and drawing of fine distinctions. But I am well aware of them when I leave them out, and can (and do) refer those who want the fine points to the proper sources, and can, furthermore, produce the necessary scholarly evidence for my conclusions if asked. Another is that I am not interested in studying, say, Buddhism in terms of what most Buddhists think about it—that is, as an anthropological phenomenon. I am interested in the work of those who are, and have been, its most creative exponents, and, above all, in the actual nature of the inner experiences which they describe. Thus if I am berated for a facile equation of the Buddhist *nirvana* with the Hindu *moksha*, or of Nagarjuna's *sunyata* with Shankara's Brahman, I can give excellent reasons for doing so to anyone prepared to listen for the time required. It is believed in some circles that I have seriously misrepresented Zen by failing to bring out, and indeed even questioning, the importance of the discipline of *za-zen*—or sitting in meditation for long hours—as the royal road to Buddhist enlightenment.[1] It is therefore also said—perhaps with truth—that my easy and free-floating attitude to Zen was largely responsible for the notorious "Zen boom" which flourished among artists and "pseudointellectuals" in the late 1950s, and led on to the frivolous "beat Zen" of Kerouac's *Dharma Bums*, of Franz Kline's black and white abstractions, and of John Cage's silent concerts.

From the beginning, I was never interested in being "good at Zen" in the sense of mastering a traditional discipline, as for example, in studying the piano with Schnabel to the point where my recordings of the Beethoven sonatas would be indistinguishable from his. I had already done that kind of

---

[1] This is a technical problem which I discussed at length with D. T. Suzuki and R. H. Blyth, to discover that our views on the matter were identical. Let it be said that I myself indulge in *za-zen*, not with compulsive regularity, but very frequently, and not with the idea that I am thereby making progress in wisdom, but simply for the delight of being still.

thing, and the point here is not to boast but to explain the real nature of my interest in Zen. For I had, without any formal teacher, unquestionably mastered the art of public speaking, and in the church had become as expert a liturgist as anyone. What I was after was, therefore, not so much discipline as understanding, in the way suggested by the British mathematician G. Spencer Brown in his amazingly mystical treatise, *Laws of Form*:

> To arrive at the simplest truth, as Newton knew and practised, requires *years of contemplation*. Not activity. Not reasoning. Not calculating. Not busy behaviour of any kind. Not reading. Not talking. Not making an effort. Not thinking. Simply *bearing in mind* what it is one needs to know. And yet those with the courage to tread this path to real discovery are not only offered practically no guidance on how to do so, they are actively discouraged and have to set about it in secret, pretending meanwhile to be diligently engaged in the frantic diversions and to conform with the deadening personal opinions which are being continually thrust upon them.[2]

And, so far as I was concerned, the formal study of Zen was "busy behaviour." To sit hour after hour and day after day with aching legs, to unravel Hakuin's tricky system of dealing with *koan*, to subsist on tea, pickles, and brown rice, or to master Dōgen's ritual style of life was—although as good in its own way as learning to sail—not what I needed to know.

What I saw in Zen was an intuitive way of understanding the sense of life by getting rid of silly quests and questions. The archetypal situation was when Hui-k'e asked Bodhidharma how to attain peace of mind. Bodhidharma said, "Bring your mind out, and I will pacify it." "But when I look for it," said Hui-k'e, "I can't find it." "In that case," the master concluded, "it's pacified already." Wittgenstein put it this way:

> We feel that even if *all possible* scientific questions be answered, the problems of life have still not been touched at all. Of course there is then no question left, and just this is the answer. The solution of

---

[2] G. Spencer Brown, *Laws of Form* (London: George Allen & Unwin, 1969), p. 110.

the problem of life is seen in the vanishing of this problem. (Is not this the reason why men to whom after long doubting the sense of life became clear, could not then say wherein this sense consisted?)[3]

It is thus that almost every morning, when I first awaken, I have a feeling of total clarity as to the sense of life, a feeling of myself and the universe as a matter of the utmost simplicity. "I" and "That which is" are the same. Always have been and always will be. I could say that what constitutes me is the same jazz that constitutes the cosmos, and that there is simply nothing special to be achieved, realized, or performed. And so also Emerson, in his essay on "Self-Reliance":

> These roses under my window make no reference to former roses or to better ones; they are for what they are; they exist with God today. There is no time for them. There is simply the rose; it is perfect in every moment of its existence. . . . But man postpones or remembers; he does not live in the present, but with reverted eye laments the past, or, heedless of the riches that surround him, stands on tiptoe to foresee the future. He cannot be happy and strong until he too lives with nature in the present, above time.[4]

Sokei-an Sasaki told me that reading this passage touched off his first experience of *satori*. The point made sounds negative or nihilistic only because the words are saying, as they must say of being in love or of sexual ecstasy, that they are speechless. One could say it with music, but this is expressive, not descriptive, and the trouble with industrially civilized people is that they have no gift for spontaneous music. Our music is so counted out, scaled, metered, and trickily calculated that no one but an expert may have the nerve to indulge in it lest he be accused of making a nasty noise. But we would understand the sense of life if we would sing more and say less.

I have for years been trying to show people that it is extremely important to chant spontaneously, or at least to hum, and also to dance. I have offended people who, on attending seminars to hear an internationally famous

---

[3] *Tractatus Logico-Philosophicus* (New York: Humanities Press, 1961), 6:52, 6:521.
[4] *Ralph Waldo Emerson: Essays and Lectures* (New York: Penguin, 1983), 270.

philosopher, were simply encouraged to breathe effortlessly and allow their voices to hum along a line of least resistance, like water. I have dismayed dancing partners because I would not go

One, two, one, two, three and four,
Over to the window and back to the door—

but would instead use liquid and unpremeditated rhythms which my daughter Ann can follow as if she were my shadow. Chanting, flute or drum playing, and dancing in demilitarized patterns are ideally natural forms of yoga-meditation, because they silence the hypnotic chattering of thought and give one a direct feeling of *shabda*—the basic energy or vibration of the universe. This is why Gregorian chant, for example, gives the sense of eternity so absent from metered rhythms.

I am saying all this to suggest the spirit in which I was working at the Academy of Asian Studies to start something which—based primarily on Lao-tzu and Chuang-tzu—would counterbalance, out-fox, soften, and allay the martial, mechanically marching, tick-tock, and saw-toothed jagged life-rhythm which has been rattling the world at least since the Caesars' legionnaires stamped out of Rome. Cultures, religions, and political attitudes have characteristic rhythms which must be watched and studied as carefully as a doctor feels the pulse or listens to the heartbeat. When President Eisenhower warned us to keep an eye on "the military-industrial complex" he was surely hearing the danger to life in this marching and mechanical rhythm which jolts, fractures, and interrupts everything organic, oceanic, and vegetative, and is being beaten out by people who do not realize that Earth is for all its creatures and not merely for human beings. I knew that I could not preach against this rhythm, because the style of preaching is its own bombast, but that I must rather woo it—like Orpheus—with a different music.

Zen, because of its association with the *banzai-bushido* spirit of the samurai, might have seemed an unlikely ally in this project. But I had learned from D. T. Suzuki, Sokei-an, and later, Sabro Hasegawa that Zen is basically Taoism—the water-course way of life—and that it attempted to tame samurai brigands precisely by showing them that the utmost perfection in swordsmanship and archery was to fence without a sword and shoot without an

arrow. In other words, if you practice fencing, archery, or judo by Zen methods the attainment of real skill puts you in a state of consciousness where
you are so free from egocentric desire that warfare ceases to have any point.
This is what happened to the master swordsman Miyamoto Musashi under
the tutelage of the Zen priest Takuan.

In the autumn of 1952 the Academy of Asian Studies ran out of funds. Our
financial angel had bad luck in his business and couldn't pay our salaries. Spiegelberg resigned as director and went back to full-time teaching at Stanford, but I,
having nothing else to do, decided that the Academy was an adventure too interesting to be abandoned, and slipped by default (as always seems to happen to
me) into the position of its administrator. By this time the Academy had moved
from the financial district to a splendidly rambling old mansion on Broadway
Street in Pacific Heights, overlooking the Golden Gate, the hills of Marin, and
Angel Island. From then until the autumn of 1956, I managed to keep this
strangely offbeat and exciting project alive with the help of a gifted, if desperate, multiracial faculty and a cluster of amazingly devoted students.

I have already spoken of the intellectual stimulation given to me by Leo
Johnson and Pierre Grimes. There was also help in most practical and material ways, first, from my secretary Lois Thille, a tall, queenly, and humorous girl who worked for a pittance, and who had all the fascination of a lapsed
Catholic for the spiritual mischief we were up to. There were three student
house-managers who attended to janitorial services, kitchen maintenance,
and structural repairs, and kept fending off city officials who suspected us of
being a disreputable commune in violation of building codes and health reg-
ulations. Crist Lovdjieff, who was later to be dubbed "the Saint of San
Quentin" by Eldridge Cleaver in *Soul on Ice*, was and still is an essentially
holy person, and I use that word in its strict sense to designate not so much
moral rectitude as a quality of devotion and dedication, of simplicity and
sincerity, which makes one just a little scared. Later, he taught in the school
of the San Quentin "correctional facility,"[5] organized courses in comparative

[5] This is California officialese for "jail," comparable to "impaired vertical clearance" for
"low bridge," and "entering vehicular crossing" for "bridge begins."

religion in which I sometimes took part, and has now become a quiet guru who is highly respected by the troubled young people of this city. Claude Dahlenberg had studied with me at Northwestern—a calm and mighty Swede with a relaxed, amused attitude to the world, who later traveled in Japan, and became a Zen priest working with the *roshi* Shunryu Suzuki. Students at the Academy would sometimes say, "If you want to know what Zen is about, talk to the janitor, Claude. Don't bother to see Alan Watts upstairs." William Swartley was an enthusiast, who came to us fresh from India to study Sanskrit, Tantric yoga, Zen, and just about anything we had to offer; and apart from his studies, he helped us in such practical matters as reconstructing the interior of the building (and much, much more) with an energy and zest seldom seen. His interests eventually moved in the direction of interpersonal psychology and encounter groups, in which field he is now the undoubted and widely acclaimed leader in Philadelphia.

Among our students at this time there were also Michael Murphy and Richard Price, who together founded the Esalen Institute at Big Sur; Richard Hittleman, who subsequently taught Yoga to the nation on television; and on occasion, Gary Snyder the poet, who first appeared unaccountably and amazingly dressed in a formal black suit, British style, with a neatly rolled umbrella, but who later emerged in history as Japhy Ryder—the Buddhist-beatnik hero of Kerouac's *Dharma Bums*—in a characterization which hardly begins to do him justice. I am not Gary's teacher. He studied Chinese at the University of California with Shih-hsiang Chen and Zen at Daitokuji in Kyoto with Goto and Oda; but when I am dead I would like to be able to say that he is carrying on everything I hold most dearly, though with a different style. To put it in another way, my only regret is that I cannot formally claim him as my spiritual successor. He did it all on his own, but nevertheless he *is* just exactly what I have been trying to *say*. For Gary is tougher, more disciplined, and more physically competent than I, but he embodies these virtues without rubbing them in, and I can only say that a universe which has manifested Gary Snyder could never be called a failure.

Yet how many people in England, for instance, know who Gary Snyder is? I used to think that London was the center of the world, and that movements and personages discussed in the *New Statesman* or the *Times Literary*

Supplement were "what's going on" and "where it's at." But now history has become so global that it has no discernible theater, and "what's going on" is so thoroughly reported that no individual can possibly keep track of it or make sense of it. Comprehensible and absorbable history must be reduced to vast generalizations, as when some years ago Arnold Toynbee said that when the history of our time is written a thousand years hence, it will stress not so much the war in Vietnam, the conflict of capitalism and communism, or racial strife, but rather the interpenetration of Christianity and Buddhism. If that is true, the events and the people I am talking about will be in the mainstream of history, if at that time the art of history remains possible or seems important. I am not suggesting that a thousand years from now we shall be reduced to barbarism or have wiped ourselves off the planet, but that we may no longer find history significant. Happy—it has been said—are the people who have no history, and it could be that by then we shall have developed a high civilization which has mastered the art of living in the present.

Naturally, the Academy was in touch with the great Chinese community of San Francisco. Chingwah Lee, its antiquarian and public relations officer, used to talk with us and sometimes lend me objects of art from his considerable collection. There was, however, a large and active Chinese Buddhist group whose leaders came to study with us, who wined and dined us with the most sumptuous hospitality, whose physicians took care of our ailments, and from whom—in working over such texts as the *T'an Ching*, or *Sutra of the Sixth Patriarch*—I learned a great amount of written Chinese. These lovable and generous people were, however, bending over backward to be Rotarian Americans and, with the exception of their diet, had forgotten the taste of Chinese culture. They could have afforded Sung paintings and Han statuary but instead preferred enormous television sets, and such works of Chinese art as they displayed were deplorable clichés. I was aesthetically baffled in trying to show them the grandeur of T'ang and Sung, as also in attempting to warn them that a protestantized Buddhism would have small appeal for the West. The same was true of the Japanese Buddhist communities, which were falling between the two stools of archaic and mechanical ritualism, on the one hand, and rationalized modernism, on the other, so that their younger Jaycee-type members had the heebijeebies when their priests chanted the sutras, and preferred instead to sing:

> Buddha loves me, this I know
> For the sutra tells me so.

They were incapable of seeing that this kind of Buddhism gave no substantial alternative to what was already being offered in the Presbyterian and Methodist churches.

Finally, however, the Soto Zen Temple, then lodged in an abandoned synagogue on Bush Street, got the message—first under Hodo Tobase and later under Shunryu Suzuki. They saw that there was no future in being a circumscribed service center for the Japanese community, for the superstitious and sentimental old folks or for their over-Americanized second- and third-generation children. They saw that what was needed was an authentic and intelligent school for Zen practice designed for Westerners, and one of the people who passed this message over was Tobase's young assistant priest, Kazumitsu Kato, with whom I spent hours and hours studying the *Rinẕai Roku* (a celebrated Zen text of the T'ang dynasty) and the teachings of Bankei, the seventeenth-century Japanese master who, for me, represents Zen at its best.[6] Kato-san was a magnificent cook and also a musician, with whom I discussed the emotional impressions which he received from Western music and I from Japanese, amid much laughter, since we found that our respective impressions were often far from what the composers intended. However, under Shunryu Suzuki the Soto Temple blossomed into the thriving Zen Center to which was later added the Zen Mountain Center at Tassajara Springs, far beyond the end of the Carmel Valley. But aside from its priests, there are hardly any other Japanese people involved!

---

[6] Bankei (1622–1693) was a contemporary of Hakuin and for some time *roshi* at the Myoshinji monastery in Kyoto. Translations of his informal talks on Zen, directed especially to lay people, may be found in D. T. Suzuki's *Living by Zen* (Pasadena, Calif.: P. D. and Ione Perkins, 1949), and in Lucien Stryk, ed., *World of the Buddha* (New York: Doubleday & Co., 1968). When accused of misinterpreting Zen, I refer people to his observations.

During 1954 we were visited by the Japanese artist and printmaker Sabro (i.e. Saburo) Hasegawa, whom I invited immediately to join the faculty. For Sabro was an ideal mixture of Parisian bohemian and traditional Zen-Taoist Japanese, with a touch of samurai dignity and austerity. On the one hand, he might be lounging on the floor, drinking brandy and discussing outrageous new techniques for creating spontaneous abstractions (such as allowing ink-soaked woolen thread to drool over absorbent paper), while on the other, he might be conducting tea ceremony according to the superb technique of his master, So-shu Sen of the Kankyu-an school. Often when Lois and I were unduly harassed with administrative problems he would wander into my office in the middle of the afternoon and invite us to take time out for tea. He had an adjoining room which he and William Swartley had converted into an astonishing burlap-walled cross between San Francisco Victorian and Japanese *shibui*, where the enshrined image of Buddha was a piece of driftwood that had originally been the lathe-turned leg of a very ordinary wooden chair. And there the three of us would sit on the floor and, with easy conversation, watch him spoon powdered green tea into a primitive Korean rice-bowl, cover it with boiling water from a bamboo ladle, and then whisk it into a potion which has been called "the froth of the liquid jade." Lois used to say that one tea with Sabro was worth fifteen visits to a psychiatrist.

Few lecturers can keep me awake, but Sabro was one of them—despite his slow, quiet, and pensive way of talking—for every sentence was like an aphorism from Lao-tzu. Sometimes they were formal lectures (invariably crowded) in the main auditorium, sometimes talks over the table in the communal dining room, and sometimes observations at tea ceremony. But he taught us about Bankei's Taoist style of Zen, about the technique of *haiku* poetry, about calligraphy with the brush, and about the art of the "controlled accident." In Japan he had collected driftwood, especially some pieces from a wrecked boat, which he then used as modular blocks for monoprints wherein he gave a certain organized control to the wandering patterns of the grain in the wood. He explained how the grain followed those same water-course patterns that we admire in clouds, drifting smoke, marble, jade, and flames, and how one might so flow with one's own nature as to live each moment of life with the same grace. When students pressed him to define all this more precisely he would sometimes shout out, "What's the matter with you? Can't you *feel*?"

When not in his Parisian mood—for he had studied painting in Paris— he would always wear a kimono, even on the street, and from him I learned to make this my own everyday attire. For he further explained that Western clothes do not follow the nature, the Tao, of woven cloth. We tailor cloth to fit the shapes of our bodies, whereas if we let it hang loosely and follow its own flow, it confers upon us both comfort and dignity. For this elegance, or grace, of going along in accordance with the flow of things he taught us the word *furyu* (literally, "wind-flow," the Chinese *feng-liu*), and showed its difference from sloppiness by pointing out how it combined relaxation and lack of hurry with alert presence of mind and aesthetic intelligence. Complications arose here because the Japanese way of saying "alert presence of mind" is *mushin*, which, literally, means "no-mind" or absence of self-consciousness.

His presence brought a new dimension into our work because, through him, our students were exposed not only to verbal information about Far Eastern cultures but also to the actual practice of *sumi-e* or black-ink painting, of calligraphy in Chinese, of *bonseki* or the appreciation of natural rocks, and of *cha-no-yu*, the tea ceremony. One day he took an ordinary housepainter's brush and, on a four-foot scroll, wrote for me the Chinese characters for one, two and three—no more than six horizontal lines, so spaced as to stop anyone's attention. D. T. Suzuki was about to visit us, and I said I would hang it in my office for the occasion. Sabro remarked, "I hope he won't notice it."

This calm, easy, dignified, and somehow lonely wind-following man evoked such love and respect from us all that he soon had a considerable following, and we arranged for exhibitions of his work at Gump's gallery in San Francisco, at the Oakland Art Museum, and the Willard Gallery in New York, so that he was certainly on the way to becoming an artist of great reputation. But today I realize, with a curious shock, that he has been forgotten, and that perhaps this was exactly what he would have wished. "I hope he won't notice it." He told me that whereas Hakuin had left eighty spiritual successors, Bankei had left none, and that this precisely was his excellence.

The wild geese do not intend to cast their reflection;

The water has no mind to retain their image.

Towards the end of 1956 it was found that he had cancer of the sinuses, and he died tragically—I would even say horribly—early in 1957, after radical surgery had removed much of the inside of his face. He had the gravest doubts as to the wisdom of submitting himself to Western medicine, but as a responsible official and administrator of a public institution I could not advise him otherwise. Once his condition was known, the pressure upon him to resort to the great medical resources of the University of California was irresistible. But I will never be sure that it was wise. There are cleaner ways out.

In retrospect one can see that the Academy of Asian Studies was a transitional institution emerging from the failure of universities and churches to satisfy important spiritual needs. It was a bridge between the idea of a graduate school and the idea of a "growth center," such as the Esalen Institute, of which there are now more than a hundred in North America. But in those days we were still troubled with the elaborate nonsense of accreditation, degrees, and academic status, so that, to put these matters in order, we had negotiated with the College of the Pacific in Stockton to be adopted as their off-campus graduate school of Asian studies. At that time the College was still recovering from being an educational institution of the Methodist Church, and its officials had all the vacuous and hearty earnestness so characteristic of that religion. They had but one other graduate school—of Education—and the institution was virtually governed from the registrar's office, which took especial pride in the efficiency and rigor of its nit-picking bureaucracy. Thus the administration had no experience even of a traditionally academic graduate school, much less of the weird and irregular spiritual adventures that most of our own faculty and students had in mind.

It must be remembered that the academic study of "alien cultures" has its background in missionary endeavor and colonial administration. Its attitude of scientific objectivity towards them, of description without participation or enthusiasm, reflects our habitual assumption of spiritual superiority (even when we are no longer religious) and our fear of "fraternizing with the natives." Thus nothing is more troublesome to a department of anthropology than a field-worker who "goes native" and forgets to keep his mind coldly aloof. He is said to have lost his objectivity, which is actually no more than a way of describing things in accord with the metaphysical preconceptions of Western culture, so that the following of scientific methods in Asian or African studies is not necessarily a release from narrow cultural provincialism. Thus our participatory approach to these cultures was as strange to Orientalists at the University of California as it was disturbing to Methodists at the College of the Pacific.

Furthermore, I think it will now be clear that my own approach to Asian philosophy was part of an individual philosophical quest. I am not interested in Buddhism or Taoism as particular entities or subjects to be studied and defined in such a way that one must avoid "mixing up" one's thinking about Buddhism with interests in quantum theory, psychoanalysis, Gestalt psychology, semantics, and aesthetics, or in Eckhart, Goethe, Whitehead, Jung, or Krishnamurti. I feel about academic "subjects" just as the Balinese feel about "Art" when they say, "We have no Art: we just do everything as well as possible." It was the same, too, for such a scientist as Gregory Bateson, whom I met at this time, when he was resident ethnologist at the Palo Alto Veterans' Hospital, attached to Stanford University.[7] He explained that in conducting a course of study he would give three or four set lectures about specific topics or methods, and for the rest of the semester simply discuss whatever happened to be of interest to him at the time. In this way his students were able to join in the experience of a creative imagination in process: actually doing science instead of merely learning about it or preparing for it.

In a similar way, I would announce in the formal catalogue the offering of a course in Lao-tzu or Chinese Zen, and simply make sure that the students had access to the relevant literature, that they understood its historical background, and were familiar with its main technical terms. For the rest, I would use the original texts as a basis for rambling reflections that might take us into Tantric yoga, optical illusions, metalinguistics, biological systems-theory,

---

[7] He was then preoccupied with the relation of communications theory to psychiatry, and had just published, with Jurgen Ruesch, that remarkable study of the "double bind" in logic and human relations, *Communication: The Social Matrix of Psychiatry*.

and hypnosis. I would bring in seemingly unrelated guest lecturers or demonstrators, such as S. I. Hayakawa on semantics, Hilde Elsberg and Charlotte Selver on sensory-awareness training, or Lloyd Saxton on hypnosis in clinical psychology. From the standpoint of the conventional academic drudge all this was a vague hodgepodge and an undisciplined syncretism, but it has always seemed to me that no intelligent person should restrict himself to artificially segregated fields of spiritual or intellectual adventure. Our understanding of the world cannot be ruled by the university's departmental politics, which—if they had had their way—would have strangled such interor multidisciplinary inquiries as biophysics, cybernetics, astrophysics, mathematical logic, and cultural anthropology. Culture is an active, present process which involves the formation of relationships between all things known to us, and the narrow specialist is its servant and informant, not its arbiter. It must proceed at all levels in the university, which otherwise becomes a mere multiversity, and it is this which is the true hodgepodge. Who—if anyone—decides what *are* the relevant departments of knowledge?

By and large our students wanted no more than to get by in the world of supposedly practical affairs. They had no ambitions for working with the Department of State, and still less for making fortunes in commerce with the Far East. They might, in a one-eyed way, be thinking that a Ph.D. would be useful in getting a teaching position, as a reasonably interesting way of supplying bread and butter. But the other eye was on something else—the thing variously called *moksha*, *bodhi*, *kaivalya*, or *satori* in the Asian religions, which is the wisdom of a transformed consciousness, of liberation from that exclusive identification of oneself with personality which overlays and conceals the basic sensation in the very back of the mind: the sensation of being identical with the universe, which is said to be the "oceanic feeling" of babies in the womb. Some call this regression, in the sense of a spineless collapse of the thrust of life, though I have always seen it as a foundation for this thrust, without which the business of life must be conducted in a spirit of panic or "quiet desperation." (Isn't it possible that space itself is an amniotic fluid?)

It was in this spirit that we invited such visitors to the Academy as D. T. Suzuki, Swami Ramdas (a bubbling *bhakti yogi*), G. P. Malalasekera, the

Bikkhu Pannananda from Thailand, the Zen master Asahina Sogen from Kamakura, the Thera (Elder) Dharmawara from Cambodia, and Ruth Sasaki, who entranced the whole student body with her formal and definitive lecture on the use of *koan* in Zen meditation. It was also in this quest that, early in the summer of 1955, I took a whole group of students on a pilgrimage to Ojai to talk with Krishnamurti—a memorable joy-ride which included an all-night drive from the College of the Pacific in Stockton to Ojai, where we camped in an orchard of loquat, grapefruit, and lemon trees, and ended up in a pearly twilight on a serene beach at Carpinteria, at the sight of which everyone heaved a long sigh of relief and said, "Why, this is it." We made a fire of driftwood, and, close to midnight, a shoal of grunion fish came running into shore. Claude caught them in his hands and roasted them on the fire, and probably none of us ever recovered from this temptation to the life of the beachcomber. Substitute for clock time the rhythm of the waves and their long, easy, interminable sighing. Forget the dates of the days, weeks, and months, and go simply by the sun, the moon, and the seasons. Catch fish and get free, second-day vegetables from a neighboring market.

But in those mid-1950s neither the College of the Pacific nor the Academy's own board of trustees (who contributed virtually nothing to its maintenance except their names) were interested in questions of human identity and the transformation of consciousness. I am not a man of business for the simple reason that the calculations and paperwork of business bore me to death, and therefore I had gone naively ahead for three years raising funds for the institution, teaching, and doing the academic administration without fully realizing that our official substructure was worthless. We were running a very lively enterprise, but our official sponsors were embarrassed and uninterested, and would neither assist the work nor get out of the way. By the end of 1956 it was becoming clear that I was as much out of place in the groves of academe as in the Church, that I was never, never going to be an organization man, and that I must make up my mind finally to go it alone.

Naturally, this troubled me. There were voices from the past echoing in my skull: "Alan, why can't you be like everyone else? Why are you so weird? Why don't you come down to earth and face reality?" Furthermore my then wife, Dorothy, although she had supported me in my resolve to work independently, was nevertheless putting more and more pressure on me to suburbanize myself, to live a more ordinary life, to mow the lawn, play baseball with the children, and abandon my far-out bohemian friends. We had then a rather pleasant house in Mill Valley, which had formerly been a garden nursery, with an expansive lawn, four great pine trees, twenty-seven fruit trees, four children—and the school just over the fence, and nice neighbors, and a Volkswagen bus, and an automatic dishwasher, and lots of cats, and chickens, and a stream, and a tiled bathroom (which I had fixed my-self), and a cozy library with a *shoji* ceiling made by Roger Somers, and— in short—a colossal family enterprise in which I should never have allowed myself to be involved.

Thus in the spring of 1957 I left the Academy to its trustees, who then appointed the venerable Theosophist Ernest Wood as its president. But the job was beyond the powers of this wonderful but failing old man, and after the College of the Pacific severed relations a year or so later, the project faded into dismal obscurity. And then Haridas Chaudhuri went off on his own and replaced it with the California Academy of Asian Studies, which is where something of the original tradition of the work is now alive and kick-ing quite interestingly. From this time on I have, as Puck Humphreys put it, "lived by my wits"—which is, I believe, a slightly pejorative expression for managing to live without any established position and thus getting by, even successfully, without really deserving to do so. I found that, for me, it is the ideal way, for as things now stand the independent author or artist has a free-dom in his work which few others enjoy. He is not tied to any particular place; he does not have to keep regular hours, or worry about faculty meet-ings and university politics; he does not have to kowtow to professional unions, like doctors and musicians, nor spend his days being nasty to people, like lawyers.

The author tends, therefore, to be an individualist in politics, and, in the American scene, finds it hard to decide whether the right wing or the left con-stitutes the greater threat to his liberty. Thus in one sense of the word I am apolitical: I cannot find enthusiasm for any particular ideology, party, state, or nation, and I believe, furthermore, that these are obsolete types of organiza-tion which increasingly work against the real interests of real people. On the other hand, I am intensely interested in specific political and economic problems: in developing an ecologically sound technology, in getting it understood that the dollar is something like an inch (not wealth, but a measure of wealth), in showing that people must be paid for work done on their behalf by machinery, and in the drastic reform of prisons and mental hospitals.

In this way of life it becomes increasingly impossible to distinguish work from play, or business life from social life, for almost everything is grist for a philosopher's mill, and I am quite sure that I would continue my present way of life even if I amassed a great fortune. At home I write, and otherwise roam about the country giving lectures and conducting seminars, or informal conferences. I make it very clear to those who attend that my role is more that of physician than of minister, for the former works to get rid of his clients and the latter to keep them in a permanent following. I insist that, after a certain time, they will have heard all the important things I have to say, and that having received the message they should hang up the phone. Because of this, most of my personal friends are former students who have ceased attending lectures and graduated from discipleship, although some of them still stop by for the entertainment. Just as I am not in competition with university professors for their jobs, I am not in competition with gurus or psychotherapists for their work with individual students or patients. I see my work simply as one of philosophical and spiritual stimulation, and refer those who want to work with a guru or psychotherapist to others—for whose existence as essential partners in what I am doing I am most grateful.

Like everything else, this profession also has its drawbacks. For one thing, anyone who speaks as a mystic and who discourses on the merely institutional or conventional reality of the ego-personality is expected to behave as a nonentity. By the same kind of reasoning, ministers and teachers are grossly underpaid on the assumption that they are not in their particular lines of work "for money." Yet no one can succeed as an independent author, or as a teacher or minister, without a flair for drama and for coming on strongly as a personality, and by success I mean not only the financial reward but also effective communication. Strength of personality—even though you yourself know very well that it is a big act—is always mistaken for an "ego-trip," and, in the mystic, for a contradiction of everything you are saying. But, supposing that "genuine mystics" actually exist, I have never known one who was not a unique and interesting individual, whereas the true egoist, who fully believes in his own separate reality, is invariably a bore. All interesting people have charisma and, whatever their personal faults, express a gift or grace or power that comes from beyond themselves, be it demonic or divine. For this reason philosophies or religions, like Buddhism, which deny full reality to the ego-personality cannot, as one might suppose, go into political partnership with any form of totalitarianism or collectivism where the individual is reduced to a cog in the social machine. This is one reason why people of intense spirituality will not serve in armies. As the universe manifests itself as an infinite variety of patterns and forms, the more any individual realizes himself to be one with that universe, the more of an individual he becomes. The five fingers move independently only because of their union with the hand, the arm, the body, and the organism-environment field.

Another drawback is that a philosopher-teacher is invariably confused with a missionary-preacher with a vocation to improve the world and do good to others, and thus his personal and private life is an object of amazing curiosity and minute scrutiny. I have the greatest difficulty in making it clear that I do not regard myself as something other than the world, which can stand aside from that world, and then tell it what it ought to be—as a sort of independent critic from some other universe. I regard my philosophizing simply as an attempt to describe what is happening in the world, and this describing, in turn, as an action of the world. If this description suggests any changes in thought or behavior, I regard these suggestions, not so much as my personal recommendations, but as integral parts of the world's own growth process. In other words, I regard my work as the spontaneous arisal of a vitamin or nutrient which the world happens to need at this time, and which it is producing through me and many others.

CHAPTER TWELVE

OTHER SELVES

If I were to be accused of being in love with myself, I would want to know rather specifically just what this "myself" is, and to see a bill of particulars. For as I think over the things that I love, very few of them would be conventionally describable as myself. I spend only negligible time looking in the mirror. I like the sound of my own voice, but because listening to my own tape recordings takes up as much time as to make them, I audition them only very occasionally. I enjoy reading my own books, but do so only to keep track of what I have said, and always have the vague feeling that someone else much brighter than I has written them. Furthermore, if Aristotle was right in feeling that contemplation is the goal of action, there should be the same satisfaction in contemplating what one has created as in digesting a good meal. But when I read my own English I am always aware that this language was given to me by others, and that I am indebted to them not only for phrases and rhythms, but also for many of the ideas with which I am playing.

It can, of course, be argued epistemologically that every experience or sensation that I love is myself, in the sense that it is a state or vibration of my own nervous system. But when you press this argument to its logical conclusion, *all* experiences are vibrations of your own organism, so that it is hard to draw any line between knowledge of yourself and knowledge of the world. So do I love the woman or do I love myself when I put my lips on hers and feel the eager electricity that flows from her body? Is there a difference between loving music and loving what music does to *me*, when I listen to a baroque ensemble and dance to it? And who or what am I loving when I send an arrow soaring into the sky, or watch cormorants flying low along the sea, or walk among pine trees on a hot day, sniffing the air?

For, at this point, the story of my life becomes inseparable from the story of my friends, so that I must explain myself by speaking of others. Work at the Academy put me in touch with a number of people who became so much part of my life that I would not be myself without them. For one thing, I found an older sister, who came there to audit the courses in Chinese art, philosophy, and poetry—a woman from Yorkshire, who by way of Montreal, New York, and the Panama Canal had sailed to San Francisco with the idea of going on to China—whose poetic imagination had been captured by the Golden Gate and its hills, and who had therefore settled for living on the edge of Chinatown when, in 1926, it was far more Chinese than it is today. But when I first met her, Elsa Gidlow was living at Fairfax on the fringes of Mount Tamalpais, and by a coincidence of the "Net" her companion, Isabel Grenfell Quallo, was the handsome daughter of an African princess and the missionary-explorer George Grenfell—and she had been one of my mother's pupils at Walthamstow Hall, the school for missionaries' daughters in Sevenoaks. Isabel had come a long way from that scene, but this odd and utterly unexpected connection somehow put both of them in my family.

From the first meeting Elsa enchanted me, in the strict sense of that word, which is that of a witch casting a spell. But I could not quite make out at first at which band on the spectrum of love I should meet her. She was sixteen years older than I, reserved and gentle, with the beauty of a lithe and very self-respecting cat. Indeed, she went about with a Siamese cat named Lao, who rode obediently on her shoulder like Wotan's raven. Superficially, she suggested that she was a very respectable and demure maiden lady, but someone had put raven's blood in her mother's milk. She wore a cloak and a soft velvet beret, and had a knowing smile. Her library replicated my own to such an extent that I could talk to her as one having the same literary background, and she shared all my own attitudes about the Tao of nature and freedom from the bombastic Father-God of the uptight Christians and Jews. She had inherited a charisma from a Celtic white witch and nature mystic named Ella Young, who had lived for many years beside the sand dunes south of Pismo Beach—even before the days when Chester Alan (Gavin) Arthur III, grandson of that President, had resided there among attendant soothsayers and yogis as King of the Dunes. Naturally, I considered an erotic relationship with Elsa, but I soon saw that we were to meet on the green and not the red band of the spectrum, where intense friendship lies between vermilion lust and violet *agape*, and that she was to fulfill exactly the role in my life that would have been taken by a very companionable older sister.

I have invented the word "goeswith" to mean the inseparable relationship which lies between different aspects of the same thing or process, as between front and back, the magnetic poles, solid and space, male and female, bees and flowers. Elsa invariably goeswith a garden. She learned from Ella Young—if she did not know it before—that flowers and vegetables, trees and mountains, animals and birds, are *people* and must be treated as such. She introduced me to Ella one evening at her house in Fairfax, and this frail, transparent, bewitching old lady talked to us, like a true shaman, about the personalities of mountains, and about talking to the weather and to wild animals, and we reminisced on a film we had both seen (about 1926) of an attempt to climb Everest, embellished with scenes of Tibetan dancing. And I was puzzled and disquieted because my wife, Dorothy, seemed to recoil from such talk as a scientist washing her hands from the contamination of superstition. Yet the evidence is growing that certain people have green thumbs because they love and talk to their plants, and it seems that plants have intensely sensitive responses to human behavior which can be recorded by the electroencephalograph. It escapes the notice of many well-educated people that the scientific establishment always runs the danger of becoming a rigidly authoritarian religion, a church excommunicating heretics such as Wilhelm Reich, Velikovsky, and Timothy Leary. In this church it is high dogma that everything outside the human skull is relatively stupid and unfeeling, and that animistic religions, such as Shinto, which attribute life and spirit to rocks and rivers, represent the lowest form of intellectual development. Meanwhile, such an imaginative enthusiast for science as Arthur Clarke speculates about vast electronic intelligences located in the galactic center. But the angels may be growing in your window boxes.

Shortly after I met her, Elsa moved from Fairfax to a knoll in the Tamalpais foothills overlooking Muir Woods, a forest of giant redwoods about a

mile inland from the Pacific on the western slope of the coastal range. Here
she, and Roger Somers the Carpenter (of whom I shall have much more to
say), discovered a run-down farm on land almost entirely surrounded by
state park, consisting of two splendid barns and two wretched, unimaginative, slummy dwellings all too characteristic of rural California. With her
skill as a gardener and his as an architect they transformed this area into a paradise, a Garden of Eden, so that a dry land of clay, scrub oak, sage brush, and
eucalyptus became a haunt for hummingbirds. All this they accomplished
with imagination and muscle, for they had nothing to speak of in the way of
money, and thus their place does not have the swell, sleek niftiness of such
expensive paradises as East Hampton, Nassau, Diamond Head, and Ascona.
It has what people who are only rich find so frustrating, because you cannot
buy it with money.

   She made a central patio, of sundecks sliding into a courtyard surrounded
with flowers and cactus plants and a lemon tree and many kinds of fuchsias
and strange little lantern-flowers with pointed caps like Tibetan lamas, and encircled all this with a kitchen garden of beans and lettuce, cabbages and straw-
berries, and New Zealand spinach—the whole protected from wind by a
grove of eucalyptus with their dense clusters of bamboolike leaves rustling
a hundred feet above. As I have said, I am a lover of gardens, but not a gardener, and cannot be relied upon to take care of a patch of fertile land larger
than half a tennis court, if that. But Elsa, who is now over seventy, is of slight
build and, without seeming to have any muscle at all, takes care of weeding,
digging, hoeing, pruning, and shoveling compost, and undertakes all this
with minute attention to the principles of nature, and thus without use of
nasty chemicals and pesticides. Her pesticide-in-chief is always the resident
Siamese cat, who takes care of the gophers. She understands also the complex
alchemy and ecology of plants in such a way as to protect her vegetable crops
with insect-repellent weeds, and is, indeed, such a master of her art that
young men come to work and study with her.

   Elsa is, furthermore, a poet of what I call the Clear School, though she
is by no means so well known as such other clear poets as Alice Meynell,
Walter de la Mare, Emily Dickinson, Kenneth Rexroth, Karl Shapiro, Jean Burden, and Eric Barker (to name but a few) who, while employing traditional

rhythms, say what they have to say with an easy, natural clarity which avoids both clichés and obscure allusions or bizarre, far-fetched images.

> Let the wild swan singing go,
> This is no bird to hold:
> No clutch can check that flight
> From cold to cold.
>
> And let the wild swan come
> In his fury and light.
> The lift of his wing is Now;
> The wing-dip, Night.

And, in connection with something I shall have to say about babies later on:

> Mountain at dayfall,
> Star-drinking lake.
> On mere gurgling baby
> Big with its own unknown—
> Quite ordinary phenomena
> Makes seers of them, although
> They stand cool before pomps,
> Panoplies, the bloated great
> and other vulgar wonders.

Just as it is difficult, if not impossible, to write real poetry about religion and philosophy (since to do so you must borrow all your images from the "secular" world of nature), it is difficult to write vividly erotic poetry without being vulgar, yet this is Elsa's particular achievement.

Kenneth Rexroth, whom I met about the same time, is a special version of the rough diamond, for he comes on with a voice at once refined and gritty, and appears to have a testy and sometimes haughty attitude to both life and literature. But, as I see it, the truth of the matter is that although he should never read his own poetry out loud, he is one of the finest poets of our time, and is a person of quite extraordinary compassion and learning—since his enormous and well-studied personal library includes all the literatures of the world, Oriental as well as Western. Once when he was reviewing books on radio station KPFA, and making the recording in his own home, a canary began to provide background music, lilting and trilling with all its might. There was a pause in the talk, and then a sudden crash. Rexroth came back to the microphone with, "That's enough of *that!*" Had he annihilated the canary or just slammed the door? One might suppose that a sensitive poet would have enjoyed the accompaniment or even let the bird take over. But then there would have been no comedy. Rexroth's writing covers such an enormous field (and I am speaking not so much of his poetry as of his critical essays and his autobiography) that it is a little difficult to identify his basic *Weltanschauung*. He has been much more than poet laureate to the Wobblies and the anarchists, and is much too cosmopolitan to be identified with the Beat Generation. Try, rather, the idea of taking T. S. Eliot and pushing him all the way over into Mahayana Buddhism without taking away his fascination with Christian mysticism, and season it all with a spirit of intense, if cynical, social concern.

It was also at this time that I came to know another poet of the West, James Broughton, who likewise belongs to the Clear School but with a unique touch of whimsy. People find it hard to understand him because of his peculiar ability to be funny about such profound matters as religion without being either irreverent or unsympathetic. He has dedicated to me a whole series of poems about Zen which some mistake for satirical lampoons, but in which he has actually caught the essential spirit of what Zen is all about.[1] He is entirely a person after my own heart, with an elfin face and big horned eyebrows, who dresses outlandishly and elegantly with cloaks, high-buttoned jackets, embroidered vests, and rare pieces of Amerindian jewelry without giving the least impression of taking himself seriously. He just lets his imagination run riot, with impeccable taste and debonair unconcern for what the stolid may think of him.

He studied with me, informally, when I gave seminars after leaving the Academy, understood exactly what I was saying, and came back with a poem entitled "Those Old Zen Blues: or, After the Seminar" which began:

---

[1] See the section "Gods and Little Fishes," Part 8 of his collected poems, *A Long Undressing* (New York: The Jargon Society, 1971).

> *It's not because it is.*
> *It's not because it isn't.*
> *It is because it is*
> *because it's not at all.*

And went on:

> There's nothing in heaven, nothing in hell,
> and nothing is what I am.
> Something is where it always was
> but it doesn't give a damn.

He made up a parody of the *haiku* called the "High Kuku," such as:

> You always think I'm greener elsewhere,
> said the Grass.
> Well, sometimes, I am.

> When I gave up trying to understand,
> said the Camel's Eye to the Needle,
> then I began to get the point.

> Going around in theological circles,
> said the Dove,
> God must get very dizzy.

> I like where I'm sitting,
> said the Toad.
> What else is a toadstool for?

And then there was "Buddha Land: A Zen Spiritual"—

> I hear the happy sound of
> one hand clapping
> that old hand clapping
> that big hand clapping—
> I hear the happy sound of
> one hand clapping
> all the way to Buddha Land.

Koan Baby, don't you cry, don't you cry!
Koan Baby, don't you cry!

These quotations may not give an idea of James's more sophisticated poetry, for which one must read *A Long Undressing*, but my point is that he is a sort of Buddhist John Betjeman with, however, the same Anglo-Catholic under-tones—surprising for one born and raised in Modesto, California. Yet he goes much deeper than Betjeman because he is closer to the child, having the sense that the everyday world is not only marvelous but magical—that is, uncanny in a way that is not so much disquieting as holy and nonsensical. You pick up a seashell not just because it is pretty, but because its twirled perfection and the way the light comes through its walls remind you of the most important thing you have ever forgotten.

> I heard in the shell
> all the hymns of hell,
> I heard all the angels crying,
> I heard the earth
> in pangs of birth
> and all the galaxies dying....
>
> I heard in the shell
> the throb of each cell
> from flower and rock and feather.
> But loudest of all
> rang the quiet call
> of Yes and No singing together.

How basic can you get?

James is also the maker of numerous films—very well known to con-noisseurs of this art—in which he manages to flip from themes that are fop-pishly elegant, cute, smart, and affectatious to things that are suddenly profound and numinous, in such a way that the contrast shakes you into ele-mental laughter. This is really the dialogue between James's deliberately and yet innocently staged personality and his deeper self, which is an astonished child of three years visited by an angel who taught him the art of poetry.

And then one day James introduced me to a lady named Suzanna—a swinging, sassy, Titian-haired artist and designer who popped right out of his grandfather's California gold-rush days with a warm and motherly heart—and asked me to join them in holy matrimony. I had been accustomed to James as a bachelor, living in a house of weathered wood on Stinson Beach, where I would sometimes go simply to get away from being suburbanized. I found that Suzanna was somehow a feminine counterpart of James, that her external personality was a good-humored joke behind which was a woman of great aesthetic perception and *joie de vivre*. He gave a house party at a lonely inn on the coast near Mendocino, in the course of which we performed a marriage ceremony so elaborately designed as to ritual and costume that everyone expected it to be nothing more than a pleasant and frivolous drama. The couple were presented by their respective analysts—James by Joseph Henderson, and Suzanna by Elizabeth Osterman, both psychiatrists and students of Jung. In fact, I regard Joseph as Jung's principal successor. He gives the impression of being an amazingly wise owl who, like Lao-tzu, achieves everything by doing nothing, and is thus one of the few psychiatrists who can help dangerously crazy people. Elizabeth—a gentle, mature, and noble blonde—after the wedding ceremony danced with Roger Somers. Now Roger, in the colossal exuberance of his dancing, has been known to grab people by the hair and swing them around his head. But after dancing with Elizabeth he said, "Wow...that woman scared me! I have never danced with anyone who trusted me so perfectly."

So the ceremony was a fantastically symbolic, multireligious rite, followed by the Nuptial Mass in Latin, in which I was assisted by two lady acolytes vested in white chasubles, and before the thing was half under way people began to get wet eyes, recognizing that it was all for real, which proved again that American Christians and Jews have no idea what they are missing in being squeamish about ritual magic.

I should have met Roger Somers in Evanston, for that was his home and he was in school there when I was chaplain at Northwestern. But it was through Gordon Onslow-Ford that he turned up at the Academy and began sitting in on my lectures. As a student of Frank Lloyd Wright he was a carpenter-architect with a religious attitude to his work. He had realized that man is not separable from his environment, and that because this includes his house, his house must be harmonious with his character. Roger can shape wood almost as if it were water—which it is when you consider the patterns of its grain, for a tree is a two-sourced river stilled into wood. Roger just doesn't like straight lines, which, in my book, is a virtue because the world itself is a ballful of wiggles, and human beings must outgrow the idea of trying to straighten it out. So he has designed houses like seashells and mushrooms and apples, and he does his work with such gusto that while he charges more per hour than anyone else he does it in half the time. He handles his medium with sheer glee, and he keeps at it day after day. In this sense he is one of the most responsible people in the world.

But he is also an incarnation of the Greek god Pan, if you can imagine Pan based on a bull instead of a goat; and don't forget that Pan means "All." For his physique is formidable, his grizzly hair sticks out like short horns, and his energy is endless. He plays the saxophone, the oboe, and all kinds of drums. He dances—free form—like a maniac, and his shrieks of delight can be heard all over the hill where, next door to Elsa, he created a pleasure-house out of a run-down shack. Under this two-horned Chinese-style roof is a true *living* room, part of which is a stage enclosed with Japanese *shoji* with inside variable multicolored lighting, a circular moon-viewing window looking out on a blossoming quince tree, a ceiling that can be raised or lowered, straw matting on the floor, and in the central alcove an ornate black-and-gold lacquer *butsudan*, or Buddhist household shrine, from Japan. Beyond this stage-cum-sanctuary is a slate-floored area with gold and redwood walls, a sunken dining table so that you can eat comfortably sitting on the floor, and the inside wireworks of an upright piano embedded in the wall. In this room—long before the days of the Beatles and the great rock bands, the light shows, and joyous freak-outs—we danced and drummed and chanted and howled to our hearts' content, and, in so doing, discovered a *yoga*, a joining with the energy of the universe, which, for me, became a fundamental religious exercise.

Roger-rock became so ecstatic that a neighbor, convinced that the most outrageous orgies were in progress, would regularly summon the police, who would arrive only to find Roger and his wife, perhaps another couple, and two respectable elderly ladies, all sitting quietly in a Japanese shrine-room. This is doubtless due to the now archaic terror which Anglo-Saxon colonists feel at the blood-pulse of hand-beaten drums, imagining that Zulus or Apaches must again be on the warpath. Perhaps, in a way, they are.

It should be added that Roger's kitchen is surrounded by a soffit, just exactly a centimeter higher than his own head, from which is projected a rectangular crown of wooden thorns—for this house is not for any man taller than himself. He has a basic sense of territory and knows that land, rather than money, is *real* estate, and in this respect he exhibits a completely honest and guiltless selfishness which makes him all the more sociable, because he will not deceive you as to the limits of his generosity. Roger also has the belly-laugh of one who knows that boys will always be boys, and though he is not a bookish man and would feel awkward on a rostrum, he is nonetheless lucid and eloquent in explaining his philosophy of art and life. He understood it by himself, but he got the words and the structure of it from me and from David Hunter, whom I shall next introduce. Hundreds of people, including the great and the famous, have spent evenings in Roger's joyhouse and have learned how to be exuberant without feeling foolish or ashamed.

Imagine, for a moment, that you are a rather ordinary person thinking it might be fun to join a drama group and take part in an amateur presentation of *Twelfth Night* or *Lady Windermere's Fan*. You find that the public school system is offering an adult evening class in drama, at Pacific High School in the very best district of San Francisco. You go to the bare gymnasium to find yourself in the presence of a tall, long-headed, and extremely handsome lanky fellow, quiet in manner, who asks you to lie on the floor, close your eyes, and listen. Meanwhile, he is sitting on the edge of the stage, picking over a pile of rags which he is knotting together into a long string. "Listen," he says. "Just become aware of all the sounds that are going on ... without trying to think what they are, without naming them. Listen in the same way as you would listen to music ... not asking what it *means*. ... And as I talk, just listen to the sound of my voice and forget about the meaning of the words. ... Are these sounds outside your head, or inside? ... And find out whether your ears are willing and happy in listening to these sounds ... and whether the sounds themselves want to be heard by your ears. ... If there is some resistance, find out where that resistance is ... and how it feels."

More experiments of this kind would follow. You would be invited to explore the feeling of how you move an arm from one position to another, or to stop dominating your voice and let the vocal chords groan on their own. There was never any explanation of why these experiments were being made, for David wanted people to learn to stop asking such silly questions. After half an hour of this he would call everyone to the stage to rehearse the play. It was David Hunter's own play, *The Orange Seller*, which he read, small section by small section, from a bulky manuscript; he had the actors go through it, repeat it, and then would arbitrarily alter the text if he felt so inclined. If an actor needed coaching in a particular gesture, he would draw his or her attention not only to the specific bodily movement, but also to what was seen as the eyes swept across the floor in making a turn—the shadows, the patches of light, the dust, the grain in the wood.

David's dramatic methods so awakened his students as to what is actually going on, as distinct from what is said to be going on, that they changed their lives about, rearranged their marriages, and altered their vocations. The school board got wind of the fact that something most peculiar was happening under their auspices, and sent an investigator to one of his classes. He found the students sitting on the floor, in two rows, facing one another and pointing their index fingers at one another, while David was saying, "Now see if your finger wants to touch your partner's finger. Be aware of what would be involved in moving your finger to touch the other. Find out whether your partner's finger wants to be touched, and if there is no reluctance allow the fingers to meet." The investigator returned to the board and screamed, "Hypnotism!" Whereupon David was ordered to teach drama properly, or desist. He desisted, and set out on a journey around the world.

But he has come back, and is still teaching people in San Francisco to "get with it," where "it" designates the world of nonverbal happenings which we usually call the physical or material world, without realizing that these words are loaded with philosophical prejudice. The sound of a frog jumping into an old pond is "Plop!" This "Plop!" isn't physical, material, mental, or spiritual, for "Plop!" isn't a philosophical category. "Plop!" is just "Plop!" This is the simplest thing in the world but the hardest to explain. If you understand it you can see that this "Plop!" is all-of-a-piece with a thousand galaxies.

David Hunter, who was introduced to me by Hilde Elsberg, is one of the pioneers in a movement—originating from many different sources—that has come to be known by the awkward name of Sensory Awareness. We never could find a good name for it because it deals with the nameless, the ineffable, and with what Korzybski amusingly termed the "unspeakable" world, that is, with "Plop!" Hilde further introduced me to Charlotte Selver, from New York, since both she and Charlotte had learned this mysterious art from Elsa Gindler, in Berlin, who had discovered it all by herself in the forests, whither she had retreated to let nature take its course when pronounced incurably tuberculous. She just lost herself among the pine trees with the thought that "what came by itself can go by itself." She just became quiet and felt what was going on with every nerve-end in her body, and then responded to it in the sense of letting the response happen. This is not the same thing as going limp, like a wet rag over a clothesline. When the eyes are in focus they are neither strained nor mushily bleary, but simply alert without stiffness. This was Elsa Gindler's attitude to everything going on inside and around her, and in this way she managed to get her ego out of the way of her organism-environment and let *it* run the show, and it was thus that she not only recovered from tuberculosis but also discovered the way of life that Lao-tzu had found centuries before. It was for this reason that, though they had no historical connection with Chinese philosophy, I introduced both Hilde and David to students at the Academy, and conducted many seminars conjointly with Charlotte, mostly at her studio in New York.

It is important that this work which derives from Elsa Gindler not be confused with eurhythmy, dance therapy, or any kind of gymnastics, and especially not with German balletomania of the twenties—with all those sexless nudes in lovely postures trailing filmy scarves. The Gindler method is much more a way of meditation. In has nothing to do with posturing, exercising, or disciplining "the body"—considered as an entity different from oneself—in any preconceived way. True, the work is done on the floor, the women may be wearing leotards, and thus the scene looks superficially gymnastic. But the principle is to find out what one is actually feeling all over and everywhere, without naming it, and then to respond to it in such a way that the act of responding is no longer separated from the act of feeling. As Spencer Brown put it, you no longer distinguish between the universe and your action upon it. How is one to explain that this is very difficult to do because it is so easy? That the easiest thing in the world requires a long period of devoted practice undertaken without worry or consideration of how long it may take? So many people think they can be natural and spontaneous just by goofing off in a tasteless and vulgar way, which is not being natural but, on the contrary, is following very artificially the precise opposite of what is demanded by social convention and propriety. There are, thus, many "liberated barbarians" among us who are actually the most devoted slaves of puritanical and repressive conventions.[2]

Both Hilde and Charlotte are refined and highly cultured ladies in the European tradition, and they each have a different and peculiar genius for doing the same work. Hilde went to India and sat at the feet of that amazing sun-god Sri Ramana Maharshi or Arunachala, for whom I have always had tremendous respect, and it was from Hilde that I learned most about him. Yet the major influence in Hilde's life was C. G. Jung, even though she had not worked with him personally, and she was thus closely associated with the whole confraternity of Jungians in Los Angeles and San Francisco; a peculiar and fascinating people for whom I have the greatest affection, even though I am an outsider who has not undergone analysis.

Both Hilde and her charming friend, the analyst Renée Brand, put gentle pressure upon me to go through the analytic process. Several years before I had tried it, for about two months, with a Freudian; but in this I had the same experience as Jano—who worked at it for a much longer time—that it ended up with the analysts asking *our* advice. To which Jano responded, "Sure, we'll go on talking, if you'll meet with me in the Saint Regis Bar and not in your office." But analysis is not really a system. It is an intimate personal relationship, and when, as usual, it is paid for, it is actually—like marriage—

---

[2] It is in rather the same way that subtle theologians of the Eastern Orthodox Church realize that Protestants are "crypto-Papists," or hidden Papists, who identify themselves by their opposition to what is done in Rome, and not by anything splendid and magnificent which they have brought forth on their own. Thus when, for some reason, a Catholic priest addressed a letter to a Scottish Presbyterian dominie, and dated it "Thursday, November 1, All Saints Day," the dominie replied with a letter dated "Tuesday, November 6, Washing Day." This is funny only because the dominie gets away with the oneupmanship of being cleverly nasty.

a most delicate and refined form of prostitution. Make no mistake: I have said that prostitutes are as honorable as nurses, and when the right analyst meets the right patient wonderful things can happen. Of all the analysts I have known, Jung himself was the only one with whom I would have wanted to have a love affair on such a level. Snobbish, perhaps, but it can't be helped.

Charlotte Selver was originally a Wittgenstein from the Ruhr Valley, educated in Munich, and of the same family as the philosopher, and she, like the philosopher himself, and Hilde and Renée Brand and Spiegelberg and more of my friends than I can count had all fled from Hitler. Fascist states always destroy themselves by getting rid of their best minds. When I first knew her, Charlotte lived in a sunny studio on West Fifty-seventh Street, overlooking a pleasantly treed and bepigeoned courtyard which echoed with footsteps and the cultivated screams of would-be opera singers studying with voice teachers. Although she had her own financial and administrative problems, her studio was a place of peace, Bauhaus furnished, and set about with filigreelike dried grasses and magical stones. In the ideal circumstance of working with a very small group of students in her bare, grey-carpeted studio-room, Charlotte exudes a bewitching tranquillity, or shall I say, a profoundly interesting stillness. She can take absolutely anything—the floor, a ball, a rock, a bamboo pole, a glass of water, or a piece of bread—and get you to relate to it in such a way that the harsh dualism of what you do and what happens to you is transcended. She puts you in love with the simple fact of physical existence. Charlotte could possibly be the only person in the world who actually keeps a real live skeleton in her closet, for there it is, dangling from the clothes pole, along with all the rubber balls, mats, bean-bags, rocks, and other weird props of her profession. She uses it to show people the harmony of their bones. Once, when conducting seminars together, we had to open a joint bank account, and the manager of the bank across the street asked her to identify her line of business. There was a deep silence. "Oh," I said, "she's a consultant." "A consultant in what?" More silence, in which the man began to get annoyed. I just shrugged my shoulders and said, "Call it physical education." Charlotte cringed.

Like all of us, Charlotte has moods, but you can tell them by the way she parts her hair. If she parts it in the middle and lets it hang down straight on either side, you know that she is Frau Professor (from Munich), rather strict and demanding. But if she parts it to one side, you know that she is a skittish lady from Vienna who will waltz with you; and it must have been in this mood that she captivated another philosophical carpenter, Charles Brooks—son of Van Wyck Brooks—who in the late fifties maintained an enormous studio and workshop in a Greenwich Village loft. Here Charlotte and I and our students would repair after seminars for Charles's excellent cooking and for music and dancing, and in due course Charlotte and Charles fell in love (and got married)—precisely at the same time as I was falling in love with a lady of unobtrusively aristocratic appearance, blond, Roman-nosed, thoughtful, and attentive, with open eyes rather than a frown, who kept turning up at our seminars.

That part of the story must wait. But my association with the work of Charlotte Selver and Hilde Elsberg was, though unacknowledged at the time, one of the main sources of what is—at least from a literary point of view—the best book I have written. This was *Nature, Man, and Woman*, written during the summer of 1957.[3] This must go on the record of gratitude, even though neither Charlotte nor Hilde would recognize me as one of their formal and apostolically successed students. That, as I have said, has never been my way because the shaman cannot be a priest. *Nature, Man, and Woman* was written a year after *The Way of Zen*, into which I put all my love of Chinese scholarship. I could spend days on end exploring Chinese diction-aries, working through ancient Taoist and Buddhist texts, and practicing calligraphy with the brush, but that neither earns a living nor enables one to communicate with the myriads of literate nonscholars who increasingly constitute our world, and with whom scholars—if they have anything valuable to say—must learn to speak. *The Way of Zen*, which was a minor best-seller, was criticized by the Zen priest Sohaku Ogata as a portrait of a cat made by

---

[3] There was also another influence on this book. It can be discovered by a cryptographic study of the dedicatory poem, which will give the clue to a name on p. 329 of the present volume. *Nature, Man, and Woman* had the peculiar honor of being translated into German under the pompedantical title of *Das Missverständnis des Geistes*, though when it came out in paperback, they sensibly reverted to *Natur, Mann und Frau*.

someone who had intended to paint a tiger. But indeed, one of the Zen master Sengai's paintings shows a tiger being scared by a cat.

Throughout my work in San Francisco I was increasingly involved with the people of Big Sur, and took any excuse I could find to get down to those pelican-haunted rocks, aromatic grasses, and floating mountains. When I travel I usually have to pay my way by the equivalent of singing for my supper, and so it was that Margaret Lial, Laverne Allen, and Nathaniel and Margaret Owings arranged seminars in their homes. These were so regular that the place Big Sur and the custom of informal seminars about These Things became so connected as to result in the founding of the Esalen Institute by Michael Murphy and Richard Price (named after the Amerindian tribe which once lived there). In fact I gave the first seminar they held, and have returned repeatedly to work with them, not only because the atmosphere and their hot sulphur baths are seductive, but because I believe that they are doing something absolutely important for the future of both education and religion.

Esalen represents education for its own sake, beyond school, without diplomas, and concerning matters which are fundamental to life but not ordinarily studied in academies. These are matters of what is vulgarly called "nitty-gritty," the utterly basic questions of our relationships to others, to ourselves, and to cosmic existence. Talk it out; feel it out; get down to the roots of what is really happening. This naturally involves religion, philosophy, psychotherapy, and as yet unclassified disciplines which have to do with direct experience of mental and physical reality. But whereas most nonsectarian groups are, in fact, sectarian, Esalen manages to remain open to astonishingly diverse points of view, despite the fact that its faculty has included such strong and persuasive personalities as Fritz Perls, Abraham Maslow, Carl Rogers, Virginia Satir, and Ida Rolfe, to mention but a few. It has been copied all over North America as well as in Europe. Its methods have been studied by government agencies and great business corporations, and its techniques are beginning to be found in churches and universities.

But what has really kept me returning to Big Sur is, again, people—especially those who live or have lived on Partington Ridge . . . and Bill and Loly Fassett's joyous restaurant Nepenthe (with dancing around the outdoor fire at night)[4] ... and cooking over coals of oak-bark at Margaret Lial's retreat in Coastlands, and searching for jade along the beaches with Janet Crew (who climbs as surely as a mountain goat) ... and eating fresh abalone with fried potatoes for breakfast with Emil White, and sampling the extraordinary wine from Ruby Hill with Henry Miller ... and doing tea ceremony with Douglas Madsen at his house on the edge of a precipice, and devouring an enormous roast of wild boar (which tastes like very rich duck) with Harrydick Ross ... and, on foggy evenings, listening to Susan Porter reciting ancient Celtic myths, and drinking sorrel soup from a cauldron with Maria Wallace in a perilously perched shack at Anderson Creek. Not all of these names, dear reader, may be familiar to you; but to me they are like music.

I never felt that I knew Henry Miller really well, for though he is tremendously outgoing in his books I found him somewhat shy in person, even though we agreed over so many matters of taste and philosophy. I feel, however, that his great books are *The Colossus of Maroussi*, *Remember to Remember*, and *The Smile at the Foot of the Ladder*, for his erotic works have failed to arouse my prurient interests, though that may not have been his purpose in writing them. But Henry, like Jean Varda, is a bohemian of the European style, with the same atmosphere of bright color, wine, cheese, good bread, sunlight, and women of passion and intelligence. Henry seems to live inside a painting by Matisse.

Just above his house on Partington Ridge I finally found Maud Oakes. Jano and I have a private club which we call "Over Sixty," and which consists of women beyond that age, such as Elsa Gidlow, who get livelier as they get older. I have the feeling, though it sounds Ogden Nashish, that Maud has never been bored. Nevertheless, she has lived alone for as long as I have known her, and certainly not because people have no desire for her company. It is just because she has so many interests and so much to do by way of reading, writing, gardening, building, cooking, and traveling that any husband would have been a nuisance. Maud is an exemplar of the saying that

---

[4] And with Kim Novak as a partner, just for one round. She dances as well as she acts and generally adorns the landscape.

to be interesting you must be interested. Strongly influenced by Jung and long connected with the Bollingen Foundation, Maud is an amateur metaphysical anthropologist, using the word "amateur" in its proper sense of one who is a lover of an art or science without making it a profession. She has lived among the Navajos and the ancient tribes of Guatemala, and her home is filled with magical objects from all over the world—masks, charms, kachinas, ritual rattles, buddhas—all of which, as is somehow not the case in museums, retain their powers.

Maud has, above all things, the rare and curious virtue of being utterly outspoken without being offensive. It is all the more easy to relate to her for the simple reason that you know exactly where you stand with her, and that if she doesn't want you around she'll let you know. Just because she has overcome the compulsion of trying to please, she pleases. There have been times when I needed very much to "get away from it all," whereupon Maud has invited us to spend a few days with her. These have invariably been rich and fascinating experiences, not only because of her scholarly and philosophical interests, but because her conversation is often punctuated with a belly-laugh and the exclamation, "I love it!" Her house, right on the edge of the ridge, looks down a straight thousand feet to the ocean, and though it is a place where the rains can fall upwards in winter, the usual atmosphere is one of softly colored light, westward-looking, and full of exhilarating space. If I could fly, I would take off from Maud's terrace and drift away with the bulbous flat-bottomed clouds to the South Sea Islands. But then I would also want to take her place along with me, for this is one of those points from which the desire to travel is more interesting than traveling.

It was at dinner at this house—Big Star Way—that I first met her neighbor, Louisa Jenkins, another and most important member of our Over Sixty Club. Louisa, like Dame Julian of Norwich and Thomas Traherne, is a Christian nature-mystic, and in the dispensation of grace, as channeled through Christianity, these people come all too infrequently. Aside from certain heraldic symbols—Christ as the Lamb, Saint Mark as the Lion, Saint Luke as the Bull, and Saint John as the Phoenix—Christianity does not allow animals in heaven, and the same is, I believe, the case with Judaism and Islam. Even Buddhists have the opinion that *nirvana* can be realized only from the human state, and this excludes both animals and gods, though both have the opportunity to be reborn as men. But Louisa has a mystical fascination with all the plays and patterns of nature; for the designs of ferns and feathers and fishbones, for the architecture of skulls and shells, and for the construction of grasses, flowers, and seeds. She is one of the great masters of mosaic and collage, especially as applied in liturgical art, but her studio is adorned with birds' wings, nautilus shells, pieces of quartz, dried rattlesnake grass, liquidinous driftwood, and prints made with *sumi* ink off the scales of live fish. She therefore embodies a possible solution to my basic theological problem: How can the God of the Christians be the architect of the natural universe? She works on it through the theology of Teilhard de Chardin and the metaphysical engineering of Buckminster Fuller, and therefore talking about things with Louisa is always like looking at the lights in an opal or watching fan coral under water or studying the foliage of maidenhair fern. Penetrating this, and looking at the lives of human beings as she looks at the forms of nature, she finds God there, saying, as he said to Dame Julian, "See! I am God; see! I am in all thing; see! I do all thing; see! I never lift mine hands off my works, nor ever shall, without end; see! I lead all thing to the end I ordained it to from without beginning, by the same Might, Wisdom and Love whereby I made it. How should anything be amiss?"

To illustrate her genius: once when we were dining with her a small white porcelain Japanese saké cup was broken in two. On clearing up afterwards, Jano was about to throw it away, but Louisa insisted on saving the pieces. Some days later we received an exquisitely primitive brown ceramic mask in the form of a plaque. The two halves of the cup were the eyelids.

One of the special marvels of Big Sur is Jack Dawn. (That isn't his real name, for he likes to be anonymous.) He has the same eye for nature as Louisa, and is likewise a formidable artist in wire and metal, as well as a carpenter and builder, and a gardener for love of whom lettuces, beans, and tomatoes do their utmost and become colossal without any forcing. With regard to people, Jack is a loving cynic. He deplores modern civilization as an ecological disaster, but instead of just grumbling he does something about it in the way of living and teaching others to live without it, or with as little of it as possible. Many times I have walked with him about that country, fascinated with his explanations of how the ecosystem works—although he would not use a word like that, for his knowledge of it is immediate and not from the laboratory. He will pick up a seed pod, open it, and point out the detailed marvels of its architecture, or explain the territorial imperatives of bees, or the habits of abalone, or how to look at a forest as an interdependent community. On one of our walks we observed an enormous weed covered with fat and flourishing greenfly. A day or two later we passed it again, to discover weed and greenfly nothing but grey dust on a dry stalk. "That," he said, "could very well happen to us."

Jack has a special way of keeping to himself. Only with the greatest reluctance will he leave Big Sur. He spends most of his time in the practical arts of carpentry and horticulture, and though he is well read in philosophy, poetry, and Oriental mysticism, he stays aloof from the multitudes of seekers and enthusiasts who flock to Esalen. Nevertheless, the great Fritz Perls—master of Gestalt therapy and incarnation of a Hasidic Jehovah—once said that he had to regard Jack as his guru. I have known him rather as the most congenial of friends with whom I have gone through all the mutual problems of raising children, and of negotiating the weird double bind of the American family—in which the father is expected to be an authority but is not allowed to be. Both of us are outsiders from Europe, but he can be much more stern and testy in his attitude to children and subordinates than I.

For on many occasions we used to stay with him in Big Sur and amalgamate our families, often climbing down the rocks for picnics on a deserted beach. On the way from San Francisco we would pick up a large salmon from Anastasia's fish market on the wharf at Monterey and then, on the beach, make a fireplace with large stones and driftwood to roast the fish. Once, when we had eaten it down to the bare bones, his oldest son (then about seven) took the remains and cast them ceremoniously back into the ocean, as he explained, "To make another one." Unconsciously, he was repeating a ritual of the Northwestern Amerindians.

These vignettes of people-in-their-environments may explain why I continue to regard the coastal ranges of California as home, even though we are beleaguered by bulldozers and superhighways and trashy housing developments (even worse than the horrors of North London), and jillions of private automobiles, and vast supermarkets selling chemical food and slithery-shiny cups and glasses and basins of soft sick-green plastic, and myriads of grubby unemployed youngsters hitching rides along the roads just to be somewhere else (though some of them are gentle and kind like wandering holy men), and an astonishing lack of public transportation. For this is a land destroying its wealth with money, and will end up with nothing to eat but numbers. But in the meantime—which is still the eternal now—I am lucky. The wind is bringing a thin mist up the valley. There is no one in sight but an old goat, who comes out of the forest and dances on top of a vast, lonely rock. She has lived here for ten years.

CHAPTER THIRTEEN

BREAKTHROUGH

N ow to go on with the theme of loving oneself, and its paradoxes, it is
well known that—for men especially—the forties are a "dangerous"
decade, because if they have been well brought up, it takes them this long to
realize that one sometimes owes it to other people to be selfish. I have often
made the joke about one spouse asking the other, "Darling, do you really
love me?" and being answered, "Well, I'm doing my best to do so." For
dutiful love is invariably, if secretly, resented by both partners to the arrangement, and children raised in so false an atmosphere are done no service. If
they do not rebel they will emulate the hypocrisy, so that the sin of their
fathers will be visited upon them to the third and fourth generations. Permanence may fairly be expected of marriages contracted and families raised
under the ancient system of parental arrangement, for then the partners are
not required to feel romantic love for each other. But modern marriage involves the impossible anomaly, the veritable contradiction in terms of basing
a legal and social contract on the essentially mystical and spontaneous act of
falling in love. The partners to such folly are sometimes lucky, and that is the
best that can be said for it. They may sometimes become wise in the ways of
the human heart by suffering each other, but such wisdom may also be
learned in a concentration camp.

At the age of forty-five I broke out of this wall-to-wall trap, even though
it was a hard shock to myself and to all concerned. But I did it with a will, and
thus discovered who were my real friends. In due course I became closer to
them, and indeed to friends in general, than had hitherto been possible for
me. For I found myself among people who were not embarrassed to express

their feelings, who were not ashamed to show warmth, exuberance, and earthy *joie de vivre*, whereas I had been slipping into the emotional constipation peculiarly characteristic of genteel academia—the mock modesty, the studied objectivity, the cautious opinion, and the horror of enthusiasm. I found, too, that these friends had always considered me a little distant and difficult to know, and had charitably put it down to British reserve. Thus on my escape from the suburban dormitory culture I found Roger Somers, Elsa Gidlow, Maud Oakes, James Broughton, and Charlotte Selver right beside me. So it was that I found a new self, fleeing to Roger's pad in the Tamalpais hills, where we could strip to the waist, bang on drums, dance, and chant through most of the night, or accompanying Charlotte to similar uproars in Charlie Brooks's Greenwich Village loft on Saturday nights after we had worked all day on our joint seminars.

From today's perspective this may not seem any great thing, and, looking back upon it, one might be tempted to feel like a snake contemplating a former skin, or wife regarding her wedding dress which, twenty years ago, was a splendid costume. Yet remember that, at least in those days, college professors and their wives had no truck with such revels, and confined their musical experiences to listening to classical records, playing the piano, or participating in chamber music. I cast no aspersion on these accomplishments, but they make no provision for spontaneous rapture, and exclude from participation anyone not a good musical technician. But, as I have said, *everyone* needs some form of musical utterance, particularly of the kind which permits one to let go without inhibition. Once this energy is allowed to flow it can, of course, be channeled and disciplined; but in these revels we were not attempting to be musical performers—only to enjoy ourselves—and for me, this sudden return to primitivity was a glorious and important release.

In all this my companion was the lady I had been watching while I talked in Charlotte's studio, whom I approached rather gently and subtly, and with whom I went wandering about the streets of the Village, to Chumley's and the Grand Ticino, and to the diminutive shops of her friends who sold musical instruments, strange jewelry, and those timeless woolen textiles from Oaxaca and Peru. Mary Jane (or Jano, as she had called herself from babyhood) was from the mountains of Wyoming, but was well versed in the urbane ways of the world through serving as the first woman reporter on the *Kansas City Star*—reveling in the musical aspects of the black subculture of that city—and through several years' sojourn in New York spent mostly as chief public-relations lady for Mobil. The catalyst that brought us together was Korzybski's General Semantics, she being a director of the New York chapter of this discipline, which had invited me to tell them about the mysteries of Zen. Thereafter she was as relentlessly drawn into Chinese nature-mysticism and Charlotte's Western-grown Taoism as I was fascinated by her voice, her gestures, the humor in her eyes, her knowledge of painting, of music, of colors and textures, her skill in the art of the love-letter, and her general embodiment of something I had been looking for all down my ages to be chief traveling companion—though my first idea was to whisk her off to a lonely shack by the Pacific, where we could sit on foggy nights by a log fire and talk over a bottle of red wine. Which was just what happened. Elsa let us have her hill cottage in Fairfax, an out-of-the-way village to the north of Tamalpais which, in times past, has often served as a congenial retreat for out-of-the-way people.

In this sanctuary, known only to closest friends, I compiled *This Is It*, a collection of essays on Zen and spiritual experience, and wrote both *Psychotherapy East and West* and *The Joyous Cosmology*. Here, where Elsa had left a garden on the hill, and where the northern sky across the valley glowed green at twilight, the world woke up for me. Jano has a capacity for aesthetic absorption which reaches into pure ecstasy—in the convolutions of a leaf, the light in a drop of water, the shadows of a glass in the sun, patterns of smoke, grain in wood, mottle in polished stone. Together in this cottage we slowed down time. We watched the sun blazing from a glass of white wine and watered the garden at sunset, when the slanting light turns flowers and leaves into bloodstone and jade. We studied the forms of shells and ferns, crystals and teazels, water-flow, galaxies, radiolaria, and each other's eyes, and looked down through those jewels to the god and the goddess that may be seen within even when the doubting expression on the face is saying, "What, *me*?" We danced to Bach and Vivaldi, and listened to Ravi Shankar taking hold of the primordial sound of the universe and rippling it with his fingers into all the shapes, patterns, and rhythms of nature.

We found a lonely road across the mountain whereby we could reach the knoll in the valley where Roger and Elsa lived without passing through built-up country, or go on down to Stinson Beach to watch the sea birds and collect sand-dollars with James Broughton—a road along lakes, through forests, and over high grassy slopes from which one could look across the Pacific to the Farallone Islands; where we would stop and listen to the loneliness and the meadowlarks. I remember once coming upon Jano, standing alone, and looking through the fence into Elsa's garden like the child who has just discovered a hidden paradise through a hitherto unnoticed gate in a wall or break in a hedge, though in this oft-repeated fantasy the child finds that on returning again to the scene, the gate has vanished. I put my arms around her from behind and whispered, "But to this one you shall return!"

In our conventionally scandalous situation we naturally kept unconventional company, and it was Gavin Arthur who first pointed out how such a style of life protected one from false friends. In those days Gavin lived in poverty, but the several humble apartments in which he lived seemed all the same, since he invariably covered the walls from floor to ceiling with innumerable photographs of friends—celebrities, relatives, gurus, and magicians—interspersed with mandalas, colorful astrological charts, and brilliant metaphysical posters. Of these friends and associates he would tell lovingly cynical, ribald, and fantastic anecdotes to keep his guests in stitches, all with a slight lisp in his soft, cultured voice. For Gavin is a supernexus in the "Net" through whom thousands of interesting people have somehow been woven together. Today, though feeble in frame, he has come to fame and some affluence because of the sudden and even astonishing popularity of astrology among young people, who now throng to his apartment in San Francisco. His heroes are Walt Whitman, Edward Carpenter, Havelock Ellis, and Stewart Edward White, and he is unpedantically learned in all the byways of occultism and parapsychology. He seems to come—both as a libertarian and as an occultist—from the last turn of the centuries, from the days of H. P. Blavatsky, Annie Besant, W. B. Yeats, George Russell, Aleister Crowley, Rudolph Steiner, and Algernon Blackwood—and the echoes of former lives in Atlantis, Egypt, India, and medieval Provence murmur through his conversation.

We have had many friendly arguments about astrology and the reincarnation hypothesis, since I have maintained that he believes in them for the wrong reasons and that, in any case, their relevance to the way of the mystic is only tangential. Once, back in 1939 and 1940, I went in heavily for astrology, but found its mythological aspect far more interesting than its practical application. Of the latter I have grave doubts, and attribute its successful prognostications more to the intuition of the individual astrologer than to the science itself. Reincarnation I find easy to understand, though I am more fascinated by the mysteries of eternity than those of time, and feel that the former must be found in the present rather than the future. Reincarnation is, I think, sufficiently explained by the constant repetition of specific patterns which one finds throughout nature, but which escape our attention when the rhythm of repetition is extremely slow. Following the Aristotelian idea that the soul is the *form* of the body, I think of my soul as pattern rather than substance. In both senses of the phrase, it is the form that matters; and forms can repeat themselves in both space and time without any substantial linkage between them, as the atoms of the hand form the hand without being tied together with strings. Successive waves that look alike are waves in the single field of water, but they do not push or cause each other. Closely examined by the physicist, water itself turns out to be wavicles. We cannot imagine how we would describe any basic substance of stuff in all these forms, even were we able to detect it.

Now I am writing of the year 1960, and it will be remembered that this was when—in San Francisco in particular—there were the first signs of an astonishing change of attitude among young people which, despite its excesses and self-caricatures, had spread far over the world by the end of the decade. In a way, it started with the Beat Generation, and though I appear under a pseudonym in Kerouac's *Dharma Bums*, Jano and I were *in* this milieu rather than *of* it, and I was somewhat severe with it in my essay *Beat Zen, Square Zen, and Zen* which appeared in the *Chicago Review* in 1958. But Jack Kerouac, Lawrence Ferlinghetti, and especially Gary Snyder and Allen Ginsberg, were now among our friends. Jack—a second Thomas Wolfe—was a warm and affectionate dog who eventually succumbed to the bottle, but the others were more serious artists and, speaking at least of Gary and Allen, more disciplined yogis. Allen is a rabbinic *sadhu* who can at need transform himself into an astute and hardheaded lawyer, and only this combination of fearless holiness, blazing compassion, and clear intellect has prevented him from being jailed or shot long ago. There was a night in Gavin's apartment when we chanted sutras together for hours, Allen ringing the time with his little Indian finger-cymbals, and through this purely sonic communion, with the glee that Allen puts into it, we somehow reached each other more deeply than in verbal exchanges. There was a time, too, when we chanted the *Dharani of the Great Compassionate One* all the way down New York's Second Avenue in a Volkswagen bus.

For some reason OM and the chanting of OM has always struck the press and Middle Americans as something to be laughed off—like the Islamic prayer rug and the Tibetan praying wheel—and it may be that the boys in Cairo speak with equal flippancy of some of their weird brethren who turn Christian and go and get themselves watered—as if *that* would do any good. But when the musical *Hair* opened in San Francisco I was invited on stage before the curtain went up to lead the cast in mantra-chanting, and today most of my college audiences are disappointed if I do not give some time to exercises in meditation and the chant. No one is more astonished at this than I. In my work of interpreting Oriental ways to the West I was pressing a button in expectation of a buzz, but instead there was an explosion. Others, of course, were pressing buttons on the same circuit, but I could not have believed—even in 1960—that, say, Richard Hittleman, who studied with us at the Academy, would be conducting a national television program on yoga, that numerous colleges would be giving courses on meditation and Oriental philosophy for undergraduates, that this country would be supporting thriving Zen monasteries and Hindu *ashrams*, that the *I Ching* would be selling in hundreds of thousands, and that—wonder of wonders—sections of the Episcopal Church would be consulting me about contemplative retreats and the use of mantras in liturgy.

The power of something so apparently simple—and so seemingly absurd—as mantra- and OM-chanting is that it fosters a relaxed concentration on pure sound, as distinct from words, ideas, and abstractions, and thus brings attention to bear on reality itself. Now the ears bring reality to us entirely as process, as flowing vibration, and we hear this energy emerging from silence in the immediate moment and then echoing away into memory and the past; just as the world emerges instantly and spontaneously from space and no-thingness, which is as essential to energy as negative electricity is to positive. To the eyes and the fingers the world seems more static, rendering it less easy to understand that a mountain is actually a vibration.

The Beat Generation was aggressively dowdy and slovenly, and lacked *gaieté d'esprit*. Patrons of the Co-Existence Bagel Shop on Grant Avenue went about in shaggy blue-jeans with their feet bare and grimy and their hair in pony-tails, and overuse of marijuana made them withdrawn and morose, even if internally beatific. (The style appeared again at the end of the decade, after the collapse of Haight-Ashbury and the dispersion of the Flower Children.) But in the circles in which we were then moving—in San Francisco, Los Angeles, and New York—something else was on the way, in religion, in music, in ethics and sexuality, in our attitudes to nature, and in our whole style of life. We took courage and began to swing. For there was an energy in the air that cannot entirely be attributed to the revelations of LSD, an energy which manifested itself on the surface as color and imagination in clothing, in a rebirth of poetry, in the rhythms of rock-and-roll and in fascination for Hindu music, in social gatherings where people were no longer afraid to touch one another and show affection (so that even men greeted one another with embraces), and in a general letting down of hair, both figurative and literal. One by one I watched this change coming over my friends as if they had been initiated into a mystery and were suddenly "in the know" about something not expressly defined.

As I saw it subjectively, from my own limited point of view, all this started before the shrine in Roger's home, in the spacious house which Henry and Virginia Denison had built on top of the Hollywood hills, in Charlie Brooks's loft, and in Jean Varda's Sausalito studio on the ferryboat S.S. *Vallejo*, where Jano and I joined him as shipmates in 1961—taking over the part of the boat which had formerly been the atelier of Gordon Onslow-Ford. This was before the founding of Esalen in Big Sur and the proliferation of growth centers, before the Hippies and the Flower Children and the great days of the *San Francisco Oracle*, before Maharishi Mahesh turned on

the Beatles to Transcendental Meditation, before Bob Dylan brought serious
poetry back into popular music, and before Timothy Leary and Richard
Alpert scared Harvard and the nation at large with LSD and the slogan,
"Turn on, tune in, and drop out."[1]

I had, then, the feeling that from these centers, from these environments
in which I felt especially free to be myself, waves were spreading to find response in an enormous number of people; helped by the fact that something
similar was coming from other centers as well. And I should add that the
energy that came from these centers was as much sucked out as blown out.
Ever since I had dropped out of the formal teaching profession in 1957,
invitations came out of the blue to talk about Zen in particular and Oriental
philosophy in general at such places as Columbia, Harvard, Yale Medical
School, Cornell, Chicago, and Rochester as well as at Cambridge and the
Jung Institute in Zürich. In the United States I found these lectures attended
by unexpectedly large student audiences, and the whole thing snowballed to
the point where I began to fear that I might be accused of corrupting the
youth of Athens. For in this period I was also making a series of programs
for National Educational Television, entitled "Eastern Wisdom and Modern Life"—which have been rebroadcast about the country ever since—in
the course of which I discovered that it was much more fun to do television
than to watch it. For with the help of Richard Moore and Robert Hagopian
of KQED in San Francisco and their enthusiastic technicians, we worked out
a way of doing these shows without rehearsal, so that it came to the point
where I had no more to do than walk into the studio and begin. We also got
rid of the tiresome classroom atmosphere of educational television—the
desk, bookshelves, and blackboard—and set the show in a Japanese garden
fabricated from little more than a papier-mâché rock, pebbles strewn on the
concrete floor, and a few bamboos.

---

[1] Though I shall return to the subject, I can see now that LSD and other psychedelic substances simply triggered an explosion of interest in the mystical aspect of religion that was
building up (*a*) through increasing contact with Oriental cultures, and (*b*) because of the
arid theology and whipping-dead-horse preaching of standard-brand Judaism and Christianity.

I had long felt that formal lectures and classes were less than satisfactory ways of studying these matters, and therefore borrowed from C. G. Jung the technique of the informal seminar, in which a relatively small group of students will meet, say, for a whole weekend, for sessions in which an hour's lecture is followed by another hour of free discussion, affording also opportunity for personal conversation with members of the group betweentimes. These lectures are for interpretation rather than information, for it has always seemed to me that facts are more easily communicated and remembered from books than from lectures. For this reason I always talk spontaneously, with no other preparation than my general reading and thinking, and preselection of the themes to be discussed. Notes embarrass me, and the reading of papers for subsequent publication I find abominable. For my writing and my speaking are entirely different techniques. Writing is slow and careful, at the rate of about two double-spaced typewritten pages an hour, but with few corrections. I write in spurts with long pauses for a strange kind of nonverbal pondering which suddenly transforms itself into articulate sentences. But speaking flows easily, though the meaning is expressed, not simply by the words, but by the pauses, gestures, and inflections of voice which cannot be reproduced on paper. This is an art in which I have never had any formal training, and I would be quite at a loss to teach anyone else how to do it. It simply happens as if I were possessed by a spirit. Perhaps what I am talking about in words and thoughts is the interval between thoughts, just as in music one hears melody not so much from the tones themselves as from the intervals between them.

For this reason I cannot dictate books, and do not allow my lectures to be transcribed, but only to be recorded on tape. Transcription is so laborious that I would rather begin anew and write an article. However, it was Henry (or Sandy) Jacobs who persuaded me about this time that tapes would become just as important as books, so that he became keeper of the archives of my recordings. Now Sandy, like Roger, was from Evanston and equally a genius-misfit in that suburban middle-class environment. He resembles a young version of my father, but with long hair, can mimic any kind of voice, and has a bizarre multilevel sense of humor which may be heard at best in his record *The Wide Weird World of Shorty Petterstein* (World Pacific). With

Jordan Belsen, the filmmaker, he invented Vortex, an audiovisual presentation in a planetarium or other domed auditorium where kaleidoscopic abstractions on the dome were harmonized with electronic and other forms
of music from speakers surrounding the audience. Shortly after Sabro
Hasegawa's death in 1957, Sandy took one look at his exquisite daughter,
Sumire, and promptly married her; and it was thus that Sumire and I made
two records of *haiku* and other types of Japanese poetry, she doing the Japanese and I the English, with background improvisations by Vincent Delgado
on the *koto* and *shakuhachi*.

Sandy records everything and is, in fact, seldom seen without a Nagra
slung over his shoulder. Thereafter he will put weirdly disparate scenes together, such as the hysterically funny situation of an *Encyclopaedia Britannica*
salesman making his pitch to a recording of hypnosis induction which he has
accidentally dialed on the telephone. In replaying tapes for editing, it is all
too easy to confuse what comes after with what went before, just because
you already heard it on the first run, and Sandy can rework these confusions
of sequence into mazes where the sense of time is garbled beyond all hope,
and the participants are involved in a time-trap from which there is no escape
except pulling the cord. In more serious moments he designs and installs audiovisual systems.

Like myself, Sandy is a Westerner semi-Orientalized, though, with
Sumire as his wife, he has gone further into the material aspect of this process,
having a home with two Japanese bathtubs (one inside and one out), and
cuisine that is famous in that Sumire is an undoubted master, not only of
Japanese cooking, but also of Chinese, Indonesian, Indian, and French. Furthermore, he has great knowledge of the ethnic music of Asia and Africa,
and through him I came more and more under the spell of the music of India,
with its long flowing and pulsing phrases against the droning *tambura*, deep
and mysterious for all its monotony; its sense of "far-off-ness" which the
Japanese call *yugen*—as when wild geese are seen and lost in the clouds; and
the feeling that I have heard this music long, long ago, somewhere beyond
childhood. For all its technical difficulty it is performed in a spirit of relaxed
enthusiasm, as when the drummer and the soloist on sitar or sarod laugh-
ingly challenge one another to variations on ever more complex rhythms.

By contrast the Western orchestra is stiff, serious, and colorlessly and uncomfortably dressed.

Ever since starting work at the Academy in 1951 I had been making visits to Los Angeles, mostly by car, often stopping on the way at Carmel, Big Sur, Santa Barbara, and Ojai, since in all these places groups would regularly assemble for seminars—mostly in private homes. And what homes! I can still smell the logs burning in Margaret Lial's music-haunted cottage at Coastlands in Big Sur, with the fog closing in at night. And there was Alice Erving's glass palace in Montecito, where house and garden seemed mysteriously inseparable, and this generous and scholarly lady (she read classical Greek) entertained us to thick steaks from the indoor barbecue and fabulous quantities of vodka. And the house which Neutra designed for Jim Moore in Ojai, with its great lily pool where frogs accompanied my lectures; his Bavarian wife Erica, pleasingly plump and vivacious, and skilled in many arts of healing; their cat, rejoicing in the name of Ratzapetz; and Jim himself, to all appearances a retired and conservative businessman, but beneath, an ardent student of Krishnamurti and a whimsically humorous sage. There was also Robert Balzer's Japanese fantasy, high on the Hollywood hills, with polished wooden corridors, white carpets, Chinese statuary, and a screen by Sesshu, where this celebrated gourmet, chef, winemaster, and Buddhist entertained us one evening to an imitation of Merce Cunningham dancing to the music of John Cage, prancing to a metrical jig with an unfastened silk kimono trailing behind him, and darting every so often to the piano to scramble a few notes.

As time went on most of my Los Angeles seminars were conducted in the bookshop run by Harry Hill and Jack Brown, opposite the Ambassador Hotel, where, in addition to regular books-of-the-month, they kept a large stock of esoterica. These two men were my indefatigable helpers and agents in a time when money was scarce; they put me in touch with more students and friends than I can count, so that writing about my network of associates in Los Angeles is a technical impossibility. Everything dissolves into a blur of gliding along freeways to symphonic music and chattering through parties of colorful people in terraced houses hidden in canyons. But again, as time went on, things centered about the hospitality of Henry Denison, once a monk of the Vedanta Society, who, with his former wife Virginia, had constructed that memorable home above the smog, overlooking the pine-bordered lake which serves as the Hollywood reservoir.

Henry, in style if not in material power, is an undoubted aristocrat: tall, gentle, courteous, urbane, and literate, but entirely relaxed in acceptance of his wondrously crazy friends. Yet at the deepest level he has devoted his life to a relentless and many-pathed quest for ultimate wisdom and enlightenment, so that for some years now he has virtually vanished into India. I miss him. I wish I could show him that what he is looking for is not in India but in himself, and obvious for all to see. But he will not believe me because I am not a guru, and all gurus represent an endless "come-on" where

Veil after veil shall lift, but there must be
    Veil upon veil behind—

until they bring us by our own desperation to absolute surrender.

Virginia I call the Yummy Yogi, because she teaches *hatha* yoga and her own physical form is an eloquent testimony to the worth of her discipline. I suspect that some people have had difficulty in taking so glamorous a woman seriously as a yoga teacher, but it has struck me that she is one of the few all-out-in-front no-nonsense gurus that I have met, for she knows her work and does it effectively without mystification, and is so refreshingly earthy and human about it that her work is not befuddled with the flattery and adulation of starry-eyed disciples. Shortly after I met Henry and Virginia they agreed upon an enviably civilized and amicable parting of the ways, so that she was replaced in his household by his present wife, Ruth, a very blond fräulein who—after harrowing adventures—escaped from East Prussia during the Russian occupation. Rutschen exhibits an imperfect mastery of English to its best possible advantage—*die schönste langwitch*—a Germanized English so utterly funny that no one wants to correct her, all the more so since it goes along with a personality so audaciously adventurous, sexy, practical, and religious.

Whenever we came to Los Angeles she, or Virginia, or both of them together, would stage far-into-the-night parties at which the guests might include Aldous and Laura Huxley, Marlon Brando, John Saxon, Lew Ayres,

Anaïs Nin, Zen master Joshu Sasaki, and a fascinating cast—this is Holly-wood—of psychiatrists, physicians, artists, writers, dancers, and hippies who, in this context, somehow managed not to bore each other. Many of us would sleep on cushions on the floor and then continue the party at breakfast. What we gathered for was simply conversation, and this way of passing an evening is so much to my liking that I find myself going only rarely to the theater, the cinema, and the concert hall. In this I am, I suppose, at a cultural disadvan-tage, but I find the drama in which I participate more interesting than the drama I merely watch. Certainly, in gatherings of this kind I like to hold the floor, but only until anyone else brings up something of greater interest, when I will become a rapt and silent listener. No one could resist listening to Aldous Huxley, even if only to the elegance of his voice and his use of language, with that recurrent phrase "really *most* extraordinary" spoken with cultivated and scholarly detachment apropos of some curious phenomenon of hypnosis, art history, neurology, optics, or exotic religion. And I will stop and listen any time to Oscar Janiger, psychiatrist and pharmacologist, who, as a frequent guest of the Denisons, will relate—not without humor—his latest explorations of the puzzle of the nervous system, or spin fantasies about a new kind of cocktail bar based on the fact that alcohol is more eas-ily assimilated through the rectum than by mouth. Oscar (known to his friends as Oz, being a wizard) is one of those relatively few psychiatrists who will take on people with real healthy psychoses instead of wasting all his time piddling around with measly little neurotics, for he has an infectious en-thusiasm for his profession and must do much for his patients just by the atmosphere of his intense interest in life. I was one of his mescaline guinea-pigs during his long investigation of psychoactive drugs, on which he has contributed extensively to the learned journals, and, for all his learning, he does not use it to impress or pontificate but to sweep you along into his own delight in his work.

Another doctor in the Denison entourage is the eye surgeon James Macy, who lives in a houseboat somewhere on the maze of harbors north of Long Beach. As he is one of my students who graduated into being a close friend, I seek him out on all possible occasions simply to enjoy his attitude to life. For Jim has been gloriously preserved, in spite of all the temptations of his

profession, from growing up (I was about to put a period here) into anything resembling solemn and serious maturity, and has a style of conversation, embellished with a colorful vocabulary which somehow gives the
impression of the strictly ludicrous side of the shit having just hit the fan.
Without knowing it, he is a born comedian—or whatever it is one calls a
player in farces—and, though his ancestors are Welsh, his appearance suggests origins in Beirut or Baghdad.

But for no one would I stop talking more readily than Jean Varda. He
must have been sixty-five when I first really got to know him—at the time
when Jano and I moved to the ferryboat *Vallejo* and into the influence of his
sunlit, multicolored, Aegean-flavored studio, with the dhow *Perfidia*, lateen-
rigged, tied up alongside. Jean, or Yanko, was a Greek born in Smyrna, but
who had lived so long in France, England, and California that he boasted
speaking all his languages with a foreign accent. His principal art was collage,
done with brilliant scraps of cloth on plywood, in which—according to his
own story—he started out to be a charlatan and became an artist in spite of
himself. His passion, in art as in life, was translucent color. He insisted that
black was not to be found in nature, and that shadows must be seen in color
or not at all. He would reproach any woman who came to his studio dressed
in black. He was a visionary who saw the entire universe as a manifestation
of light, and denounced Leonardo da Vinci and Rembrandt for bringing mud
and grime into painting, though to Yanko's eyes ordinary natural mud was
a scintillation of minute jewels.

In this studio, and aboard the *Perfidia* when we sailed the Bay on Sundays, Yanko literally held court, sitting in a great peacock-style wicker chair
at the head of a long, rough table stained with paint and red wine. He worked,
as I do, very early in the morning, and as I sat at my typewriter I would hear
him hammering and rustling about in his studio. A little after eight I would
often light a cigar and wander over for coffee with him, to be greeted with,
"My God, Alan, you smoke like a paratrooper. Come now ... tell me, tell me,
what is new? What profundities have you discovered? What mischief have
you perpetrated? What beautiful woman have you seduced?" Even at this
hour there would often be others at the table—his current mistress, or young
men helping him with boat construction; and as the day went on a stream of

visitors would be in and out—diplomats, professors, ballerinas, fishermen, pirates, and models—for hour after hour of multilingual badinage. By lunchtime there were jugs of wine, Jack cheese, and sourdough bread on the table, and towards evening Yanko would get together lamb or fish with olives and peppers, vine leaves and lemons, eggplant and onions, and seemingly toss off Greek and French dishes, mixing salad in an immense wooden bowl whose original use had been in the casting of wheels for railroad cars. He insisted that the lettuce be handled with reverent delicacy, and upbraided Gavin Arthur for allegedly preparing salads in which the lettuce had first been trampled with riding-boots.

All the while he would regale us with anecdotes, real and imaginary, and outrageous commentaries on art, women, museum curators, nautical adventures, and strange inventions—such as the Perfect Chair, which some insane craftsman had designed from plaster casts of the bottoms of senators, stockbrokers, judges, archbishops, opera singers, duchesses, bootblacks, bookies, and Bulgarians, thus arriving at a cast of the ideal bottom for a seat which fitted no one. He would play about with Greek compounds, and assert that an artist must have not only sympathy and empathy, but also peripathy, catapathy, apopathy, anapathy, parapathy, metapathy, bathypathy, and apathy. He especially detested museum curators, whom he accused of a conspiracy to destroy vision with canvases slurped with tar, asphalt, axle-grease, and bituminous coal-dust mixed with cow dung. He told us of a metaphysical machine which he had patented (it became more complicated every time he talked about it), without ever divulging its operation or purpose. He expatiated on the two schools of contemporary artists, the Bumblepuppies and the Mumblepuppies, and explained that the perfect formula for the brand-name of any product was to use obscene terms from foreign languages—for example, the derivation of Coca-Cola from *caca culo*. He talked of the clarity and luminosity of the air in Greece, told ribald tales of the monks of Mount Athos, excoriated Turks and Bulgarians, related tragic stories of lives and love-affairs ruined by horoscopy, explained how to make *avgolemono* soup, and assured us that he was an absolutely trustworthy fellow except in two very small matters: words and deeds. All this came out with passion, exuberance, exaggeration, indignation, childlike enthusiasm, and mock-malice from this stocky, white-haired unrepentant bohemian in a bright pink T-shirt, bald on top and so moustached as to look like a benevolent Gurdjieff.

One sat on benches beside the long table, looking across the water to Angel Island through clusters of masts, and on the sill of the great window were his sculptural constructions made from decorative bottles glued atop one another and filled with colored liquids. The candlesticks were adorned with bright-winged *garuda* figures from Bali, and on the kitchen counter stood a huge wooden hare, carved by Oliver Andrews. To one side was a puppet theater exhibiting a stuffed iguana made into a gold-and-green dragon. The ceiling lights hung from a monstrous wooden cutout of an amphisbaenic turtle, and by the stone fireplace (embellished with dark green bottle-bottoms) stood a formidable and dangerous trident which Yanko would carry on ceremonial occasions, crowned and robed as the representative of Poseidon. For nothing pleased him more than riotous costume parties, usually organized by court poet and master of ceremonies Victor DiSuvero, for which as many as four hundred people would gather on the boat or on a neighboring beach, and at which Varda-Poseidon would preside with an entourage of comely handmaidens in attendance. For Yanko—with discrimination—adored women. For many years—almost until I suggested that he take up the theme of the Celestial City—his collages were entirely of courtly women, as if the mosaics of Ravenna had gone slightly cubist. It was, indeed, rumored that society ladies of San Francisco would send their more beautiful daughters to him for initiation into the arts of love, though when I told him of this he discounted it—with a sly grin, blushing a little.

On fine Sunday mornings he would gather friends together for—often somewhat perilous—jaunts on the *Perfidia*, Yanko being a stubbornly proud sailor who would permit no motor aboard his boat, so that we were often becalmed or carried away by strong tides. Yet *Perfidia* was the bravest boat on the Bay, with eyes on the prow, a broad band of vivid red below the gunwales, and a honey-colored lateen sail. There was room aboard for at least a dozen passengers, often including such notable beauties as Anne Ryan, Henrietta DiSuvero, Clare Wiles, and Ruth Costello, dressed in their brightest and supplied with loaves and cold chicken and gallons of wine. Seeing this craft gliding in full sail by the wooded cliffs of Belvedere, it was impossible to believe that this was the United States and not the islands of Greece.

There were those, of course, who considered Yanko an impostor and a show-off, but I think they were merely jealous of him. I cannot understand this dislike of showing off, especially when—like Yanko—one does it with a certain humorous gaiety and lack of seriousness. When people are too modest and self-effacing the color goes out of life, the cities are drab and the citizenry shabby and morose; and it always strikes me that those who resent showing off have a peculiarly unrelaxed attitude to their own egos. I lived alongside Yanko for ten years and absorbed all that I could of his spirit. I never had the slightest trouble from him. When he could not pay for the utilities, he would give us a painting, and now I wish we had taken more of them and let the money go. For he lived, on purpose, close to poverty so that he need keep no records, pay no taxes, nor possess resources for which anyone could sue him. He was only disconsolate that the art world virtually ignored his work, which began to get due recognition only when he was close to death.

A year or so before he died he had a stroke which impaired the peripheral vision of his left eye. When I saw him the day after, he said, "Alan, I am afraid to tell this to most of my friends because they will think I am crazy. But I was quite sure I was going to die, even that I was dead. It was astonishing! It was an apotheosis! I found myself somewhere where I and everything else were transformed into a warm, golden light, where there were formless presences welcoming and assuring me, like angels. How can I say it? All this was much more real than ordinary life, which now seems like a dream, so that I can't possibly be afraid of death any more. Can you understand that I knew for sure that this golden light, this divinity which I became, is the real thing? That this world in which you and I are talking is just a shadow? That we haven't anything to worry about at all—ever? And my God, how can this have happened to *me*? Alan, you know I am a scoundrel and a lecherous man. Tell me, what do you think? Am I nuts? Was I hallucinated? If they wouldn't think I was quite mad I would recommend *everyone* to have a stroke." Several months later he went to La Paz in Baja California to spend the winter in the sun. In January 1971 he took off for Mexico City, and before leaving, treated a group of friends to drinks in the bar at the airport. But when he got off the plane in Mexico City, seven thousand feet above La Paz, the change of altitude was too much. He dropped dead of a heart attack. Six hundred people attended his funeral.

We mourned, not for him, but for ourselves that this radiance, this colossal *joie de vivre*, had left us. The Gate Five community of the Sausalito waterfront has been dreary ever since. The hippies have been replaced by "freaks," who look like peasants from a depressed area of Hungary. Perhaps they are not to be blamed, for the industrial system offers few jobs that any self-respecting person wants to do, and the intelligent young are sick to death of a way of life that wastes and squanders material for the production of baubles and bombs. But consider that Yanko, too, had no job and nothing to mention in the way of money. Nevertheless, he has left waves. He did more than anyone else to release me from pomposity, from submitting to false modesty, and from knuckling under to the general fear of the colorful and all that it signifies.

To go back. A year after Jano and I moved onto the boat, we and a group of friends created the Society for Comparative Philosophy to sponsor my own work, and to use the spacious studio for seminars and for a library to shelter my thousands of books. Over the years we also raised funds to assist others working along the same lines, and brought in, to conduct seminars, the Lama Anagarika Govinda, Charlotte Selver, Krishnamurti, Douglas Harding, and the Lama Chögyam Trungpa. I have a mild ambition to create something which will carry on, in some respects, where the Bollingen Foundation left off, since most of the great foundations are stuffy and unimaginative and do not support weird scholars investigating Amerindian mysticism or Tibetan iconography. But this may well change, for the new decade is seeing a remarkable revival of interest in magic, witchcraft, alchemy, astrology and mythology which is invading even the universities and creating the suspicion that the worldview of modern science may itself have been a peculiar form of myth. Science itself, by investigating alpha-waves, antimatter, holes in space, psychopharmacology, and the dynamics of waves and cycles, may be hoisted by its own petard to the confrontation of a universe very different from what we now imagine, and its pandits may say with the Los Angeles entomologist first hearing of von Fritsch's discovery of bee language, "I have the most passionate reluctance in accepting this evidence." For it does indeed seem that many scientists have a religious fervor and a vested interest in demonstrating that nature is *only* a rather inefficient machine—to which they must paradoxically ascribe their own boastedly superior intelligences. My own interest, however, remains with the mystical rather than the occult, for having seen what we have done with ordinary technology I am troubled by what black magic we might commit with psychotechnology.

I have said, however, that my ambition for creating a philosophical foundation is mild, for it has become by strong impression that human institutions and collectivities, as distinct from individual people, are impervious to grace. This is no more than a tentative opinion, but I feel that nations, churches, political parties, classes, and formal associations of almost all kinds operate at the lowest level of intelligence and moral sensibility. This is, in part, because they are not organized as an individual is organized. They act upon rules and verbal communications which, when compared with the organic nervous system, are of extreme crudity. It is this which gives us the feeling that most social problems are too complicated, for, in the same way, the human body would seem too complicated were it not that the nervous system—as distinct from conscious attention and memory—can handle an immense number of variables at the same time. Societies, insofar as they are restricted to linear, strung out, forms of communication, can handle very few variables. Therefore governments and corporations, in attempting to keep up with the infinitely varied and multidimensional process of nature, resort to words on paper—to laws, reports, and other records—which would take lifetimes for any intelligent being to read, much less assimilate. Yet for all these mountains of paper covered in small print, only a tiny amount of natural process has been described, and we do not really know whether what we select for description are actually the most important features of the process. In other words, our social organizations are not organic.

As they become more complex and computerized they become less organic, because their code of communication—however fast and complex—rests on a basic confusion of symbol with reality, of words and numbers with natural events. When natural process is represented in words, it appears that there are separable things and events which may be dealt with individually, one by one. There are not. In nature each event implies, or "goeswith," all other events in varying degrees of relevance, and we have only the sketchiest notions of how those degrees may be measured—for how often do the most momentous events arise from the most trivial? A chance meeting precipitates a marriage, and an accident in a laboratory touches off a major scientific discovery. I feel, therefore, that we have long been involved in an unworkable and destructive method of managing both the social order and the natural environment, and that our main hope of finding something better will be through study of the nervous system itself—and by some other way than representing it as a mechanical process. Until we find some such alternative (and I may be saying that we must learn to develop our intuitive rather than our intellectual faculties) I have little hope for constructive, large-scale social changes. Society will remain a swamp redeemed only by some relatively few individual plants of fruitful beauty.

Yet it is not difficult for me to be in a state of consciousness where all such problems dissolve. I see that nature makes no real errors; that man and his institutions are as natural as anything else; and, furthermore, that my complaints about any situation are as natural as the idea that I have no reason to complain. Of course this curiously exhilarating feeling implies no specific course of action, and may therefore be dismissed as worthless philosophy or mysticism. But, on the other hand, no one has yet come up with a philosophy, a set of general principles or laws, which *does* provide adequate rules for action, without first having to be modified into chaos with exceptions. And the sharper one's intellect, the faster one finds reason to take exception to any general principle. Thus we began the study of Greek in school by learning the conjugation of regular verbs, only to discover that the verbs most commonly used were irregular. As a language becomes rich with usage and idiom it strays from grammar, or rather from description by grammarians, and must be learned by ear. So, too, life must be played by ear—which is only to say that we must trust, not symbolic rules and linear principles, but our brains or natures. Yet this must bring one back to the faith that nature makes no mistake.

In such a universe a decision which results in one's own death is not a mistake: it is simply a way of dying at the right moment.

But nothing can be right in a universe where nothing can be wrong, and every perception is an awareness of contrast, of a right/wrong, is/isn't, bright/dark, hard/soft situation. If this is the very nature of awareness, any and every circumstance, however fortunate, will have to be experienced as a good/bad or plus/minus in order to be experienced at all. By such reflections I think myself into silence and, by writing, help others similarly spellbound by thoughts and words to come to silence—which is the realization that a linear code cannot justly represent a nonlinear world. But this intellectual silence is not failure, defeat, or suicide. It is a return to that naked awareness, that vision unclouded by commentary, which we enjoyed as babies in the days when we saw no difference between knower and known, deed and happening. This time, however, we are babies reborn—babies who remember all the rules and tricks of human games and can therefore communicate with other people as if we were normal adults. We can also feel, as a just-born baby cannot, compassion for their confusions.

Now, from the standpoint of the wise-baby the confusions of the normal adult world cannot be straightened out without becoming even more confused. There is no solution except to regain the baby's vision and so realize that the confusions are not really serious, but only the games whereby adults pass the time and pretend to be important. Seen thus, the world becomes immeasurably rich in color and detail because we no longer ignore aspects of life which adults pass over and screen out in their haste after serious matters. As in music, the point of life is its pattern at every stage of its development, and in a world where there is neither self nor other, the only identity is just This—which is all, which is energy, which is God by no name.

CHAPTER FOURTEEN

THE SOUL-SEARCHERS

To go back to the baby's vision of the world is, in psychoanalytic jargon, regression; and in the Freudian religion, as also in the Christian religion, this is sickness or sin, which are in practice the same. According to Freudian doctrine a baby's state of consciousness is the "oceanic feeling" in which there is no differentiation between I and All, so that the baby—poor deluded thing—feels omnipotent and is unable to discriminate between what matters and what doesn't. Growth and maturation are defined in terms of differentiation, as the emergence of the articulate ego from the primal id, where the latter is considered as an amorphous, blubbering, and energetically lecherous sludge. This growth is forced and encouraged by the superego, which is an implant from all the full-grown egos surrounding the baby, particularly its parents, who in turn had superegos implanted by their parents, so that there has really been no way of knowing whether this kind of development should be called growth or cancer. However, powerful people with sticks and guns call it growth, and most others agree with them. In fairness it must be admitted that a few psychoanalysts, including Erik Erikson, have recognized that regression may sometimes be important in the service of maturation. This was also true of Freud's sadly neglected colleague and contemporary Georg Groddeck, who called the id the It, and had great respect for it.

It is curious that psychoanalysts and most psychiatrists continue faithfully in the Christian, Islamic, and Judaic tradition of persecuting those who, including Jesus Christ, experience and express some form of identity with God—common and acceptable as this experience is in India and most of

Asia. Thus in tangling with psychiatrists it is of the utmost importance to avoid mention of such experiences, even of religion, and especially of weird religions. It is *prima facie* evidence of insanity, and few psychiatrists are able to distinguish between a megalomaniac who thinks he is Jesus Christ and a genuine mystic who is a simple person without erudition. For a genuine and simple mystic, like the Japanese Zen monk Ryokan, may be so naive and whimsical as to have difficulty in being recognized—in an unsympathetic social environment—for anything but a poor fool. It seems probable that some people grow up without ever losing their oceanic consciousness, and so never know what it is to be a fully confused adult.

Nevertheless, since the age of eighteen or thereabouts I have kept my eye on the practice of psychotherapy. It has seemed to me a possible aperture through which Western people might catch a glimpse of something beyond the iron firmament of their mechanized world. From the beginning, I was interested in the work of C. G. Jung, and also in Groddeck, Havelock Ellis, Eric Graham Howe, and G. R. Heyer, all of whom, without any formal psychotherapy, rescued me from the sexual confusions of adolescence and specifically from guilt in sexual pleasure. I have already mentioned one brief experience in actual psychotherapy—at the age of thirty-four—with a Freudian psychiatrist who was the only analyst in the area. I was so bored with the whole process that I began telling the doctor things which took his mind off the subject. I did not fall for the ploy that this was resisting therapy, for this is the same line a priest will offer when he attributes your intellectual doubts to unwillingness to repent of sins or, in other words, to cower before your small boy's conscience. And I must confess that I still find the psychotherapeutic process boring, whether on the giving end or the receiving, and thus have considerable admiration for therapists who spend their working lives at this often very merciful task. I have the same admiration for dentists. I don't know how they can do it unless they can manage to think of themselves as jewelers and workers in ivory. For like reason I also admire the guru, in the strict sense of one who gives personal direction to individuals in their spiritual development.

The Freudian method of analysis never appealed to me, though I would neither deny its usefulness nor the tremendous importance of Freud himself, especially when one considers the wider cultural implications of his thought as discussed, for example, with Norman O. Brown in his *Life Against Death*. I agree with Brown that practical psychoanalysis on the couch has become an ignoble compromise, to the extent that it attempts to relieve sexual inhibitions and at the same time accord mock-respect to the more lugubrious social conventions. Accordingly, the psychoanalytic religion exhibits no true delight in sexuality, no appreciation of its metaphysical wonder, and no realization of the value of the child's vision of the world. Sex, one would think, is a necessary and hygienic relief of pressure, similar to a bowel movement in that it is not really very nice. There is no thought of making sex into a fine art like *haute cuisine*, and the obvious connections between sex and religion are, on the whole, taken to mean that religious phenomena are *only* perversions of sex, and not very interesting sex at that. One could hardly imagine an important New York analyst dancing in the nude with his (or her) loved one, garlanded with flowers, to the music of African drums or even a Viennese waltz, much less practicing Tantric yoga.

To overcome the association of sex with guilt it was enough for me only to read Havelock Ellis and Georg Groddeck, and since then such problems as I have had seem to have arisen from the qualms and proprieties of other people, who take my lighthearted joy in this aspect of life for lack of maturity and serious commitment. But when we get heavily serious about either sex or religion there follow crimes of passion, suicides, bitter divorces, inquisitions, and holy wars—all of which are signs of imbecility rather than sincere conviction.

Personally, I have been more troubled by social attitudes to the child than to sexuality, and have already explained my difficulty in relating to children—especially my own children—as soon as they are of an age to go to school, since I am unable to represent the image which society expects of a father. In the present social context, to have a child is, as Spencer Brown has remarked, like going out into the street and offering the first person you meet room and board, health care and education, for twenty years. But it is, I think, school rather than biological accident which makes the child a stranger in the house, for in an industrial civilization children are not invited to work alongside their parents in offices and factories as might be expected on a farm or in a family workshop. School offers them the prospect of doing better and going higher than their parents, and this presents a weird problem to a parent who has already "done better and gone higher," especially in some scholarly or literary pursuit. I am torn between being a co-conspirator with my children and protecting myself from the social opprobrium that would ensue, particularly when it comes from within the family. The new "free schools" are bound to make initial mistakes, but they are a welcome step in the direction of ending the conflict between ties of blood and ties of personal interest when such schools are operated by groups of like-minded parents who do not have to commute to their work—which is still a tall order. On the other hand, generation gaposis might well be preferred to thousands of family schools run by Bible-bangers and other uptight persons who would neither spare the rod nor encourage freedom of thought and feeling.

It must now be obvious that, all along, I have been at odds with our social resistance to what Jung called the values of feeling and intuition as distinct from those of intellect and sensation, where the last signifies order and competence in handling the physical aspects of life: a good relationship to things. Jung called this resistance a cramp in consciousness, unknowingly, perhaps, using an exact equivalent of the Sanskrit *sankocha* or "contraction" which goes along with the sensation of the ego. For it has struck me that my ego is a marriage between my (necessarily false) image or concept of myself, and the chronic muscular tension which a child learns in *trying* to do things which must happen spontaneously: to love, to sleep, to attend, to have bowel movements, and to control crying, pouting, or blushing. But muscular tension does not necessarily assist neural efficiency, for it hinders rather than helps when we strain our eyes to see and furrow our brows to concentrate. Yet we are forever scratching our heads, clenching our fists and jaws, holding our breath, and tightening our rectal muscles in order to will or to keep control of our feelings, and the vague persistence of this tension becomes the substantial referent of the word "I," and the image the emotional and conceptual referent. A futility married to an illusion!

Throughout most of his life Jung did not see this, for he considered ego as the central organizing principle of consciousness, bewitched by the grammatical convention that the verb must have a subject, and that knowing requires a knower, whereas William James saw that "I" might be a designation of position like the words "this" and "here." As I was skeptical of Jung's reification (or "thingifying") of the ego, I was likewise dubious of his and Freud's use of the noun "the unconscious" for what Lance Whyte has better termed "unconscious process with conscious aspects," avoiding Whitehead's "fallacy of misplaced concreteness." But what fascinated me about Jung from the beginning was his idea that the unconscious process could be supraindividual or "collective" and that it represented an archetypal wisdom from which individuality could flower instead of being forcibly dragged up by the superego. It seems obvious that we should inherit the formative processes of the psyche just as we inherit those of the body, and that they should, at least initially, be as unconscious to us as our genes. Indeed, the genes and the "collective unconscious" may be the same process described from two different viewpoints.

Still more impressive was Jung's attitude to the *yin* (or dark aspect of the unconscious), his feeling that psychic integration was largely an acceptance and assimilation of the devil in ourselves by the power of love. He was pointing out a razor-edged path between repressing the dark aspect and going overboard for it, a path which took the risk of "allowing things to happen in the psyche." Through Jung, I understood that in repressing my devils and animals I would be cutting myself off from the manure for my flower, and that these dark forces would then issue in such forms as righteous cruelty and the fascination with "dirty" sexuality. Furthermore, Jung was the one leading psychotherapist who, in his time, took a positive and intelligent attitude to religion and mythology, and realized—with some important reservations—what we could learn from Eastern spirituality. Anyone who has read my books from *The Legacy of Asia* (1937) to *Psychotherapy East and West* (1961) will see what a vast influence Jung has had on my work, and how my enthusiasm for Oriental wisdom has been disciplined by his celebrated commentary on Richard Wilhelm's translation of *The Secret of the Golden Flower*. Over those years I read everything Jung wrote as soon as it was translated, including many of the privately circulated volumes of the transcriptions of his seminars, in which he could speak freely without fear for his scientific reputation as a physician, and thus go deeply into such disreputable subjects as astrology, alchemy, and *kundalini* yoga.

It was not until 1958 that I met Jung himself (I had once heard him lecture in London, around 1937), though I had known many of his principal students: H. G. Baynes, Michael Fordham, Charles Taylor, Olga Fröbe-Kapteyn, Joseph Henderson, and several others. But by the time I met Jung I had been exposed to another and very different approach to psychotherapy by Gregory Bateson, who had just begun work as consulting ethnologist at the Palo Alto Veterans' Hospital when I first came to California. He had been hired for the express purpose of keeping his colleagues on their toes by exercising themselves with his gentle and tentative but ever-questioning intellect. Gregory does one the mystifying courtesy of assuming that one is as bright as he, and thus it is sometimes difficult to follow the subtlety of his thought. This very large, informal, and somewhat shy Englishman has the special ability of spotting basic patterns in human and animal behavior and of pointing out where they exhibit logical contradictions and paradoxes. He began, therefore, to look for the roots of neuroses and psychoses in the context of social communication. One could say that he worked out a communications-theory approach to psychiatry in which the unconscious was not so much the psyche as the unexamined network of relationships in which every individual finds himself.

He discovered that the principal trouble-spot in our patterns of communication, especially in the family, was the "double bind"—that is, a two-level message in which the levels are in mutual contradiction. Thus the double bind has the logical form of the statement "I am lying," which is false if true and true if false. As between parents and children or husbands and wives, it takes the general form of a command to do what will be acceptable only if it is done voluntarily or spontaneously, as in "You must love me." For example, the wife complains to the husband that she is being taken for granted because during all their two years of marriage he has never taken her to the movies, whereas when they were courting he took her every week. The following night he comes home and suggests, "What about a movie tonight?" But she replies, "You're only suggesting it because I complained." The husband therefore finds himself in a damned-if-you-do-and-damned-if-you-don't situation, from which he can escape only if he can show her the contradiction. If, however, the individual so double-bound (as is usually so with a child) does not or cannot rise above it, there follows a state of anxiety comparable to the trembling of an electric bell which is so wired that the "on" signal turns it off and the "off" signal turns it on. Gregory further observed that schizophrenic children were commonly found in families which played this game on them.

I saw immediately that the double bind was characteristic of religious injunctions. "Thou shalt love the Lord thy God." "As Catholics we are bound to believe that..." "You must have Grace." "You cannot get it by seeking; you cannot get it by nonseeking." "Be unselfish." "Be unselfconscious." "Be natural." Gregory picked my brains on the techniques of Zen, and began to formulate the idea that successful psychotherapy might also, homeopathically, employ the double bind so as to create a *reductio ad absurdum* of a patient's life situation, and thus snap him out of it. I saw that this was equivalent to the Buddha's enjoining his disciples to stop desiring, which would of course put them in a state of desiring not to desire, which has the same logical form as trying to bite one's own teeth. If, then, I discover that I *cannot*, by any means, let go of myself (or at best only make an imitation of having done so), the message is that there is no "I" separate from me—that is, from the stream of thoughts and sensations which form the content of consciousness. This at once explodes the difference between the knower and the known, upon which we base such injunctions as "You must love" or "You must not desire."[1] This would seem to leave the stream uncontrolled by depriving the flow of thoughts of any thinker, unless it is realized that there never was a thinker, either to control thoughts or be controlled by them, other than the illusory self-image and the futile straining of muscles. Obviously this leaves a lot of questions, but I have done my best to answer them in other books.

The Jungians, also, were interested in Zen, and in the spring of 1958 I was invited to give some lectures at the C. G. Jung Institute in Zürich—an

---

[1] I do not know if anyone has pointed out that Bateson's theory of schizophrenia supports Ronald Laing's, as explained in his *Politics of Experience* (New York: Pantheon Books, 1967), where he suggests that schizophrenia may be at once a reaction against an impossible social context and a form of spontaneous therapy, if properly assisted by an understanding therapist.

invitation which also gave me my first opportunity to return to England in twenty years. On taking this journey I discovered that my old sensation of depression in moving eastwards had disappeared. Despite World War II, the England that I knew had changed little. Why, there were even advertisements painted on sheets of metal that had adorned Chislehurst Station since I was a child! The general quality of cooking had improved considerably, perhaps because of the unavailability of servants, and though I had imagined that much smoking had ruined my taste for apples, peas, and potatoes, the fruits and vegetables of our Chislehurst garden tasted the same as ever, and I realized that true potatoes are simply not to be found in America, even in kitchen gardens. And for the first time I saw, as many others have seen, that England is a peculiarly agreeable land for any reasonably affluent adult male if one agrees to play the game of detached courtesy, undemonstrative friendship, and quiet, contemplative enjoyment of such basics as chestnut trees in flower, pubs and good beer, pork pies, the London *Times*, the general feeling of lived-in-ness, and the small, special, and ever-changing sky.

I detected a feeling of peace that flowed from an agreeable lack of ambition, but also a blasé weariness that came from lack of imagination. I felt that many of my friends had remained, intellectually and spiritually, exactly where I had left them; that students showed little thirst for knowledge; that the publishing business was dreary and tired from the sense that the market had reached its limit, and that one's efforts were destined to be wittily damned with faint praise in the *Times Literary Supplement*; that authors and journalists were heavily preoccupied with nostalgia for the imperial past; and that the academic world, at least in the sphere of my own interests, was a tower of decaying ivory.[2] I had the honor of being asked, by the joint faculties on theology, anthropology, and Oriental studies, to lecture at

---

[2] I must make a notable exception for the work in the history of Chinese science over which Joseph Needham presides at Cambridge, a work both ambitious and imaginative, and which continues to swell the volumes of his *Science and Civilization in China*. I didn't meet Needham himself until 1962, when he proved, as I had expected, to be my ideal of a scholar in that he combines immense learning with genuine enthusiasm for his subject, which involves him in a colossal range of interests. He is, above all, an excellent listener who even takes notes during a conversation.

Cambridge, and never in my life met such an unresponsive audience—as was quite the reverse in Zürich.

Nevertheless, my basic respect for English literary standards leaves me truly puzzled, and even alarmed, at the continuing indifference of this country to my own work—and it is not as if the land were still enthralled by Anglican theology and the morals of the Victorian bourgeoisie. England exhibits an extraordinary degree of civil liberty and freedom of expression, and retains a unique tolerance of eccentricity, but I am most reluctantly forced to believe that its intellectual life is elegantly shallow. In America, for all the lack of style and background, there is passionate interest in things which a philosopher considers essential and deep, whereas the British persuade themselves, quite falsely, that they have heard all this before. In the domain of serious philosophy they continue to thumb the edge of the logical positivist sword, which helps them only to be condescendingly boring. To be a literary success one must be a retired general or faded aristocrat writing memoirs in several volumes, which is an exaggeration offered me by a London publisher.

I was thus agreeably amazed to be thoroughly unbored in stolid, commercial Zürich; partly, perhaps, because I was taken in hand by a most interestingly crazy (if inamorous) young woman who would have been an artist of some fame had she not taken her own life several years later. Sonya showed me the town, went boating with me on the lake, introduced me to snails, cheese fondue, and beef tartare, and showed an eye for beauty in things and places that normal people would simply ignore. She had, alas, been abandoned by the psychotherapeutic pandits as hopelessly psychotic, but she taught me, nevertheless, to listen and enter into a conversation that was quite off the rails of orthodox sanity. I became quite fond of her, but felt the association was a mark against me among the elite of the Institute, on the principle, I suppose, that anthropologists must not befriend natives in the psychotic jungle. It is, perhaps, understandable that psychiatrists are abnormally afraid of losing their own minds, but it seems that their patients are more in need of friendship than professionally sterilized therapy.

The C. G. Jung Institute is in a pleasant part of the Old Town, sonorous with big, booming bells and the rumble of streetcars. There seem to be scholarly bookshops on almost every street, and cafés serving good if unimaginative food to the University literati, who conduct their real intellectual business in these civilized surroundings. Here, as in other Jungian circles, there was a "hangout of bluestockings," that is, a company of elderly, refined, and extremely well-educated ladies of formidable appearance who set the tone of the Institute, mingled with young men and women from all over Europe and America studying to be psychotherapists. They managed to constitute a fascinating audience, and after the first lecture we adjourned to a café where I was introduced to Dr. Medard Boss, a professor of psychiatry at the University, who had traveled in India and had been initiated by a Tantric guru in Kashmir.[3] He expressed amazement that I had explained the doctrine of *maya* as he had received it from his teacher, and wondered how I could have stumbled upon what he took to be an esoteric tradition, almost unknown to Western scholars. I could say only that my view of the doctrine was unusual, in that I understood *maya*—the illusion of duality and separateness—to arise from our concepts rather than our senses, and that enlightenment did not therefore imply the disappearance of nature from before our eyes. The enlightened one sees the world that others see, but does not conceive it in the way others do, as a collection of separate things other than himself. For when we get the actual sense of depth from a drawing in perspective, the concept is overruling the eyes, and Adelbert Ames had constructed a whole series of experiments demonstrating that we see what we believe rather than believe what we see. I had, of course, been explaining to the Institute my long-held view that mystical experience is not intended to dissolve our vision of the natural universe into a featureless void or a blinding light, since the great mystics I have known seemed quite clearly aware of their surroundings.

Some days later I went out to Jung's home at Küsnacht and met the old master in his summerhouse on the edge of the lake, where we talked for two hours about everything from Sanskrit words for the unconscious to the sex life of swans. I found Jung an even greater, more intuitive, more humorous,

---

[3] See his excellent book *A Psychiatrist Discovers India* (Chester Springs, Pa.: Dufour Editions; London: Rider & Co., 1965).

and deeper person than I had expected from his writings. He asked me how I was getting along at the Institute, and was careful to explain that he himself was not a Jungian and that he had had no intention of promulgating a particular system of psychotherapy. He had simply followed his intuition and written down his findings as they came along, never intending that his concepts should be more than heuristic devices in a work where the living individual counts for more than any technique.

As our conversation turned to his interest in Oriental philosophy, he told me of his difficulty in finding any term in Hindu or Buddhist philosophy exactly parallel to the idea of the unconscious. I suggested that the nearest thing would be the Mahayanist term *alaya-vijñana*, the "store-consciousness," which, somewhat like his collective unconscious, was the supraindividual origin of those archetypal forms or concepts which we use in making sense of the universe. I pointed out that Suzuki had sometimes used the phrase "the unconscious" in a very different way, to translate the Japanese *mushin* ("no-mind") which, so far from being unconscious, was a highly aware un*self* consciousness. He was so open, eager, and twinkly-eyed in his comments and questions that I had the temerity to tell him that I thought the very term "*the* unconscious" was unfortunate, and went into the whole linguistic problem of using nouns for processes and having verbs caused by subjects. I said that I thought he was confusing things by considering the ego the center of consciousness because, even sticking to his own terminology and the noun-verb system of grammar, he would surely have to say that consciousness was a function of the unconscious, and that therefore you couldn't very well call it "unconscious." The difficulty was rather that the light of consciousness doesn't illumine its own source; that it is a scanning process, like a thin beam, which can only focus on one small area at a time—and how could we call to memory things we had never noticed unless the unconscious were in some way conscious apart from the scanning beam? He seemed intensely interested in this, probably because, as I understood, he had rather recently had his own experience of cosmic consciousness transcending the ego (this inelegant terminology is only for shorthand), which he mentions at the end of *Memories, Dreams, Reflections*.

The discussion of linguistics and scanning led us into the subject of the influence of communications theory and computer mechanics on American psychology—a question raised still more fully a few days later in a conversation with Professor Benedetti of Basel. Jung, Benedetti, Boss, and several others had the feeling that American psychology had always a tendency to be brashly mechanical and lacking in those "finer feelings" which Europeans commonly accuse Americans of ignoring. I interposed, however, that those who made really thorough studies of mechanical analogues of the mind, such as Bateson and Wiener, were the first to recognize their limitations. Several years later I could have cited the case of John Lilly, who went so deeply into the computer analogy, and with such a gifted intellect, that he came to a *ne plus ultra* of intellectual formulation and had to save his sanity by passing into occultism, though keeping his scientific wits very much about him.[4] But Jung could have predicted the uncritical "Uprush of unconscious contents" which now both fascinates and confuses American youth as an inevitable reaction to the cult of conscious control in technology and behaviorism.

When it was time for me to leave we walked out of the summerhouse and looked at the swans on the lake.

"Isn't it true," I asked, "that swans are monogamous?"

"Oh yes," he said, "but there's a funny thing about their mating for the first time. They invariably begin by picking a fight until they discover what they are supposed to be doing.

"Yes," he added, "the swans here have been of great help to some of my female homosexual patients."

Thinking back, I am trying to remember what Jung told *me*, for I was tremendously impressed by his warmth, his intelligence, and his sense of fun. But I realize that he spent almost the whole time asking questions, which was natural for a great psychotherapist. The same kind of thing happened when my friend Margaret Tilly, the San Francisco pianist, went to him to discuss therapy with music. He asked her to go straight ahead with the therapy, using him as the patient. Shortly afterwards, Jung's daughter said to Margaret, "Perhaps you don't realize that you did something very important for me and my father. I have always loved music, but he has never understood it, and

---

[4] See his *Programming and Metaprogramming in the Human Biocomputer* (Berkeley, Calif.: Portola Institute, n.d.) and his *Center of the Cyclone* (New York: Julian Press, 1972).

this was a barrier between us. Your coming has changed all that, and I don't know how to thank you."

Towards the end of my stay in Zürich I had dinner with Karlfried von Dürckheim, a former German diplomat who had studied Zen in Japan and had begun to operate a school of meditation in the Black Forest. Anyone who has never met such a person might think me snobbish in saying that he was a true nobleman—unselfconsciously and by long tradition perfect in speech and courtesy—Keyserling's ideal of the *grand seigneur*. But there was much more to him than that, as I shall try to show in what he told me about his work, and which I remember almost verbatim.

"A great deal of my present work," he said, "is in helping people who underwent great spiritual crises during the war. We know, of course, that sometimes, in extreme circumstances, people have a natural *satori* or spiritual awakening when it appears that all is finished for them—and they accept it. This happened often in the war, and when those who lived through it tried to tell the tale to their friends it was shrugged off as some kind of hallucination, a brief fit of insanity in a desperate situation. When these people come to me, as they often do, I have the happy opportunity of showing them that, for once in their lives, they were truly sane.

"There were three typical ways in which these crises came about. You heard the whistle of a bomb falling straight at you, and knew that this was quite certainly the end. You accepted it, and quite suddenly the whole universe made sense. All problems, all questions vanished, and you understood that there was no 'you' other than the eternal. But the bomb was a dud, and you lived to remember the experience. . . . You were in a concentration camp, and you had been there so long that you were fully convinced that you would stay there for the rest of your life. Finally, you had to accept it, and in that moment you understood everything. . . . You were a displaced refugee far from home. You had utterly lost your friends and relatives, your possessions, your job, your very identity, and saw no hope of regaining them. You accepted it, and suddenly you were as light as a feather and as free as the air."

I had heard similar stories of *kamikaze* pilots who miraculously survived, and should add a parallel experience of my own which I recorded in *This Is It*, and which happened in a dream when I was about eight.

I was sick at the time and almost delirious with fever, and in the dream I found myself attached face-downward and spreadeagled to an immense ball of steel which was spinning about the earth. I knew in this dream with complete certainty that I was doomed to be spun in this sickening and terrifying whirl forever and ever, and the conviction was so intense that there was nothing for it but to give up—for this was hell itself and nothing lay before me but a literal everlastingness of pain. But in the moment when I surrendered, the ball seemed to strike against a mountain and disintegrate, and the next thing I knew [still in the dream] was that I was sitting on a stretch of warm sand with nothing left of the ball except crumpled fragments of sheet-metal scattered around me.

I have traveled no further east than Zürich, except to Ceylon and Japan which I approached from the West. I went there again, with Jano and my father in 1962, when we drove from Paris to Rome and back, and gave my father his first view of real mountains. He had always loved to read about mountaineering, especially in the Himalayas. Just at the top of the Saint Gotthard Pass we came out of the clouds to see a blazing white peak above us, and he was as happy as a child as we zigzagged down into Ticino where the Alps, like a garden wall, bounce back the sun on the castles, monasteries, villas, gardens, and cypress trees above the lakes. But why do I specially like Zürich? The natives are serious, industrious, and stuffy, and have converted the beautiful hilltop cathedral into a lecture hall, with chairs turned to face the pulpit, standing at one side of the nave. Nevertheless, Zürich has a certain luminosity and I find its place-names musical—Zollikon, Limmatquai, Gemeindestrasse. Also, it is far enough east for some of its towers to show signs of bulging into the onion dome of Russia.

On returning to America I was introduced to psychiatric adventures of a very different order, for Aldous Huxley had recently published *Doors of Perception* about his experiment with mescaline, and had by this time gone on to explore the mysteries of LSD. Gerald Heard had joined him in these investigations, and in my conversations with them I noticed a marked change of spiritual attitude. To put it briefly, they had ceased to be Manicheans. Their vision of the divine now included nature, and they had become more relaxed and humane, so that I found myself talking to men of my own persuasion. Yet it struck me as highly improbable that a true spiritual experience could follow from ingesting a particular chemical. Visions and ecstasies, yes. A taste of the mystical, like swimming with waterwings, perhaps. And perhaps a reawakening for someone who had made the journey before, or an insight for a person well practiced in something like Yoga or Zen.

Nevertheless, on these "inner planes" I am of an adventurous nature, and am willing to give most things a try. Both Aldous and my former student at the Academy, mathematician John Whittelsey, were in touch with Keith Ditman, psychiatrist in charge of LSD research at the UCLA department of neuropsychiatry. John was working with him as statistician in a project designed both to test the effect of the drug on alcoholics and to make a map of its effects on the human organism. So many of their subjects had reported states of consciousness that read like accounts of mystical experience that they were interested in trying it out on "experts" in this field, even though a mystic is never really expert in the same way as a neurologist or a philologist, for his work is not a cataloguing of objects. But I qualified as an expert insofar as I had also a considerable intellectual knowledge of the psychology and philosophy of religion: a knowledge that subsequently protected me from the more dangerous aspects of this adventure, giving me a compass and something of a map for this wild territory. Furthermore, I trusted Keith Ditman. He wasn't scared, like so many Jungians, of the unconscious. Nor was he foolhardy, but seemed level-headed, cautious, tentative in opinion, yet lively, bright-eyed, and intensely interested in his work.

We made, then, an initial experiment at Keith's office in Beverly Hills in which I was joined by Edwin Halsey, formerly private secretary to Ananda Coomaraswamy, and then teaching comparative religions at Claremont. We each took one hundred micrograms of d-lysergic acid diethylamide-25, courtesy of the Sandoz Company, and set out on an eight-hour exploration. For me the journey was hilariously beautiful—as if I and all my perceptions had been transformed into a marvelous arabesque or multidimensional maze in which everything became transparent, translucent, and reverberant with double and triple meanings. Every detail of perception became vivid and important, even ums and ers and throat-clearing when someone read poetry, and time slowed down in such a way that people going about their business outside seemed demented in failing to see that the destination of life is this eternal moment. We walked across the street to a white, Spanish-style church, surrounded with olive trees and gleaming in the sun against a sky of absolute, primordial blue, and saw the grass and the plants as inexplicably geometrized in every detail so as to suggest that nothing in nature was disordered. We went back and looked at a volume of Chinese and Japanese *sumi*, or black-ink paintings, all of which seemed to be perfectly accurate photographs. There were even highlights and shadows on Mu'ch'i's persimmons that were certainly not intended by the artist. At one time Edwin felt somewhat overwhelmed and remarked, "I just can't wait until I'm little old me again, sitting in a bar." In the meantime he was looking like an incarnation of Apollo in a supernatural necktie, contemplatively holding an orange lily.[5]

All in all my first experience was aesthetic rather than mystical, and then and there—which is, alas, rather characteristic of me—I made a tape for broadcast saying that I had looked into this phenomenon and found it most interesting, but hardly what I would call mystical. This tape was heard by two psychiatrists at the Langley-Porter Clinic in San Francisco, Sterling Bunnell and Michael Agron, who thought I should reconsider my views. After all, I had made only one experiment and there was something of an art to getting it really working. It was thus that Bunnell set me off on a series of experiments which I have recorded in *The Joyous Cosmology*, and in the course of which I was reluctantly compelled to admit that—at least in my own case—

---

[5] Several years later he was killed in an automobile accident on his way to Ajijic in Mexico, where he had made his home. And so went into obscurity a most extraordinary and brilliant man, who wrote a book that no one would publish (his Harvard Ph.D. dissertation) on history as a subjective illusion, based on the conflicting views of modern critics of the New Testament. He was both a scholar and an artist in life from whose conversation and criticism of my work I profited greatly. However, his liberal views were too much both for Reed College and for Claremont, where he was refused preferment and tenure—unless, as he was once told, he would settle down and marry a nice Episcopalian girl.

LSD had brought me into an undeniably mystical state of consciousness. But oddly, considering my absorption in Zen at the time, the flavor of these experiences was Hindu rather than Chinese. Somehow the atmosphere of Hindu mythology and imagery slid into them, suggesting at the same time that Hindu philosophy was a local form of a sort of undercover wisdom, inconceivably ancient, which everyone knows in the back of his mind but will not admit. This wisdom was simultaneously holy and disreputable, and therefore necessarily esoteric, and it came in the dress of a totally logical, obvious, and basic common sense.

In sum I would say that LSD, and such other psychedelic substances as mescaline, psilocybin, and hashish, confer polar vision; by which I mean that the basic pairs of opposites, the positive and the negative, are seen as the different poles of a single magnet or circuit. This knowledge is repressed in any culture that accentuates the positive, and is thus a strict taboo. It carries Gestalt psychology, which insists on the mutual interdependence of figure and background, to its logical conclusion in every aspect of life and thought; so that the voluntary and the involuntary, knowing and the known, birth and decay, good and evil, outline and inline, self and other, solid and space, motion and rest, light and darkness, are seen as aspects of a single and completely perfect process. The implication of this may be that there is nothing in life to be gained or attained that is not already here and now, an implication thoroughly disturbing to any philosophy or culture which is seriously playing the game which I have called White *Must* Win.

Polar vision is thus undoubtedly dangerous—but so is electricity, so are knives, and so is language. When an immature person experiences the identity of the voluntary and the involuntary, he may feel, on the one hand, utterly powerless, or on the other, equal to the Hebrew-Christian God. If the former, he may panic from the sense that no one is in charge of things. If the latter, he may contract offensive megalomania. Nevertheless, he has had immediate experience of the fact that each one of us is an organism-environment field, of which the two aspects, individual and world, can be separated only for purposes of discussion. If such a person sees thus clearly the mutuality of good and evil, he may jump to the conclusion that ethical principles are so relative as to be without validity—which might be utterly demoralizing for any repressed adolescent. Fortunately for me, my God was not so much the Hebrew-Christian autocrat as the Chinese Tao, "which loves and nourishes all things, but does not lord it over them."

I hesitated a long time before writing *The Joyous Cosmology*, considering the dangers of letting the general public be further aware of this potent alchemy. But since Aldous had already let the cat out of the bag in *Doors of Perception* and *Heaven and Hell*, and the subject was already under discussion both in psychiatric journals and in the public press, I decided that more needed to be said, mainly to soothe public alarm and to do what I could to forestall the disasters that would follow from legal repression. For I was seriously alarmed at the psychedelic equivalents of bathtub gin, and of the prospect of these chemicals, uncontrolled in dosage and content, being bootlegged for use in inappropriate settings without any competent supervision whatsoever. I maintained that, for lack of any better solution, they should be restricted for psychiatric prescription. But the state and federal governments were as stupid as I had feared, and by passing unenforceable laws against LSD not only drove it underground but prevented proper research. Such laws are unenforceable because any competent chemist can manufacture LSD, or a close equivalent, and the substance can be disguised as anything from aspirin to blotting-paper. It has been painted on the thin pages of a small Bible, and eaten sheet by sheet. But as a result of this terror, the injudicious use of LSD (often mixed with strychnine or belladonna or quite dangerous psychedelics) has afflicted uncounted young people with paranoid, megalomaniac, and schizoid symptoms.

I see this disaster in the larger context of American prohibitionism, which has done more than anything else to corrupt the police and foster disrespect for law, and which our economic pressure has, in the special problem of drug abuse, spread to the rest of the world. Although my views on this matter may be considered extreme, I feel that in any society where the powers of Church and State are separate, the State is without either right or wisdom in enforcing sumptuary laws against crimes which have no complaining victims. When the police are asked to be armed clergymen enforcing ecclesiastical codes of morality, all the proscribed sins of the flesh, of lust and luxury, become—since we are legislating against human nature—exceedingly profitable ventures for criminal organizations which can pay both the police and the politicians to stay out of trouble. Those who cannot pay constitute about one-third of the population of our overcrowded and hopelessly mismanaged prisons, and the business of their trial by due process delays and overtaxes the courts beyond all reason. These are nomogenic crimes, caused by bad laws, just as iatrogenic diseases are caused by bad doctoring. The offenders seldom feel guilty but often positively righteous in their opposition to this legal hypocrisy, and so emerge from prison loathing and despising the social order more than ever.

I speak with passion on this problem because I have often served as a consultant to the staffs of state institutions for mental and moral deviants, such as the institutional hells which the State of California maintains at San Quentin, Vacaville, Atascadero, and Napa—to mention only those I have visited, and knowing that they are considerably worse in other parts of the country, and most especially in those states afflicted with religious fanaticism. Relative to our own times, the prosecution of sumptuary laws is as tyrannical as any of the excesses of the Holy Inquisition or the Star Chamber.

My retrospective attitude to LSD is that when one has received the message, one hangs up the phone. I think I have learned from it as much as I can, and, for my own sake, would not be sorry if I could never use it again. But it is not, I believe, generally known that very many of those who had constructive experiences with LSD, or other psychedelics, have turned from drugs to spiritual disciplines—abandoning their water-wings and learning to swim. Without the catalytic experience of the drug they might never have come to this point, and thus my feeling about psychedelic chemicals, as about most other drugs (despite the vague sense of the word), is that they should serve as medicine rather than diet.

In was again through Aldous that I first heard of a Dr. Leary of Harvard University who was doing experimental work with the drug psilocybin, derived from a mushroom that had long been used for religious purposes by some of the Indians of Mexico. From the detached and scholarly flavor of Aldous's account of this work I was expecting Timothy Leary to be a formidable pandit, but the man I first met in a New York restaurant was an extremely charming Irishman who wore a hearing-aid as stylishly as if it had been a monocle. Nothing could then have told me that anyone so friendly and intelligent would become one of the most outlawed people in the world, a fugitive from justice charged with the sin of Socrates, and all upon the legal pretext of possessing trivial amounts of marijuana.

It so happened that Timothy was working under a department of the University that had long been of interest to me, the Department of Social Relations, which had been established by Henry Murray. On several occasions I had visited Murray's domain, at 7 Divinity Avenue, and been entertained at luncheons where, as host, he showed a special genius for arousing intelligent conversation and for making other people appear at their best. In his company there would turn up—it might be—I. A. Richards, Mircea Eliade, Clyde Kluckhohn, or Jerome Bruner for such civilized intellectual discourse as is all too rarely heard in academic circles, where it now seems a point of honor to keep off one's subject and discuss the trivia of departmental politics. But these gentlemen were ashamed neither of their scholarship nor their personalities, and on one occasion—over an old-fashioned before lunch—I distinctly heard Richards remarking, "Well, as a matter of course, I always regard myself as the perfect human being." I was so delighted with Murray's milieu that, with the assistance of a wealthy friend, I managed to get myself a two-year fellowship for travel and study under his and the University's dispensation—a breather which gave me time to compile *The Two Hands of God* and to write *Beyond Theology*.

The time I could actually spend at Harvard was all too brief, for this is a university so assured of its intellectual reputation that its faculty can afford to be adventurous. But—even at Harvard—you must draw the line somewhere, and Timothy did not know just where that was. Whenever I was in Cambridge I kept closely in touch with him and with his associates Richard Alpert and Ralph Metzner, for—quite aside from the particular fascinations of chemical mysticism—these were the most lively and imaginative people in the department other than Murray himself, who watched their doings with deep and constructively critical interest even after his official retirement.

I was also interested in the work of B. F. Skinner, wondering how so absolute a determinist could write a utopia, *Walden Two*, and digging into his beautifully reasoned writings until I discovered the flaw in his system. This

I explained in a lecture which Skinner, though I had forewarned him in person, did not attend.[6] I saw that his reasoning was still haunted by the ghost of man as a something—presumably a conscious ego—determined by environmental and other forces, for it makes no sense to speak of a determinism unless there is some passive object which is determined. But his own reasoning made it clear, not so much that human behavior was determined by other forces, but rather that it could not be described apart from those forces and was, indeed, inseparable from them. It did not seem to have occurred to him that "cause" and "effect" are simply two phases of, or two ways of looking at, one and the same event. It is not, then, that effects (in this case human behaviors) are determined by their causes. The point is that when events are fully and properly described they will be found to involve and contain processes which were at first thought separate from them, and were thus called causes as distinct from effects. Taken to his logical conclusion, Skinner is not saying that man is determined *by* nature, as something external to him: he is actually saying that man *is* nature, and is describing a process which is neither determined nor determining. He simply provides reason for the essentially mystical view that man and universe are inseparable.

Such problems were involved in my attempts to work out an intellectual structure for what Timothy and his friends were experiencing in their psychedelic states of consciousness. For I saw that their enthusiasm for these states was leading them further and further away from the ideals of rational objectivity to which the department and the University were committed; especially as the department had recently acquired a computer and was going overboard for the statistical approach to psychology. On the one hand, I was trying to persuade Timothy's clan to keep command of intellectual rigor, and to express their experiences in terms that people bending over backward to be scientific would understand. On the other hand, I was trying to get such conservatives as David McClelland, Murray's successor, and Skinner to see that the so-called "transactional" description of man as an

---

[6] "The Individual as Man-World," *The Psychedelic Review*, Vol. 1, No. 1 (Cambridge, Mass.: June 1963).

organism-environment field was a theoretical description of what the nature-mystic experiences immediately, whereas most scientists continue to experience themselves as separate and detached observers, determined or otherwise. Their feelings lag far behind their theoretical views, for psychologists, in particular, are still under the emotional sway of Newtonian mechanics, and their personal feelings of identity have not yet been modified by quantum mechanics and field theory.

But Timothy could not contain himself, and it seemed to him more and more that, in practice, the procedures of scientific objectivity and rigor were simply an academic ritual designed to convince the university establishment that your work was dull and trivial enough to be considered "sound." It so happens that psychedelic chemicals make one curiously sensitive to pomposity. Anyone talking memorandumese, or religious or political rhetoric, or anyone waxing enthusiastic about a product in which he does not believe, sounds so ridiculous that you cannot keep a straight face: one excellent reason why no government can tolerate a "turned-on" populace. Both Timothy and Richard Alpert began to see, furthermore, that a distinguished academic career was not all that important, since the university was already an obsolete institution representing the nineteenth-century mythology of scientific naturalism. But when one arrives at this point of view after, if not because of, "taking drugs," it becomes impossible to maintain rational discourse with the establishment, even though some of its more distinguished brains are pickled in alcohol. Thus things came to the point where Timothy and Richard were as suspect as if they had been lobotomized or become Jehovah's Witnesses.

I was present at the dinner party where Timothy finally agreed with David McClelland to withdraw experimentation with drugs from his work under the department. David was making the point that they had become too enthusiastic about their work to preserve scientific integrity, and with this I was in partial agreement, because to be intellectually honest you must be able to come to terms with any intelligible criticism of your ideas. When I have received inspirations during an LSD session, I have always reviewed them subsequently in the light of cold sobriety, in which some, but by no means all, of them appear to be nonsense. But David was going so far as to insist that no one with a religious commitment could really do scientific work in psychology, and this so amazed me that I protested, "Now, David, are you seriously saying that, for example, a very sober, honest, and devoted Quaker, well educated and straight from Philadelphia, could not be entrusted with scientific work?" I do not remember his reaction, but I was unaware at the time that he himself was a concerned Quaker.

What followed is now a matter of history. Timothy and Richard continued their experiments unofficially, and scandalized the University authorities by including undergraduates in their work. Henry Murray, however, with a wise look on his face, reminisced about the days when psychoanalysis first struck Harvard, and what an uproar of indignation had come to pass when a psychoanalyzed faculty member had committed suicide. Nevertheless, I myself began to be concerned, if mildly, at the direction of Timothy's enthusiasm, for to his own circle of friends and students he had become a charismatic religious leader who, well trained as he was in psychology, knew very little about religion and mysticism and their pitfalls. The uninstructed adventurer with psychedelics, as with Zen or yoga or any other mystical discipline, is an easy victim of what Jung calls "inflation," of the messianic megalomania that comes from misunderstanding the experience of union with God. It leads to the initial mistake of casting pearls before swine, and, as time went on, I was dismayed to see Timothy converting himself into a popular store-front messiah with his name in lights, advocating psychedelic experience as a new world-religion. He was moving to a head-on collision with the established religions of biblical theocracy and scientific mechanism, and simply asking for martyrdom.

Life with Timothy, as I saw it in his communes at Newton Center and Millbrook, was never dull, even though it was hard to understand how people who had witnessed the splendors of psychedelic vision could be so aesthetically blind as to live in relative squalor, with perpetually unmade beds, unswept floors, and hideously decrepit furnishings. It could be, I suppose, that being turned-on all the time is like looking through a teleidoscope: it makes far more interesting patterns out of messes (such as dirty ashtrays) than out of such orderly scenes as neatly arranged books in shelves. But Timothy was the center of a vortex which pulled in the intellectually and spiritually adventurous from all quarters, and in his entourage student hip-pies jostled with millionaires and eminent professors, while to spend an evening with him in New York City or Los Angeles was to be swept from one exotically sumptuous apartment to another.

Through all this, Timothy himself remained an essentially humorous, kindly, lovable, and (in some directions) intellectually brilliant person, and therefore it was utterly incongruous—however predictable—to become aware of the grim watchfulness of police in the background. Now nothing so easily deranges people using psychedelics as a paranoid atmosphere, so that by their intervention the police created the very evils from which they were supposed to be protecting us. In the early days when LSD, psilocybin, and mescaline were used more or less legitimately among reasonably mature people, there was little trouble with "bum trips," and episodes of anxiety were usually turned into occasions for insight. But when federal and state authorities began their systematic persecution, the fears invoked to justify it became self-fulfilling prophecies, and there was now real reason for a para-noid atmosphere in all experiments conducted outside the sterile and clini-cal surroundings of psychiatric hospitals. Although Timothy won a case in the Supreme Court which technically quashed the federal law against possessing and using (but not against importing) marijuana, the state laws remained in force, and he was harassed wherever he went, until finally imprisoned without bail with so many technical charges against him that there was nothing for it but to escape and seek such asylum in exile as he could find.

Richard Alpert, who in all this had played a much quieter role, also went into exile, but in another way. While visiting India he realized that he had come to the end of the identity as a psychologist which he had thus far played, so much so that he could not envisage any normal role or career for himself in the United States. Furthermore, he felt as I did that he had learned all that he could get from psychedelics, and that what remained was actually to live out the life of freedom from worldly games and anxieties. He therefore took the name of Baba Ram Dass, and came back as a white-robed and bearded *sannyasin*, full of laughter and energy, dedicated simply to living in the eter-nal now. And, as might be expected, people raised their eyebrows and shook their heads, saying that the old showman was playing another game, or, alas, what drugs had done to such a promising young scientist, or that it was just great to be a *sannyasin* with an independent income. But I felt that he had done just the right thing for himself. I spent many hours with him and sensed that he was genuinely happy, that his intelligence was as sharp as ever, and that he was confident enough in what he was doing not to try to persuade me to follow his example. Certainly he was having great pleasure in the multitudes of young people who came to listen to him, but in this respect he and I are alike, for we enjoy thinking out loud with an appreciative and intelligent audience just as we enjoy landscape or music. But would he be going about in a white robe if he were really sincere? Indeed yes. For in a country where a philosopher's sincerity is measured by the ordinariness of his dress, I too will sometimes wear a kimono or sarong in public, lest, like Billy Graham, I should attract an enormous following of dangerously serious and humorless people.

Now, in retrospect, it must be said that the Psychedelic Decade of the sixties has really begun to awaken psychotherapists from their studiedly pedestrian and reductionist attitudes to life. Here I am using the word "psychedelic" to mean all "mind-manifesting" processes: not only chemicals, but also philosophies, neurological experiments, and spiritual disciplines. At the beginning of the decade one felt that so many psychiatrists saw themselves as guardians of an official reality which might be described as the world seen on a bleak Monday morning. They saw a good orientation to reality as coping—as having a normal heterosexual (and preferably monogamous) sex life, a "mature adult relationship" as it was called; as being able to drive a car and hold down a nine-to-five job; as being able to recall the product of 9 and 7 without hesitation; and as being able to participate in group activities and show qualities of initiative and leadership.

It was, as I remember, in 1959 that I was asked to speak before a meeting of the American Psychiatric Association in Los Angeles. Learned statistical papers had dragged on and on, overtime, and my turn came when we were already late for lunch. I abandoned my prepared remarks (being what the press calls a textual deviate) and said:

"Gentlemen, this is not going to be a scientific paper because I am a simple philosopher, not a psychiatrist, and you are hungry for lunch. We philosophers are very grateful to you for showing us the unconscious emotional bases of some of our ideas, but the time is coming for us to show you the unconscious intellectual assumptions behind some of yours. Psychiatric literature is full of unexamined metaphysics. Even Jung, who is so readily repudiated for his 'mysticism,' bends over backward to avoid metaphysical considerations on the pretext that he is strictly a physician and a scientist. This is impossible. Every human being is a metaphysician just as every philosopher has appetites and emotions—and by this I mean that we all have certain basic assumptions about the good life and the nature of reality. Even the typical businessman who asserts that he is a practical fellow unconcerned with higher things declares thereby that he is a pragmatist or a positivist, and not a very thoughtful one at that.

"I wonder, then, how much consideration you give to the fact that most of your own assumptions about the good life and reality come directly from the scientific naturalism of the nineteenth century, from the strictly metaphysical hypothesis that the universe is a mechanism obeying Newtonian laws, and that there is no other god beside it. Psychoanalysis, which is actually psychohydraulics following Newton's mechanics, begins from the mystical assertion that the psychosexual energy of the unconscious is a blind and stupid outrush of pure lust, following Haeckel's notion that the universe at large is a manifestation of primordially oafish and undiscriminating energy. It should be obvious to you that this is an opinion for which there has never been the least evidence, and which, furthermore, ignores the evidence that we ourselves, supposedly making intelligent remarks, are manifestations of that same energy.

"On the basis of this unexamined, derogatory, and shaky opinion as to the nature of biological and physical energy, some of your psychoanalytic members have this morning dubbed all the so-called mystical states of consciousness as 'regressive,' as leading one back to a dissolution of the individual intelligence in an acid bath of amniotic fluid, reducing it to featureless identity with this—your First Cause—mess of blindly libidinous energy. Now, until you have found some substantial evidence for your metaphysics you will have to admit that you have no way of knowing which end of your universe is up, so that in the meantime you should abstain from easy conclusions as to which directions are progressive and which regressive. [*Laughter*]"

It had always seemed to me that, by and large, psychotherapists lacked the metaphysical dimension; in other words, that they affected the mentality of insurance clerks and lived in a world scrubbed and disinfected of all mystery, magic, color, music, and awe, with no place in the heart for the sound of a distant gong in a high and hidden valley. This is an exaggeration from which I will except most of the Jungians and such occasional freaks as Groddeck, Prinzhorn, G. R. Heyer, Wilhelm Reich, and others less well known. Thus, writing of American psychology in 1954, Abraham Maslow remarked that it was

> overpragmatic, over-Puritan, and overpurposeful. . . . No textbooks have chapters on fun and gaiety, on leisure and meditation, on loafing and puttering, on aimless, useless, and purposeless activity. . . . American psychology is busily occupying itself with only half of life to the neglect of the other—and perhaps most important—half.[7]

The publication of my *Psychotherapy East and West* and *Joyous Cosmology* early in the sixties brought me into public and private discussion with many leading members of the psychiatric profession, and I was astonished at what seemed to be their actual terror of unusual states of consciousness. I had thought that psychiatrists should have been as familiar with these wildernesses and unexplored territories of the mind as Indian guides, but as I perused something like the two huge volumes of *The American Handbook of Psychiatry*, I found only maps of the soul as primitive as ancient maps of the world. There were vaguely outlined emptinesses called Schizophrenia, Hysteria, and Catatonia, accompanied with little more solid information than "Here be dragons and cameleopards." At a party in New York I fell into conversation with one of that city's most eminent analysts, and as soon as he learned that I had experimented with LSD his personality became surgically professional. He donned his mask and rubber gloves and addressed

---

[7] *Motivation and Personality* (New York: Harper & Row, Publishers, 1954), pp. 291–92.

me as a specimen, wanting to know all the surface details of perceptual and kinesthetic alterations, which I could see him fitting into place zip, pop, and clunk with his keenly calipered mind. I took part in a televised debate on "Open End," with David Susskind trying to moderate between the two factions of psychedelic enthusiasts and establishment psychiatrists, and in the ensuing uproar and confusion of passions I found myself flung into the position of moderator, telling both sides that they had no basis in evidence for their respective fanaticisms.

In all these contacts I began to feel that the only psychiatrists who had any solid information were such neurologists as David Rioch, of Walter Reed, and Karl Pribram, of Stanford. They could tell me things I didn't know and were the first to admit how little they knew, for they were realizing the odd fact that their brains were more intelligent than their minds or, to say the least, that the human nervous system was of such a high order of complexity that we were only just beginning to organize it in terms of conscious thought. I sat in on an intimate seminar with Pribram in which he explained in most careful detail how the brain is no mere reflector of the external world, but how its structure almost creates the forms and patterns that we see, selecting them from an immeasurable spectrum of vibrations as the hands of a harpist pluck chords and melodies from a spectrum of strings. For Karl Pribram is working on the most delicate epistemological puzzle: how the brain evokes a world which is simultaneously the world which it is in, and to wonder, therefore, whether the brain evokes the brain.[8] Put it in metaphysical terms, psychological terms, physical terms, or neurological terms: it is always the same. How can we know what we know without knowing knowing?

This question must be answered, if it can ever be answered, before it can make any sense at all to say that reality is material, mental, electrical, spiritual, a fact, a dream, or anything else. But always, in contemplating this conundrum, a peculiar feeling comes over me, as if I couldn't remember my own name which is right on the tip of my tongue. It really does make one

---

[8] See his *Languages of the Brain* (Englewood Cliffs, N.J.: Prentice-Hall, 1971).

wonder if, after all...if...

Anyhow, at the end of these ten years I have the impression that the psychiatric world has opened up to the possibility that there are more things in heaven and earth than were dreamed of in its philosophy. Orthodox psychoanalysis has appeared more and more to be a religious cult and institutional psychiatry a system of brainwashing. The field is giving way to movements and techniques increasingly free from the tacit metaphysics of nineteenth-century mechanism: Humanistic Psychology, Transpersonal Psychology, Gestalt Therapy, Transactional Psychology, Encounter Therapy, Psychosynthesis (Assagioli), Bioenergetics (Reich), and a dozen more interesting approaches with awkward names.

Historians and social commentators will try to discover from any autobiographer how much he has influenced the movements of his time and how much they have influenced him. I can say only that as I get older I get back into that strange childlike feeling of not being able to draw any certain line between the world and my own action upon it, and I wonder if this is also felt by people who have never been in the public eye or had any claim to influence. A very ordinary person might have the impression that there are millions of himself, and that all of them, as one, are doing just what it is in humanity—that is, in himself—to do. In this way he could perhaps feel more important than someone who has taken a particular view and followed a lonely path.

Part of the problem is that the closer I get to present time, the harder it is to see things in perspective. The events of twenty, thirty, and forty years ago are clearer in my mind, and seem almost closer in time than what has happened quite recently—in years that seem fantastically and excitingly crowded with people and happenings. I feel that I must wait another ten years to find out just what I was doing, in the field of psychotherapy, with Timothy Leary and Richard Alpert, Fritz Perls and Ronald Laing, Margaret Rioch and Anthony Sutich, Bernard Aaronson and Stanley Krippner, Michael Murphy and John Lilly; in theology with Bishops James Pike and John A. T. Robinson, Dom Aelred Graham and Huston Smith; and in the formation of the mystical counterculture with Lama Anagarika Govinda and Shunryu Suzuki, Allen Ginsberg and Theodore Roszak, Bernard Gunther and Gia-fu Feng, Ralph Metzner and Claudio Naranjo, Norman O. Brown and Nancy Wilson Ross, Lama Chögyam Trungpa and Ch'ung-liang Huang, Douglas Harding and G. Spencer Brown, Richard Weaver and Robert Shapiro—to mention only a few of the names and faces gathering out of the recent past to tell me that I have hardly begun this story.

CHAPTER FIFTEEN

THE SOUND OF RAIN

Although I have always been following the sun to the West, I have at last come to love the rain as well, especially in these dry California hills where the burnished grass so easily takes fire. Better still, though, are the spring and autumn rains of Japan. Despite the fascination which I have had with the Far East since reading about Dr. Fu Manchu at the age of eleven, and Lafcadio Hearn's *Gleanings in Buddha-Fields* at the age of fourteen, I didn't reach Japan until I was forty-six. From all I had heard about its frantic industrialization I was prepared to be completely disillusioned. But I went, and have returned three more times.

One would suppose that in view of my lifelong interest in Zen Buddhism I would have gone there years before—like Ruth Sasaki, Gary Snyder, and many others—to undertake the monastic discipline of living Zen, sit at the feet of a master, attain enlightenment, and come back with a certificate to prove it. I have nothing against that at all, especially if one may judge by what it has done for Gary. But that isn't my way. And when at last I did get to Japan I didn't rush off to a Zen school to gobble up all the wisdom I could. I went to look and to listen, and to see things in a way that insiders often miss; and I found what I wanted—albeit with the help of two Zen masters. It was the sound of rain.

Zen Buddhism fascinates Westerners because its way of teaching is quite unlike that of any other religion, if religion it is. It has no dogma, requires no particular belief, and neither deals in abstractions nor harps on morality. Then what, of religion or philosophy, is left? All and nothing, for Zen deals with reality—the universe—as it is, and not as it is thought about and described.

The heart of Zen is not an idea but an experience, and when that experience happens (and "happens" is just the right word) you are set free from ideas altogether. Certainly, you can still use them, but you no longer take them seriously. Picture yourself, then, as a person very earnestly concerned with making sense of life, of a world involving intense pleasure and appalling pain, and trying to understand how and why there is this weird sensation called "myself" in the middle of it all. You have heard that there is a great master, a sage, who can give you the answer; not in terms of some fancy theory, but the thing itself, so that you will never feel the same again and that sensation called "myself" will have been turned upside down and inside out. You approach the master and, perhaps with some difficulty, get an interview. You have thought out your questions most carefully, but just as you are about to open your mouth he yells "Ho!" at the top of his voice. You are nonplussed, and he asks what's puzzling you. You begin, "Well I came to ask...," but he interrupts, "And I have answered you." "But I don't..." and again "Ho!"—shouted from the depths of his belly. End of interview.

The greater part of Zen literature consists of such tales, often adding, however, that the questioner was completely satisfied. He cannot think of any more questions about life to ask, other than such simple matters as, "What time does the plane leave for San Francisco?" For this reason intelligent and adventurous Westerners have, in considerable numbers, been heading for the ancient capital of Kyoto, which has long been the main center for training in Zen.

But it was not only for Zen that I went immediately to Kyoto when I first arrived in Japan. I wanted to feel the everyday life of a city which had been soaked in Buddhism for so many centuries, not analyze it like a psychologist, categorize it like an anthropologist, or study its splendid monuments like an antiquarian. I went to gape like a yokel and simply absorb its atmosphere. We went to the district called Higashi-yama, or Eastern Hills, where buildings on narrow, winding streets overlook the rest of the city, which—unusually for Japan—are laid out in the flat grid pattern of an American city in a geographical setting which slightly resembles Los Angeles. Hills, even mountains, lie to the east, north, and west, while the south is open to Osaka, Kobe, and the sea. As in Los Angeles, the best land is in the foothills, where spring-water flows into garden pools through bamboo pipes, and though there are here many quiet and sumptuous private homes, much of the area has been occupied by temples and monasteries. Originally it belonged to feudal brigands, who were scared of the Zen priests because the priests weren't scared of them, became pious Buddhists, and made generous offerings of land.

When one goes to a city like this it is all very well to make plans to see the famous sights, but there should be plenty of time to follow one's nose, for it is through aimless wandering that the best things are found. We stayed in the *ryokan*, of Japanese-style inn, on the hill above the Miyako Hotel. To the northwest the sweeping grey-tiled roofs of the Nanzenji Zen temples float above dense clusters of pines, and to the southeast stands the huge cathedral of Chion-in, and all about are wayward cobbled lanes enclosed by roofed walls with covered gates, giving entrance to courtyards and gardens, and interspersed with small shops and restaurants. It was April, and under such a gate we took refuge from a sudden shower. The gate opened a few inches, and out came a hand proffering an umbrella, and as soon as we took it the hand was withdrawn and the gate closed. The umbrella was a *kasa* made of oiled paper—a wide circle spread out like a small roof supported on a cone of thin bamboo struts, almost as cozy as carrying your own house with you in a quiet, heavy rain. We returned it the next day.

Gutters were bubbling, and water was spilling from bronze, dragon-mouthed gargoyles at roof corners. Everywhere the soft clattering of wooden sandals like small benches with legs on the soles to keep your feet above water. Courtyards with glistening evergreen bushes and floating branches of bright green maple. The smell of Japanese cooking—soy sauce and hot saké—mixed with damp earth and the faintest suggestion, pleasant in that small a dosage, of the *benjo* or toilet which, because of the diet, smells quite different from ours. Because I need a dictionary to read most Chinese characters the signs on shops are just complex abstract designs, or it seems to me that "Mr. Matsuyama's Cafeteria" is the "Pine Mountain Harmonious Food House." Going deeper into the city we found the long, busy lane of Teramachi, or Temple Street, to nose about in the higgledy-piggledy of tiny shops that sell utensils for tea ceremony, incense, ink, writing brushes, old Chinese books, fans, Buddhist *bondieuserie*, and huge mushrooms that should be wearing pants—the whole lane buzzing and rattling with motorcycles and diminutive Toyota taxis.

With sense of time gone awry from travel by jet, I wake at four in the morning to hear what is, for me, the most magical single sound that man has made. It comes from a bronze bell some eight feet high and five feet in diameter, struck by a horizontal swinging tree-trunk, and hung close to the ground; actually more of a gong than a bell. It doesn't clang out through the sky like a church bell but booms along the ground with a note at once deep and sweet and vaguely sad, as if very very old. It sounds once and, when the hum has died away, again . . . and several times more. From the direction, I realize that this is the bell of the Nanzenji Zen monastery, signifying that, so long before sunrise, some twenty young men, skin-headed and black-robed, have begun to sit perfectly still in a quiet dark hall. When the bell finishes they will begin to intone, on a single note, the *Shingyo*, or *Heart Sutra*, which sums up everything that Buddhism has to say: *Shiki soku ʒe ku, ku soku ʒe shiki*—"What is form that is emptiness, what is emptiness that is form." Actually the language is the Japanese way of pronouncing medieval Chinese, which hardly anyone understands, and the words are chanted for their sound rather than their meaning. We shall see why.

With one side of my brain I know that these are rather bored and sleepy young men, mostly sons of priests, attending the Japanese equivalent of an ecclesiastical boys' boarding school or a Jesuit seminary. They think they ought to be there, but would really rather be chasing girls or learning to fly planes. The fine aloeswood incense, the faint candles, the sonorous gongs, and the pulsing chant are for them merely *kurai*: gloomy, musty, dank, decrepit, and old. A graveyard long gone to waste, with an old lady muttering over a stone. Only the sternest discipline will keep these boys at it. For the most part they are not, like Western seekers, *interested* in Buddhism, and they, in their turn, seldom realize that much of this seemingly esoteric discipline is simply routine drill for reluctant boys. Having been through that once, in school at Canterbury Cathedral, I have not been inclined to try it again.

But with the other side of my brain I want to be in their company, silently and unseen, with no wretched novice-master pushing me around and trying to teach me how to sit in meditation. For the antiquity and mystery of those gongs and the chant is not so much from a backward direction in time as from a vast depth inside the present, from a level of my own here-and-now being, as ancient as life itself. I wonder—what is this glamour of the mysterious and venerable East? Is it all a phony projection of my own romantic fantasies, and if so, why such fantasies? Why do Buddhist rituals and symbols evoke in me a sensation of the mysterious and the marvelous far more enthralling than any Christian equivalent, more even than astronomical revelations about the scope of distant galaxies? There is, of course, a wise-guy debunkery school of cultural anthropologists who want to insist that, seen from the familiar inside, all exotic culture-forms are just humdrum "old hat," as if Japanese and Tibetans could not feel for their traditions what we feel for Shakespere and Beethoven. There are, indeed, orchestra men bored to death with the Ninth Symphony and schoolchildren who find *Hamlet* a drag, so why should I share these Japanese novices' lack of enthusiasm for Zen? I am sure that the paternalistic discipline with which it is forced down their throats connects it with the same emotions of guilt that I felt in the presence of God the Father and Jesus Christ. It would follow, then, that my enchantment with Zen and Buddhism is that their forms are, for me, free from this kind of static, and thus that through them I can approach the mysteries of the universe without having to feel like a small boy being bawled out because it is good for me.

Anyhow, I am not a small boy. I have five grandchildren, and thus am no longer liable to be impressed by grandfathers. Nevertheless, as I look back I could be inclined to feel that I have lived a sloppy, inconsiderate, wasteful, cowardly, and undisciplined life, only getting away with it by having a certain charm and a big gift of the gab. Yet what am I supposed to do, now, about *that*! A realistic look at myself, aged fifty-seven, tells me that if I am that, that's what I am, and shall doubtless continue to be. I myself and my friends and my family are going to have to put up with it, just as they put up with the rain. I could, of course, tell myself that in so feeling I am casting away my humanity, the only thing which makes me different from a machine, which is supposedly the effort of will to take control of myself and change.

This might be fine if one knew precisely what would be a change for the better. If I would become more Christlike, I should remember that the Crusades and the Holy Inquisition were conducted in his name. If I would practice asceticism, I should bear it in mind that Hitler was quite an ascetic. If I would cultivate bravery, I should consider that Dillinger was brave. If I would observe sobriety, I should recall that Bertrand Russell put down a fifth of whiskey daily, and if I would find it in myself to be chaste, I should meditate upon Sri Hari Krishna and the Gopi maidens, and twit myself that I once had the privilege of sharing a mistress with one of the holiest men in the land. The difficulty is that our waking and attentive consciousness scans the world myopically, one thing, one bit, one fragment after another, so that our impressions of life are strung out in a thin, scrawny thread, lining up small beads of information; whereas nature itself is a stupendously complex pattern where everything is happening altogether everywhere at once. What we know of it is only what we can laboriously line up and review along the thread of this watchfulness. Better not to interfere with myself: it could set off an earthquake. Perhaps there is an entirely different way of being responsible and compassionate.

To keep the Zen monks company, I light a stick of incense, sit down on the *tatami* mat, and begin the ink-and-brush meditation. Some people have passions for ancient weapons, crystal eggs, or effigies of owls; mine is for Chinese ink and writing brushes. I can't stay away from Kyukyodo on Teramachi, where, the day before, I had bought several small slabs of black ink, each in a box of plain white wood, interestingly perfumed, and embossed with gold ideographs; and also a large and somewhat expensive brush, some three-quarters of an inch in diameter with hairs coming to a fine point. But the first step is to make tea for wakefulness, and for this there is nothing better than *ma-cha*, the finely powdered green tea used for ceremonial tea-drinking. A small amount is put in the bottom of a roughly glazed bowl, covered with hot water, and whirled into a jade-green froth with a bamboo whisk. Although it tastes vaguely of Guinness stout, it smells of straw matting and freshly planed wood. And then I begin to rub the ink easily back and forth, on a black stone cut like a small swimming-pool with a short deep end and a long shallow end, and filled with water. It takes fifteen minutes or more, during which there is nothing in my consciousness except the increasingly oily texture of the liquid, the mountain-forest smell of the incense, and the continuing sound of soft rain on the roof. Wide awake but with hardly a thought in my head I stroke and roll the brush in the black liquid, and then, with a certain unhurried suddenness, write ten Chinese characters on a long scroll of absorbent paper. They say:

In the midst of the rain, seeing the sun;
From the depths of the fire, spooning clear water.

That day we go down to Sanjusangendo, a long barn of a building which contains one thousand and one images of an astonishing hermaphroditic being known as Kannon, the Watchful Lord, and revered popularly as the Goddess of Compassion. One thousand of these images are life-size standing figures, each with eight arms, lined up along five or six platforms which run the entire length of an inside wall down the center of the building. But at mid-point there is the one extra figure, sitting on a lotus throne with eleven heads in a tall column and exactly one thousand arms forming an aureole about the figure. Most of the hands are empty, but at least a hundred of them hold various objects—bells, wands, flowers, thunderbolts, daggers, conch trumpets, flags, books, rosaries, staves, and bottles—instruments which this cosmic millipede is manipulating all at once without having to stop to think about any one of them in particular. It is in the same way that my nervous system manages the multitudinous functions of my body, and the energy of the universe appears simultaneously in myriads of patterns and forms, all working together in an ecological balance of unthinkable complexity. For you cannot truly think of one without thinking of the others, just as the earth implies the sun, and the sun implies the galaxy. To think of one alone is to have your mind caught or hung up on it so that you miss the movement of the whole, and this is what Buddhists mean by ignorance (ignore-ance) and consequent attachment to worldly things. This means any particular thing, such as myself, considered as separate or separable from the rest, and attachment in this sense is almost exactly what we now call a "hang-up." Spiritual myopia. Not seeing the forest for the trees. Killing flies with DDT and forgetting about the fish and the birds. Thus in passing judgments of praise and blame upon myself I forget that I am like one of Kannon's hands—a function of the universe. If my conscious mind had eleven heads and one thousand arms I might know what I was talking about. But my conscious mind is but one small operation of my nervous system.

When the rains stopped, Jano and I took a day off for meditation at Nanzenji, not in the temple itself, but on the forested hillside behind it, where we sat on the steps of some ancient nobleman's tomb, supplying ourselves with the kit for ceremonial tea and a thermos bottle of hot saké. Zen meditation is a trickily simple affair, for it consists only in watching everything that is happening, including your own thoughts and your breathing, without comment. After a while thinking, or talking to yourself, drops away and you find that there is no "yourself" other than everything which is going on, both inside and outside the skin. Your consciousness, your breathing, and your feelings are all the same process as the wind, the trees growing, the insects buzzing, the water flowing, and the distant prattle of the city. All this is a single many-featured "happening," a perpetual *now* without either past or future, and you are aware of it with the rapt fascination of a child dropping pebbles into a stream. The trick—which cannot be forced—is to be in this state of consciousness all the time, even when you are filling out tax forms or being angry. Experiences move through this consciousness as tracklessly as the reflections of flying birds on water, and, as a Zen poem says—

The bamboo shadows
sweep the stairs,
but raise no dust.

In this state it seemed that the whole city of Kyoto—with its thousands of shops and businesses, its streetcars, schools, temples, taxis, crooks, policemen, politicians, monks, geisha-girls, salesmen, firemen, waitresses, fish vendors, students, and bulging *sumo* wrestlers—was no other than the thousand-armed body of Kannon. And a curious feature of this state is that all details are as clearly etched as in a perfectly focused photograph. Even mist appears as its millions of individual droplets of moisture, each containing the reflections of all the others: a haze of jewels. I can have the feeling "self" only in relation to, and by contrast with, the feeling "other." In the same way, I am what I am only in relation to what everything else is. The Japanese call this *ji-ji-mu-ge*, which means that between every thing-event (*ji*) and every other thing-event there is no (*mu*) barrier (*ge*). Each implies all, and all implies each.

Our "contact man" in Kyoto is the Zen priest Sohaku Ogata, who is in charge of the subtemple of Chotoku-in (the House of Long Virtue) on the precincts of the great monastery of Shokokuji, maintaining it as a hospice for Western students of Zen. We had met years before in Chicago when he was studying at the Divinity School of the University and I was at Northwestern. Ogata-sensei[1] and his marvelous wife, whom Louisa Jenkins has designated a Japanese National Treasure, receive guests in their temple and guide us to restaurants, *no* plays, gardens, *aikido* demonstrations, and anything we want to see. He is a Zen monk right out of a painting by Sengai, having a shaved gourd-shaped head and a great laugh, and he speaks fluent English with a heavy but delightful Japanese accent. I wonder if his *bejetaburanch* (vegetable lunch) will take its place along with *dorai kuriningu* (dry cleaning) in the ever-growing vocabulary of Nihonglish. Incidentally, the rule for—widely understood—Nihonglish is to speak English without separating your teeth, to omit the definite and indefinite articles, and to insert a vowel sound after every consonant. Substitute *r* for *l*, *b* for *v*, and pronounce the long *o*, as in "note," as *aw*, as in "claw." We are now in Kyawtaw.

Ogata-sensei arranged to get us into Ryoanji—the Temple of the Dragon Hermitage—after visiting hours, so that we could see the rock-and-sand garden in the stillness before twilight, when all the tourists and swarms

---

[1] *Sensei*, or "teacher," is a convenient and allowable form of address for a Japanese Buddhist priest, although in Zen an official master is called *roshi*. I refuse to address Buddhist priests, even in writing, as "The Reverend," and no clergyman of any religion should be addressed as "Reverend X" or spoken of as "a reverend." This depressing word is an adjective, not a noun, and its use as a noun displays the same absence of education as calling one's congressman "Honorable Smith." In writing, a clergyman is correctly addressed as "The Reverend John Brown" and in speech he may be referred to as "The Reverend Mister, Doctor, or Father Brown." I follow the British custom of using the adjectival form "The Venerable" for Buddhist priests, since the word is relatively free of religious stink.

of schoolchildren had left. These gardens are strictly called "dry landscapes," and though everyone has seen photographs of this one at Ryoanji they give little idea of the place itself. It reduced us to immediate silence. The camera cannot grasp the whole scene, from the tops of the pines in the background to the whole long stone-edged rectangle of raked river sand with its nine island rocks arranged by miraculously controlled accident upon their beds of moss. One sees islands in a stretch of ocean, or perhaps just rocks on a beach, and the rocks are so scattered as to suggest vast space in the sand. There is nothing for it but to sit on the long veranda and absorb. *Yugen.* "To wander on and on in a forest without thought of return; to watch wild geese seen, and hidden again, in the clouds; to gaze out at ships going hidden by distant islands."

The garden must be seen in its total setting: the low, roofed, and damp-mottled wall along one side, with the pines above; the calm, horizontal temple buildings with their sliding screens; the luminous deep-green moss garden just around the corner; the incense, the birds, the far-off traffic, the quiet.

Less well known, and little troubled by tourists, is a comparable garden at Nanzenji designed by Kobori Enshu, and another, marvelously designed but not quite so happily situated, in the Honzan at Daitokuji. Guidebooks and loquacious priests have invented all kinds of symbolic meanings (which may be entirely ignored) for these creations. Such considerations stand in the way of realizing that they are astonishing demonstrations of the power of emptiness, and even that is saying too much. Lao-tzu explained that the usefulness of a window is not so much in the frame as in the empty space which admits light to the house. But people of the West, with their heavily overloaded ideas of God, will easily confuse the Buddhist and Taoist feeling for cosmic emptiness with nihilism—the hostile, sour-grapes attitude to the world implicit in the mechanist metaphysics of blind energy—which is hardly to be found in the Orient at all.

It is curious that Shinto, to judge from its architecture, has almost more feeling for creative emptiness than Buddhism. Exoterically, at least, Shinto or *kami-no-michi* (the way of the spirits) is the cult of Japanese patriotism and nationalism, and one feels this strongly at the National Shrine at Ise, but more because of the officious and impolite guards than anything else. But there are no guards at the even more venerable and splendid Taisha at Izumo on the west coast, where the architecture of the shrine shows a subtle Chinese influence. As with most Shinto shrines, the roofs are thatched and the ridgepole is supported in V-shaped extensions of the terminal roof-beams as if the prototype had been a tent or some house of palm wattles from the South Sea Islands. The buildings are austere structures of unpainted wood, but so proportioned and varied in texture as to be sanctuaries of clean-swept serenity for dignified rites oddly reminiscent of the style of the Church of England. At Izumo the buildings surround clear, cobbled courtyards containing other, sacred and unapproachable, buildings like boxes within boxes; and though there may be a sword and a bronze mirror in the holy of holies, one has the feeling that all this is emptiness containing emptiness. Suzuki once told me that he suspected, but could not prove, a connection between Shinto and Taoism. After all, the word is the Japanese pronunciation of the Chinese *shen-tao*, which may be understood as the Tao of divine spirit, or simply of intelligence or energy.

Kyoto must contain thousands of tiny, tucked-away restaurants and bars in narrow streets and alleys, and also has long arcades of small shops selling colorful stacks of dried fish, huge radishes, persimmons, all types of seaweed—dried or pickled—octopuses, squid, sea bream, tuna, globefish, soybean curd, leeks, eggplant, and a multitude of vegetables, pickles, and pastes that I have not yet identified. I wish I had my own kitchen there, though I am happy to sample the restaurants, particularly the bar-type ones for *sushi, tempura,* and *yakitori* where the food is prepared right before you. Hidden away somewhere near Kawaramachi and Shijo (River Street and Fourth Avenue) is an exclusive *sushi*-bar frequented by gourmets. *Sushi* are small rice patties topped with green mustard and a slice of raw fish—tuna, eel, sea bream, squid, octopus—or caviar or cooked shrimp, and served with thin slices of fresh ginger. The bar here is an immense slab of plain, silky-textured white wood, and one is served by four young men in blue-and-white bandannas with the bows tied to resemble horns. There is room for about ten customers; you make your own selections from the fish stacked before you on a bed of ice, and the *sushi* are formed with lightning-deft gestures and laid in front of you on a sloping shelf of black lacquer. Fine saké is served in pleasingly generous cups from white porcelain bottles. One such restaurant, which serves both *sushi* and *yakitori* (miniature kabobs on bamboo skewers), calls itself a *dojo* or gymnasium for saké drinking, and here the cups are not only generous—as distinct from the usual minuscule one-sip cups—but the bottles mighty. Unlike the Americans, the Japanese have no sense of guilt whatsoever about drinking, and this goes for priests as well as laymen. I remember Kato-san telling me about his Zen teacher: "Today I had retter from my teacher. Ah so! My teacher he very drunk. Much, much saké. He rive in ronery tempuru high up in mountain. Onry way to keep warm."

I do not, alas, speak much Japanese; only enough to direct taxis and order food in restaurants, helped out with Chinese characters on a scratch pad. Unfortunately the Japanese and the English find each other's languages so difficult that we can only talk like children, giving a false if amusing impression of our mentalities.

I do wonder if this attitude to alcohol (a name given to the liquid by Muslims, who forbid it) accounts for the fact that I have never seen anyone nasty-drunk, as distinct from happy-drunk, on saké, which is about as strong as sherry. The Chinese drink far more fearsome liquors, most of which taste like a mixture of paint remover and perfume (though I once had a dark brown substance as good as Benedictine), and seem to give alcohol an entirely innocent association with poetry and music (*raku*), which is written in the same way as "happiness." Doubtless these people become alcoholics in the clinical sense, but I suspect that what we call a "problem drinker" is as much a product of social context as of mere booze. Since to be drunk in Japan, and old China, is not considered a disgrace, no one drinks because he is miserable about drinking or in simple defiance of stuffily sober friends and relatives. The Japanese also observe the interesting and salutary social rule that nothing counts which is said in a bar.

What is perhaps most unfamiliar to us is the Far Eastern connoisseurship of tea, which includes not only appreciation of its many varieties and ways of preparation, but also of its effects on the mind. I am drawn, like a moth to light, to the shops on Teramachi which sell tea and utensils for the *cha-no-yu* (literally, "hot water of tea") or tea ceremony, which I have learned to conduct in the relaxed and unofficial style used by Zen monks when casually entertaining friends. There are some five main schools of the art, the most popular of which, Urasenkei, is to my mind uncomfortably stiff and over-refined, so much so that only the most accomplished master could conduct it in a relaxed and congenial way. But the Kankyu-an school is another matter. Several times I have been entertained in his home by the master of this school, So-shu Sen, and once in the tearoom of the Daitokuji Honzan. The refined naturalness and informality of his style, his ingenious choice of utensils and flower arrangements, as well as his personal atmosphere, make his offerings of *cha-no-yu* a genuine pleasure.

Mac-ha or *koi-cha*, the powdered green teas used for the ceremony, would doubtless be banned in this country if they were widely known, for, taken in strength, they are highly conducive to the states of consciousness characteristic of Zen meditation: to a serene, wide-awake clarity of which the T'ang poet Lo-t'ung has written:

> The first cup moistens my lips and throat; the second cup breaks my loneliness; the third cup searches my inmost being. . . . The fourth cup raises a slight perspiration—all the wrong of life passes away through my pores. At the fifth cup I am purified; the sixth cup calls me to the realms of the immortals. The seventh cup—ah, but I could take no more! I only feel the breath of cool wind that rises in my sleeves.

The main fascination of *cha-no-yu*, derived naturally from Zen, is that it is a ceremony without any meaning other than itself. No Buddha images or other formally religious objects are present, and veneration is accorded only to the guests, the tea, the utensils, the water, the fire, and the painting and the flowers in the alcove. Time is slowed down in calm, easy, and absorbed attention to boiling the water and serving the tea. There may be rambling conversation about matters of no urgency, but more often a contented silence such as one gets in puffing at a pipe and looking into the fire.

I have visited Kyoto four times, and will snatch at any opportunity to go there again, despite the plastic fury with which Japanese industrialism is destroying the country. Kyoto is now dominated by a colossal plastic phallus in full erection from the roof of the Station Hotel, and most "modern" buildings look as if they had been put together from sheets of acetate and crimped tin, and the whole industrial project is a frantic success because there are no squares like Japanese squares. Nevertheless, Kyoto has civic pride in its ancient traditions and monuments, so that there is some resistance to an aesthetic debacle which is perhaps the world's major illustration of the proverb that the worst is the corruption of the best.

When Oliver Andrews was there with me he remarked that Kyoto somehow reminded him of Hermann Hesse's Castalia, for, as the greatest international center of Buddhist culture, it is a curiously cosmopolitan city frequented by pleasantly eccentric people from all over the world. In Kyoto one never feels "out of things" as one can in Miami, Cape Town, Melbourne, or other such places with vast concentrations of people who have nothing very interesting to do. I have my eye on a virtually unused temple in the grounds of Nanzenji—a quiet place by the aqueduct. Will someone please let me have it for a year?

The hour's train ride into the mountains of Wakayama, east of Osaka, is like a journey through one of those long horizontal landscape scrolls called *makemono* which you roll and unroll as you go along. You move through ranges of densely forested hills, growing higher and higher, and below the forests are hundreds of wiggly terraced fields, following the contours of the slopes and many-colored with the various crops of tea, rice, millet, radishes, onions, and beans. Villages, farmhouses, and temples peek from the folds of the hills, tiled blue-grey and "belonging" in the landscape as much as the trees, since the old nonindustrial culture of Japan sees the work of man as but one of the many works of nature. The end of the line is Mount Koya, where at three thousand feet and more than a thousand years ago, the monk Kobo Daishi established a complex city of temples in the midst of the colossal Japanese sequoia trees known as cryptomeria.

I think about Koya-san as I think about Big Sur: better not to spoil it by going there to live, for in this way it remains for me an archetypal sanctuary which I enjoy all the more for not possessing and penetrating it. This is not simply a romantic illusion, for were it so all distant views would be false, and no face would be seen correctly except with a microscope. Looked at from the right psychological distance Koya-san *is* a Shangrila, just as far-off hills are indeed blue. Both places and people should thus be respected and enjoyed in not inspecting them too closely with a vulgar, nosy, and intrusive attitude. Here the style of Buddhism is called Shingon and is closely related to Vajrayana, the ritualistic and magical Buddhism of Tibet, so that in this place I am more than ever affected by the supposedly phony mysteriousness of Asian religion. Of course I know as a matter of information that most of the priests are going through the motions and have forgotten the meaning, that the young seminarists are just dutifully following their fathers' tracks, and that the economic *raison d'être* of this temple-city is to be a tourist-trap and a mortuary. All this I deliberately overlook.

Our headquarters is a temple not far from the station yet surrounded by forest. The buildings enclose a garden of miniature hills, with pine trees, rocks, and pools, and the rooms are separated by gold screens painted with bamboo trees and tigers. In the dark shrine hall the principal image is of Fudo Bosatsu, the Fire Bodhisattva of Immovable Intelligence, presiding over a huge array of memorial tablets, subordinate images, gongs, drums, vessels, and innumerable ritual objects that have no English names. Because we are here with a group of my students, the priest allows us to use this place for early-morning meditation, and sometimes one of his assistants will join us to celebrate the *goma* or Fire Ceremony in Fudo's honor, which is a most refined form of ritual magic. We do not, of course, understand it, and perhaps the priest doesn't either, but I simply have to admit that these Buddhist mysteries enchant me in the same way as people are enchanted by the particular features of a beautiful woman or by the style of a favorite musician. I don't approach them in a pious way, like the little old ladies, because I think they're a manifestation of cosmic fun, and I just have never been able to be pious in the serious downcast-eyes meaning of the word. Nor do I approach them as a scholar, for I have just enough scholarship in matters Buddhist to know when the rest of it will bore me, and I sometimes suspect that taking a scholarly attitude to a subject is a lame excuse for doing what you secretly enjoy for no good reason.

So in that little temple they have a huge, bowl-shaped bronze gong, and there amid the smell of incense and by the light of glimmering lamps, I like to start up its vast, deep voice and let my own run with it to intone the mantric syllables OM-MA-NI-PA-DME-HUM. If I had the nerve I would keep that up for a couple of hours, but would be thought pious or mad, whereas I am simply enjoying the go of it. Then, again, Shingon Buddhism is not at all like other forms of Buddhism, for its chief object of veneration is not the historic Buddha, Gautama, but the supercosmic Great Sun Buddha who, with his four subordinate Buddhas of the Four Quarters, personifies that No-thingness which is simultaneously the ground of the universe and our own inmost nature. These so-called *dhyani* Buddhas have weird and musical names— nothing at all familiar and customarily bandied about, like God, Jesus Christ, Jehovah, and Allah, but names that have the same ring of strange immensity as those given to the stars: Aldebaran, Fomalhaut, Altair, Betelgeuse, and Arcturus. The central figure, Buddha of the Sun, is called in Sanskrit Mahavairocana, in Japanese Dainichi Nyorai, and then clockwise from the east to the north come Akshobhya (Ashuku Nyorai), Ratnasambhava (Hosho Nyorai), Amitabha (Amida Nyorai), and Amoghasiddhi (Fukujoju Nyorai). In painting and statuary they are displayed in the mandala form, with Mahavairocana in the center and the others surrounding him like the petals of a flower—crowned, aureoled, jeweled, and seated on lotus thrones amid attendant Bodhisattvas—and you must imagine them as radiating from the ultimate back of your mind, where the eyes cannot look and thought cannot reach.

The city-village of Koya-san is a large cluster of temples surrounding a few shops and restaurants, all standing among pine, cedar, and cryptomeria trees, including also an enormous cemetery and a splendid museum of Buddhist art. To my delight I found one or two shops selling the magical tools and objects of Shingon ritual, and there acquired a heavy brass "diamond thunderbolt," which the Tibetans call a *dorje*, a brass *shakujo* or ceremonial rattle, and an esoteric book of incantations and finely drawn symbolic letters in the Chinese way of writing Sanskrit. Everywhere is the smell of pine needles underfoot and, as one passes temples, of *jinko*, the fine aloeswood incense which D. T. Suzuki called "the smell of Buddhism." But the point of Shingon is "to realize Buddha in this body," and as I look at the temple architecture and the imagery and symbolism I get the odd feeling that it is at once electronic and neurological. The masts on the pagodas are topped with a flaming golden ball and surrounded with nine metal rings, suggesting an early type of transmission mast for television, and the ever-present *dorje*, or thunderbolt-scepter, has five claws at each end with points barely touching, as if about to generate electric sparks. And there are diagrams of *kshetra*, of "fields," containing hundreds of Buddha-figures like some organism with massed eyes, or nerve-endings, or contact points, where again each implies all because "body of Buddha" means the whole universe.

Thus "to realize Buddha in this body" is to realize that you yourself are in fact the universe. You are not, as parents and teachers are wont to imply, a mere stranger on probation in the scheme of things; you are rather a sort of nerve-ending through which the universe is taking a peek at itself, which is why, deep down inside, almost everyone has a vague sense of eternity. Few dare admit this because it would amount to believing that you are God, and God in our culture is the cosmic Boss, so that anyone imagining himself to be God is deemed either blasphemous or insane. But for Buddhists this is no problem because they do not have this particular idea of God, and so also are not troubled by the notion of sin and everlasting damnation. Their picture of the universe is not political, not a kingdom ruled by a monarch, but rather an organism in which every part is a "doing" of the whole, so that everything that happens to you is understood as your own *karma*, or "doing." Thus when things go wrong you have no one but yourself to blame. You are not a sinner but a fool, so try another way.

Now I have always found this a highly civilized and humane point of view. For Westerners, the only real alternative to the boss-God religion has been the so-called "scientific" view of the universe as a system of essentially stupid objects. This comes from looking at things in a coldly withdrawn way as in studying the behavior of machinery, while in physiology and psychology we turn this attitude inwardly upon ourselves—only to become objectionable objects to our own gaze. If this mechanical view of life gets rid of horrors about sin and guilt, it also gets rid of any real reason for sympathy or kindness. From the standpoint of mechanical efficiency all feelings and emotions are just obstructive static, and when we are through with poisoning the air there will be every reason for replacing ourselves with steady-state electronic mechanisms that require no atmosphere and do nothing but solve mathematical problems. The objective attitude to oneself is finally suicidal, and it is not, therefore, surprising that the grandest flower of our technology is the hydrogen bomb.

But when Buddhists look very deeply into themselves they ask, "But who is looking?" They come up with an answer which has been hard to understand, essentially because of a language problem. For the Japanese word *ku* (translating the Sanskrit *sunya*) has the sense of sky, space, or emptiness, but when it is used for the root of one's own consciousness it means also the finally mysterious and inconceivable. Not so much emptiness or darkness as the way the head looks to its own eyes. This is the meaning of the flaming crystal ball atop the pagoda mast, which in Zen is said to be "like an eye that sees, but does not see itself." *Ku* is therefore "clarity" as of vision or hearing, and nothing is so mysterious as clarity even though we speak of clearing up mysteries. For exactly *what* is clarity itself? Could it be well-defined form? Crystal-clear form? Then, as the *Heart Sutra* says, *ku* is *shiki*—transparency is form.

Unburdened by a Christian upbringing, Gary Snyder has the humorous attitude to religion so characteristic of Zen. We found him in a Japanese-style cottage, close to the Daitokuji monastery in Kyoto, where he was making a twelve-year study of the Zen way of life. He is like a wiry Chinese sage with high cheekbones, twinkling eyes, and a thin beard, and the recipe for his character requires a mixture of Oregon woodsman, seaman, Amerindian shaman, Oriental scholar, San Francisco hippie, and swinging monk, who takes tough discipline with a light heart. He seems to be gently keen about almost everything, and needs no affectation to make himself interesting. He has taken to wife Masa, a beautiful but gutsy Japanese girl from the southern islands, who looks you straight in the eye, does not simper and giggle, gives no mock humility, yet has a quiet naturalness. Their living room is adorned with two large and colorful scrolls bearing those Shingon diagrams of multitudinous Buddha-figures, and so abounds with Buddhist ceremonial tools that Gary called it "the safest place in the galaxy."

After we have taken a communal bath in a huge cauldron over a wood fire, much saké is downed, and apropos of *ku*, the clear void, Gary suggests that we incorporate the "Null and Void Guaranty and Trust Company" with the slogan, "Register your absence with us; you *can* take it with you!" Later, I had some business cards printed for him to this effect, naming him as the company's nonrepresentative. I wonder, why is it that we can't stop laughing at the notion that none of us really exists, and that the walloping concreteness of all the hard facts to be faced is an energetic performance of nothingness?

The joke derives from the fact that, although Westerners speak of "conquering space," they have a radical prejudice and a positive blind spot with respect to the importance of nothingness. They balk at it as people used to balk at thinking of the world as round. To them, nothingness is the awful-awful, the end, the demise which, we most fervently hope, is not to be the ultimate destiny of man and the universe. Yet this is due to a freaky lapse in our logic which affects our theology, our science, our philosophy, and our most vivid emotions. No one seems to have realized that you can't have something without nothing. How can you know "is" without understanding "isn't"? Try to imagine a solid without any space through and around it. Try to imagine space without any solid, including yourself, within it. For if something implies nothing, then nothing—in turn—implies something. To be or not to be is *not* the question, for reality, like electricity, is a pulsation of positive and negative energy. The big bang with which this universe is supposed to have started was, as they say in Zen, "the Void gnashing its teeth." Put in more scientific jargon: Every approach to the limit of absolute inertia condenses by inversion into a departure from the limit of absolute energy. Flip—total void equals big bang.

Stated in bare words this looks too simple. Yet I regard it as my most important philosophical discovery, and if we could understand it thoroughly, we would no longer have the horrors about death, darkness, night, silence, and the unknown. But the remaining question is how to get one's feelings, those easy victims of habit, to recognize that it takes nothing to start something.

All over Japan one finds temples on the sides of hills and mountains that are approached by stone stairways ascending through forests of coniferous trees with the monotony of their dark pillars relieved by the light frivolity of maples and ferns. These stairways, flanked by stone lanterns and moss-covered images of Bodhisattvas, are usually reached through massive wooden gates, roofed in the Chinese style, and richly embellished with carvings of dragons, clouds, and birds. Two or three flights may lead to another such gate, beyond which is the quiet courtyard of the main temple—a horned and sweeping roof of dull blue-grey tiles supported on hefty wooden pillars; the whole building rather long and low, the eaves extending so far beyond the walls that the roof seems to float. Inside, beyond the uncluttered floor of straw mats, is an altar of gold-and-black lacquer, set about with candlesticks, golden replicas of lotus flowers in vases, and bronze bowls for offerings. At the center, before the Buddha-image, an orange rests on a presentation tray, and beside it is a burner filled with sand upon which powdered incense has been laid out in the form of a complex Sanskrit letter, burning slowly from brown to black. The Buddha, "old goldenface," looks down from within his leaf-shaped aureole, not exactly with a smile nor with indifference, but with completely unselfconscious calm. Although these formal features are repeated again and again, and are familiar the world over from their colossal embodiment at Kamakura, I am never tired of them.

Out behind the temple another staircase goes higher into the forest, suggesting that one has not yet come to the end of the mystery. Climbing, one reaches not a Chinese gate but a *torii*, a Shinto arch that originally served as a perch for sacred birds, and this gives access to a plain wooden shrine with a thatched roof. Looking inside one is faced—and given pause—by nothing more than a mirror, a disk of polished bronze on a lacquered stand. Yet that is not quite that, for behind this the stairway goes on, narrower and less imposing, winding up through the trees to come out into a level clearing planted with rows of stone and wooden posts inscribed with Chinese characters. The obvious message seems to be that it all comes to this—the cemetery. But as you are about to conclude that the tedious and depressing moral of this ascent is that "the paths of glory lead but to the grave," it appears that there is still another stepway, rough and little used, going yet higher. You climb on. The path levels out a little, and then vanishes. Put into *haiku*—

This is all there is;
the path comes to an end
among the parsley.

Perhaps I can express this Buddhist fascination for the mystery of nothingness in another way. If we get rid of all wishful thinking and dubious metaphysical speculations, we can hardly doubt that—at a time not too distant—each one of us will simply cease to be. It won't be like going into darkness forever, for there will be neither darkness, nor time, nor sense of futility, nor anyone to feel anything about it. Try as best you can to imagine this, and keep at it. The universe will, supposedly, be going on as usual, but for each individual it will be as if it had never happened at all; and even that is saying too much, because there won't be anyone for whom it never happened. Make this prospect as real as possible: the one total certainty. You will be as if you had never existed, which was, however, the way you were before you did exist—and not only you but everything else. Nevertheless, with such an improbable past, here we are. We begin from nothing and end in nothing. You can say that again. Think it over and over, trying to conceive the fact of coming to never having existed. After a while you will begin to feel rather weird, as if this very apparent something that you are is at the same time nothing at all. Indeed, you seem to be rather firmly and certainly grounded in nothingness, much as your sight seems to emerge from that total blankness behind your eyes. The weird feeling goes with the fact that you are being introduced to a new common sense, a new logic, in which you are beginning to realize the identity of *ku* and *shiki*, void and form. All of a sudden it will strike you that this nothingness is the most potent, magical, basic, and reliable thing you ever thought of, and that the reason you can't form the slightest idea of it is that it's yourself. But not the self you thought you were.

Whenever I am in Kyoto I seem to meet unexpected friends from home, and, in connection with what I have just been trying to describe, I shall never forget a long night spent with Dom Aelred Graham and David Padwa in the *ryokan* above the Miyako. Dom Aelred was then Prior of the Benedictine house at Portsmouth, Rhode Island, undertaking a spiritual pilgrimage to Asia with his disciple Harold Talbot. I had introduced them to each other some years before after a remarkable meeting with Harold, then aged seventeen, in New York. Harold, after a brief correspondence, had invited me to lunch at one of the best French restaurants in town. He appeared to know the headwaiter, and ordered the luncheon and the wine with the taste of an experienced gourmet. Thereafter he involved me in a theological discussion of quite amazing profundity, in the course of which he disclosed that, after going to Harvard, he intended to become a Trappist monk. I considered that such a remarkably cultured young man was much more of a Benedictine than a Trappist, for most Benedictines I have known have an urbane and assured serenity which comes both from being the oldest order in the Church and from their preoccupations with scholarship and art as well as the spiritual life. I cannot imagine a fanatical Benedictine. So I urged him to look up Dom Aelred as soon as he went to Harvard, and everything worked out as I had hoped, although Harold remained a layman.

Dom Aelred is an Englishman from Ampleforth Abbey in Yorkshire and entirely my idea of what a Benedictine should be: holy and relaxed, with all the freedom that comes from mastery of a great tradition. He had recently published *Zen Catholicism*, a book symptomatic of the growing catholicity of Catholicism in a select circle of the Church's most gifted theologians and scholars. (Thomas Merton, for example, really understood what Zen is all about, and wrote most admirably of Chuang-tzu's Taoism.) At the time of this meeting in Kyoto, Dom Aelred as going to see the Dalai Lama in India and on his way was getting into discussion with several of the great Buddhist priests of Japan, not to convert but to learn, for it seems that those who go deeply into almost any of the great spiritual traditions come to the same place and find themselves talking the same language.

David Padwa was on vacation from being a director of the Xerox Corporation, having had the sense to "drop out" after a swift and remarkable career in law and business, exemplifying the saying that the secret of the mastery of life is to know when to stop. He came to Kyoto from India, carrying nothing but a knapsack and a copy of the *Lankavatara Sutra*, and it should be said here that his home in New York contains the world's coziest library, comprising a most respectable collection of works on Mahayana Buddhism and Tibetan iconography.

Having settled into the *ryokan*, all four of us made ourselves comfortable on the *tatami*, with an adequate supply of saké, and went into an all-night discussion. Now not all discussions are arguments, or kickings around of ideas, or emotional encounters. It is possible, in dialogue, to conduct a sort of *jñana* yoga which gets down to the rock-bottom of one's common sense, one's basic ideas, one's fundamental logic, and, indeed, the very moorings of one's sanity. We started, I think, from trying to get behind Dom Aelred's Thomist premises about God as "necessary Being" and talked very frankly about the feelings we had in connection with such ideas, especially as they came into our respective spiritual disciplines. I wondered about Saint Thomas's tremendous respect for the negative theology of Saint Dionysius, who had insisted that the highest knowledge of God was in "unknowing," in leaving behind every single trace of a concept of reality, including Being itself, and what this meant in terms of a state of consciousness. David literally and figuratively let down his hair—for he has extraordinary hair. He can smooth it so compactly against his head that he passes easily as a straight type, and then he can let it out into thick masses of curls to look like a wild man, like a dervish with flashing black eyes and an unnerving sense of humor. That evening he was wrapped in a Hindu monk's shawl of yellow cotton printed all over with red Sanskrit invocations.

David went into a discourse on the relativity of all concepts and ideas that made our heads swim. He reduced all basics to babble. He developed the epistemological impasse of knowing about knowing to demonstrate that we knew nothing at all about anything, that survival was a whim, time a hallucination, and sanity a majority consensus of the blind. He was like a trapeze artist at a hundred feet with no net, playing with his own sanity over an abyss of absolute madness, which—who knows?—might be a viable life-form if we could ever decide what we meant by viable. He showed that the act of making sense between each other had, in itself, no more sense than the gurgle of a stream. With the whole of his own remarkable intellect he tore every intellectual canon to shreds—and all this without bitterness or hostility, in the feeling of a joyous and terrible dance, for he seemed to be Shiva doing the *tandava* dance that brings all the worlds to an end.

Dom Aelred listened and listened, obviously cooking inside. For David was repeating, in a modern way, the dialectical process that the Madhyamika school of Nagarjuna had worked out as an intellectual approach to enlightenment by teasing the mind completely out of thought. In effect, this can bring about the same *paravritti* or flip at the root of consciousness as the contemplation of one's eventual nothingness. If the process sounds like a flight of philosophical fancy, I should stress the warning that our intellects do not function in a psychological vacuum or watertight compartment, and that we should not risk untying our conceptual moorings unless we are prepared to weather considerable confusion and anxiety. But once the critical point of the "flip" is passed and the identity of form and void is clear, one's consciousness of form is *in* the clear. That is to say, when grounded on "nothingness" one's zest for life is astonishing.

On the far west side of Kyoto is the village of Nagaoka. Here, some years ago, there was established a Zen school, not for regular monks but for college students, so that they might combine Zen practice with their academic courses. Though the buildings are relatively new, the damp climate of Japan fosters rapid growth of moss, and the patina of antiquity forms quickly. These buildings, and their garden, are in the most exquisite Zen taste: uncluttered but not bare, white but not garish, brown but not drab. (The wooden passage-floors, though stained, show all the grain and have been polished with long slithering of stockinged feet.) Gary, Jano, and I are received by the *roshi*, or master, Morimoto-san and his student successor, Gisen-san, in a spacious room where that adjective does not mean simply large or adequate. It is a room so designed that its empty spaces are a positive feature of its beauty: the paper *shoji* windows and sliding wall-screens are not mere background but, by their proportions and playing with light, are what is there to be seen.

Morimoto is so ancient and frail as to seem transparent, whereas Gisen—with his rich black hair and rounded sensuous features—looks more Latin than Japanese, though he serves us ceremonial tea, then saké, and then dinner with such perfection of refined Zen style—of slow and relaxed formality—that I find myself deposited, dreamwise, into some sort of Buddhist heaven designed by Sesshu and Rikyu. Meanwhile, Gary interprets my conversation with Morimoto so expertly that I hardly remember him as an intermediary. There is some preliminary talk about the possibilities of intelligent action without thinking—as when Kannon uses a thousand arms. In Zen this is called *munen* ("no-thought") and I would describe it as using the brain rather than the conscious mind with its linear limitations. Someone suggests that this is like the skill of Japanese carpenters, who can make astonishing constructions measuring by eye alone, without yardsticks or blueprints. So I ask, "But what about the skill of making a blueprint without using a previous blueprint?" My point is, of course, that conscious thinking is one of the thousand arms. We don't think before we think, and we don't know how we think: we just do it. That is the Zen of thinking. Morimoto makes no immediate comment, but goes after my question in a roundabout way.

For what I am really asking is whether there is a conflict between Zen meditation and the intellectual life, since his school was attempting to provide for both. But can one be in the state of *munen* while reading? He replies that, for college students, he goes about teaching Zen in a new way. "Instead of asking them to meditate on the sound of one hand, I ask them what is the first word in the dictionary." And, of course, there isn't one: since every word requires other words to define it, the dictionary is circular. I remember trying, as a small boy, to write down the pronunciation of the letters of the alphabet. This is obviously impossible for just the same reason that words and ideas can never lead us to reality. Yet although you can't take a bath in the word "water," the word itself is an event in the real world—not wet but noisy.

"Any book will do for studying Zen," Morimoto went on. "You can use the dictionary, or *Alice in Wonderland*... even the Bible. There's no real point in going to all the trouble to translate our old Chinese texts about Zen—not if you're serious about understanding real Zen. The sound of rain needs no translation."

Though the conversation went on for some time, that remark—as we now say—blew my mind. At the end of the evening Gisen produced a *nyoi*, a Zen master's ritual scepter, this one made of smooth dark wood in the shape of a butterfly's proboscis, and presented it to me with the remark, "This for Western Zen master!"

And then, the following morning, Gary and I arose at dawn and went to the Daitokuji monastery for the *teisho*, or formal lecture, to be given by Sesso Oda, then the presiding *roshi*. It is announced by a tremendous drumming, a monk using a stick on a large upright wooden drum having the skin secured by big upholsterers' nails. He pounds it to the rhythm of a bouncing ball, with

variations, crescendos, and diminuendos, and sometimes circulates the stick
across the heads of the nails to make a sound like a speedboat. We assembled
in the great rectangular hall and sat on the mats, monks on one side, guests on
the other, facing, and everyone was given a copy of the textbook for the lecture: a Chinese text about the teachings of a T'ang dynasty master. Knowing
that I had studied this work, Gary found the place for me, and then the *roshi*
entered wearing scarlet-and-gold brocade robes, dangling a rosary from his
wrist, and holding a white horsetail flywhisk. He solemnly mounted a throne
facing the Buddha-image across the hall, for these lectures are actually to be
understood as conversations between the master and the Buddha. At the sound
of a gong the head monk intoned, "*Ma-ka-hannya-ha-ra-mi-ta-shin-gyo,*" and
to the heavy pulse of a wooden drum everyone chanted the *Heart Sutra.*

This done, the *roshi* began to speak in a low voice, and the monks to
doze off into sleep. There is an art to this, for they must remain sitting upright as if in meditation, and the head monk must have the trick of waking
up exactly two minutes before the lecture ends, so as to ring the bell. This is
sleeping Zen. About halfway through the lecture, rain began to fall in tor-
rents, and the pelting on the roof drowned all other sounds for at least five
minutes. But the *roshi* didn't stop. He didn't raise his voice. He went straight
on with his inaudible lecture. The story is told of another master who, years
before, had been about to begin the lecture when a bird started singing. When
it stopped he announced that the lecture had been given.

Long after this I was talking to Ali Akbar Khan, the sarod player, who is
generally regarded as the greatest living master of Indian music. I have a particular personal admiration for him, for he is at once holy and sensuous, a complete man. Wine and woman go with his song; a song of unsurpassed technique
which he also uses as a type of yoga-meditation in which—if one can use temporal language about things eternal—he is very advanced. Discussing this, he
dropped the remark, "All music is in the understanding of one note."

Now this really ought not to be explained. But if you just listen, relating
yourself to the world entirely through the sense of hearing, you will find yourself in a universe where reality—pure sound—comes immediately out of
silence and emptiness, echoing away as memory in the labyrinths of the brain.
In this universe everything flows backward from the present and vanishes,

like the wake of a ship; the present comes out of nothing, and you cannot hear any self that is listening. This can be done with all the senses, but most easily with the ears. Simply listen, then, to the rain. Listen to what Buddhists call its "suchness"—its *tathata* or da-da-da. Like all classical music, it means nothing except itself, for only inferior music mimics other sounds or is *about* anything other than music. There is no "message" in a Bach fugue. So, too, when an ancient Zen master was asked about the meaning of Buddhism he replied, "If there is any meaning in it, I myself am not liberated." For when you have really heard the sound of rain you can hear, and see and feel, everything else in the same way—as needing no translation, as being just that which it is, though it may be impossible to say what. I have tried for years, as a philosopher, but in words it comes out all wrong: in black and white with no color. It comes out that life is a perfectly and absolutely meaningless happening—nothing but a display of endlessly variegated vibrations, neither good nor evil, right nor wrong—a display which, though marvelously woven together, is like a Rorschach blot upon which we are projecting the fantasies of personality, purpose, history, religion, law, science, evolution, and even the basic instinct to survive. And this projection is, in turn, part of the happening. Thus when you try to pin it down you get the banality of formal nihilism, wherein the universe is seen as "a tale told by an idiot, full of sound and fury, signifying nothing."

But this sense of "turning to ashes in one's mouth" is the result of trying to grasp something which can only come to you of itself. Trying to catch the meaning of the universe in terms of some religious, philosophical, or moral system is really like asking Bach or Ali Akbar to explain their music in words. They can explain it only by continuing to play, and you must listen until you understand, get with it, and go with it—and the same is true of the music of the vibrations. The vibrations can go so high on the scale of pain that we have to go into zero, and the way can be made richly horrible by thinking to ourselves, "This ought not to happen"—"It was all that bastard's fault"—"I am being punished for my sins"—"How could God let this happen to me?" When you say the music is abominable, listen to the sound of your own complaint. Above all, simply listen, and I (for the time being) will be silent.

INDEX

Page numbers in *italic* type refer to illustrations.

ABOUT THE AUTHOR

Alan Watts was born in England in 1915 and received his early education at King's School, Canterbury, and the Buddhist Lodge in London, where he met Zen scholar D. T. Suzuki. He received a master's degree from Seabury-Western Theological Seminary in Illinois and an honorary doctorate of divinity from the University of Vermont.

He published his first book, *The Spirit of Zen*, at the age of twenty-one and went on to write more than twenty other books, including *The Way of Zen*, *The Wisdom of Insecurity*, and *The Book: On the Taboo against Knowing Who You Are*. In addition to being an acclaimed author and philosopher, Watts was an Episcopalian minister, a professor, a graduate-school dean, and a research fellow at Harvard University. In the early 1960s, he moved to California and began holding seminars and lectures throughout the United States. He died at his mountain retreat near Muir Woods in 1973.